To Improve the Academy

To Improve the Academy

Resources for Faculty, Instructional, and Organizational Development

VOLUME 25

Douglas Reimondo Robertson, Editor
Northern Kentucky University

Linda B. Nilson, Associate Editor
Clemson University

POD NETWORK
Professional and Organizational Development Network in Higher Education

ANKER PUBLISHING COMPANY, INC.
Bolton, Massachusetts

To Improve the Academy
Resources for Faculty, Instructional, and Organizational Development

Volume 25

ISBN 13: 978-1-933371-08-5

Composition by Lyn Rodger, Deerfoot Studios
Cover design by Boynton Hue Studio

Anker Publishing Company, Inc.
563 Main Street
P.O. Box 249
Bolton, MA 01740-0249 USA

www.ankerpub.com

To Improve the Academy

To Improve the Academy is published annually by the Professional and Organizational Network in Higher Education (POD) through Anker Publishing Company, and is abstracted in ERIC documents and in Higher Education Abstracts.

Ordering Information

The annual volume of *To Improve the Academy* is distributed to members at the POD conference in the autumn of each year. To order or to obtain ordering information, contact:

Anker Publishing Company, Inc.
P. O. Box 249
Bolton, MA 01740–0249
Voice 978-779-6190
Fax 978-779-6366
Email info@ankerpub.com
Web www.ankerpub.com

Permission to Copy

The contents of *To Improve the Academy* are copyrighted to protect the authors. Nevertheless, consistent with the networking and resource-sharing functions of POD, readers are encouraged to reproduce articles and cases from *To Improve the Academy* for educational use, as long as the source is identified.

Instructions to Contributors for the Next Volume

Anyone interested in the issues related to instructional, faculty, and organizational development in higher education may submit manuscripts. Manuscripts are submitted to the current editors in December of each year and sent through a blind peer-review process. Correspondence, including requests for information about guidelines and submission of manuscripts for Volume 26, should be directed to:

Douglas Reimondo Robertson, Ph.D.
Assistant Provost, Professional and Organizational Development Center
Northern Kentucky University
Steely Library, Suite 220
Highland Heights, KY 41099
Voice 859-572-1354
Mobile 859-630-4467
Fax 859-572-1387
Email robertsond2@nku.edu

Mission Statement

As revised and accepted by the POD Core Committee, April 2, 2004.

Statement of Purpose

The Professional and Organizational Development Network in Higher Education is an association of higher education professionals dedicated to enhancing teaching and learning by supporting educational developers and leaders in higher education.

The Professional and Organizational Development Network in Higher Education encourages the advocacy of the ongoing enhancement of teaching and learning through faculty, TA, instructional, and organizational development. To this end, it supports the work of educational developers and champions their importance to the academic enterprise.

Vision Statement

During the 21st century, the Professional and Organizational Development Network in Higher Education will expand guidelines for educational development, build strong alliances with sister organizations, and encourage developer exchanges and research projects to improve teaching and learning.

Values

The Professional and Organizational Development Network in Higher Education is committed to:

- Personal, faculty, instructional, and organizational development

- Humane and collaborative organizations and administrations
- Diverse perspectives and a diverse membership
- Supportive educational development networks on the local, regional, national, and international levels
- Advocacy for improved teaching and learning in the academy through programs for faculty, administrators, and graduate students
- The identification and collection of a strong and accessible body of research on development theories and practices
- The establishment of guidelines for ethical practice
- The increasingly useful and thorough assessment and evaluation of practice and research

Programs, Publications, and Activities

The Professional and Organizational Development Network in Higher Education offers members and interested individuals the following benefits:

- An annual conference designed to promote professional and personal growth, nurture innovation and change, stimulate important research projects, and enable participants to exchange ideas and broaden professional networks
- An annual membership directory and networking guide
- Publications in print and in electronic form
- Access to the POD web site and listserv

Membership, Conference, and Programs Information

For information contact:
Hoag Holmgren, Executive Director
The POD Network
P. O. Box 3318
Nederland, CO 80566
Voice 303-258-9532
Fax 303-258-7377
Email podnetwork@podweb.org

Table of Contents

Section IV: Instructional and Curricular Development

Section V: Faculty Careers

About the Authors

The Editors

Douglas Reimondo Robertson is assistant provost and professor at Northern Kentucky University. He has helped to start or reorganize four university professional development centers (Portland State University, University of Nevada–Las Vegas, Eastern Kentucky University, and Northern Kentucky University). He is senior editor of the book series on better teaching for New Forums Press, as well as a current or past member of the editorial boards for *Innovative Higher Education, Journal for Excellence in College Teaching,* and *Kentucky Journal for Excellence in College Teaching and Learning.* He is a Fulbright senior specialist candidate and a frequent consultant and speaker at colleges, universities, and a diverse array of other organizations. He has authored or co-edited five books including *Making Time, Making Change: Avoiding Overload in College Teaching* (New Forums Press, 2003) and *Self-Directed Growth* (Brunner-Routledge, 1988). He can be reached at robertsond2@nku.edu.

Linda B. Nilson is founding director of Clemson University's Office of Teaching Effectiveness and Innovation. She recently co-edited *Enhancing Learning with Laptops in the Classroom* (Jossey-Bass, 2005) and revised her bestselling guidebook *Teaching at Its Best: A Research-Based Resource for College Instructors* (Anker, 2003), now in its second edition. In addition to teaching a graduate course on college teaching, she leads faculty workshops at universities and conferences both nationally and internationally. Before coming to Clemson, she directed teaching centers at Vanderbilt University and the University of California–Riverside, and was on the sociology faculty at the University of California–Los Angeles. She can be reached at nilson@clemson.edu.

The Contributors

Laura L. B. Border holds her doctorate in French literature and has worked in faculty and graduate student professional development for 20 years. She directs the award-winning Graduate Teacher Program and the Colorado Preparing Future Faculty Network at the University of Colorado–Boulder.

Laura is past president of POD and served for several terms on its Core Committee as well as initiated the TA/Graduate Student Professional Development Committee. She can be reached at laura.border@colorado.edu.

Maura Borrego is assistant professor of engineering education at Virginia Tech. She holds an M.S. and Ph.D. in materials science and engineering from Stanford University. Her current research interests center around interdisciplinary collaboration in engineering education, including studies of the collaborative relationships between engineers and education researchers and how engineering faculty learn educational research methods. She can be reached at mborrego@vt.edu.

Robert G. Bringle is Chancellor's Professor of Psychology and Philanthropic Studies and director of the Center for Service and Learning at Indiana University–Purdue University Indianapolis. His books include *With Service in Mind* (APA, 1998), *Colleges and Universities as Citizens* (Allyn and Bacon, 1999), and *The Measure of Service Learning* (APA, 2003). Robert received the Ehrlich Award for Service Learning and an honorary doctorate from the University of the Free State, South Africa, for his scholarly work on civic engagement and service-learning. He received his Ph.D. in social psychology from the University of Massachusetts. He can be reached at rbringle@iupui.edu.

Stephen D. Brookfield is Distinguished University Professor at the University of St. Thomas. Since beginning teaching in 1970, he has worked in England, Canada, Australia, and the United States, teaching in a variety of college settings. He has written or edited ten books on adult learning, teaching, and critical thinking, four of which have won the Cyril O. Houle World Award for Literature in Adult Education (1986, 1989, 1996, and 2005). He also won the 1986 Imogene Okes Award for Outstanding Research in Adult Education. His work has been translated into German, Finnish, and Chinese. He can be reached at sdbrookfield@stthomas.edu.

Patti H. Clayton is director of the North Carolina State Service-Learning Program and an instructor in the College of Humanities and Social Sciences. She serves as senior scholar with the Center for Service and Learning at Indiana University–Purdue University Indianapolis and coordinator of the North Carolina Campus Compact Research and Scholarship Initiative. Her scholarly work focuses on faculty development, critical reflection, assessment of student learning, and student leadership in service-learning, and she is the author of *Connection on the Ice: Environmental Ethics in Theory and Practice* (Temple University Press, 1998). She received her Ph.D. in ecology curriculum from the University of North Carolina–Chapel Hill. She can be reached at patti_clayton@ncsu.edu.

Constance E. Cook, a political scientist, is director of the Center for Research on Learning and Teaching at the University of Michigan (U-M), as well as associate professor of education and adjunct associate professor of political science. She previously served as executive assistant to the U-M president, coordinator of FIPSE's Comprehensive Program at the U.S. Department of Education, and associate professor at Albion College. Her most recent book concerns federal higher education policy. Presently, she writes about teaching improvement strategies. She can be reached at cecook@umich.edu.

Miriam Rosalyn Diamond is associate director of the Searle Center for Teaching Excellence at Northwestern University, where she facilitates training programs in North America and abroad. She is coauthor of *Chalk Talk: E-Advice from Jonas Chalk, Legendary College Teacher* (New Forums Press, 2004). She received her Ph.D. in educational processes and her M.A. in counseling psychology, and she teaches courses in both disciplines. Her other interests include adult development, holistic approaches to teaching and learning, and outcomes of active learning approaches. She can be reached at miriam-diamond@northwestern.edu.

Michele DiPietro is associate director of the Eberly Center for Teaching Excellence and an instructor in the Department of Statistics at Carnegie Mellon University. His professional work focuses on graduate student professional development and issues of diversity in the classroom, among other things. His scholarly interests include the impact of tragic events in the classroom, how millennial students experience college, student ratings of instruction, classroom climate issues for LGBTQ students, and statistics education. He is a member of POD's Core Committee for 2005–2008. He can be reached at dipietro@andrew.cmu.edu.

Shari Ellertson is assessment consultant for the Division of Student Affairs at the University of Wisconsin–Stevens Point. She previously served in administrative roles at North Dakota State University, Minnesota State University Moorhead, and Iowa State University (ISU). At ISU, she worked with the learning communities program, which is regarded as one of the top programs in the country. Her interests include faculty development, learning communities and other student success programs, and assessment and evaluation in higher education. She can be reached at sellerts@uwsp.edu.

Peter Felten is associate professor and director of the Center for the Advancement of Teaching and Learning at Elon University. As a historian, he teaches about race, education, and politics in the United States. Peter's research explores questions about learning, teaching, emotion, and visual culture. His newest project considers the implications of including undergraduates as partners with faculty in the scholarship of teaching and learning. He can be reached at pfelten@elon.edu.

Peter Frederick is a consultant in diversity education, teaching and learning, and faculty development. A recipient of the 2001 Eugene Asher Distinguished Teaching Award from the American Historical Association, his love of interactive, inclusive teaching began at the University of California–Berkeley and at California State University–Hayward in the 1960s, and then at Wabash College for 35 years. From 2004–2006, Peter was Distinguished Visiting Professor and Chair of American Cultural Studies and founding co-facilitator with Mary James of the Center for Intercultural Learning and Teaching at Heritage University. He can be reached at frederip@wabash.edu.

Jeff Froyd is a research professor in the Center for Teaching Excellence and director of academic development at Texas A&M University. He was project director for the Foundation Coalition, one of the NSF Engineering Education Coalitions, and project director for Changing Faculty through Learning Communities, sponsored by the NSF Research on Gender in Science and Engineering Program. Presently, he is working on several curriculum development projects in engineering and science. He can be reached at froyd@tamu.edu.

Eugene V. Gallagher is the Rosemary Park Professor of Religious Studies at Connecticut College. He is also the founding director and current faculty fellow of its Center for Teaching and Learning. Eugene is an American Academy of Religion (AAR) Excellence in Teaching Award winner (2001) as well as a CASE/Carnegie Professor of the Year for Connecticut (2003). He currently chairs the AAR's Committee on Teaching and Learning. A specialist in new religions, Eugene is the author, most recently, of *The New Religious Movements Experience in America* (Greenwood Press, 2004). He regularly works with departments and colleges on issues concerning teaching. He can be reached at evgal@conncoll.edu.

Blake Godkin is an instructor for the Leadership Development Center at Texas A&M University and also serves as the personal development coordinator for the university's Department of Honors. He has developed and delivered courses in creative problem solving, futurism, teamwork, and change leadership. Blake's research interests include creative approaches to problem solving, futurist approaches to higher education, and the application of creativity to emergency management. He is presently completing a Ph.D. in educational psychology with an emphasis on creativity. He can be reached at bgodkin@tamu.edu.

Adalet Baris Gunersel, born and raised in Istanbul, majored in English and German at Oberlin College. She has been a correspondent for the Turkish newspaper *The Republic* since 2003. Her articles written during one year in Rio de Janeiro were compiled into a book, *A Year in Rio*, and published in 2005 in Turkey. She is presently working on her Ph.D. in educational psychology at Texas A&M University and is a research assistant at the university's Center for Teaching Excellence. She can be reached at bgunersel@tamu.edu.

Julie A. Hatcher is associate director of the Center for Service and Learning at Indiana University–Purdue University Indianapolis, an instructor in the School of Liberal Arts, and a doctoral student in philanthropic studies. Her scholarly work has focused on the institutionalization of service-learning in higher education, the use of reflection activities in service-learning courses, the implications of John Dewey's philosophy for undergraduate education, guidebooks and resources for faculty, and institutional issues associated with enhancing and assessing civic engagement. She can be reached at jhatcher@iupui.edu.

bell hooks is a writer, cultural critic, feminist theorist, and the author of more than twenty-five books, including two on teaching: *Teaching to Transgress: Education as the Practice of Freedom* (Routledge, 1994) and *Teaching Community: A Pedagogy of Hope* (Routledge, 2003). She has been on the faculties of Yale University, Oberlin College, and City College in New York City, and is currently Distinguished Writer-in-Residence at Berea College. Born Gloria Jean Watkins in Hopkinsville, Kentucky, she changed her name to bell hooks to honor her mother and grandmother.

Therese A. Huston is the founding director of the Center for Excellence in Teaching and Learning and adjunct faculty in psychology at Seattle University, where she consults with faculty and leads workshops on teaching, learning, and faculty development. Her current research interests focus on faculty satisfaction and the impact of physical appearance (race, age, etc.) in the classroom. She is a program co-chair for POD's 2006 conference and has a Ph.D. in cognitive psychology from Carnegie Mellon University. She can be reached at hustont@seattleu.edu.

Mary James teaches at Heritage University, where she also served as director of the Academic Skills Center for 15 years. She was part of the team that designed the Heritage Core, a general college requirement that combines intercultural communication with intensive writing practice. In addition to teaching the Heritage Core, writing, and literature courses, she currently serves as cofacilitator of the Center for Intercultural Learning and Teaching, which she founded with Peter Frederick. She can be reached at james_m@heritage.edu.

Alan Kalish is director of faculty and TA development and adjunct assistant professor of education policy and leadership at The Ohio State University. He previously served as the founding director of the Center for Teaching and Learning at California State University–Sacramento and associate director of the Teaching Resources Center at Indiana University, where he earned his Ph.D. in English. His research interests include the transition from graduate school to faculty life and the scholarship of teaching and learning on educational development. He can be reached at kalish.3@osu.edu.

Sean Patrick Knowlton is a humanities reference and instruction librarian with the faculty rank of assistant professor at the University of Colorado–Boulder. His collection responsibilities include Spanish and Portuguese languages and literatures, comparative literature, and humanities and social sciences reference. He received his undergraduate degree in education (Spanish) from the University of North Carolina–Chapel Hill, where he also completed an M.A. in Hispanic literature and an M.S. in library science. He can be reached at sean.knowlton@colorado.edu.

James M. Lang is associate professor of English at Assumption College, where he teaches courses in nonfiction writing and contemporary British literature. He is the author of *Life on the Tenure Track: Lessons from the First Year* (Johns Hopkins, 2005), and he writes a monthly column about teaching and learning for *The Chronicle of Higher Education*. He gives frequent lectures and workshops on teaching and higher education for graduate students and new faculty. He can be reached at lang@assumption.edu.

Jean Layne works as a program coordinator and instructional consultant in the Center for Teaching Excellence and the Division of Academic Development at Texas A&M University. Her professional interests include how people learn and how the evolution from novice to expert occurs within the disciplines. She can be reached at j-layne@tamu.edu.

Mary McCord is associate professor of computer information systems at Central Missouri State University. After an entrepreneurial career in oil and gas production, she received her Ph.D. in business administration from the University of Oklahoma. Her research areas include e-commerce, service-learning, and team-based learning. She presently teaches management of information systems through the Integrative Business Experience Program, which combines team-based learning methods with real-world business endeavors. She can be reached at mccord@cmsu1.cmsu.edu.

Larry K. Michaelsen is David Ross Boyd Professor Emeritus at the University of Oklahoma, professor of management at Central Missouri State University, a Carnegie scholar, a Fulbright senior scholar (Indonesia and Korea), and former editor of the *Journal of Management Education*. He has received numerous college, university, and national awards for his outstanding teaching and for his pioneering work in developing and disseminating two powerful and widely acclaimed active learning strategies: Team-Based Learning and the Integrative Business Experience. He can be reached at lmichaelsen@cmsu1.cmsu.edu.

Barbara J. Millis is director of the Excellence in Teaching Program at the University of Nevada–Reno. She received her Ph.D. in English literature from Florida State University. She is a sought-after workshop presenter and speaker, giving six invited keynotes in 2005. Overall, she has offered workshops at more than 300 conferences, colleges, and universities. Barbara has also published numerous articles and two books, *Cooperative Learning for Higher Education Faculty* with coauthor Philip Cottell (Oryx, 1998) and *Using Simulations to Enhance Learning in Higher Education* with coauthor John Hertel (Stylus, 2002). She can be reached at millis@unr.edu.

Edward Nuhfer is director of the Center for Teaching and Learning and professor of geology at Idaho State University, where he enjoys teaching, writing, hiking, skiing, biking, and fine conversations over coffee. He devised student management teams, knowledge surveys, and, with other faculty developers and faculty, founded Boot Camp for Profs®, a faculty development retreat based on the fractal model. The camp is in its 14th year and is held each summer in Leadville, Colorado. He can be reached at nuhfed@isu.edu.

Kathleen F. O'Donovan has been an education specialist with the Center for Teaching and Learning Services at the University of Minnesota since 1998. She previously owned and operated a consulting firm and served clients in the areas of leadership development, change management, and cross-cultural communication. She earned her Ph.D. from the University of Minnesota in foreign language education/adult education. Her research interests center on transformational learning, reflective practice, and issues associated with internationalizing undergraduate courses. She can be reached at odono004@umn.edu.

Christopher O'Neal, a biologist, is Center for Research on Learning and Teaching coordinator for faculty development in the science, technology, engineering, and math disciplines at the University of Michigan. Chris has contributed to the design and development of workshops on active learning, teaching problem-solving skills, engaging students, curriculum revision, the scholarship of teaching and learning, clinical instruction, and implementation of team-based learning. He also helps to coordinate the university's Preparing Future Faculty programs. He can be reached at coneal@umich.edu.

Mathew L. Ouellett is associate director of the Center for Teaching at the University of Massachusetts–Amherst. In this capacity Mathew works to implement a broad range of teaching development programs for faculty members and graduate students across the disciplines, with special emphases on diversity and organizational change. He is a summer lecturer in the Smith College School for Social Work and, most recently, editor of the book *Teaching Inclusively* (New Forums Press, 2005). He can be reached at mlo@acad.umass.edu.

Allison Pingree is director of the Center for Teaching and assistant professor of medical education and administration at Vanderbilt University. She teaches in women's and gender studies and in American studies, and is co-leading a project on "Music, Religion, and the South: An Interdisciplinary Scholarship of Teaching and Learning," sponsored by Vanderbilt's Center for the Study of Religion and Culture. Additional interests include the relationship between cognitive and affective learning and leadership and organizational change. She can be reached at allison.pingree@vanderbilt.edu.

Kathryn M. Plank is associate director of faculty and TA development and an adjunct assistant professor in the School of Educational Policy and Leadership at The Ohio State University. She received a Ph.D. in English from Pennsylvania State University, where she also worked for several years as associate director of the Center for Excellence in Learning and Teaching. Her interests include program assessment in educational development, diversity and gender issues in higher education, teaching with technology, and literature and medicine. She can be reached at plank.28@osu.edu.

Michael Reder is director of Connecticut College's Center for Teaching and Learning. He chairs the POD Small College Committee and has run a variety of workshops on small college teaching and learning, including starting successful centers and creating programs that address the needs of untenured faculty. He consults regularly on these topics and on writing at small liberal arts colleges. He has served on the faculty of the National Institute for New Faculty Developers. He teaches courses on contemporary literature, culture, and theory in the English department. He is the author of several chapters on Salman Rushdie, and is the editor of *Conversations with Salman Rushdie* (University Press of Mississippi, 2000), a collection of interviews. He can be reached at reder@conncoll.edu.

Shelley Z. Reuter is assistant professor of sociology at Concordia University in Canada, where she teaches both large classes and seminars in the areas of health and medicine, knowledge, contemporary and feminist theories, and race and ethnicity. She received her Ph.D. from Queen's University–Kingston. She can be reached at sreuter@alcor.concordia.ca.

R. Eugene Rice is senior scholar at the American Association of Colleges and Universities. For 10 years, he served as scholar-in-residence and director of the Forum on Faculty Roles and Rewards and the New Pathways projects at the American Association for Higher Education (AAHE). Before moving to AAHE, Gene was vice president and dean of the faculty at Antioch College. Prior to his work at Antioch, he was senior fellow at the Carnegie Foundation for the Advancement of Teaching, collaborating with the late Ernest Boyer on the Carnegie Report *Scholarship Reconsidered*. In *Change* magazine's 1998 survey of America's higher education leaders, Gene was recognized as one of a small group of "idea leaders" whose work has made a difference nationally. He can be reached at rice@aacu.org.

John H. Schuh is Distinguished Professor of Educational Leadership and Policy Studies at Iowa State University. Previously he held administrative and faculty assignments at Wichita State University, Indiana University–Bloomington, and Arizona State University. John is the author, coauthor, or editor of more than 200 publications, including 24 books and monographs. He is editor of the *New Directions for Student Services* sourcebook series and associate editor of the *Journal of College Student Development*. He can be reached at jschuh@iastate.edu.

Mei-Yau Shih is coordinator of teaching technologies in the Center for Teaching at the University of Massachusetts–Amherst. She is responsible for faculty technology development programs and helping faculty integrate instructional technology into teaching and learning. Mei-Yau also teaches a graduate course in the School of Education and sits on campus and system advisory and governance councils that set practices and policies for effective use of instructional technology. She received her Ph.D. in educational technology in 1991 and an M.A. in journalism and mass communications in 1987 from the University of Northern Colorado. Before joining the Center for Teaching in August 1998, Mei-Yau was associate academic dean, associate professor, and director of the telecommunications program at Westmar University. She can be reached at mshih@acad.umass.edu.

Steve R. Simmons is Morse-Alumni Teaching Professor of Agronomy and Plant Genetics at the University of Minnesota, where he has served since

1977. His degrees are from Purdue University (B.S.), Colorado State University (M.S.), and the University of Minnesota (Ph.D.). His academic and pedagogical interests include agricultural ecology, experiential learning, and decision case-based education. He conducts workshops and retreats for memoir writing for personal and professional reflection at Minnesota and other universities. He can be reached at ssimmons@umn.edu.

Nancy Simpson is director of the Center for Teaching Excellence at Texas A&M University. In addition to working with faculty on teaching and learning, she teaches introductory mathematics courses and graduate education courses. She has been involved with faculty development initiatives, including the Wakonse Foundation's Conference on College Teaching and the Pew-funded Peer Review of Teaching Project. She is currently directing an NSF-funded project that helps math and science faculty to use writing as a learning and assessment tool. She can be reached at n-simpson@tamu.edu.

Karl A. Smith is Morse-Alumni Distinguished Teaching Professor and Professor of Civil Engineering at the University of Minnesota. His teaching and research interests include building rigorous research capabilities in engineering education; the role of cooperation in learning and design; project and knowledge management and leadership; problem formulation, modeling, and knowledge engineering; and faculty and TA development. Karl has bachelor's and master's degrees in metallurgical engineering from Michigan Technological University and a Ph.D. in educational psychology from the University of Minnesota. He can be reached at ksmith@umn.edu.

Mary Deane Sorcinelli is associate provost for faculty development, director of the Center for Teaching, and associate professor in the Department of Educational Policy, Research, and Administration at the University of Massachusetts–Amherst. Mary Deane has worked at individual, departmental, school, campus-wide, national, and international levels to encourage support and recognition for good teaching. She publishes widely in the areas of academic career development, teaching improvement and evaluation, and faculty development. She directs a number of external faculty development grants and teaches regularly. She can be reached at msorcinelli@acad.umass.edu.

Marjory A. Stewart is a doctoral candidate in higher education administration in the Department of Educational Policy, Research, and Administration at the University of Massachusetts–Amherst. She is former coordinator of the Center for Teaching's post-tenure review faculty development grants program, PMYR Grants for Teaching Enhancement. Prior to beginning her doctoral studies, she served as vice president for instruction at Massachusetts Bay Community College. She can be reached at stewartm@acad.umass.edu.

Ruth A. Streveler is assistant professor in the Department of Engineering Education at Purdue University. Prior to that, she was director of the Center for Engineering Education at the Colorado School of Mines. She has been co-principle investigator in several NSF-funded projects, including Conducting Rigorous Research in Engineering Education: Creating a Community of Practice (DUE–0341127). She can be reached at rastreve@purdue.edu.

Mary Wright, a sociologist, is coordinator for Graduate Student Instructor (GSI) Initiatives in the Center for Research in Learning and Teaching (CRLT) at the University of Michigan. Mary's work at CRLT focuses on GSI development and Preparing Future Faculty programs. She has developed workshops on critical thinking, academic interviewing, mentoring, instructional technology, classroom management, and classroom conflict. Mary has published on university teaching cultures, experiential learning, preparing future faculty programs, and teaching and learning in sociology and qualitative methods courses. She can be reached at mcwright@umich.edu.

Preface

This silver anniversary edition of *To Improve the Academy* was a profoundly communal act, and many people deserve acknowledgement. First, I would like to thank my colleagues who submitted their good work for review, and I encourage them to continue to do so no matter what the outcome of the review process. Growing the scholarship of educational development depends on our willingness to make our work public, to put it into a form that can be shared, and to submit it to peer review. I applaud all of you who submitted your work for taking the risk and for contributing importantly to the process of developing our field's literature.

Reviewing six or more papers in a short time during the holiday season is no small feat, especially with an already overflowing plate. Deserving high praise for thoughtful and prompt manuscript evaluation is the review panel for this silver anniversary edition: Danilo Baylen, Donna Bird, Phyllis Blumberg, Jeanette Clausen, Francine Glazer, Judy Grace, Patrice Gray, Wayne Jacobson, Frances Johnson, Kathleen Kane, Diana Kelly, Joseph "Mick" LaLopa, Jean Layne, Virginia Lee, Vilma Mesa, Edward Nuhfer, Leslie Ortquist-Ahrens, Donna Petherbridge, Nancy Polk, Gerald Ratliff, Jen Schoepke, Judy Silverstrone, Kathleen Smith, Margaret Snooks, and Mary Wright.

Special thanks go to Associate Editor Linda Nilson, whose publishing and editorial acumen contributed importantly to the development of this volume. She dispatched close edits of the many chapters assigned to her with sure-handed wisdom and remarkable speed. Her effervescent intelligence, good humor, and rock-solid friendship buoyed this project throughout.

At Anker Publishing, Carolyn Dumore deserves recognition for her charming responsiveness and competence, as well as Jim Anker for his personable leadership over the years. The relationship with Anker has been reliably pleasant and productive.

Accomplishing a project of this size is virtually impossible without the support of one's institution, and I have been blessed with strong support at Northern Kentucky University (NKU), where I serve as assistant provost for professional development. The support at the executive level has been extraordinary. In particular, I would like to thank President James Votruba, who is without doubt one of the most intellectually curious and civically principled university presidents I have ever met, always ready to discuss an idea, particularly if it is about contributing to a community; Vice President for Academic Affairs and Provost Gail Wells, a wise and brilliant academic leader who despite heavy administrative demands maintains an active intellectual life, reading broadly and voraciously; and Vice Provost for University Programs Paul Reichardt, who serves as an exemplary scholar-leader with his effective administration, active scholarship and teaching, and steadfast collegiality. In the climate set by NKU's executive leadership, being an administrator and editing a scholarly volume are seen as compatible and commendable, which is certainly not true at every college and university.

As director of the Professional and Organizational Development Center at NKU, I would also like to thank the center's professional staff: Patty Wilsey, coordinator; Laura Brenner, research assistant; Sarah Mann, online educational development consultant; Jim Nilson, web educational development consultant; Megan Downing, associate director; and the corps of student workers. As individuals and as a group, they have adjusted their own work in order to accommodate my periodic need to focus on this project. I want to single out Patty Wilsey for high praise. Essentially, Patty was the project coordinator and showed extraordinary patience, dedication, and creativity as she developed and managed Access databases that recorded and tracked every aspect of the project. Without her dependable competence, cleverness, and wit, I would surely have been lost on this project and many others.

Finally, I want to express gratitude for being blessed with a family that teaches me so much about living and loving: especially my daughter, Maura Eileen Robertson, who begins her all-consuming career in middle school this year but still finds space in her head and heart for her dad; and my wife, Sue Robertson Reimondo, who, besides being my best friend, is the director of counseling and psychological services at Berea College and a good friend to many.

Douglas Reimondo Robertson
Northern Kentucky University
Highland Heights, Kentucky
April 2006

Introduction

Without Contraries there is no progression.
—William Blake (1790/1963, p. 3)

[T]he human soul is always moving outward into the objective world and inward into itself; & this movement is double because the human soul would not be conscious were it not suspended between contraries, the greater the contrast, the more intense the consciousness.
—William Butler Yeats (1921/1940, p. 824)

Contrast creates energy that can fuel both growth and destruction. How do we channel this energy to growth? The secret lies in generative paradox, where difference flourishes and stimulates others to develop, where within an overarching integration around core identity there's a whole lot of shakin' going on. So I was not surprised when recent research revealed that one of three essential qualities of generative cities is tolerance (the other two being talent and technology) (Florida, 2002, 2005). Apparently, human groups who achieve and maintain generative paradox (true difference in synergistical relationship) develop, attract, and flourish. Yeats (1921/1940) spoke of the human soul, but his words apply equally well to human groups: "The greater the contrast, the more intense the consciousness" (p. 824). I believe that this intensification of consciousness might have been what Blake (1790/1963) had in mind when he wrote, "Without Contraries there is no progression" (p. 3).

POD is a human group that began with an intense consciousness three decades ago (i.e., with plenty of contraries married together more or less harmoniously). I would argue that POD's consciousness has shown Blakean "progression" through the intervening years as we have added and integrated ever more contrasts within a unifying identity. We are large; we are small. We are researchers; we are administrators. We are teachers; we are staff. We are complex units with permanent professionals; we are half-time reassigned. We are established; we are new. We are research institutions; we are teaching institutions. We want ideas; we want practices. We want research; we want techniques. We are specialists; we are generalists. We want to focus on teaching; we want to focus on leadership. A POD gathering is typically an extraordinary combination of earnest confrontation and peaceful regard, hard work and whimsy.

This silver anniversary edition of *To Improve the Academy* reflects POD's consciousness in many ways with its diverse array of topics and contributors. As I look back 25 years, I see that three of the contributors to the inaugural volume (edited by Sandra Cheldelin and Stephen Scholl) have contributed to this anniversary edition: R. Eugene Rice, Mary Deane Sorcinelli, and Peter Frederick. We celebrate these important continuities and the wisdom that they bring. Also among these continuities are two central dialectics: concrete-abstract and reflective-active. The contents of that first volume clearly covered the full range of these fundamental dialectics, as do the contents of this volume. An anniversary volume should honor its traditions, and one of POD's hallowed conventions is innovation. Indeed, its steadfast appreciation of creativity is admired by many POD members. So along with familiar themes, this silver anniversary edition includes material that may strike some readers as new and challenging.

Section I: Educational Development and the Sociological Imagination

This section takes its name from sociologist C. Wright Mills (1959) who coined the term *sociological imagination* to describe the ability to compellingly connect individual experience to social structure, biography to history, and personal troubles to social issues. Not everyone is blessed with a keen sociological imagination, and we are fortunate to have three exemplars here.

Chapter 1. R. Eugene Rice, a leading senior voice in American higher education, pauses to review his career-long work with the evolving faculty role and to connect that work with larger national developments, including the birth and maturation of POD.

Chapter 2. bell hooks, arguably among the most influential living American intellectuals, presents her reflections in a "talking chapter" (reminiscent of her "talking book" with Cornel West [hooks & West, 1991]) where she reveals, among other things, details of what she means by "engaged pedagogy" and how it can be applied to faculty as well as students.

Chapter 3. James M. Lang turns the insightful, narrative brilliance with which he described his first year on the tenure track (Lang, 2005) to articulating his journey through all six years to the tenure decision (which he was awarded). These three reflections collectively cover a lot of ground and touch provocatively on many important issues in educational development and higher education in general.

Section II: Paradigms

This section takes its name from a concept in Kuhn's (1970) hugely influential book *The Structure of Scientific Revolutions,* which demonstrates with stunning historical material the simple yet easily forgotten point that everyone, including sophisticated professionals like scientists (and educational developers), has a perspective (or paradigm) that functions in and out of our awareness (mostly out) to construct our realities. In other words, we are all human beings, and human beings can do no better than to make up reality as best they can. Immaculate perception is a myth. This section contains two fascinating and potentially powerful paradigms for readers to consider: critical theory and chaos theory.

Chapter 4. Widely read and highly regarded author Stephen D. Brookfield extends his most recent book (Brookfield, 2005), an insightful discussion of critical theory and adult education, to the specific context of faculty development. He articulates key tenets of critical theory and discusses with typical wit and candor his encounters and strategies with regard to promoting faculty discussion of these ideas.

Chapter 5. Edward Nuhfer explains fractals, a central concept from chaos theory, and suggests how generative that concept can be in higher education, specifically in faculty evaluation and holistic faculty development. Chaos theory is serving as an important new metaphor for more effective strategic planning (Cutright, 2001, 2006), and its application to instructional design (a similar endeavor to strategic planning, only on a different scale and in a different context) is a natural extension. Chaos theory has yet to be applied in a major publication to the teaching process: design, implementation, evaluation, and redesign. This chapter provides a significant first step in that direction.

Section III: Educational Development and the Scholarship of Teaching and Learning

This section comprises four chapters that address systematic inquiry into various aspects of educators' intentional learning programs and activities (i.e., the scholarship of teaching and learning). In *Scholarship Reconsidered,* Ernest Boyer (1990) introduced the phrase "scholarship of teaching" as one of four equally valuable faculty scholarships. He wanted to relax the death grip on the faculty reward system held by research (or more precisely, publication, the measure having surpassed in importance that which it originally measured). Boyer's impact was far reaching and deep as many institutions adopted this framework and language and "Boyerized" their policies regarding faculty roles and rewards. The "scholarship of teaching" sounded good, but Boyer left its meaning unclear. Was it the scholarship required for the teacher to acquire and organize content for a course (traditional content-driven, disciplinary scholarship applied within the context of a course)? Or was it scholarship related to effectively facilitating the learning of that content (for most disciplines, a new, instructionally driven scholarship about the teaching and learning of that disciplinary scholarship)? Discussion over the last 15 years has largely settled this question in favor of the latter, and the "scholarship of teaching" has become the "scholarship of teaching *and learning*" (SoTL).

Chapter 6. Peter Felten, Alan Kalish, Allison Pingree, and Kathryn M. Plank argue that practice-oriented educational developers should make the same journey that they recommend for teaching faculty from mere practice to studying systematically the outcomes of their practice. In other words, educational developers should apply the scholarship of teaching and learning to educational development itself. They provide ideas and examples of how busy educational developers might go about doing this research.

Chapter 7. Nancy Simpson, Jean Layne, Adalet Baris Gunersel, Blake Godkin, and Jeff Froyd report the results of a fascinating study of the developmental impacts on faculty who participate in a program to improve student learning in the natural and mathematical sciences, which provides an excellent example of just what the authors of the previous chapter recommend: SoTL applied to educational development.

Chapter 8. Constance E. Cook, Mary Wright, and Christopher O'Neal provide another fine example of a center's SoTL, in this case using action research to focus on teaching assistants in gateway science courses. This chapter clearly articulates and exemplifies steps in the action research process as well as six useful principles for centers wanting to pursue this scholarship.

Chapter 9. Ruth A. Streveler, Maura Borrego, and Karl A. Smith provide an intriguing account of educational developers doing the scholarship of teaching and learning (conducting outcomes research on an educational development program) with engineering faculty.

Section IV: Instructional and Curricular Development

This section contains six chapters that focus on specific practices and issues related to improving curriculum and instruction.

Chapter 10. Barbara J. Millis explains how complex group work (five cooperative learning techniques) can be used effectively in short classes.

Chapter 11. Peter Frederick and Mary James share a riveting discussion and illustration of best practices in moving beyond rhetoric to truly realizing highly functioning multicultural learning environments.

Chapter 12. Miriam Rosalyn Diamond points out that the ethical challenges that inevitably accompany college teaching demand the attention of educational developers and teaching faculty, and she compares and contrasts the responses of American and British faculty to a workshop that addressed these ethical challenges.

Chapter 13. Therese A. Huston and Michele DiPietro discuss research and its implications for education developers regarding typical instructor responses to collective tragedy (e.g., September 11, 2001, Hurricane Katrina in 2005) and students' perceptions of the most helpful instructor responses.

Chapter 14. Shelley Z. Reuter delineates a process for teaching students to succeed at leading seminar discussions, an endeavor that is developmental for student seminar leaders and for the seminar.

Chapter 15. Larry K. Michaelsen and Mary McCord present outcomes research and recommendations based on extensive experience with a multicourse, integrative, problem-based curriculum where business students use real dollars to create and implement an actual startup business as well as a community service project.

Section V: Faculty Careers

This section includes six chapters that focus on various aspects of faculty development, vitality, and reward at different stages of the faculty career.

Chapter 16. Robert G. Bringle, Julie A. Hatcher, and Patti H. Clayton provide an important service to educational developers with a rich discussion of the nature of engaged faculty work, its development, and documentation. As Boyer's (1996) fifth overarching scholarship, the scholarship of engagement, becomes increasingly integrated into institutional cultures, educational developers may find this chapter to be an invaluable resource as they are called upon to help their institutions promote engaged faculty work by assisting their institutions' faculty to learn how to do it and how to document it for reward.

Chapter 17. Mary Deane Sorcinelli, Mei-Yau Shih, Mathew L. Ouellett, and Marjory Stewart provide a significant contribution to the literature with their evaluation research of an innovative program that addresses the difficult challenge of combining faculty evaluation and faculty development (normally like oil and water) within the context of post-tenure review.

Chapter 18. Shari Ellertson and John H. Schuh illuminate the potentially remarkable impact on revitalizing mid-career faculty through their work with student learning communities. This chapter demonstrates that this increasingly common tool for enhancing student learning and retention (student learning communities) can have significant value for both student and faculty development.

Chapter 19. Kathleen F. O'Donovan and Steve R. Simmons describe an exciting memoir-writing program that guides and supports faculty, particularly senior faculty, in reflecting deeply on their experiences and in making meaning from those experiences.

Chapter 20. Michael Reder and Eugene V. Gallagher report on the procedures and outcomes of an important experiment in a small college environment with a yearlong new faculty mentoring program that features peer mentors (second- and third-year faculty).

Chapter 21. Sean Patrick Knowlton and Laura L. B. Border discuss a promising program in the professional development of graduate students by supporting the exploration of careers (in this case academic librarianship) that may provide attractive alternatives to the usual discipline-based faculty tracks but about which graduate students may be unaware.

The chapters in this silver anniversary edition of *To Improve the Academy* reflect the diversity of its readership and of POD's membership. Like POD, I find the mix satisfying. Paraphrasing Eleanor Roosevelt, if I were asked what is the best thing that one can expect in editing a book, I would say the privilege of readers finding the book useful. I hope that you find this volume satisfying, as I do, but most of all, I hope that you find it useful.

References

Blake, W. (1963). *The marriage of heaven and hell.* Coral Gable, FL: University of Miami Press. (Original work published 1790)

Boyer, E. L. (1990). *Scholarship reconsidered: Priorities of the professoriate.* Princeton, NJ: Carnegie Foundation for the Advancement of Teaching.

Boyer, E. L. (1996, Spring). The scholarship of engagement. *Journal of Public Service & Outreach, 1*(1), 11–20.

Brookfield, S. D. (2005). *The power of critical theory: Liberating adult learning and teaching.* San Francisco, CA: Jossey-Bass.

Cutright, M. (Ed.). (2001). *Chaos theory and higher education: Leadership, planning, and policy.* New York, NY: Peter Lang.

Cutright, M. (2006). A different way to approach the future: Using chaos theory to improve planning. In S. Chadwick-Blossey & D. R. Robertson (Eds.), *To improve the academy: Vol. 24. Resources for faculty, instructional, and organizational development* (pp. 44–61). Bolton, MA: Anker.

Florida, R. (2002). *The rise of the creative class: . . . And how it's transforming work, leisure, community, and everyday life.* New York, NY: Basic Books.

Florida, R. (2005). *The flight of the creative class: The new global competition for talent.* New York, NY: HarperCollins.

hooks, b., & West, C. (1991). *Breaking bread: Insurgent black intellectual life.* Boston, MA: South End Press.

Kuhn, T. S. (1970). *The structure of scientific revolutions* (2nd ed.). Chicago, IL: University of Chicago Press.

Lang, J. M. (2005). *Life on the tenure track: Lessons from the first year.* Baltimore, MD: Johns Hopkins University Press.

Mills, C. W. (1959). *The sociological imagination.* New York, NY: Oxford University Press.

Yeats, W. B. (1940). The second coming. In P. Allt & R. K. Alspach (Eds.), *The variorum edition of the poems of W. B. Yeats* (pp. 823–825). New York, NY: Macmillan. (Original work published 1921)

Ethical Guidelines for Educational Developers

Preamble

Educational developers, as professionals, have a unique opportunity and a special responsibility to contribute to improving the quality of teaching and learning in higher education. As members of the academic community, we are subject to all the codes of conduct and ethical guidelines that already exist for those who work or study on our campuses and in our respective disciplinary associations. In addition, we have special ethical responsibilities because of the unique and privileged access we have to people and information, often sensitive information. This document provides general guidelines that can and should inform the practice of everyone working in these development roles.

Individuals who work as educational developers come from many different disciplinary areas. Some of us work in this field on a part-time basis, or for a short time; for others, this is our full-time career. The nature of our responsibilities and prerogatives as developers varies with our position in the organization, our experience, and our interests and talents, as well as with the special characteristics of our institutions. This document attempts to provide general ethical guidelines that should apply to most developers across a variety of settings.

Ethical guidelines indicate a consensus among practitioners about the ideals that should inform our practice as professionals, as well as those behaviors that we would identify as misconduct. Between ideals and misconduct is an area of dilemmas: where each of our choices seems equally right or wrong; or where our different roles and/or responsibilities place competing—if not incompatible—demands on us; or where certain behaviors may seem questionable but there is no consensus that those behaviors are misconduct.

It is our hope that these guidelines will complement individual statements of philosophy and mission and that they will be useful to educational developers in the following ways:

- In promoting ethical practice by describing the ideals of our practice

- In providing a model for thinking through situations which contain conflicting choices or questionable behavior
- In identifying those specific behaviors which we agree represent professional misconduct

Responsibilities to Clients

- Provide services to everyone within our mandate, provided that we are able to serve them responsibly
- Treat clients fairly, respecting their uniqueness, their fundamental rights, dignity, and worth, and their right to set objectives and make decisions
- Continue services only as long as the client is benefiting, discontinuing service by mutual consent; suggest other resources to meet needs we cannot or should not address
- Maintain appropriate boundaries in the relationship; avoid exploiting the relationship in any way; be clear with ourselves and our clients about our role
- Protect all privileged information and get informed consent from our client before using or referring publicly to his or her case in such a way that the person could possibly be identified

Competence and Integrity

Behavior

- Clarify professional roles and obligations
- Accept appropriate responsibility for our behavior
- Don't make false or intentionally misleading statements
- Avoid the distortion and misuse of our work
- When providing services at the behest of a third party, clarify our roles and responsibilities with each party from the outset
- Model ethical behavior with coworkers and supervisees and in the larger community
- Accept appropriate responsibility for the behavior of those we supervise

Skills and Boundaries

- Be reflective and self-critical in our practice; strive to be aware of our own belief system, values, biases, needs, and the effect of these on our work
- Incorporate diverse points of view
- Know and act in consonance with our purpose, mandate, and philosophy, integrating them insofar as possible
- Ensure that we have the institutional freedom to do our job ethically
- Don't allow personal or private interests to conflict or appear to conflict with professional duties or the client's needs
- Continually seek out knowledge, skills, and resources to undergird and expand our practice
- Consult with other professionals when we lack the experience or training for a particular case or endeavor and in order to prevent and avoid unethical conduct
- Know and work within the boundaries of our competence and our time limitations
- Take care of our personal welfare so we can take care of others

Others' Rights

- Be receptive to different styles and approaches to teaching and learning and to others' professional roles and functions
- Respect the rights of others to hold values, attitudes, and opinions different from our own
- Respect the right of the client to refuse our services or to ask for the services of another
- Work against harassment and discrimination of any kind, including race, gender, class, religion, sexual orientation, age, nationality, etc.
- Be aware of various power relationships with clients (e.g., power based on position or on information); don't abuse our power

Confidentiality

- Keep confidential the identity of our clients, as well as our observations, interactions, or conclusions related to specific individuals or cases
- Know the legal requirements regarding appropriate and inappropriate professional confidentiality (e.g., for cases of murder, suicide, or gross misconduct)
- Store and dispose of records in a safe way; comply with institutional, state, and federal regulations about storing and ownership of records
- Conduct discreet conversations among professional colleagues; don't discuss clients in public places

Responsibilities to the Profession

- Attribute materials and ideas to their authors or creators
- Contribute ideas, experience, and knowledge to colleagues
- Respond promptly to requests from colleagues
- Respect your colleagues and acknowledge their differences
- Work positively for the development of individuals and the profession
- Cooperate with other units and professionals involved in development efforts
- Be an advocate for our institutional and professional mission
- Take responsibility when you become aware of gross unethical conduct in the profession.

Conflicts Arising From Multiple Responsibilities, Constituents, Relationships, Loyalties

We are responsible to the institution, faculty, graduate students, undergraduate students, and our own ethical values. These multiple responsibilities and relationships to various constituencies, together with competing loyalties, can lead to conflicting ethical responsibilities, for example, when:

- An instructor is teaching extremely poorly, and the students are suffering seriously as a result

  Conflict: responsibility of confidentiality to client teacher versus responsibility to students and institution to take some immediate action

- A faculty member wants to know how a TA, with whom we are working, is doing in his or her work with us or in the classroom

  Conflict: responding to faculty's legitimate concern versus confidentiality with TA

- We know firsthand that a professor is making racist, sexist remarks or is sexually harassing a student
  Conflict: confidentiality with professor versus institutional and personal ethical responsibilities, along with responsibility to students

- A fine teacher is coming up for tenure, has worked with our center or program for two years, and asks for a letter to the tenure committee

  Conflict: confidentiality rules versus our commitment to advocate for good teaching on campus and in tenure decisions

In such instances, we need to practice sensitive and sensible confidentiality:

- Consult in confidence with other professionals when we have conflicting or confusing ethical choices

- Break confidentiality in cases of potential suicide, murder, or gross misconduct; in such cases, to do nothing is to do something

- Inform the other person or persons when we have to break confidentiality, unless to do so would be to jeopardize our safety or the safety of someone else

- Decide cases of questionable practice individually, after first informing ourselves, to the best of our ability, of all the ramifications of our actions; work to determine when we will act or not act, while being mindful of the rules and regulations of the institution and the relevant legal requirements.

Conflicts Arising From Multiple Roles

As educational developers, we often assume or are assigned roles which might be characterized as, for example, teaching police, doctor, coach, teacher, or advocate, among others. We endeavor to provide a "safe place" for our clients; we are at the same time an institutional model and a guardian or a conscience for good teaching. These multiple roles can also lead to ethical conflicts.

Some educational developers, for example, serve both as faculty developers and as faculty members. As faculty we are on review committees, but through our faculty development work have access to information that probably is not public but is important to the cases involved. Given these multiple roles, it is important always to clarify our role for ourselves, and for those with whom and for whom we are working. When necessary, recuse ourselves.

Summative Evaluation

A particular case of multiple roles needing guidelines is the summative evaluation of teaching. Faculty and administrators (chairs, deans, etc.) have the responsibility for the assessment of teaching for personnel decisions.

In general, educational developers do not make summative judgments about an individual's teaching. In particular, we should never perform the role of developer and summative evaluator concurrently for the same individual, other than with that person's explicit consent and with proper declaration to any panel or committee. However, we may provide assessment tools, collect student evaluations, help individuals prepare dossiers, educate those who make summative decisions, and critique evaluation systems.

Conclusion

These guidelines are an attempt to define ethical behaviors for the current practice of our profession. The core committee welcomes comments and suggestions as we continue to refine this document in light of the changes and issues confronting us as educational developers in higher education. The guidelines will be updated on a periodic basis.

We would like to thank our many colleagues who offered their thoughtful comments on earlier drafts.

In creating this document, we have referred to and borrowed from the ethical guidelines of the following organizations: American Psychological Association, American Association for Marriage and Family Therapy, Guidance Counselors, Society for Teaching and Learning in Higher Education, Staff and Educational Development Association.

Prepared by Mintz, Smith, & Warren, January 1999. Revised March 1999, September 1999, and March 2000.

Section I

Educational Development and the Sociological Imagination

1

It All Started in the Sixties: Movements for Change Across the Decades–A Personal Journey

R. Eugene Rice
Association of American Colleges and Universities

A combination of memoir and social commentary, this chapter explores changes in higher education throughout five decades—1960s: utopian quest for learning communities; 1970s: faculty development movement; 1980s: focus on the academic workplace; 1990s: broadening the understanding of scholarship; and 2000s: new pathways and the engaged campus. This chapter provides a context for the careers and work of faculty, academic administrators, and faculty development specialists (both new and experienced) as well as for POD.

Many of us involved with the Professional and Organizational Development Network in Higher Education in its beginning years can trace our attraction to the 1960s. The civil rights movement inspired the press for institutional change with authentic moral confidence. The rapid expansion of higher education and the incredible growth during that decade sowed seeds of hope and provided genuine opportunities. Our horizons of expectation broadened. The free speech movement on the Berkeley campus was a fundamental challenge to academic authority. Students were demanding to be heard; the shift from teaching to learning was put in motion—the classroom would never be the same. The empowering—if naïve—words often attributed to Goethe were cited frequently and with conviction:

> Whatever you do, or dream you can, begin it.
> Boldness has genius, power, and magic in it.
> Begin it now.

During those heady days, I remember being inspired by Ralph Waldo Emerson's famous address "The American Scholar." Oliver Wendell Holmes came to regard the essay as "our intellectual Declaration of Independence." In that 1837 address Emerson raised the question I have pursued—or been pursued by—through most of my career: "What is the work of the scholar in a vibrant changing democracy?" It is a question that has its own intellectual tradition running from Emerson and Dewey to Richard Rorty and Cornel West. In the sixties this question and the larger issue, the relationship between education and democracy, took on new life. Dewey's ideas were resuscitated; he had taken the key elements of democracy—freedom and equality—and given them new meaning. On campuses in the 1960s, freedom became not just freedom *from* (e.g., tyranny and oppression) but freedom *to*—freedom to grow and develop, freedom to learn, as individuals, as institutions, and as a country. It is the kind of freedom James Baldwin (1963) wrote about in *The Fire Next Time,* where he reflects on "our racial nightmare." There he speaks of the freedom and opportunity to "achieve our country and change the history of the world" (p. 119). Dewey also gave new meaning to equality: not just to be treated in the same way, but to celebrate our differences and learn from one another, to confront our differences and build a rich mosaic that strengthens our democracy and our humanity.

As we are frequently reminded, the utopian idealism of the sixties was countered by a dark side, the strong opposition to the civil rights movement and a ravaging war in Vietnam. The darkest days came in 1968 with the assassinations of the two public figures holding out the brightest promise for the future—Martin Luther King, Jr. and Robert F. Kennedy.

Higher education itself emerged from the yeasty period of the 1960s with deep structural contradictions. Burton Clark (1987), one of the several talented sociologists devoted to understanding this period, writes of the "paradox of academic work." On the one hand is the structured hierarchy and competition leading to a higher education system that depends on research and is the "envy of the world" (p. 98), and on the other is a diverse and inclusively open system that requires that attention be paid to the quality of teaching and student learning. Clark's conclusion from his perch in a research university borders on the cynical: "This is the way the system operates." He warns that

> Statesmen bent on major repairs soon find that their categorical imperatives, couched in the "musts" and "shoulds" of the rhetoric of reform, stumble over an inability to state "how" the incentives that decisively affect the behavior of institutions and professors might be changed. (p. 100)

The movements for change that I propose to trace through the decades beginning with the 1960s are ones in which I participated and that provided the scaffolding for my career. This is a personal journey shared, I am sure, by many who found themselves affiliated at one time or other with POD, AAHE (American Association for Higher Education), AAC&U (American Association of Colleges and Universities), or other groups coming together to try to make a difference. Our conversations, I am confident, have been saturated with "musts" and "shoulds" (the rhetoric of reform) and have roots going back to the sixties. The movements shaping my life and work over the decades are these:

- 1960s: Utopian Quest for Learning Communities
- 1970s: Faculty Development Movement
- 1980s: Focus on the Academic Workplace
- 1990s: Broadening the Understanding of Scholarship
- 2000s: New Pathways and the Engaged Campus

I have been asked to be autobiographical. I do this with reluctance, not only because I run the risk of reflecting the self-absorption that is a special flaw of academic males in my age cohort, but because I am one of a group of senior faculty who were in fact especially privileged—structurally and demographically advantaged. The year I was born there were fewer babies born in the U.S. than at any other time in the century—born, as they would say in the business school, with a competitive advantage. The public high schools in Denver were unusually strong academically. When I graduated from college, major fellowships were available for those of us willing to consider college teaching as a career. Women were prohibited from applying for the fellowship (Danforth) that paid my way through to the Ph.D., and the number of minority candidates encouraged by their circumstances to apply was few. In the mid-sixties, when I was searching for my first faculty appointment, it was a buyer's market; colleges and universities were expanding in an unprecedented way. When I came up for tenure the process was not particularly onerous; in fact, tenure was often used to entice faculty with competitive offers to stay—a far cry from the present situation.

The professional advantage of my age cohort was a structural one, rooted in long-standing social injustices. This privileged experience often makes it difficult for senior faculty leaders to understand the very trying situations faced by today's early-career faculty or to envision a different kind of future for the professoriate. With this disclaimer I will proceed on my "personal journey" through the decades that frame my experience.

1960s: Utopian Quest for Learning Communities

Beginning a Cluster College

In their book *The Perpetual Dream,* Grant and Riesman (1978) caught the gist of what was so seductive about the experimental college in the 1960s. The winds of change erupting during the decade fanned the embers of utopian longing for community that had always been latent in American aspirations for higher education, and small experimental colleges began to appear across the landscape—365 by one count. California, as you might expect, provided especially volatile terrain.

In 1964, I began my teaching at Raymond College, the first of the cluster colleges at the University of the Pacific. It was intentionally patterned after Oxford and Cambridge: students graduated in three years, required liberal arts (one-third humanities, one-third social science, one-third math and natural science) with no majors, no grades (narrative evaluations), and High Table every Wednesday with the faculty on a raised platform in the Great Hall. The provost and a number of the faculty lived in the quad. Jerry Gaff (whose first book was on the cluster colleges) and I had offices across the hall from each another in one of the student residences. We were a close community—probably too close—and the "Hawthorne effect" was overwhelming.

Despite the utopian ethos, the experimental colleges of the 1960s were, by and large, counterrevolutionary. They came into being in opposition to the dominance of the large research-oriented universities—what Jencks and Riesman described in 1968 as *The Academic Revolution.* What they were opposed to was the rise of an academic hegemony dominated by an increasingly professionalized, research-oriented, discipline-driven, specialized faculty. The counter vision was a more intimate, democratic, student-oriented learning community. There was a Camelot quality to these places, and for a time wonderfully dynamic learning communities took shape. This dream informed my participation and that of many of my colleagues in the reform movements I want to trace across the following decades. It was the resilience of that vision—chastened and more nuanced—that later took me to another experiment, Antioch College, to try my hand at being dean of the faculty.

The vision of the learning community lives on explicitly in the much more pragmatic, diverse, and cost-effective learning communities that are now thriving across most states and sectors of higher education and have joined together to form a major national movement. It is no accident that this movement is rooted in The Evergreen State College experiment.

1970s: Faculty Development Movement

A Study of Danforth Fellows in Mid-Career

In the 1970s, the focus of my work shifted to what became known as the faculty development movement and my membership on one of the early Core Committees that formed POD. In 1974, I went to the Danforth Foundation as a program officer and conducted a study of "Danforth Fellows in Mid-Career." The results were published as the lead article in the first volume of *To Improve the Academy.* That I ended up marrying one of the editors of that volume, Sandra Cheldelin, is probably a pivotal sign of the times and certainly the transformative event in the development of this faculty member—for which I will be forever grateful. I will refrain from discussing favoritism or objective peer review in this silver anniversary edition of the publication.

Maintaining the vitality of faculty had only recently emerged as a national concern. In fact, it was in 1974 that the influential booklet *Faculty Development in a Time of Retrenchment* (Group for Human Development in Higher Education) was published and launched what was to become a national movement. The academic job market had virtually shut down, particularly in liberal arts fields. At the annual AAHE meeting in 1974, Russell Edgerton convened foundation officers to discuss the issue; many—Lilly, Kellogg, Ford, and Danforth—had already funded several faculty-oriented projects. I remember debating, however, whether the concern for faculty development would last beyond the life of the grants.

Fortunately, there was a long-term research effort that was about to appear on the scene and make adult development a national preoccupation. Daniel Levinson's work on adult development had an enormous heuristic impact. His book, *The Seasons in a Man's Life* (Levinson, Darrow, Klein, Levinson, & McKee,1978), was widely read and emulated. Gail Sheehy borrowed from it in writing *Passages* (1976) and launched a very lucrative career. What youth, the "identity crisis," and Erik Erikson were to the 1960s, the mid-life transition, generativity, mentoring, and Daniel Levinson became in the 1970s.

In spring 1975, and again in 1976, the Danforth Foundation invited 300 Danforth Fellowship recipients to a weeklong "Workshop on the Profession of Teaching." Daniel Levinson, William Perry, Herman Blake, and Robert Menges (a formative leader in the early days of POD) took the roles of master teachers. In preparation for the workshops, each fellow was sent the statement of personal and professional aspiration each had submitted when applying for this highly competitive national fellowship as seniors in college, some 10, 15, and even 20 years earlier. They were also sent an article by Levinson sketching out his theory of adult development and were asked to write a reflective essay on the relationship between their stated aspirations and what had actually happened in their lives over the intervening years. In reviewing the study, I was surprised at the number of themes that have persisted over time.

- The disappointment of so many in the absence of colleagueship among faculty. They had anticipated joining a community of scholars and failed to find it.
- The widespread perception of a disconnection between faculty work and the larger purposes of society.
- The sense of institutional drift in higher education.

As an English professor from a large state university in the Midwest put it:

> My profession seems to me to flounder, to have lost faith in its old models and to be unable to find new ones. The result of floundering is a loss of cohesiveness and therefore a constant strain on intellect and emotion. Having lost the common ground that should nourish us, each individual has to invent his profession for himself.

Included in the study was a group of Graduate Fellowship for Women recipients (a program for women started belatedly in the 1960s after years of their being excluded from the competition). These women wrote of their struggles to integrate the personal and professional aspects of their lives as particularly difficult. In reviewing this study, it struck me that one of the major changes confronting faculty in the years since the 1960s is the dominance of the dual-career relationship. We have done very little to address the multitude of problems introduced by this change in the personal side of life. The work on these issues now being sponsored by the Sloan Foundation is especially important.

In my years of working on faculty issues, it was the time spent coping with developmental themes in faculty lives that was most satisfying. During this time, I began to teach a course titled "To Love and Work." I taught it to both traditional-age undergraduates and to what were referred to then as new adult learners. In addition, it was a central theme in my work with faculty. The attention to developmental issues needs to be reinvigorated and built into practice in the field of faculty development. Recent efforts with post-tenure review and later-life career planning could provide the occasion.

1980s: Focus on the Academic Workplace

Organizational Development

In the 1980s, my work and interests shifted from personal and professional development to organizational development. This shift took place in both my local and more cosmopolitan work—in my teaching and research. This integration of the two was one way I coped with the perennial problem of inquisitive faculty who spread themselves too thin. I also moved from the experimental college at the University of the Pacific to the Department of Sociology and took on for a time the role of department chair.

The major study occupying my time in the mid-1980s dealt with the academic workplace in liberal arts institutions conducted for the Council of Independent Colleges (CIC). It gave me the opportunity to work closely with Ann Austin just as she was beginning her career. This study had a large quantitative research component but was also applied—a kind of action research. Ann did the hard quantitative work, and I organized a series of case studies of colleges that were identified in the study as having high faculty morale and satisfaction.

This work was intriguing to me not only because it allowed me to work with small, church-related colleges similar to the one from which I graduated (Pasadena College), but also because it involved working with other disciplines and professionals. We drew heavily on a creative career research project launched by schools of organization and management. The names of Schein, Driver, Van Mannen, Baylin, and Kolb will be familiar.

The organizational factors we identified as contributing to better faculty morale and satisfaction were

- A distinctive organizational culture
- Participatory leadership
- Organizational momentum
- Identification with the institution

Another key characteristic sustaining strong faculty morale and satisfaction emerging from the CIC study was "a broader definition of scholarship." These small colleges had found ways to recognize and reward the scholarly work of faculty that included but went well beyond specialized disciplinary research and publication. It was my preoccupation with this issue that later led to my going to the Carnegie Foundation for the Advancement of Teaching and participating with Ernest Boyer (1990) in the preparation of the Carnegie Report *Scholarship Reconsidered: Priorities of the Professoriate.*

Another impetus that helped shape where I was going with the enlarged understanding of scholarship was an article I prepared in 1986 for my disciplinary journal, *Teaching Sociology*, titled "The Academic Profession in Transition: Toward a New Social Fiction." It was in writing that article, and through the deliberations of a wonderful seminar organized by the American Sociological Association to critique the offerings being considered for the journal, that the scaffolding for the ideas informing my work at Carnegie and later as director of AAHE's Forum on Faculty Roles and Rewards took form.

I am convinced that much about life is shaped by socially constructed fictions, patterns of meaning that cohere at a particular time and place. In preparing the article on the academic profession in transition, I took my lead from the American poet Wallace Stevens (1977):

> The final belief is to believe in a fiction, which you know to be a fiction, there being nothing else. The exquisite truth is to know that it is a fiction and that you believe in it willingly. (p. 163)

Nowhere in the contemporary world do these socially constructed fictions have more power in our lives than in the professions. During that expansionist period in the 1960s in American higher education, a powerful fiction, an image of what it meant to be an academic professional, became firmly established among faculty. It was often reflected in institutional policies, shaped the graduate school experience of many of us, and—most insidiously—became solidly engrained in the way in which we thought about ourselves as professionals. This social fiction had a number of elements; some could be traced back to Oxford and Cambridge, others to Scotland, and most assuredly to the influence of the German universities, but during that heyday of affluence and expansion several came together to form what I tagged the "assumptive world of the academic professional." The controlling elements were these:

- Research is the central professional endeavor and the focus of academic life.
- Quality in the profession is maintained by peer review and professional autonomy.
- Knowledge is pursued for its own sake.
- The pursuit of knowledge is best organized by discipline.
- Reputations are established in national and international professional associations (not locally).

- Professional rewards and mobility accrue to those who persistently accentuate their specializations.
- The distinctive task of the academic professional is the pursuit of cognitive truth.

This image of what it meant to be a scholar becomes normative for most faculty, dominating our thinking about our work, and specifically about what counts as scholarship.

In 1988, I went to the Carnegie Foundation for a two-year period that proved to be a significant turning point in my career. This generative transition was facilitated by the institution in which I had taught for 24 years and the faithfulness of a genuine mentor. Over the years, the University of the Pacific had consistently supported my more cosmopolitan career. When I would receive invitations to go to Washington, DC, or to work on various national projects, I was generously encouraged and would return, excited to be back. I loved teaching and working with undergraduates. The mentor was my undergraduate teacher Warren Bryan (Dick) Martin. When I was a graduate student, I met him crossing Harvard Square, and he invited me to join him in starting an experimental college in California. I accepted without ever visiting the campus for an interview. Dick was later the director of the Danforth Fellowship Program, inviting me there, and then senior scholar at the Carnegie Foundation. More important than the contacts he provided were the intellectual challenges and friendship over the years.

1990s: Broadening the Understanding of Scholarship

Making a Place for the New American Scholar

In 1990, when I left the Carnegie Foundation for Antioch College, the manuscript calling for a broader conception of the scholarly work of faculty was titled "The New American Scholar." I had been intrigued with Antioch since my earliest involvement with the experimental college movement in the 1960s and knew that it was envisioned as a "laboratory of democracy" which, since the inventive work of Arthur Morgan in the 1920s, had struggled to relate intellectual reflection in the liberal arts to the practical work of building a democratic society. The institutional mission was so congruent with my vision of what faculty ought to be doing that when I was approached about applying for the position of vice president and dean of the faculty I could not resist.

I am glad I stayed as long as I did in a predominantly faculty role; it helped me better understand the changing nature of faculty work and increased my legitimacy when speaking about it. I am also grateful, however, for the experience as a chief academic officer. Some things are so complicated and "messy" that they can only be learned from experience. It also helped to have thoughtful colleagues such as Alan Guskin and Michael Bassis when working through the school's severe financial challenges and the contentiousness of faculty, students, and staff who take democratic aspirations seriously.

In 1994, I moved to Washington, DC, and to AAHE. No one could ask for a better platform from which to pursue the agenda I envisioned while at Carnegie—"Making a Place for the New American Scholar"—than to be director of the Forum on Faculty Roles and Rewards. Russ Edgerton, president of AAHE, and an imaginative group of major university provosts founded the forum with significant support from the Fund for the Improvement of Postsecondary Education. From the beginning there was a strategy in place for effecting change on local campuses. Colleges and universities were encouraged to send "teams" of faculty leaders and academic administrators to an annual conference to work on faculty-related issues central to the mission of the institution. Provosts knew that the initiative of their offices would not be enough, but that team members interacting with one another across administrative and faculty lines and with participants from other institutions struggling with similar issues, in the company of key resource people, could make a difference.

The first conference of which I had responsibility was titled "From 'My Work' to 'Our Work': Realigning Faculty Work with College and University Purposes." It took on the critical issue of an atomized faculty culture and the need to collaborate. In 1998, Peter Senge introduced the conference theme, "Faculty Work in Learning Organizations," and initiated a new way of thinking about faculty work. The year 2000 was the 10th anniversary of the publication of *Scholarship Reconsidered.* The new president of the Carnegie Foundation, Lee Shulman, was the lead speaker and the theme was "*Scholarship Reconsidered* Reconsidered." We had an attendance of 1,500, and an opportunity to take stock of what had happened since the publication of the report calling for a broader definition of scholarly work.

When *Scholarship Reconsidered* appeared in 1990, it immediately struck a responsive cord, becoming the bestselling publication in the history of the Carnegie Foundation. The primary agenda of the forum was driven by the issues raised in the Carnegie report about the nature of scholarly work, the changing faculty role, and criteria to be used in making decisions about tenure and promotion. Ernest Boyer's leadership was critical in drawing widespread attention to the report and its agenda. Few others had the national visibility, legitimacy, persuasiveness, and audacity required to effectively take on the task of redefining the meaning of scholarship and raising substantive questions about the relationship between faculty priorities and institutional missions. The report had an ongoing life—"legs" as they say—because Russ Edgerton and the extraordinary staff of AAHE had enough foresight to develop an organizational initiative such as the forum to ensure that the ideas it sparked would not disappear. It was a pleasure to be at the confluence of these events.

The effort to broaden the definition of scholarship generated a large number of campus-based initiatives and a widespread national debate. Whether the effort will result in a movement that permanently changes the academic landscape, only time will tell. Under the leadership of Lee Schulman, Pat Hutchings, and Mary Huber, the Carnegie Foundation has put the scholarship of teaching and learning on the map, and Campus Compact has advanced the scholarship of engagement in creative ways. KerryAnn O'Meara and I (2005) have edited an inquiry aimed at assessing the impact of the work that has been done since the publication of the 1990 report. A series of impressive campus-based studies and a survey of the provosts of all four-year institutions support the claim that the broader definition of scholarship is being given serious consideration and is reflected in the tenure and promotion guidelines of the majority of colleges and universities. The study also demonstrated that the press for faculty research is being ratcheted up and prestige ranks continue to have an invidious influence. As Ernest Lynton put it, many institutions are continuing to strive to be what they are not, and "falling short of what they could be," guaranteed to be second rate.

2000s: New Pathways and the Engaged Campus

The symmetry of my essay is breaking down as I move into the new century and a decade that is incomplete. However, there are two movements in which I have been involved that are gaining momentum: one, the development of new pathways in faculty work—which I find perilous—and the other, the engaged campus—which I find most promising.

One of the lines of work pursued by the Forum on Faculty Roles and Rewards was called "New Pathways: Academic Careers for the 21st Century." The project began by producing 14 studies of different dimensions of faculty work, ranging from tenure to part-time faculty. The New Pathways Working Papers generated widespread discussion—and some rather sharp controversy—

about the future of academic work. The tenure discussions were particularly discordant. I was disappointed at the extent of the "turf" protection in the profession and the lack of openness. I came away with the sense that the fissures between the collegial culture of the faculty and the growing managerial culture were so divisive that unless we can cultivate a more collaborative culture—building on the strengths of both—higher education is going to suffer immensely.

The "Heeding New Voices" study in the New Pathways series (written with Mary Deane Sorcinelli and Ann Austin, 2000) provided insights into the perceptions of early-career faculty that were quite startling. In group interviews conducted across the country, junior faculty repeatedly reported a sense of being overwhelmed, of having—and this phrase was used frequently—an "overloaded plate." The older "assumptive world of the academic profession" I referred to earlier is still normative, but to that work are all the new reform agendas that have been added: the new demands on teaching and engagement, assessment, learning communities, service-learning, the list goes on. The question was raised time and again about whether the academic career we have encouraged to develop will attract the best of a new generation—is it viable?

For both individual and institutional reasons, new pathways are being developed with very little long-range planning. Full-time, nontenure-track appointments are proliferating with no one taking responsibility. Part-time faculty are added and dropped in an almost capricious way; they do the bulk of our teaching with very little faculty development support. Intentionally developed new pathways are much needed.

"Unbundling of the faculty role" is emerging as a key issue. Advances in instructional technology are driving this in settings such as the Open University in the UK and the for-profit institutions springing up in the U.S. Teams of experts—not all of whom are faculty—design online courses in a digital environment, making the unbundling not only possible but perhaps even inevitable. Learning communities involve student affairs personnel, librarians, and housing officers, as well as what we think of as traditional faculty, in the collaborative instructional processes. How faculty in these unbundled settings are rewarded represents a major challenge for the future. I am willing to argue that in the next ten years many faculty will have individualized contracts that are renegotiated every three to five years.

The idea of the "complete scholar" that I have contended for will be a possibility only over the length of one's professional career as one develops different aspects of one's scholarly self at different times. My concern for continuity, institutional memory, and a sense of the whole among faculty leaders is clearly losing ground at a time when—given the rapidity of change—it is most needed. I am confident, however, that in the future the sense of wholeness will be more collective and not as highly individualized as it is now. There is a lot of discussion of "new networks for learning" incorporating a wide variety of academic staff as well as off-campus personnel and resources working collaboratively. In my more optimistic moments, I see us moving toward new forms of reintegration, beyond the narrow specializations and organizational silos characterizing our work now. Doing this without losing the enormous benefits of our highly specialized world will be the challenge. Much of the work on new pathways will make them less hierarchical and more democratic. The big question is this: Will we have a two-tiered system with the nontenured, flexible, collaborative, inclusive appointments—more oriented toward teaching and community engagement—being on one level, and the more elite, tenured, research-oriented appointments being on another? There is some indication that we are already moving in this direction and that the second tier will be composed of more women and have a larger percentage of minorities.

The other movement that is rapidly gaining momentum is the engaged campus, with its emphasis on the scholarship of engagement. In February 2006, I attended a Wingspread Conference sponsored by the Johnson Foundation titled "Engagement in Higher Education: Building a Federation for Action." So many activities around civic and community engagement have blossomed lately that a national call for coordination and collaboration has gone out. The press for greater involvement in public life comes from two contradictory directions. On the one hand, there is the charge that the academy—and particularly the faculty—have become seriously disengaged, hustling for private gain with little concern for the public good. On the other hand, it is being argued that academic knowledge has never been more important to the life of the community, region, state, and global society. After all, the economies of the world are learning based and knowledge driven. Both sides acknowledge that the scholarship of engagement is not being adequately recognized and rewarded, that colleges and universities have failed to fully communicate what is being done to make the connection, and that the walls of our institutions need to be more permeable.

This movement calls for a fundamental change in our epistemological assumptions. No longer can we assume that knowledge is generated in academic settings and applied or exported; the generation and exchange of knowledge need to be multidirectional—a two-way street. Donald Schön and Lee Shulman have made the case for honoring the "wisdom of practice."

If this movement is going to take hold, the relationship between cosmopolitan and local knowledge needs to be more fully explored; local knowledge is undervalued in the academy. Engaged, democratic pedagogy that is active, contextual, and value driven is getting a lot of attention and will be a key element in invigorating this movement. The enduring vitality of service-learning across the disciplines is making a major contribution to this development. Community-based research that has been around for years in various disciplines and professional pockets is now gaining visibility and is beginning to be coordinated nationally. The importance of making academic knowledge accessible can no longer be avoided. We have been irresponsible in the way we have used language. Public scholars are beginning to speak out and community partners are not only demanding to be heard, but to become full and legitimate participants in the pursuit and generation of knowledge.

The academy has never been good at relating theory and practice, and only with the advent of service-learning have we begun—on a larger scale—to generate a creative interchange between intellectual reflection and active practice. Only recently, in reading one of the Beat poets, Gary Snyder (1990), and his reflections on the power of meditative practice in the Buddhist tradition, have I come to a fuller appreciation of practice. He writes, "Practice is the path.... Practice puts you out there where the unknown happens, where you encounter surprise" (p. 153). We need more "surprise" of this sort in our colleges and universities and in our personal lives.

Allow me to close by quoting another poet whose lines I have probably cited in public much too often. These words are to my mind this culture's best commentary on the meaning of work and a fitting conclusion to these very personal reflections. They are the closing lines of Robert Frost's (1949) "Two Tramps in Mud Time":

> Only where love and need are one,
> And the work is play for mortal stakes
> Is the deed every really done
> For Heaven and the future's sakes. (p. 359)

For those participating in the movements for change discussed here, work has not been play, although there have been some wonderful moments. I am confident, however, that important needs are being met by the work we have loved and it is making a difference.

References

Baldwin, J. (1963). *The fire next time.* New York, NY: Modern Library.

Boyer, E. L. (1990). *Scholarship reconsidered: Priorities of the professoriate.* Princeton, NJ: Carnegie Foundation for the Advancement of Teaching.

Clark, B. R. (1987). *The academic life: Small worlds, different worlds.* Princeton, NJ: Carnegie Foundation for the Advancement of Teaching.

Frost, R. (1949). *Complete poems of Robert Frost.* New York, NY: Henry Holt & Company.

Grant, G., & Riesman, D. (1978). *The perpetual dream: Reform and experiment in the American college.* Chicago, IL: University of Chicago Press.

Group for Human Development in Higher Education. (1974). *Faculty development in a time of retrenchment.* New York, NY: Change Magazine Press.

Jencks, C., & Riesman, D. (1968). *The academic revolution.* New York, NY: Doubleday.

Levinson, D. J., with Darrow, C. N., Klein, E. B., Levinson, M. H., & McKee, B. (1978). *The seasons of a man's life.* New York, NY: Ballantine Books.

O'Meara, K. A., & Rice, R. E. (2005). *Faculty priorities reconsidered: Rewarding multiple forms of scholarship.* San Francisco, CA: Jossey-Bass.

Rice, R. E. (1986, January). The academic profession in transition: Toward a new social fiction. *Teaching Sociology, 14*(1), 12–23.

Rice, R. E., Sorcinelli, M. D., & Austin, A. E. (2000). *Heeding new voices: Academic careers for a new generation.* Washington, DC: American Association for Higher Education.

Sheehy, G. (1976). *Passages: Predictable crises of adult life.* New York, NY: Bantam Books.

Snyder, G. (1990). *The practice of the wild.* San Francisco, CA: North Point Press.

Stevens, W. (1977). *Opus posthumous* (S. F. Morse, Ed.). New York, NY: Alfred A. Knopf.

2

Living Engagement

bell hooks
Berea College

Douglas Reimondo Robertson
Northern Kentucky University

In this "talking chapter" bell hooks reveals, through dialogue about her thoughts and experiences related to college teaching and learning, a profound and robust perspective on what could be called "deep" faculty development. Topics include engaged pedagogy, therapeutic conversations, spiritual practice, difference, conflict, and love.

> To engage in dialogue is one of the simplest ways we can begin as teachers, scholars, and critical thinkers to cross boundaries, the barriers that may or may not be erected by race, gender, class, professional standing, and a host of other differences. (hooks, 1994, p. 130)

October 7, 2005, bell hooks's dining room.

DR: To get started, could you summarize your approach to teaching, what you have called "engaged pedagogy"? What have been some major influences on the development of that perspective?

bh: Perhaps the most influential scholar in relationship to my teaching has been Paolo Freire, coupled with the kind of people who taught me in the segregated schools of the south—the black men and women who were my teachers, who were teaching in resistance, who were teaching at a time when segregation was saying that black children don't deserve the right to learn to read and think and to have teachers who were deeply and profoundly committed. When I think about where I learned my love of Shakespeare, it was in those segregated black schools that did not have equal resources. They didn't really even have libraries because library science schools were some of the most racist. Black females couldn't be librarians and it was unheard of for black males. We had only a white librarian who would visit our school once a week. In that atmosphere, learning had such an incredibly precious and engaged element to it. The feeling that learning can transform your life is what led me to Freire and to principles of engaged pedagogy, which talk about the classroom as a community for mutual growth. That is the foundation of my sense of what learning is all about, that it's all about growing and living. So I've always wanted to teach in such a way that unites theory and practice and that enhances students' ability to live in the world more fully.

DR: In *Teaching to Transgress* (hooks, 1994) you write,

> Progressive, holistic education, "engaged pedagogy" is more demanding than conventional critical or feminist pedagogy. For, unlike these two teaching practices, it emphasizes well-being. That means that teachers must be actively committed to a process of self-actualization that promotes their own well-being if they are to teach in a manner that empowers students. (p. 15)

Faculty who feel overloaded might benefit from some examples of how you set boundaries and attend to your own well-being as a part of your professional practice.

bh: I am a big proponent of therapy. For one, I think that many of us who are intellectuals or academics have often been rewarded for the nourishing of our minds, but not for the nourishing of our psychological well-being. So I think we can be as damaged, if not more so, than a general population in relation to well-being because usually we've been encouraged all our lives to cultivate smarts above all else. We've all encountered professors who lacked basic social skills, and it's not my experience that someone who lacks basic social skills—basic skills of communication—is really a dynamic and wonderful teacher in the classroom. It's one of the myths of genius that one can be this almost sociopathic person who is withholding, withdrawing—all of those things—but somehow be this great person in the classroom. I had no experience of that. Lots of my thinking about teaching really has also emerged from my experience as a student, my sense that often teachers were acting out of their own ego-centered issues, insecurities, and neuroses. So I think that a teacher's being engaged in processes of critical self-examination, whether with therapists or in therapeutic conversation with colleagues, is important. I have lots of conversations with colleagues just about how we're doing. Here, where I teach at Berea College, one of my favorite colleagues, a younger African-American woman, has been preparing for tenure, and we've had many conversations. I had no such person in my life, an elder who had gone through this experience and who's able to talk to her about balance, about how to best get the packages together, get everything done in ways that don't wear us down psychologically and emotionally. I think those kinds of therapeutic conversations can be part of a general well-being. We get together at least two or more times a week for lunch. That's one of the pleasures of teaching at a small college, in a small town. It doesn't require a big loss of time to get together. I think those things aid in creating a space where our well-being, as professors and teachers, is considered vital—where I can say to her or she to me, "You know, you seem really overextended, overtly tired, what's happening, what's going on?"

DR: It strikes me that college teaching is a helping profession. It's one of the few helping professions, or the only one I can think of, that doesn't emphasize the well-being of the practitioner as an important professional tenet. Which is part of what I hear you saying about college teaching.

bh: Absolutely. Which is why, I think, I've drawn so much on spiritual practice. In the world of spiritual practice with a "spiritual teacher," as in Buddhism, the teacher is expected to have mastered certain arts of self-development and self-awareness. *Mindful awareness* would be the term we would use within Buddhism. For me, it's been helpful to bring that thinking about what it is to be a teacher into the realm of classroom teaching because we often think of the teacher as someone who's a split personality, not as someone who is whole in mind, body, and spirit.

DR: Related to that, it seems to me that the teacher needs to love the self and love the other, or the student, simultaneously. Some experience that need as an antagonistic contradiction, and others experience it as a generative paradox where, by doing both, one feeds the other. Can you comment on that?

bh: The question of love is intriguing because it presupposes the existence of self-love in the teacher, which automatically reverberates back to your question about well-being. Certainly, in many of the ways that I feel I've grown psychologically in the last 20 years of my life, a lot of that has had to do with the kind of example I wanted to set for my students. I would include growing in the practice of love of myself, which is particularly challenging, I think, as a woman teacher working in a world that is still predominantly male-governed and patriarchal in its thinking, whether that thinking is coming from males or females. It's rugged terrain for feminist women and men and for that practice of self-love that I think automatically dovetails into good practice with our students. I want to be really clear that when I think about love, I think of a combination of six things: care, commitment, knowledge, responsibility, respect, and trust. How do we bring those into the classroom? How do I bring the quality of love when working with a student whom I may find really awful, whom I may in fact not like, but of whom I can still think about how I can best serve? It's great to be at Berea College, an institution that privileges three things: learning, labor, and service. We are not ashamed to identify ourselves and our students as people who give service. I may best "love" a student by suggesting that I am not the right teacher or my class is not the right class for him or her. I think that it's a hard decision to come to in a climate of free choice, free speech, to say that to a student. We all have had those students who annoy us to death because they disrupt, they take over, they try to deflect attention away from the subject matter at hand. How do you cope with that in a loving way so that it doesn't fragment your learning community or make learning impossible? There, I think, is the highest challenge of how one works with the practice of love in the classroom.

DR: The challenge, if I may paraphrase, would be of trying to respond to the individual and to the whole group at the same time.

bh: When you said that, I thought about Mary Rose O'Reilley's (1998) book, *Radical Presence: Teaching as Contemplative Practice.* She talks so much in this little book about being on the path of love by our presence and how we work with the classroom and what we bring into it. It really is challenging. She talks particularly about those of us who are English teachers who she sees as storytellers in that in many ways we're bringing to the classroom a vision of how to be disciplined storytellers and how to create community around the art and act of storytelling. She says,

> We are like old shamans sitting around the fire scaring people half to death, or saving their lives, or healing their hearts. . . . I teach literature and writing, so in my classes it is a two-way

street: I tell stories and I listen to stories. It's quite a weird job for a grown-up. (p. 25)

DR: Is this ability to love the self and the other effectively and simultaneously essentially Gilligan's (1982) third level in developing the capacity to care? It seems to me that what engaged pedagogy is about is learning to love in this way in the professional role of a teacher. Is that something a faculty developer should be helping faculty learn to do?

bh: Absolutely. These questions have come up so much around issues of diversity and multiculturalism. As I've tried to write about in my two teaching books (hooks, 1994, 2003), many of us entered classrooms where we were told, "Oh, we want to be diverse; we want to have multiculturalism," without any preparation for how to deal with difference. How will we deal with the student who comes from a background that you know nothing about or that you may even have some aversion to? The best work that I see being done around faculty development is precisely work that allows people to come to the table to talk about these issues in ways that open up that space for the personal to meet with the theoretical. Early on in the feminist classroom practically everyone was white, and practically everyone was female. In many ways that allowed for a much easier task than what is before us now, where our classrooms are often really diverse. Recently a professor said to me, "I had this class with a small number of men. I went out of my way to make them feel welcome and to really let them know that their perspectives were desired." But in her class evaluations, the majority of the female students said, "You were too hard on the guys." She was really concerned: "How do I address this issue when I felt that I was already bending over backward not to alienate these two or three male students?" I think that the kind of faculty development that allows people to bring concrete problems like that to the table is so much about the practice of love. In the last five years, I pretty much have served as a catalyst for faculty development at different institutions. At Southwestern University in Texas, I had a core group of faculty whom I worked with where we brought issues of concern. Some of them were about religion. What do you do when you're a non-believing professor but you teach at an institution where most of your students are religious? That creates conflict. You're gay, but your students think homosexuality is evil. How do we deal with those concrete things? To me, those are as much faculty development issues as whether we are publishing enough or whether we're getting adequate enrollments. I think that the more sophisticated learning institutions are trying to bring people together in ways that allow faculty to develop those parts of themselves—those awarenesses around difference, identity, nationality—where they may simply have felt they don't know what to do.

DR: I want to situate this next question within a real event. Recently I was conducting a faculty workshop at a self-described public ivy, a respected university, and the workshop topic was helping students to develop critical thinking while they learn disciplinary content and skills, a common challenge. The workshop was on facilitating this paradigmatic transition in students from dualistic thinking, where the epistemological authority is invested in agents outside the self, to a committed relativism, where the epistemological authority and responsibility lie within the self. The self is seen as someone constructing a reality among whole communities of other selves doing the same thing as best they can. It was about helping students to make that kind of developmental shift. Toward the end of the workshop, a new assistant professor raised her hand and asked me what professors are supposed to do if they themselves operate dualistically. How could she be expected to promote this kind of thinking if she herself did not think that way? In the audience, I saw some other faculty heads nod. Given any developmental model, most people inflate their developmental level, and I thought her candor and courage were remarkable, especially in a group setting. What do you make of this faculty member's question, "If I don't have critical consciousness, how can I be expected to help students to develop it?"

bh: I think that's exactly why bringing these issues to bear on faculty development is so crucial. Most of us have been trained in western metaphysical, dualistic, binary thinking. Then, whammo! Suddenly we have talk of diversity, multiculturalism, post-colonialism, anti-racism. People's modes of learning are called into question, without the training that would help them to undo those modes of learning or even to see the wisdom of undoing them. So that again is why these are all such crucial issues for faculty development. Often what happens is we end up with subcultures within institutions where you have a radicalized faculty, usually women's studies, black studies, gay and queer studies, attempting to do the work of reading against the grain, reading against biases. And then you have another institution that is informed by imperialist, white-supremacist, capitalist, patriarchal thinking that just goes on. The question is, how do we reeducate professors who may indeed be closed-minded when it comes to thinking in new ways about the subjects we teach?

DR: That's the nut to crack, and I hope you've got some suggestions. If you create these reflective spaces that you talked about before—faculty development as a place to reflect together and to problem solve and to help each other grow—often the people who come, in my experience, are already highly developed and are desiring to develop further. How do you get those other faculty to become involved? With students you've got the power of grades. You can create assignments that make them encounter difference. How do you do that with a faculty?

bh: Sophisticated institutions have had to find ways to make that type of faculty development mandatory, and to reward it: you take this seminar in the summertime, and you get extra pay. Or, you take this faculty development course, and you have a one-course release. There are lots of ways to build into structures the time and rewards for faculty development. I think one of the amazing aspects of being a teacher right now is that there are so many unemployed teachers. We really have a body of people available so that faculty could have much more time off to reflect and to work on these issues, if our institutions were more flexible. To my way of thinking, there is no reason why any of us in the academy shouldn't be able to take leave without pay whenever we want to because there are so many people desperate to find jobs, and there is the space for that. We have to be clear and honest about the fact that certain types of pedagogy, engaged pedagogy especially, take a lot of energy. There is a feeling at times of burning out or simply not having the energy. One thing about the old styles of teaching, particularly the banking system, is that they don't require a lot of energy. I remember in my early years at Stanford, we would joke about the aged, white, male professors who would bring the yellowed notes that they had been using for 10 and 15 years to give their lectures. There was an element of rote, and it didn't really require all that much. Engaged pedagogy requires one to be fully present, which makes it so similar to contemplative practice. It requires hands-on labor in the classroom, even in just that small gesture of getting to know who you are teaching. One of the issues I face in my feminism course is that there are often more people there than the hour can absorb. I'm always struck that if we do the business of hearing everyone's voice, we've eaten up a substantial amount of our time together. Yet it's continually essential to creating not only that learning community but allowing people to gauge what is interesting to them in the classroom, what they're learning. I always begin class by asking what students have been thinking about, if anything, from the class before. What stimulated them? How did they take it into their everyday life?

DR: Have you encountered situations where there are just more people whom you are teaching than time allows and that the pedagogy has to change? Or do you stick with the pedagogy no matter what?

bh: I think that pedagogy has to always be, in a sense, improvisational in relationship to who is present, who the audience is, and that one has to be aware of what's possible. In that sense, the teacher as a kind of guru has to be able to intimate early on, step into that space, what needs to be done. I think it's a rare professor who can create in a monological way a sense of community and learning. I believe it is usually that mutual spark between professor and student, or students, that allows for the passion of learning to erupt and spread. Certainly, we are constantly challenged. When I began public lecturing, it became really clear to me that the idea that I could take a fixed lecture and make it work in every location was ridiculous. In fact, there has to be some kind of organic communication between me and the learners. When I give a talk, the audience often has different levels of learners. I just recently gave a talk in my hometown [Hopkinsville, Kentucky] at the community college. You have the people who are coming from an institution where they are taking a course on postmodernism; you have a group of people coming from feminist theory; and then you have my parents and people I went to high school with who just want to see what I'm about. What is the lesson plan that addresses all those people? Usually it's a multiple lesson plan. It's polyvocal. It's not one way that can address, speak, to all those audiences. There's a way in which it is about reading quickly. I think of it as exceptional sports, often like exceptional basketball players, what they do. Yes, there are rules to the game that we all apply. At the same time, one has to have unique moves, plays, strategies that are about addressing the team that you are up against or that you're playing with whether in a noncompetitive way or a competitive way.

DR: That's so important, that organic metaphor, especially in an age where through the side door of technology and online course delivery there's an emphasis, especially among administrators, on instructional design, which is a more prepackaged approach. I know that there's rhetoric of flexibility, but in my experience, such a difference exists between that kind of instructional design and the organic stance that you are talking about.

bh: When I first did faculty development with a colleague, Chandra Talpade Mohanty, at Oberlin, we were really surprised to find how open faculty were and that a lot of people simply didn't know what to do. Over the years, I've shared in faculty development simple writing exercises that I use with students. People who didn't think that they could have certain kinds of energies in their classrooms found, "Yes, I can do that; I can have that; it's not something so special or so like you have to be the particularly gifted teacher to do that." That's one reason why faculty development is so crucial. We can move away from the idea that it's individuals' unique gifted qualities that allow them to bring certain skills into the classroom. Rather, there are certain skills that we can all learn together, how to use them, and how to use them while applying our particular personalities and unique styles to those skills because not everybody will be able to do things in the same way.

DR: Helping a faculty member to move from a banking model to a learning facilitation model of teaching is probably tantamount in magnitude to that shift from dualism to committed relativism in students. It's a big paradigmatic shift. It strikes me that there's a transition process in this shift that starts with an ending period, where the person realizes that they can't keep teaching in the same old way. Despite all their resistance, they finally realize that their way of teaching is not cutting it, "It's not making me happy; it's not making the students happy; students aren't learning much or well; I've got to change." Typically, they haven't got the new perspective in place and gelled. There's a disorienting neutral zone where they don't have faith in the old paradigm and they can't quite see the new one yet. In the classroom, that's what we help students to do—to make these shifts where the authority comes into the self and they start taking existential responsibility to choose their knowledge. I think that in the profound sense of faculty development that you're talking about, true development, we're helping some faculty members to make a shift of that magnitude. Do you view it that way?

bh: Actually, that's one of the tremendously positive gifts that the feminist classroom has given to all of our classrooms across the nation by bringing that personal-is-political element and awakening people to greater awareness of how we can use our persons—our personal histories, experiences—to enhance learning. I think that a lot of professors stuck in the old modes of knowing were able to realize that, "Oh, gee, these alternative ways of knowing are attracting students and giving them energy, and we have to implement some of those ways in our own styles of teaching." I think that's been an important gift from the feminist teacher to the overall classroom that is often not honored. Frequently, male colleagues were threatened by me because students would rather take, for example, my Faulkner class because of the kind of teaching strategies that would be used rather than Faulkner taught by someone else who was using the old banking system. It's not that as people who like to put down the different modes of knowing and teaching would say, "Oh, it's easier." One of the things that people engaged in critical pedagogy and feminist thinking brought to the classroom was the basic idea that learning could be enlivening, that learning would not be this deadening process, would not be boring, but that it in fact would make you want to be more engaged and would lead students to want to be more engaged. I think there are many colleagues who saw that and thought, "Well, I'll have to try to incorporate some of this into how I do things because I don't want to be sitting here with no students while they are all in these other classes that are saying to them there is a different way to learn."

DR: A lot of what faculty developers experience is faculty who come in with a kind of banking frame around faculty development: "Just give me the material quick; no liberation here. I just need content quick. I've got 20 minutes over lunch. Do a quick presentation, and I'm out of here." Often, that sits within an administrative context where faculty development efforts need to put up big participation numbers to justify their existence. It's a structural dynamic that works against this kind of true development, which takes time, is much more labor intensive, takes a lot more effort on the faculty's part, maybe even takes some release time. In the end, this deep faculty development is much better for the university. However, it takes a while for the university and the person to get the return, and we're in a culture that has a quick return mentality.

bh: In so many ways, what we're talking about is a teaching of resistance because we implement a lot of these practices within frameworks that are actually structured in such a way that they're hostile to these practices. But the good thing is that there is always this space that can be made for development and that people will enter. I never hear of any case where a space has opened for faculty development where someone hasn't chosen to enter that space to grow. That is a positive affirmation of where, in general, teachers are. I think that teachers are wanting to know, "How can I teach in this world of crisis? How can I teach in this world of closed-mindedness? How can I teach in a world where TV is actually stronger in its pedagogical influence?" We can sit with the facts on paper, and our students will talk back to us from something that they've seen on TV. I think it's that hard wall that has led many more teachers to feel, "I'm open to new development, I'm open to new change because I feel like I'm up against a very difficult space."

DR: Would you talk about these contentious points that are out there now around politics and religion, the blue and the red states, and the cultural wars and so on?

bh: I think this goes back to the future both for faculty development and student growth. We really are going to have to have much more awareness of conflict resolution and how to engage in dialectical exchange without shattering, without falling apart. I still think that the family is the first model of community that many of us know. Within the family, most of us have not seen constructive conflict resolution. We bring that experience into those public domains of our work and our teaching and our learning. I think that the classroom of the future will have to be a far more sophisticated classroom in relation to styles of conflict resolution. How do you teach in a classroom where there are such incredibly divergent belief structures and where people often deal with those differences with aggressive negation as opposed to a spirit of open-mindedness? I think one of the requirements of the classroom to come is the radical openness that I write about in my work because when you have major differences, which we will always have any time you have genuine community, you need to know styles of conflict resolution, of negotiation, of compromise. Most of us do not come either to our graduate education or our teaching profession very well equipped to handle those things.

DR: I find so often that people presume that community means homogeneity, that there are these communities of homogeneity. What you're saying is, I think, rule one is that we as professors and faculty developers need to preach that diversity and pluralism is the basis of true community.

bh: Exactly. There is no community of homogeneity. That is the fiction. And that is the fiction that many of us are wounded within. Whether we are wounded in the fiction that all white people think alike or share in the privilege of whiteness alike, any time that we're not doing the work of sussing out the great diversity that we are learning within, we contribute to that idea that somehow those of us who are in the educational world have transcended difference, have transcended the dirtiness of difference. In fact, allowing that difference to unfold and using it in the classroom is a major positive tool, if we can learn how to do that. I've been teaching one of my hardest classes at Berea because it involves faculty, staff, students, and community people. The president and provost of our college attend regularly, and their presence has raised the question of how to have an open classroom with open discussion when you have people who are at very different points in the hierarchy present in a setting. When you have, in fact, radically different points of entry, there has to be a level of trust and courage present that one doesn't have to have in a classroom where people are on the same level of educational status, age status. These are courses that are aimed at not just faculty development but our collective development in community. It becomes hard at times. You are going to have radically different tensions, and the question becomes how to utilize those tensions so that we learn more.

DR: And that the tensions aren't bad.

bh: Absolutely.

DR: That it's a good thing actually.

bh: Or even that we get away from that binary of bad/good, but that we recognize tension as creating the energy of growth, as being stimulating, and that in fact it may be "bad" at a given moment in time in terms of how we all experience something in a classroom. In one of my Berea classes, a white woman administrator said that the group she felt least identified with was young black men, and many of the parents of young black males in that room felt very enraged and pissed off. You can't disallow that. We can't say, "Oh, this is going to be a good experience." Because, in fact, it may be a painful experience. She felt misunderstood, or maybe in that moment of spontaneous self-revelation she didn't like what she saw within herself. How do we utilize that? But we can't say it's a good moment. Or don't we feel good in this moment? Actually, don't we all feel like we'd rather be somewhere else in this moment? The question is, how do we step back from those feelings of discomfort, pain, or even grief, and allow that material to be a basis for learning?

DR: From the point of view of trying to help people to facilitate that in groups the objective is to be comfortable with it yourself so that when it comes you don't head for the hills and you do see the value of it.

bh: I am a big believer that humor is crucial for faculty development in all these settings where we are trying to deal with shifting paradigms. If we can laugh together, if we can laugh even at some of the difficulties, it's very important for creating the space of essential vulnerability that is needed for the construction of community.

DR: I want to apply this to mentoring now, and particularly among diverse faculty writ large. Many colleges and universities are really interested in developing more effective mentoring programs. You mentioned that you were mentoring a colleague at Berea. It raises the issue of best practices. What training would help mentors to do it better? Issues of cross-racial, cross-gender, cross-identity mentoring come into play here.

bh: One of the primary skills of mentoring is nurturing growth, and certainly we know in terms of gender studies and feminist studies the low value that we place on nurturing. Mentoring is always such a loaded issue for people because it truly is about nurturing growth. It means a willingness to humble oneself in relationship to someone else, both for the person who may require mentoring and for the mentor who needs to assume a leadership position. I've never wanted to be a leader in my life. It's been hard for me to feel that I have the right or the requirement to assume the role of leader, of guiding someone else. I tend to be much more focused on mutual exchange because I think our old models of mentoring had within them so much dominator-culture power breakdown of servant/served rather than an idea of service that allows for the mutual interplay between teacher/student, mentor/mentee. I think that as we nurture those new models we will hear more about how both people grow in the situation of sharing with the other person.

DR: I've had trouble with the mentor idea because it is a patriarchal notion from the get-go, from the myth. It does have a power relationship. I like this model that you are talking about, this mutual nurturing model.

bh: It's reciprocal nurturing. When we use a phrase like *reciprocal mentorship,* we embrace the idea that there is a give and take here, that it's not one person extending to another solely, but that it is about our mutual extension to one another. I've benefited from my colleague who is very junior to me. Her support and her belief in me, even her admiration of me, is important to my acclimatization here where I am a new person. It becomes part of the spirit of welcomeness. That reciprocal nature of interaction allows me to focus on what this person has given to me, as well as what I can, in fact, give to her. To bring into our faculty development vision notions of reciprocity is crucial as a counter to the old way, which was, let's face it, so much about domination, so much about subordinating yourself to the person in power, not being critical, not angering them. Once again we are in the dysfunctional family, and there can really be no free speech and no questioning of authority. Being able to highlight individuals who are actually using different ways of interaction and how that works is important. So many people are afraid that if they step outside the conventional hierarchy they're going to be misused or mistreated, or they are going to lose authority. And I think that dovetails back to some of your earlier statements about intact self-esteem. If my self-esteem is fully intact, if I am fully actualized, then I can engage in the practice of mutual actualization with others and the community because I am not threatened by the sense that someone can take something away from me. It's just so hard for us because of the way the academy is currently structured. The academy has been so much about people with levels of low psychological self-esteem using power in a dominating way and subordinating others through dehumanization, shaming, goading, one-upping, all of those things. We really have to focus on all of the little places, the little subcultures within, where people are engaged in different practices.

DR: It strikes me that if I were wanting to put together a program that was supportive of diverse faculty, I would pick people, regardless of color, gender, identity, who were nurturing teachers in the sense that we've been speaking about. That whole approach to teaching would translate well in terms of helping a colleague to grow and develop. Do you have thoughts on that?

bh: I think that people's needs are really radically different and that we're better able to mentor or to facilitate growth if we center clearly on what an individual needs. I want to step back from that gender-laden word of nurturing because there are a lot of female faculty who would appear to have "nurturing skills," but those skills may not actually be the skills that facilitate growth in an academic or intellectual setting. Those skills may lead somebody to only want to say good things and not want to say really difficult things. Recently one of my colleagues gave me her tenure self-evaluation to look at, and I felt, okay, do I really look at this and tell her what I think is not adequate or good about it, or do I do a light critique? I asked her, "What do you want? What are you comfortable with?" And in her case, she said, "I really want this to be the best it can be. Go for it!" But I think we're often afraid. We have to talk about honesty because part of what happens when people are not fully self-actualized is they will often act as though they can receive truth and then in fact be blown away when they are given a truth. I always feel that caution around colleagues who say, "I want to give you this piece of writing to read and critique." You have to be gauging both your willingness to do this but also gauging where they are in their psychological and emotional growth in order to know what can be received.

DR: I want to read to you a quote from Elizabeth Ellsworth (1989):

> If you can talk to me in ways that show you understand that your knowledge of me, the world, and the right thing to do will always be partial, interested, and potentially oppressive to others, and if I can do the same, then we can work together on shaping and reshaping alliances for constructing circumstances in which students of difference can thrive. (p. 324)

Do you think she got it right?

bh: I think that she got it right for her. I don't presume in any way the presence of oppressive anything in interaction. The assumption that somehow there will always be some kind of something about you that is oppressive to me, which seems to be one of the aspects of the quote, is not something that I would particularly agree with. For me, a big part of dominator thinking has always taught us that with the stranger, with the different, there is always threat. We could equally be saying that with the stranger, with the different, there will always be curiosity, intrigue, and the excitement of mystery. Rather than frame difference in terms of that which threatens or might potentially threaten you and let's both know that, why can't we equally frame difference as intriguing, mysterious, something you will want to seek out. I think about this reframing a lot. When I teach my course and we talk about dominator culture, how do we reframe? If dominator culture has taught us to always and only see difference as threat, how do we begin to reframe that so that we can in fact see difference as something that is positive, that has the potential to be transforming, that difference may be difficult, even painful, but that that will not necessarily lead to a bad ending?

DR: I agree with you totally there. The phrase that Ellsworth used was "potentially oppressive." So it's like a warning to me that I have to remember that when I'm doing something I might be silencing somebody without even intending to or I might be advantaging somebody over somebody else without intending to.

bh: I think that evokes for a lot of people the aura of political correctness, where you're being so careful not to say, do, or behave in any way that could be harmful, which I think has resulted for a lot of people in greater paralysis and passivity. Rather than engaging in certain kinds of difficult dialogue and exchanges, people just shut down because they feel it's too much work not to say anything that will offend anyone. Going back to humor, my humor is often "off" for my students. They don't quite get it, but I can't worry all the time about that. What we can laugh about is that they are not getting it as something they think is funny and that can be a point of commonality for us. What is sad is that so many people have forsaken the path of resistance to dominator culture precisely because they fear being controlled by the specter of political correctness: "I don't want to hurt anybody. So I won't even join the discussion. But also, I don't want to be hurt." Instead, we need to frame it that here we are, capable of taking care of ourselves, that in genuine community, which requires vulnerability, yes, there may be occasions in which people feel hurt. For example, in 2004 I taught a group of faculty, staff, and students, and one black student said, "Oh, I was out in Wal-Mart and this white woman asked me if I worked there." The black student saw this as racist, and she was very angered by it. I said, "Well, given the history of the civil rights struggle, if all you have to worry about in terms of racism is somebody thinking you work at Wal-Mart, you're really quite fortunate." But that did not go over well in the classroom. It was perceived that I was not being sensitive to her pain. But I was trying to get her to contextualize her pain and realize that people sometimes focus on small things and see them as having far greater weight than they should have in the scheme of things. Again, I think that's where so much fear of political correctness comes in because just challenging that person, momentarily, I felt I lost her, by not addressing her, "Yes, I understand that was awful for you," but instead really saying, "Well, come on, let's ask ourselves, can we really compare that to people sitting at Woolworth counters while people are spitting on them and threatening to kill them and arresting them?" We can put it into perspective and not lose our sense of proportion in relationship to domination even as we do hold people accountable for racism, for racist perspectives, and the like. Those are essential things that we need to talk about in faculty development because I think these are all the issues that faculty grapple with beyond diversity alone. The vast majority of our classes are not diverse racially. The vast majority of classes are white, and our faculties are predominantly white. But some of the same issues prevail: Who are we in that classroom and how do we deal with the differences of opinion and values that come up in that classroom setting? It's been easy for white faculty to presume a sameness in the all-white classroom that is really not there, and it can be unacknowledged if space is not made for that difference to speak itself.

DR: Sometimes, a slim line exists between feeling heard and feeling exposed. You ask your students to write reflectively and then to read aloud in class often or to speak about what they've been thinking. Also, you model it as a teacher; you disclose as a teacher. Would you talk a little about this teaching practice?

bh: I think, one, it's important to let students know what is required at the very beginning so that in choosing that class they are choosing to participate in those acts of self-revelation, so that it does not become something they didn't feel they should be required to do or they don't want to do. I've had students who choose and then still refuse. Then I have to let them know they're failing this part of their grade. But that's their choice. I am not going to try to force them to participate, but I would like them to know that this is what's required of them and of myself. We're constantly going back to the issue of self-responsibility and accountability. So much of what happens in the classroom as it is currently structured is the students' desire to be passive and to feel acted upon. Part of our enormous challenge as critical pedagogues, as people who want to teach liberation, is to first break through that idea of their passivity as a student, as someone who is without control over their destiny in the classroom, and to create that sense that they indeed are in control of their destiny. Oftentimes, I encourage students to grade themselves and then to come to me and talk about the grade. That level of self-monitoring and self-evaluation takes away that sense of the dominating teacher versus the subordinated student.

DR: As I hear you talk about your approach to teaching, it seems to me that it applies directly to faculty development work with colleagues, of trying to encourage them to see that they can take more direction in their own development. The parallels are striking to me.

bh: But that's because I think that we have to reframe our thinking about where learning takes place. In the courses that I teach that involve faculty, staff, and students, one of the first things we talk about is that learning does not simply take place in the classroom. It is also taking place in how we conduct ourselves with one another as administrators, in how I conduct myself if I'm the chair when someone who has lesser rank comes into my office. We need to view all those interactions as part of learning. Part of what's unique about Berea College is that we are governed by great commitments. One—impartial love—is the theme of my class this semester. How do we really show impartial love in our interactions and beyond the classroom? I think that we need to begin to teach faculty, administrators, and staff that learning isn't just taking place in the classroom, and service isn't just taking place in the classroom, but it's also taking place in the myriad ways in which we conduct ourselves in our actions outside the classroom. When I first met Paolo Friere, it wasn't what he was doing in the classroom or on the stage as a lecturer, but how he conducted himself as an individual where I saw him living out the truth of his theory that was so amazing and so impressive to me—and so challenging. I wanted to know how to do that, how to be that liberating teacher, whether I'm in the classroom, or whether I am going in to speak with the secretary, or whether I am going in to speak with one of the janitorial people who are busy pushing a mop as I am headed to my classroom at 8:30 in the morning. I think that is a challenge of the classroom of the future in extending the vision that development isn't just about the classroom, isn't just about faculty and students, but about our collective interaction with one another as communities of learning.

DR: Excellent.

bh: And let me just say that we particularly see that on those campuses where presidents are very proactive in promoting discussion and allowing for dissent. It is happening in many places, often not at the public ivies or the private ivies but at other schools where people are simply trying to do the right thing, to create spaces of humane and marvelous learning. Often you find administrators in those settings who are willing to dare to be different, whose own experiences are governed by affirmative values about how we should interact with one another. And so faculty development is always happening in a parallel way to what we are expecting of students in the classroom.

DR: That's excellent. It's not marginalized. It's at the center of the endeavor, and the formal leader at the top is exemplifying the same value that is being worked out in the classroom. There's alignment and consistency.

Wonderfully said. About this idea of where you have worked, I want to close our dialogue with a different line of conversation. It seems to me that you've not only lived a career of engaged pedagogy but also of engaged scholarship. You've worked long and hard as a public intellectual who struggles with problems of direct relevance to much larger communities than narrow disciplinary niches. You've commented about being an intellectual in an anti-intellectual society, and you have also made a clear distinction between being an academic and an intellectual. You've noted that your experiences taught you that being an intellectual in an academic institution, such as a university, is not always a good fit, notwithstanding the life-of-the-mind rhetoric of most colleges and universities. Can you comment on the supportiveness of the American academy for public intellectuals who practice engaged scholarship? What could be done to make colleges and universities more supportive of this kind of work? Do faculty developers have any role in helping to support engaged scholarship?

bh: I, myself, would not use the term *public intellectual.* I have no negative thoughts about it, but it's not something I've ever really felt like, "Oh, this represents me." I think usually when people use that term what they mean is, "I'm an intellectual who has been very committed to service and service outside the academy." When we talk about the future and the appreciation of academic intellectuals, we really have to talk about greater unity between learning institutions and the communities surrounding those institutions. There will be a diminishment of the value of even being at a college or university in the future if we don't have a greater effort to unite theory with practice beyond the academy. Then we will see the academic as someone useful to society beyond what they're doing in their classroom setting or their specific scholarship that 10 people may read. It's interesting that popular films like *A Beautiful Mind* or even *What the Bleep Do We Know?* have become examples of how that can be done. I mean, think of all those scientists that people are listening to in the film *What the Bleep Do We Know?* It's kind of amazing when you see just ordinary people looking at this film and learning from people that it would never have occurred to them to think, "Oh, okay, this particular physicist will have something to say to me as an ordinary person." That kind of bringing of intellectual, academic work into a public arena allows everyday people to recognize that this work contributes to the quality of their lives. Part of the tragedy, I think, of our times in our nation and in a cultural pedagogy that is ruled by conservative media is that we really exist with a lot of ignorance. It's important to cut through that arrogant ignorance. It's not just that it's ignorance. It's that there's an arrogance about it, that we don't have to know things to rule the world. I think that we will have to make great efforts as teachers, as administrators, to bring back some valuation to knowing—to knowledge itself, which means working to create better links among public schools, high schools, and university settings. Why don't we ever think about rewarding faculty development that is about going outside the university into other kinds of schools? I do a lot of programs with public libraries because I think that the public library remains one of the great bastions of where alternative ways of knowing are accessible, free to all. The most intense pedagogical challenges of my career have been those challenges that take place outside the privileged setting of the academy. Recently I did a part of a literacy program in Chicago, going to the south side of Chicago and poor neighborhoods, reading books with kids, and talking about critical thinking. I remember entering that setting, and I could palpably feel the level of suspicion directed at me because I didn't look like how a famous person should look. I didn't carry myself in a dominator-culture mode, which is how most people understand celebrity. Those challenges of moving our work and seeing our work as being relevant to a world beyond the academy are part of faculty development too, and are, I think, extraordinarily neglected.

DR: Do you think that the sense of doing something that's useful for specific communities and for larger societies is a particular burden of the public university or is it one that extends to both public and private practice?

bh: To me, it extends to all people who are engaged in practices of critical pedagogy and learning. It's just really exciting. I wish that I could adequately describe the difference between writing an important piece of literary criticism that very few people read and writing something where people feel like this utterly transformed their life. Once you do the other it's almost like the difference between sitting at a computer playing a basketball game and actually being on a basketball court, playing, having your whole body engaged, extending itself, growing. It's just such an awesome, wonderful feeling of that work you do. I'm sometimes shy of the term *public intellectual* because what always amazes me is the little laboratory of ideas that I work within is often a space that is so private, so solitary, and often so lonely. That those ideas can move out beyond that solitary space into an incredible world and be influential is for me the

> awesome quality of what one can do as a thinker, writer, intellectual, and not, in fact, that somehow one starts out in some public arena and you're testing everything there. Things are not tested there. They're not formed there. They're formed in the silences and in the space of critical reflection and contemplative practice.

Acknowledgments

We gratefully acknowledge the following colleagues who contributed to the pool of interview questions (listed alphabetically): Elizabeth Barkley, Stephen Brookfield, Constance Cook, Patricia Cranton, K. Patricia Cross, Barbara Holland, Matthew Kaplan, Sally Kuhlenschmidt, Claire Major, A. T. Miller, Mary Deane Sorcinelli, Christine Stanley, Elizabeth Tisdell, and Barbara Walvoord. Also, we thank Laura Brenner, research assistant in the Professional and Organizational Development Center at Northern Kentucky University, who so ably transformed the recorded conversation into an editable transcript.

References

hooks, b. (1994). *Teaching to transgress: Education as the practice of freedom.* New York, NY: Routledge.

hooks, b. (2003). *Teaching community: A pedagogy of hope.* New York, NY: Routledge.

Ellsworth, E. (1989, August). Why doesn't this feel empowering? Working through the repressive myths of critical pedagogy. *Harvard Educational Review, 59*(3), 297–324.

Gilligan, C. (1982). *In a different voice: Psychological theory and women's development.* Cambridge, MA: Harvard University Press.

O'Reilley, M. R. (1998). *Radical presence: Teaching as contemplative practice.* Portsmouth, NH: Boynton/Cook.

3

Surviving to Tenure

James M. Lang
Assumption College

For most new faculty, anxiousness about the tenure application begins from the first day on the job. Surviving the six intervening years on the tenure track requires a range of time- and career-management skills that new faculty may only learn piecemeal along the way. New faculty need help in five specific areas in order to survive their path down the tenure track: 1) developing teaching strategies that will fit their personalities and reach as many students as possible, 2) managing their time to allow for research and publication, 3) determining what and how many service commitments to make, 4) existing peacefully and productively with their colleagues, and 5) preparing documentation for their tenure cases from the start of their careers.

Nine days from the date I am writing these lines, in November 2005, my tenure case will be decided by the evaluation committee at my college. I am hopeful. The prospect of a substantial raise, of job security, and of a life settled into my college and community all represent significant golden apples that I would love to hold in my hands in the near future. And I shouldn't underestimate my excitement at the possibility of securing a sabbatical next year, for which I am busily lining up writing projects and conference proposals.

Whether or not tenure falls my way—and by the time I am writing the last lines of this chapter, I suspect I'll know the answer—I can say at this point that I have survived *until* tenure. And that is no mean feat. In my 2005 memoir of my first year as an English professor, I chronicle the lessons I had learned from my first year in the faculty trenches: teaching seven courses, trying to maintain my writing projects, learning about committees and service, and struggling to balance a chronic illness and the obligations of a family with two small children. Nearly five years have elapsed since the conclusion of that first year—and, God help me, three more small children have come along—and those five years have enabled me to gain some perspective on what I wrote, and on the lessons that I learned in my first year, as well as on those I hadn't yet learned.

In what follows, I will draw on my experiences over those next five years, and on my ongoing and informal study of the shape of faculty lives in the 21st century, to offer five broad guidelines for how new faculty can best survive their own paths to tenure. I wish the lessons lined up neatly, one learned or practiced per year on the tenure track, but they don't. They came to me piecemeal over the course of my 11 semesters on the tenure track, and some are lessons that I need to relearn constantly, reminding myself of them anew each semester.

No guidebook or set of rules will guarantee anyone tenure. But following these simple principles can smooth the journey and put new faculty in a position to make strong cases for themselves when they are preparing their tenure applications. These principles should also help ensure that faculty arrive at that milestone with enough sanity and energy to savor and make the most of that first post-tenure sabbatical.

In the Classroom

I suspect that most people come to teaching the way they come to parenting, if they have children. You begin by raising your children with the basic rules which governed in your own house when you were a child. My wife's family ate dessert every night, and her mother was an excellent cook, making gourmet meals for their family of four. I come from a family of seven, with a mother who cooked large, serviceable meals, and I lived with a diabetic brother. So dessert, which came once a week in our house, if that, meant a bowl full of Jell-O or some other lame pseudo-dessert. When our kids want dessert, they know which parent they should appeal to. I tell them dessert's a special treat, to be enjoyed rarely; my wife rolls her eyes at such moralizing and dishes out the ice cream.

The rules and strategies our parents used with us resemble the rules and strategies our college teachers used with us: They formed the initial limits of our imaginative horizons, confining our understanding of what was possible with our own children or our students. And my own experiences, as well as the experiences of many faculty members whose teaching I have studied or discussed with them, suggests that we often have difficulty stretching beyond the limits of the horizons formed in our youth, or in our own educational experiences.

When I was an undergraduate English major, I had three formative pedagogical experiences as a student. In a Renaissance literature class, the professor frequently told us to get in groups and discuss a question or issue that she raised at the beginning of the class. I *hated* that class. The group discussions seemed aimless and pointless, people contributed to them unequally, and I just wanted to hear what the teacher had to say.

In a general education class in theology, by contrast, the professor lectured to 100 or more students about the "Kingdom of God"—a title hardly designed to appeal to us undergraduates, who were much more focused on the kingdom of humanity. And yet, with his colored overheads (the advanced technology at that time), his amusing anecdotes and clear explanations, and his enthusiasm for his subject, he enthralled me. I rarely missed that class, despite the fact that no one took note of whether I was there or not.

Finally, in a required course for undergraduates in the College of Arts and Letters—the equally lamely titled "Ideas, Values, and Images"—the professor ran the course entirely by discussion. For each new reading we filled out a worksheet that summarized the reading and then gave our opinion of it. In class, the professor initiated the conversation, and then let us have at it. And have at it we did, much to my great pleasure. Those discussions were some of the most charged intellectual experiences of my life.

The limits of my pedagogical horizon were largely formed by these three courses and offered a simple prescription for my own teaching: be witty and entertaining in lectures; hold life-changing discussions; *never* use group work.

Sit through a week of classes with me these days, and you will see a minimal amount of lecturing, a very small time allotted for potentially life-changing discussions, and lots of group work. When students aren't working in groups or holding discussions, they might be writing in class or helping me organize facts or information about the topic for the day on the board, in anticipation of that life-changing discussion—a discussion that we sometimes never get to.

So what happened?

What happened was something I believe should happen to every faculty member at some point in their careers—and the sooner the better. In my first year of teaching, I came to the simple realization that students learn in different ways. Some students—like most of us who earn advanced degrees and teach in higher education—learn best by reading and listening to lectures. Other students learn best by participating in discussions and exercises designed by the teacher. Still others learn best when they have the chance to work with each other and to move together to meet and overcome intellectual challenges. And one student I know—and she surely can't be the only one—told me that she only learns material when she reads it aloud!

While I was smoldering in those group discussions in Renaissance literature, some of my fellow students were no doubt engaging with the text in ways I couldn't understand. And while I was happily listening and taking notes in my theology course, other students may have been nodding off, or having trouble keeping their notes caught up. Those life-changing discussions in my seminar may have seemed like pointless arguing to some of my peers.

The lesson here is simple but has important pedagogical implications: Not everyone learns the way I did, and not everyone learns the same. Therefore, however formative my educational experiences were, I need to look beyond them and consider how I can vary my teaching methods in order to reach the largest numbers of students. The only true statement about teaching that I know is that there is no one right way to teach. I would add to this the corollary that, given that, and given the different learning preferences of our students, I should teach in as many different ways as possible: lecture some, hold some discussions, structure some group activities, have students write or solve problems in class, and so on.

I used group work reluctantly in my first year of teaching, remembering my own awful experiences with it. When the student evaluations came at the end of the semester, a significant minority of students wrote that the group work days had been the best days of the course, and that I should use more of them in the future. So I followed their prescription and began to incorporate more group work into class. But I held on to the other activities as well, so that the students out there like me get to sit and listen for a bit. In a 75-minute class, I might plan three or four different activities, each of them designed to appeal to different kinds of learners.

Of course, new faculty will find that one or two styles of teaching have special appeal to them, and they may find themselves more or less talented in certain forms of teaching. But if they want to succeed in the classroom—and they want to earn the positive student evaluations that will mark that success to their tenured colleagues—they should vary their teaching methods on a regular basis, designing classes which will appeal to multiple kinds of learners.

At the Writing Desk

Poet and novelist Jay Parini (2005) argues that the best route for faculty to become productive researchers and writers is to write a little bit every day. "A little work every day," Parini says simply, "adds up" (p. B5). Parini explains that he made it a goal to write two pages of text every day, and that he often did so in the small, 20- or 30-minute spaces he found scattered throughout his day.

I read with some amusement the discussion forums in the weeks following this column, since I have always worked in precisely the way that Parini recommends. While Parini's argument had some defenders, many writers argued that publishing scholarship in such a manner was not feasible.

My reaction to the article, and to the debates that followed it, was split. On the one hand, I work precisely as Parini recommends, sometimes sitting down to write just one paragraph on my current project, for no more than five minutes, on any given day. At the same time, I agreed with the readers who responded that scholarship which required substantial research was extremely difficult to produce in this manner. The writing I do in this piecemeal fashion has always been creative writing—nonfiction essays aimed at more popular periodicals, or essays like this one about academic life (which was produced over a month of brief, daily writings). I find that producing research-based writing in my scholarly field requires longer ramp-up times before I can write—time to review my notes, to reread what I have written, to consult sources, and to craft sentences that will face more critical academic scrutiny than my creative work will.

Most faculty members will be producing scholarship of this kind, and—outside of summers and winter breaks—will find the large chunks of time necessary to produce such scholarship infrequently in their first years on the tenure track. And yet the pressures of tenure hardly allow time and space to ignore research projects until three or four years have passed by, and new faculty are settled into more predictable routines.

So what to do?

The faculty members whom I have seen successfully produce scholarship while managing demanding teaching loads take the spirit, if not the letter, of Parini's recommendation and find ways to accommodate it into their schedule. The literal recommendation to produce a piece of finished writing every day may not be feasible. But taking some action to further your scholarly project—reading a journal article, typing up a page of notes, spending a half-hour photocopying materials in the library—certainly should be. Even if new faculty accomplish five small tasks like this each week (giving themselves two off days), they will be making progress in their scholarship.

The real work of that scholarship will likely have to come on days when they can set aside larger chunks of time—breaks and holiday weekends, or an odd day in the semester when they have no grading to do and they've done all the reading, and they find themselves with a free afternoon. Eventually they will learn to foresee these chunks of time on the horizon, do the preparatory work in the days leading up to them, and set reasonable writing goals to accomplish during them.

But for me it has been equally important to acknowledge that some weeks during the semester—when, thanks to my poor planning, I have 90 essays to turn around in a 10-day time frame—will be times when I free myself from the obligation of any writing or research. In my fifteen-week semester, teaching three or four classes, I find this happens to me for three or four weeks, mostly near mid-semester. During those three or four weeks, I tell myself that I need to concentrate on my teaching for a short period of time, and I absolve myself of any guilt for doing so. That absolution makes me a more efficient grader and teacher, and allows me to return to my research or writing the following week with fresh eyes.

So much of this seems psychological, and I believe that to be true. Finding the time and energy to commit yourself to scholarship while you are teaching means accepting very limited goals for yourself and having the doggedness and the patience to meet those goals on a daily and weekly basis. A close friend of mine, and next-door office neighbor, writes in the same genre as I do. He writes in bursts, though, and doesn't sit down to write unless he sees one of those big chunks of time before him. When it came time for him to apply for tenure, he looked back over his publication record and saw that he had published only seven pieces of writing, all of them brief nonfiction essays.

"I guess I just haven't been as productive as I thought," he said to me in dismay.

My colleague is a wonderful teacher, puts in long hours at his job, and has far more natural writing talent than I do. But he recognized at that moment that his working habits had betrayed him and kept him from producing at the level he would have liked.

Your new faculty members may not be the sort of people to whom daily writing or small goal-setting comes naturally. I'm not either. Many days the last thing I want to do at 10:30 p.m. is sit down and crank out a paragraph or two on a current project; reading the newspaper or watching television always seems like a more attractive option. But as my growing family of small children left me increasingly small chunks of time in the evening to advance my writing and research, I became the sort of person for whom daily writing and limited goal-setting formed my routine.

Any new faculty member can become that sort of person too—and doing so will help make them more productive and efficient scholars, without compromising their standards in the classroom.

On Committees

Each year the nominations committee at my college sends an email to all faculty listing the college-wide committees and the open positions on each of them. We are asked to respond with our preferences for the committees on which we would like to serve. No one is obligated to serve on any committee, of course, but tenure-track faculty do have to demonstrate their willingness to contribute to the college community from their first year on the faculty.

These committees range in purpose, gravity, and time commitment from demanding curriculum-setting bodies like the Standing Committee on General Education Requirements to lighter obligations such as serving as the faculty liaison to the campus bookstore. There are dozens of committees, and as a new faculty member I had a hard time determining which ones seemed both appealing to me and not too demanding.

Of course, these college-wide committees don't represent the only opportunities we have for service—or that any new faculty member will have as well. Our department has committees on which I can serve—planning an annual dinner for our seniors, search committees, committees to craft and recraft our departmental mission statement—and every search committee on campus consists of one person outside the department, so there are always opportunities to serve on search committees for other departments.

Students, too, offer up opportunities for service commitments. Student leaders invite us to the dorms for talks or meals with students; publications and clubs need advisors; and students need faculty advisors and mentors in both formal and informal settings.

New faculty members will be faced with this same bewildering array of possibilities to demonstrate their commitment to their institution—and they know that they have to demonstrate this without allowing these obligations to push their pedagogical or scholarly priorities too far off the screen.

So how do they make this decision?

They need to keep the end in mind from the beginning. Most institutions ask that faculty who are applying for tenure write a self-evaluation as a part of that application, one that includes a listing and analysis of their service contributions. In that document, a faculty member wants to be able to put together a picture of someone who has a distinctive contribution to make to the life and community of his or her institution. This can be done by selecting service commitments, from the first year on the tenure track, which are connected by common threads.

Faculty will have trouble doing that if they randomly choose new committees on which to sit each year. Trying out some different committees in their first year or two can help give them a broader picture of how your institution works, but by their second or third year they should be settling into patterns in terms of their service commitments.

One of my colleagues, who came to our department to teach journalism and writing, has focused his commitments to the college in that area. He advises the student newspaper; he sits on the writing emphasis committee; he arranges for visiting writers to come to campus; he started a literary magazine on campus. In his self-evaluation, he was able to make a very convincing case that he has dedicated himself to raising the visibility of writing on campus and to helping our students take writing more seriously and become better writers.

In preparing this section of my self-evaluation, I found that I was not able to put together quite the same level of coherence in terms of my service commitments, and that made writing my self-evaluation, and defining my contributions to the college community, that much more difficult. I did have at least one extended thread, which spun out from a number of initiatives I had helped to develop to promote dialogue about teaching among the faculty, but I had a host of other random commitments that I had a hard time putting into a coherent few paragraphs in my self-evaluation.

New faculty should take a year or two to learn about what kinds of service obligations are available to them—serving on one or two of those strange committees if they can't make up their mind—and then figure out what they have to offer to the campus community outside the classroom, so they can build up a service résumé that presents a coherent picture of their commitments to the college or university community.

With Colleagues

During my first year as a new faculty member, I had little sense or understanding of the past or present conflicts within the department (and conflicts and unpleasant histories exist in every department). I was too buried in papers and meetings and deadlines to worry about which of my colleagues didn't like each other. As far as I could tell, everyone seemed likeable and seemed to get along with everyone else.

Late in the spring semester of my first year, an extremely contentious meeting—the nadir of which occurred when one of my colleagues looked another in the eye and said, in a voice dripping with venom, "You talk too much"—opened my eyes to the fact that the department was not the collegial paradise I had envisioned. From that point on, and especially as I found myself with more leisure time to contemplate my surroundings in my second and third years, I began to look more carefully at interactions among my colleagues and at how they spoke to one another and voted on each other's proposals in meetings. The battle lines emerged slowly, and although I could never fully understand the reasons they disliked each other, I could see who usually argued with whom.

And of course, like any human being would, I wanted to know the sordid stories that had led to the outrageous display I had seen in that meeting and that caused the air to turn a few degrees colder when certain colleagues passed each other in the hallway. By my third year I had found a colleague, a junior faculty member a couple years farther along the tenure track than me, who was more than willing to divulge as much of those sordid histories as he knew.

The information came filtered through his viewpoints, of course, and those viewpoints were strong in their support of certain members of the department, and even stronger in their condemnation of other members. Along with two other junior colleagues, I became increasingly drawn to this faculty member's perspective and to his clarifying vision of the department. He knew who was evil, who was good, and who didn't matter.

After almost every department meeting we held, we would find ourselves out with him at the bar, where he would reinterpret what we had seen and heard in the department from his perspective as the omniscient narrator. He would explain to us the "real" reasons for the arguments people were making or for the votes they were casting. These sessions became exercises in the art of hermeneutics. Everyone's comments and votes had a subtext that called for interpretation on our part, and we set about the task with a glee that I am ashamed to recollect.

The more this activity continued, the more I began to feel as if I were working in a highly antagonistic and fraught environment, one in which every word I heard from any of my colleague's lips had multiple subtexts. I recounted to my wife the theories I had developed—or had been told, more accurately—about my evil colleagues and marveled at their duplicity and ill intentions.

And, mentally and emotionally, I became consumed by these matters. I spent so much time practicing the hermeneutics of suspicion that departmental politics became more important to me than my teaching or writing. Every lunch, every time we met for drinks, every trip into the offices of one of the colleagues on our side—they all became occasions for griping and interpreting and plotting.

I was saved from all of this, fortunately, by the actions of the very colleague who had ensnared me in this web in the first place. He had lost his temper and behaved in a highly unprofessional way in that contentious meeting way back in the spring semester of my first year. I had overlooked it then; after all, I came to believe he had right on his side. But as I was most deeply caught in his perspective on the department, I began to see him lose his temper more frequently—at my colleagues, at a student, and once even at me and the other colleagues who had supported him.

After one of these events, I told him that while I supported his positions in the department, I really couldn't support him when he lost his temper and insulted my colleagues. Another cohort conveyed a similar message to him. And that was it. He retreated from all of us, friend and foe alike, and we have hardly spoken since.

Almost from the moment it happened, I felt an overpowering sense of relief. I felt as if I were breathing the free air again for the first time in years. I looked at everyone around me, in the department and the college, with a fresh pair of eyes—my own. Once I climbed out of the tunnel of his perspective, I found that the landscape of the department had changed entirely.

My colleague had convinced me that a group of my senior colleagues were in a cabal to block positive change in the department and to ruin his career. I looked more closely at their behavior over the past few years and realized that they were no more guilty of plotting than my suspicious colleague (and the rest of us) had been. I saw that my senior colleagues had a vision for the department, one that they were willing to fight for—just as I was willing to fight for my own vision of the department, or my colleague for his.

I remembered then that this was how democracy worked. I remembered too that programs or decisions that emerge from debate and discussion and compromise are usually more thoughtful and productive ones than those that emerge from exercises in groupthink. I began to value their opposing positions—even though I still disagreed with them—rather than seeing them as evidence of sinister plots to stifle us.

But most importantly, I abandoned at that point the hermeneutics of suspicion and adapted instead the hermeneutics of collegiality. The hermeneutics of collegiality rely on the premise that everyone seeks the good for both themselves and the department. They ask you to see people's proposals and statements in that light—exactly as you would want people to see your own proposals and statements. The hermeneutics of collegiality ask you to take the statements of your colleagues at face value—to assume they mean what they say. They ask you to respond in kind. The hermeneutics of collegiality don't believe in projecting hidden intentions or sinister motives onto people's statements and behaviors.

The hermeneutics of collegiality have a potential downside; new faculty may, in fact, end up working with a colleague who is undeniably selfish, or mean-spirited, or ill-intentioned. Practicing the hermeneutics of collegiality with this person may lead a new faculty member to Pollyannaish responses that open them to injury.

They should practice it nonetheless. The injuries to which they may expose themselves from practicing the hermeneutics of collegiality, in this faculty member's opinion, will be far less damaging to their career than the mental and emotional strain and exhaustion they will feel from practicing the hermeneutics of suspicion.

Jumping Through Hoops

Every new faculty member should become a pack rat.

At the landmarks of tenure and promotion, pack rats will find themselves the envy of their colleagues who like to keep their offices purged of old lesson plans, day planners, and long-forgotten computer files.

When the time came for me to produce my self-evaluation, I had kept most of my publications updated on my curriculum vita, as well as other basic information about new courses I had developed and the numbers of times I had taught each course. I remembered many of the major service commitments I had undertaken in my five years at the college, such as service on college-wide committees or search committees.

But it wasn't until I pulled my old day planners off the shelf that I remembered the times I had been invited to student dormitories to spend an evening critiquing resumes, or the film screening that I had arranged for my class but opened up to the college. I saw many events and contributions recorded in my daily log that would have otherwise escaped my attention but that contributed substantially to the picture I was trying to paint of myself as a faculty member who believed in the student-centered mission of the college and supported it with my time outside the classroom.

Electronically filed lesson plans also proved instrumental to me in making my tenure case. For each course I teach, I keep a separate folder saved on my computer, and into that folder are saved the lesson plans for every class session. Sometimes those plans are so basic that recording them seems silly; other times they include extensive lecture notes, discussion questions or issues, and handouts or worksheets I use in class.

One of the pillars upon which I rested the teaching portion of my self-evaluation was the idea that I am constantly trying new strategies in the classroom, experimenting and hoping to grow and develop as a teacher. I was able to make that case—and able to support it with an appendix full of evidence—because of all those old lesson plans I had saved, and I could return to and remember the experiments that had failed, those that had been so successful that they folded into my regular teaching routine, and those that I am still tinkering with. Tracking my own development as a teacher through that electronic pile of lesson plans, while I was writing my self-evaluation, was both a fulfilling and helpful experience.

Of course, tenure-track faculty will jump through a good half-dozen of these hoops before they write and teach and serve their way to full professor: first-year reviews, third-year reviews, tenure reviews, applications for promotion to associate and full, and perhaps even post-tenure reviews, which seem increasingly likely in all of our futures. The good news is that those hoops are clearly mapped out for new faculty members from the moment they step onto the tenure track.

They'll sail through them with less effort if they're saving and filing from day one on the job.

Coda

Today I found in my mailbox a letter from the provost indicating that the college had granted my sabbatical request for the 2006–2007 academic year. It's customary at my institution that sabbatical requests are granted before we hear official word about our tenure cases (since those cases need the stamp of approval from a variety of bodies, figurative and literal, some of which meet irregularly). But I've heard that the college withholds that information from faculty members whose cases are in trouble—so while it's not official word, it's a heck of a good sign.

Whatever happens with my case, by the time you read these words I will have survived until the close of my tenure application year—and I will have been deeply and richly contented with my life on the tenure track. I will have seen many hundreds of young people walk through the doors of my classrooms and offices, and I will have inspired some of them to think differently about their lives, to write for love and money, and to burn a novel or a poem into their memory forever. I will have spent many happy hours at my writing desk, shaping words into sentences and paragraphs and essays, an activity that gives me more personal satisfaction than anything else I know. And I will have spent a lot of time on campus, and off campus, interacting with intelligent and interesting colleagues, people who speak many languages and have traveled the world and write books and make music and study lobsters and dig for lost civilizations.

None of which is to say that I won't enjoy equally getting away from it all, and spending my sabbatical on the projects I have been rolling over in my mind for the past couple of years, projects that needed larger chunks of my time and mind than I could give them even during the summers. In my home office, I won't be far from campus physically (2.3 miles, to be exact), but in my mind I'll be on the other side of the world.

And yet still a small part of me will feel the tug of the tenure track, and the tenured track, and will miss my classrooms and my colleagues and my office at school. And when my year is up, though I'm sure I'll regret the loss of that unstructured ocean of sabbatical time, I'll be ready to return.

References

Lang, J. M. (2005). *Life on the tenure track: Lessons from the first year.* Baltimore, MD: Johns Hopkins University Press.

Parini, J. (2005, April 8). The considerable satisfaction of 2 pages a day. *The Chronicle of Higher Education,* p. B5.

Section II
Paradigms

4

A Critical Theory Perspective on Faculty Development

Stephen D. Brookfield
University of St. Thomas

This chapter argues that critical theory implies a number of conceptions and practices of teaching, and it applies a critical theory perspective to conducting faculty development. It speculates on how faculty development might be organized according to some insights drawn from critical theory, and it reviews the chief reasons why teachers resist engaging with this perspective.

My understanding of critical theory focuses on three core assumptions regarding the way the world is organized: 1) that apparently open, western democracies are actually highly unequal societies in which economic inequity, racism, and class discrimination are empirical realities; 2) that the way this state of affairs is reproduced as seeming to be normal, natural, and inevitable (thereby heading off potential challenges to the system) is through the dissemination of a dominant ideology of capitalism and the natural selection of merit assuring that the most capable and talented rise to the top; and 3) that critical theory attempts to understand this state of affairs as a prelude to changing it. Taken together, these three assumptions explain so much of what I see happening around me, in macro-political terms and also in the intimate spheres of daily life.

When this dominant ideology works effectively, it ensures that an unequal, racist, and sexist society is able to reproduce itself with minimal opposition. It functions to convince people that the world is organized the way it is for the best of all reasons and that society works in the best interests of all. Critical theory regards dominant ideology not as a value-free descriptor of whatever set of beliefs the majority of citizens live by but as inherently manipulative and duplicitous. From the perspective of critical theory, a critical adult (and, by implication, a critical teacher) is one who can discern how the ethic of capitalism, and the logic of bureaucratic rationality, pushes people into ways of living that perpetuate economic, racial, and gender oppression. Additionally, and crucially, critical theory views a critical adult as one who takes action to create more democratic, collectivist economic and social forms. Some in the tradition (e.g., Cornel West) link social change to democratic socialism, others (e.g., Erich Fromm) to socialist humanism.

Conceptions and Practices of Teaching Inherent in Critical Theory

A number of conceptions and practices of teaching seem to me to be inherent in critical theory's formulations. From Marx's 11th thesis on Feuerbach onwards, I view the theory as full of activist intent. Indeed, as Horkheimer (1972) argues in his essay defining critical theory, the theory can only be considered successful if it produces revolutionary change. Theorizing exists so that people can understand the dynamics of political, economic, racial, and cultural oppression. With that understanding they can then began to challenge these dynamics and learn to create new social forms, particularly new conditions of labor, that allow them to express their creativity. So critical theory is normatively grounded in a vision of a society in which people live collectively in ways that encourage the free exercise of their creativity without foreclosing that of others. In such a society people see their own well-being as integrally bound with that of others. They act toward each other with generosity and compassion and are ever alert to the presence of injustice, inequity, and oppression. Creating such a society can be understood as entailing a series of learning tasks: 1) learning to recognize and challenge ideology that attempts to portray the exploitation of the many by the few as a natural state of affairs, 2) learning to uncover and counter hegemony, 3) learning to unmask power, 4) learning to overcome alienation and thereby accept freedom, 5) learning to pursue liberation, 6) learning to reclaim reason, and 7) learning to practice democracy.

To teach informed by critical theory is, by implication, to teach with a specific social and political intent. Critical theorists intend that their analyses and concepts will help people create social and economic forms distinguished by a greater degree of democratic socialism. Although teaching critically has a transformative impetus, there are noticeable differences in the ways different theorists pursue this. However, one theme—the inevitably directive nature of education—remains constant across critical theory. Critical teaching begins with developing people's powers of critical thinking so that they can critique the interlocking systems of oppression embedded in contemporary society. Informed by a critical theory perspective, faculty development would have a very specific and highly political agenda. Its purpose would be to help faculty learn to see that capitalism, bureaucratic rationality, disciplinary power, automaton conformity, one-dimensional thought, and repressive tolerance all combine to exert a powerful ideological sway aimed to ensure that the current system—both within and outside their institutions—stays intact.

Helping faculty to think critically about their practice—an oft-espoused aim of faculty development programs—would take a form very different from what we see at most faculty development days. Critical theory views critical thinking as the educational implementation of ideology critique; that is, as the deliberate attempt to penetrate the ideological obfuscation that ensures that massive social inequality is accepted by the majority as the natural state of affairs. Adults who learn to conduct this kind of critique are exercising true reason; that is, reason applied to asking universal questions about how we should live. Questions considered at faculty development opportunities might be: What kind of college work arrangements and teaching practices will help faculty and students treat each other fairly and compassionately? How can we redesign teaching, staff, and faculty development, promotion and tenure, and the conduct of departmental meetings so that these encourage the expression of human creativity?

This form of critical thinking is only the beginning of critical theory's educational project, however. The point of getting people to think critically is to enable them to create true democracy—what Fromm, Marcuse, West, and others regard as the cornerstone of socialism—at both the micro and the macro level. If adults think critically in this view they will be demanding worker cooperatives, the abolition of private education, the imposition of income caps, universal access to healthcare based on need not wealth, and public ownership of corporations and utilities. Critical thinking framed by critical theory is not just a cognitive process. It is inevitably bound up with realizing and emphasizing common interests, rejecting the privatized, competitive ethic of capitalism, and preventing the emergence of inherited privilege.

Conducting faculty development in a manner informed by critical theory is, therefore, inherently political. It is political because it is intended to help people learn how to replace the exchange economy of capitalism with truly democratic socialism. For faculty within private colleges or proprietary institutions this would be particularly difficult to realize! It is also political because it makes no pretense of neutrality, though it embraces self-criticism. Finally, it is political because it is highly directive, practicing, in Baptiste's (2000) terms, a pedagogy of ethical coercion.

Methodological Approaches

Although critical theorists share a common recognition of the politically directive nature of education, they do not advance any kind of methodological orthodoxy to describe how such education should take place. However, three contrasting methodological clusters or emphases are discernible in the canon, each of which has implications for faculty development. The first of these clusters is the need to teach a structuralized worldview that analyzes private experiences and personal dilemmas as structurally produced. In faculty development terms, a structuralized worldview is one in which teachers are helped to see that individual classroom troubles (e.g., the resistance or sabotage offered by a small group of students, the need to rush through content quicker than one wishes, the imperative of teaching and grading according to a rubric developed by a team of "specialists" one has never met) are actually the result of wider structural forces. Changes in the legislature, a new policy agenda from Washington, DC, the fallout from lurid stories of the failure of higher education that make the tabloids, the prospect of winning a large grant from a local industry—all these factors shape classroom events just as much as the personal histories of the students and teachers involved. (Of course, these personal histories are structural products, too.) Faculty development would help white teachers who work mostly with black and brown students, or black teachers who work mostly with white students, understand how much of the resistance that each teacher faces has been sculpted by years of racial tension and racism.

Two theorists who strongly advocate teaching a structuralized worldview are Erich Fromm (1955) and Angela Davis (1983), though to a degree all in critical theory advocate this. Fromm's perspective as a therapist and social psychologist is that adults' intellectual development means they are much better equipped than children to realize that forces external to their own whims and inclinations shape their lives. He feels that adults' accumulated life experience provides the curricular material that can be analyzed for evidence of the impact of wider social forces. Fromm would clearly see faculty development (comprised as it is of adult participants) as a prime forum for teaching a structuralized worldview. His hope would be that teachers would then become adept at teaching this to their own students. Davis consistently urges that any teaching about women's issues must always illustrate how individual lives are shaped, and injured, by the workings of capitalism. For her, this is crucial to the development of political consciousness and to women's psychological well-being. They learn that what they thought were problems visited on them by an arbitrary fate, or the result of personal inadequacy, are in fact the predictable outcome of the workings of capitalism and patriarchy. This is a life-saving realization. For women faculty who consistently suffer from having spent extra time with students rather than closing their door to focus on their own writing, identifying patriarchy in their institutions is particularly crucial. Being denied tenure because one has taken teaching too seriously needs to be worn as a badge of honor, not as shame or self-loathing.

A second pedagogical emphasis in critical theory explores the need for abstract, conceptual reasoning—reasoning that can be applied to considering broad questions such as how to organize society fairly or what it means to treat each other ethically. Critical theorists, particularly Marcuse and Habermas, argue that critical thought is impossible if adults have learned only to focus on particulars, on the immediate features of their lives. For example, people need some basis for comparing the claims of various groups that they should be treated differently because of their history, race, culture, religion, and so on. As long as we live in association with others there has to be restrictions placed on the liberty of those who behave in ways likely to injure others. How we decide what these limits should be is based on some broad concepts of fairness or social well-being. Your right to smoke a cancer-inducing cigarette cannot be exercised regardless in a small room containing asthma, lung cancer, or emphysema sufferers. So if living socially requires the development of rules of conduct that have a level of generality beyond that of individual whims then we need to be comfortable thinking in broad, abstract terms. Deciding which rules should be followed, and how these might be established in ways that ensure their general acceptance, are matters that require a level of thought beyond that of saying, "This is what I want because it works for me in my life." Freedom, fairness, equity, liberation, the ethical use of power—all these "big" ideas are central to the critical tradition and all contain a level of universality entailing the exercise of abstract, conceptual thought.

In a faculty development context, this means asking the "big" questions about the purposes and features of teaching such as: What makes a good teacher? Why do we teach? When do we know that learning is happening? How do we define learning? What does it mean to teach ethically? How and when do we abuse our power as teachers? These are questions we all ponder as teachers, but usually this happens in private. Rarely, if ever, do they surface in a department or faculty meeting or in team-teaching. One of the few times

I have seen group conversations about these questions among teachers has been in a faculty development context when a group of teachers meets to convert a classroom course to an online format. Under the skilled guidance of an instructional developer's questions, teachers are provided with a rare opportunity to ask basic questions about what they believe is important and why this is so. They are required to clarify among themselves what it is they wish students to be able to accomplish in a course and how learning is recognized. Only once have I seen time for the consideration of such questions included as a matter of course as a regular item on the agenda of a monthly faculty meeting.

A third element stressed in some variants of critical theory is the need for adults to become "uncoupled from the stream of cultural givens" (Habermas, 1990, p. 162). This momentary separation from the demands and patterns of everyday life allows them to view society in a newly critical way. Gramsci and Marcuse argue that a temporary detachment from social life is a necessary spur to critical thought, with Marcuse conducting a sustained analysis of how separation, privacy, and isolation help people to escape one-dimensional thought. This element in critical theory receives less contemporary attention probably because privacy is now, as Marcuse admits, a resource available chiefly to the rich. Also, Marcuse's emphasis on how a powerfully estranging, private engagement with a work of art leads to the development of rebellious subjectivity smacks to some of elitism. It also raises the specter of unrestrained individualism, an element of dominant ideology that prompts deep skepticism among many of a critical cast.

In the practice of faculty development, I believe there is still a place for separation, privacy, and isolation, despite its compromised nature. One of the approaches I use in my own teaching—the emphasis on students doing private, separated, and isolated reading of original critical theory material before engaging in small group discussion of this—is applied in my faculty development work in the context of faculty reflection groups. I am a strong advocate of such reflection groups, particularly those where topics for conversation are under the control of teachers themselves. However, I do not believe that faculty developers can assume that teachers know how to participate in democratic, respectful conversations. The people who talk the loudest and longest inside such groups are often those whose social locations mean their voices get the most attention in the world outside.

I have argued in a book coauthored with Stephen Preskill (2005) that teachers do not leave their racial, class, or gender identities at the meeting room door, nor do they forget their previous participation in meetings and conversations with all the humiliations and manipulations these often entailed. For a teacher reflection group to look anything remotely like the ideal speech situation described by Habermas, its participants will need to evolve, and adhere to, rules of discourse that exemplify these features. Since the exercise of these rules cannot be left to chance, the group will have to find some way to monitor observance of these.

Because groups are often unwilling to acknowledge and confront the hierarchies and power dynamics they import into their activities, faculty developers can help illuminate these. They can consistently draw attention to the need for inclusive models of conversation such as the circle of voices, circular response, snowballing, or newsprint dialogue (Brookfield & Preskill, 2005). They can intervene in conversations to stop the most privileged and vociferous from dominating by declaring a ground rule that the next couple of minutes of conversation are reserved for those who up to now have not had a chance to contribute. They can also democratize the conversation by advocating the three-person rule. This rule holds that once someone has made a comment they are not allowed to contribute again until at least three other people have spoken. The only exception to this is if someone else in the group directly asks a speaker to say more about their original comment. Developers can also distribute to the group the results of anonymous participant evaluations if these reveal that some people feel shut down and unheard. And they can acknowledge constantly the fact of their own power and how this is being exercised to create conversational structures that equalize participation and prevent the emergence of an unofficial pecking order of contributions.

Resistance to Faculty Development Conducted in a Critical Theory Key

In this section I want to reflect on some of my own personal experiences doing faculty development in a way informed by critical theory. This experience has taught me that the one fact on which I can depend in this work is that faculty will resist, often quite strongly, viewing their teaching through the lens of this tradition. Five elements in critical theory seem to present particular problems: 1) the emphasis on Marx, 2) the critique of capitalism the theory entails, 3) the questioning of democracy (particularly the identification of the tyranny of the majority), 4) the difficult language used by critical theorists, and 5) the radical pessimism induced by constantly reading analyses that emphasize the power of dominant ideology and the way it effectively forestalls any real challenge to the system. Let me deal with these in turn, beginning with the issue of Marxophobia.

One of the first things I do when introducing a critical theory perspective is to position it as a response to Marx. I do this as a matter of scholarly honesty. Since I believe Marx's work to be the foundation and fulcrum of critical theory—its theoretical starting point—it would be disingenuous not to make this clear. Hearing this is difficult for some faculty who wonder if it means that only Marxists can make use of critical theory. The rampant Marxophobia commented on by Peter McLaren (1998) means that any body of work connecting to Marx's ideas, no matter how critically these ideas are examined, is immediately suspect. Teachers with a strong commitment to values of individuality, liberation, and creativity—the same values emphasized in Marx's manuscript on alienated labor (Fromm, 1961)—see reading Marx almost as an unpatriotic act. It is as if by opening the pages of *Marx's Concept of Man* (Fromm, 1961) one is rejecting democracy, free speech, even America itself.

It is important to say that it is not only third or fourth generations who have this difficulty. Teachers from former communist regimes who have fought in wars, suffered the loss of family members, seen the disappearance of livelihoods, and been forced into exile by those regimes also have an understandable visceral reaction to Marx's association with critical theory. It does not seem to matter how many times I point out that critical theorists unequivocally condemn the automaton conformity, surveillance, and one-dimensional thought they see in totalitarian communism, or how many times these theorists assert the primacy of true democracy. Once Marx is mentioned—unless it is to denounce anything associated with him—you have immediately created a problem in several teachers' minds.

So how to respond to this situation? One thing is to emphasize early on the self-critical nature of critical theory itself and how this critical perspective is applied to Marx's work as well as to capitalist ideology. I quote Gramsci's warning against the idolatry of Marx, Marcuse's insistence on the need to take a critical approach to critical theory, West's essay on the indispensability yet insufficiency of Marxist theory, and the blindnesses of race and gender in Marx identified by hooks, Davis, Karenga, and others. A useful resource here is Noam Chomsky's (2002) essays on "The Leninist/Capitalist Intelligentsia" and "Marxist 'Theory' and Intellectual Fakery." Chomsky, one of the most prominent leftist scholar-activists in the US, has a long record of public ideology critique, so his credibility is strong. He is scathing about the way Marxism-Leninism reveals, in his view, strong elements of authoritarianism and condescension. These are seen most prominently "in the very idea that a 'vanguard party' can, or has any right to lead the stupid masses towards some future they're too dumb to understand for themselves" (Chomsky, 2002, p. 226). Chomsky views Marx as a theorist of capitalism who has an interesting abstract model of how capitalism functions, but one that can be improved on, refined, and broadened. He says he hasn't "the foggiest idea" (Chomsky, 2002, p. 228) what "dialectics" means and admits "when I look at a page of Marxist philosophy or literary theory, I have the feeling that I could stare at it for the rest of my life and I'd never understand it" (Chomsky, 2002, p. 228). For many people, this is enormously reassuring! It is important to stress, however, that Marx should not be introduced so circumspectly as to rob his ideas of any force or power. There is a thin line between encouraging a healthy skepticism of Marx, or of any theorist, and predisposing people to dismiss him. The point is not to set him up for easy demolition, but to demonstrate that a serious reading of Marx can happen without readers feeling they somehow have to convert to Marxism.

The second source of resistance critical theory induces concerns its critique of capitalism, particularly the "single existential judgment" offered by Horkheimer (1972) that critical theory's chief project is studying how to abolish the exchange economy of capitalism. A critique of capitalism—the way it commodifies creativity and labor, makes reason its servant, reduces friendships and intimate relationships to the exchange of personality packages, and fuels spiritual malnourishment—is threaded throughout critical theory. One reason this disturbs people so much is because they recognize features of their own life in this critique. It calls into question the professional location, and by implication the professional practices, of teachers themselves.

We live in a country where capitalism is propounded as dominant ideology, as obviously a "good thing" that supports admired values of freedom, liberty, and individuality. Capitalism is lauded for the prosperity it brings, the technological advances it stimulates, and the way it disseminates the innovative spirit of entrepreneurship among the population. For those working in proprietary institutions, or private colleges that operate as nonprofit institutions, to hear a sustained critique of capitalism, and a documentation of its injuries, is highly threatening. Even faculty in public institutions find themselves increasingly in thrall to capitalist mores as they are exhorted to cut costs, increase their productivity, and become better at attracting customers (students) in an ever more competitive market place.

This is why it is important, early on, to get teachers to distinguish between capitalism's ideology and functioning and their own role in the system. One way to bring teachers to consider a critique of capitalism is through Fromm's analysis of alienation. Fromm is the critical theorist who had the greatest success introducing a Marxist-inclined analysis of American life to mainstream America itself. His outlines of the social character of capitalism with its stress on punctuality, orderliness, and pulling for the team, his analysis of the marketing orientation with its emphasis on producing attractive personality packages for exchange on the open market of relationships, and his warnings against the pull of automaton conformity are all couched in still recognizable vignettes and accessible language. As a starting point for understanding Marx, Fromm is far more appealing to suspicious teachers than, say, Gramsci or Althusser. Fromm is also very good at critiquing statist, totalitarian communism, and pointing out the automaton conformity and alienation rampant in totalitarian communist regimes.

A third source of resistance lies in critical theory's condemnation of the way democracy has been distorted to serve capitalism's interests. The radical democratic strain evident in critical theory also regards the realization of genuine democracy as blocked by the simple-minded assumption that a majority vote inevitably ensures the right course of action. Assuming that a majority vote is by definition correct is based on the belief that the choices the majority make represent the free and uncoerced realization of authentically felt needs. Critical theory argues that in reality automaton conformity, one-dimensional thought, self-surveillance, and the steering mechanisms of money and power combine to ensure that these supposedly "authentic" majority needs merely mimic dominant ideology. The radical democratic critique holds that in "comfortable, smooth, reasonable, democratic unfreedom" (Marcuse, 1964, p. 1), majority choices are by definition manipulated and compromised, uncritical expressions of needs that capitalism and bureaucratic rationality have created. Contemporary democracy is thus seen as representing the automatic tyranny of the majority, rather than an inclusive, open-ended conversation.

To hear democracy critiqued this way is very tough for a lot of teachers. They can live with a critique of capitalism, but democracy? How can that be bad? Even some who are relatively comfortable with reading critical theory become very alarmed when democracy is called into question. This makes the idea of democracy a fine example of what linguistic philosophy calls a premature ultimate; that is, a term that is held in such reverence that its invocation effectively ends any further debate or critical analysis. Teachers can get away with pedagogical murder if they justify their practice by saying they're striving to act democratically.

One response to the resistance to any critique of the majority vote model of democracy is to remind people that critical theory and democracy are not at odds. There is a radical democratic strand in critical theory that sees genuine participatory democracy as a viable political system, but believes that hegemony has co-opted and distorted this idea to reproduce the current unequal system. This stand is evident particularly in the work of Fromm, Marcuse (who says that the fact that democracy has never existed does not mean we give up its dream), Habermas, and West. In fact, West positions Marx himself as a radical democrat, arguing that Marx and Engels define communism as a struggle for democracy. This democratic emphasis is evident, in West's view, in the insistence by Marx that "ordinary people, workers, ought to have some control over the conditions of their existence, especially the conditions of their workplace" (West, 1999, p. 223). To West, this is "a profoundly democratic idea" (p. 223) and one, therefore, that can be linked to the mainstream of American ideology. Arguing that Marx is a radical democrat creates some interesting cognitive dissonance for teachers used to thinking of him as the antithesis of all that is democratic.

Finally on this point, one of the things I stress to teachers new to critical theory is the theory's central concern with freedom—a libertarian idea very honored in American ideology. For example, Habermas argues that "socialism and liberty are identical" (Dews, 1992, p. 75), a sentiment many teachers would regard as contradictory. However, Fromm, Marcuse, and Habermas in their different ways all see socialism as "an attempt . . . to indicate the necessary conditions which would have to be in place for emancipated life-forms to emerge" (Dews, 1992, p. 145)—to be free in other words. Critical theory is centrally concerned with releasing people from falsely created needs and helping them make their own free choices regarding how they wish to think and live. Framed this way it is much closer to democratic ideals than people realize. Although in many teachers' minds critical theory is essentially a socialistic discourse concerned only with economic arrangements, it can be broadened to privilege freedom as much as common ownership. To North Americans who subscribe to Marxophobia and who are wary of all things socialistic, it is the emphasis in critical theory on claiming freedom that stands the best chance of engaging their interest.

A fourth source of resistance to studying critical theory is its often impenetrable language. Marcuse is one of those who recognizes how the language of critical theory can alienate potential readers and allies. He is particularly perturbed by those who ritualistically invoke terms (proletariat, dialectics, and so on) that are "identification labels for in-groups . . . mere clichés" (Marcuse, 1972, p. 39). Mechanically repeating phrases like *emancipatory praxis* or *proletarian hegemony* can make those outside the leftist in-group even more convinced that readers of critical theorists live in some kind of fantasy world. Noam Chomsky is another on the left who is most critical of a specialized language of leftism. He declares that "whenever I hear a four-syllable word I get skeptical, because I want to make sure you can't say it in monosyllables" (Chomsky, 2002, p. 229), and he urges people to "be extremely skeptical when intellectual life constructs structures which aren't transparent" (Chomsky, 2002, p. 229). In a similar vein, hooks and Davis both argue strongly for an accessible language of critique. Both acknowledge the way everyday language has become distorted by capitalist ideology, and both are quite willing to use many terms drawn from the critical tradition. Both are willing to use autobiographical reflection as a way to ground critique in contexts that connect to readers outside academe. Davis's (1974) own autobiography and hooks's (1989, 2000) personal reflections in books such as *Talking Back* and *Where We Stand* interweave descriptions of personal episodes with theoretical analyses. Many of these episodes have to do with the excitement of stumbling over a new way of thinking—a theoretical analysis in other words—that explains something in their lives.

Both Davis and hooks believe that much of the revolutionary energy of critical theory has been dampened by its overly convoluted language. How can a teacher galvanize people's desire to question, and then act upon, their world if the language used to do this "mystifies rather than clarifies our condition" (Christian, 1990, p. 572)? This is where Gramsci's idea of the organic intellectual has a particular resonance. To be able to understand a complicated but powerful vocabulary of critique, and to be able to render this in an intelligible and meaningful way to those outside that discourse, is a crucial educational role. Erich Fromm worked to do this as do contemporary commentators such as Ira Shor (1996), Lisa Delpit (1996), Herb Kohl (2000), and Mike Rose (1999). Myles Horton's (1990) use of stories, analogies, and metaphors is one of the best implementations of this that avoided all jargon.

The final point of resistance to critical theory is caused by the radical pessimism it induces. For some people new to the tradition of reading analyses of ideological manipulation, the infinite flexibility of hegemony, the pervasiveness of automaton conformity and alienation, the invasion of the lifeworld, and so on, is like being hit over the head repeatedly with a padded mallet. There seems to be no end to the unrelieved gloom, no prospect of the clouds of oppression ever being blown away. The two worst phases for many people are when they read Foucault on the nature of surveillance and disciplinary power and Marcuse on repressive tolerance. These writings contain the same message of circumspection regarding actions that seem unequivocally hopeful or liberating. Foucault and Marcuse both warn against the easy and seductive assumption that the sincerity of a teacher's intent guarantees that his or her actions will somehow be experienced as liberating. This is sometimes very hard for activist teachers to hear.

Educators drawn to critical theory are often attracted by its oppositional stance. It seems to hold the promise of helping us overcome alienation, unmask power, or learn liberation. When adult teachers encounter an idea like repressive tolerance it seems to sap their energy. On the one hand, their studies in critical theory have created enthusiasm for the possibility of opening up the curriculum to different ideas, thereby galvanizing their own students' activism and developing their critical thinking. Then they read Marcuse's warning that broadening the curriculum often serves only to emphasize the dominance of the existing center and they feel robbed of hope. "How can we do anything," they ask, "when Marcuse says that opening things up really only closes them down further, and Foucault tells us our efforts to democratize education will be experienced as oppressive by those we're seeking to help?"

There is not a lot one can say in response to such a question. But just shrugging your shoulders is not an option either. I usually reply by talking about the importance of using whatever energy you have most effectively. More particularly, I focus on the importance of not wasting energy obsessing fretfully over things you can't control. It seems to me that teachers trying to get students to think and act critically need to be aware of the many traps that lie in wait for them. One of these is working diligently to promote practices that you feel are unequivocally positive without realizing their potentially negative consequences. To act believing you are changing the world for the better, and then to find out that the converse is the case, is horribly demoralizing. It kills the transformative impulse and induces a profoundly debilitating pessimism.

As a teacher I would rather know of the traps and dangers that lie ahead, no matter how much they might complicate matters. If I am aware of the contradictions and complications of teaching critically, then when these present themselves I am less likely to feel that I have single-handedly caused them to appear. In her book *Practice Makes Practice,* Britzman (1991) identifies the belief that "everything depends on the teacher" as one of the most enduring myths teachers learn early on in their careers. This myth holds that successes are due to your brilliance and failures to your incompetence. We need to dispel this myth with its Copernican emphasis on the teacher as the center of the universe. Given that teaching critically is a pothole-strewn highway we need to know that the reason the car is banging about in such a perilous and unpredictable manner is because of the holes already in the blacktop, not because we are unable to drive.

I realize that much of this chapter may seem far removed from the day-to-day realities of much faculty development work. For many of us, just getting teachers to show up at faculty development events is a triumph in itself. The last thing we want to do is risk scaring them away with a focus on seemingly needlessly political, overly confrontational themes. It seems to me, however, that faculty development—like teaching itself—tries to start where people are, and then to nudge them toward a different, and more critical, understanding of everyday reality. In this regard the focus of this volume on the sociological imagination is entirely appropriate. The private troubles of teachers that they bring to faculty development efforts with the hope of receiving assistance—particularly that of receiving poor evaluations from students that threaten their continued employment, merit pay, or effort to achieve tenure—provide a perfect entry to a critical theory analysis. I would argue that you cannot accurately understand the way students' ratings of instruction affect your career without appreciating the way that the dominant ideology of capitalism and bureaucratic rationality commodifies learning and teaching. According to this ideology, the value of learning can be assessed by the grade it receives. Such a grade is deemed to represent accurately the internal value of learning. In this way learning is fetishized; that is, deemed to have a standardized, internal worth that can be assigned an unequivocal value. Learning becomes equated with the production of an artifact—an essay, test, or lab—to which this value can be assigned. Similarly, teaching is also commodified—judged to be an object containing unequivocal, standardized worth that is measured by the average of student ratings. So, far from critical theory being an abstracted body of ideas of interest only to those with leftist or philosophical leanings, it is a heuristic of enduring relevance.

References

Baptiste, I. (2000, May). Beyond reason and personal integrity: Toward a pedagogy of coercive restraint. *Canadian Journal for the Study of Adult Education, 14*(1), 27–50.

Britzman, D. P. (1991). *Practice makes practice: A critical study of learning to teach.* Albany, NY: State University of New York Press.

Brookfield, S. D., & Preskill, S. (2005). *Discussion as a way of teaching: Tools and techniques for democratic classrooms* (2nd ed.). San Francisco, CA: Jossey-Bass.

Chomsky, N. (2002). *Understanding power: The indispensable Chomsky* (P. R. Mitchell & J. Schoeffel, Eds.). New York, NY: The New Press.

Christian, B. (1990). The race for theory: Science, technology and socialist feminism in the 1990s. In K. V. Hansen & I. J. Philipson (Eds.), *Women, class, and the feminist imagination: A socialist-feminist reader* (pp. 568–579). Philadelphia, PA: Temple University Press.

Davis, A. Y. (1974). *Angela Davis: An autobiography.* New York, NY: International Publishers.

Davis, A.Y. (1983). *Women, race, and class.* New York, NY: Vintage Books.

Delpit, L. D. (1996). *Other people's children: Cultural conflict in the classroom.* New York, NY: New Press.

Dews, P. (Ed.). (1992). *Autonomy and solidarity: Interviews with Jurgen Habermas* (Rev. ed.). New York, NY: Routledge.

Fromm, E. (1955). *The sane society.* New York, NY: Holt, Rinehart, & Winston.

Fromm, E. (1961). *Marx's concept of man.* New York, NY: Frederick Ungar.

Habermas, J. (1990). *Moral consciousness and communicative action* (C. Lenhardt & S. W. Nicholsen, Trans.). Cambridge, MA: MIT Press.

hooks, b. (1989). *Talking back: Thinking feminist, thinking black.* Boston, MA: South End Press.

hooks, b. (2000). *Where we stand: Class matters.* New York, NY: Routledge.

Horkheimer, M. (1972). *Critical theory: Selected essays.* New York, NY: Herder and Herder.

Horton, M. (1990). *The long haul: An autobiography.* New York, NY: Doubleday.

Kohl, H. (2000). *The discipline of hope: Learning from a lifetime of teaching.* New York, NY: New Press.

Marcuse, H. (1964). *One-dimensional man: Studies in the ideology of advanced industrial society.* Boston, MA: Beacon Press.

Marcuse, H. (1972). *Counterrevolution and revolt.* Boston, MA: Beacon Press.

McLaren, P. (1998). *Life in schools: An introduction to critical pedagogy in the foundations of education* (3rd ed.). New York, NY: Longman.

Rose, M. (1999). *Possible lives: The promise of public education in America.* New York, NY: Penguin.

Shor, I. (1996). *When students have power: Negotiating authority in a critical pedagogy.* Chicago, IL: University of Chicago Press.

West, C. (1999). Cornel West on heterosexism and transformation: An interview. In J. A. Segarra & R. Dobles (Eds.), *Learning as a political act: Struggles for learning and learning from struggles* (pp. 290–305). Cambridge, MA: Harvard University Press.

5

The ABCs of Fractal Thinking in Higher Education

Edward Nuhfer
Idaho State University

All learning establishes and often stabilizes neural networks in the brain. These carry both cognitive and affective attributes and have fractal form. Fractal networks produce many actions and products that exhibit fractal qualities. Awareness of such qualities provides a unifying key to understanding and applying educational knowledge. It represents a marked shift in perception that differs from thinking customarily employed in considering information as a specialist. This alternate perspective helps professionals in higher education draw on diverse information from specialty research and apply it more effectively.

Fractal thinking, a term coined simply for brevity, describes individuals' abilities to visualize fractal traits within teaching, learning, thinking, performance, and in assessment and management of these. My exposure to fractal thinking developed through sheer luck: a background as a natural scientist and college teacher, and a fortuitous opportunity in 1988–1989 that introduced me to fractals during the same sabbatical that introduced me to faculty development. It took a decade as a practicing developer before my own brain connected the two (literally, not figuratively, as we shall soon see). Only then did I realize how much fractal thinking had to offer to my practice and to higher education in general. Since becoming conscious of the connection, I enjoy a new fascinating insight at least monthly, which makes me passionate about sharing fractal thinking with others.

This chapter begins by providing awareness of the nature of fractal forms—the ABCs. It follows with a summary of the sparse information now relating fractals to higher education and explains why fractals should be useful. It next provides examples of application to some of the toughest problems in higher education.

The model presented is conceptual and stresses pattern recognition and visualization rather than numerical analyses. As such, it does not require mathematical training to understand and apply it. If you address the complex problems of student learning, teaching evaluations, grading, assessment of student learning, curricular development, or faculty development, you will find something of value. Fractal thinking will help you to choose efforts that will promote tackling such issues successfully and help you to foresee some reasons why particular approaches are likely destined to fail.

First, What's a Fractal?

Nature is full of fractal geometric forms that are familiar to all readers: trees, clouds, landforms such as meandering streams or continental coastlines, and biological systems such as blood vessels of the vascular system or neural networks of the brain (Liebovitch, 1998; Mandelbrot, 1982). To those in "the pre-fractal awareness stage," such forms appear impossible to quantify or to describe other than in terms such as *random, irregular,* or perhaps *confusing.* Fractal thinking brings awareness that intimidating complexity often stems from a simple source that provides a means to understand a complex challenge in surprising and deep ways. It's easiest to learn the nature of fractals by seeing a picture of a fractal form's development (see Figure 5.1).

FIGURE 5.1
Development of a Fractal Form

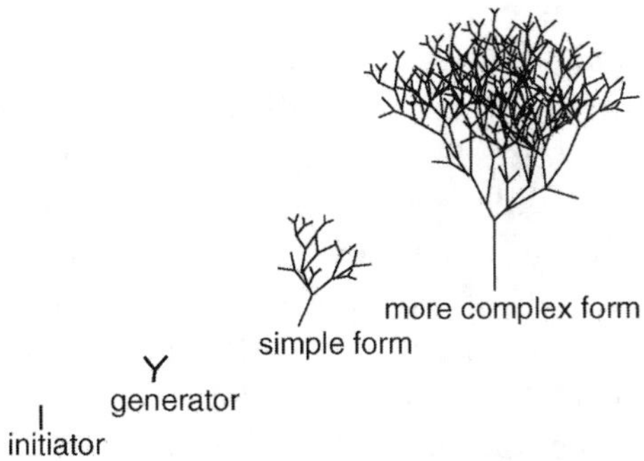

Note. From Nuhfer (2003b). The fractal form of an increasingly complex branching network is built from recursive operations on a generator in which each branch of the "Y" is replaced repeatedly with subsequent "Y" shapes.

Note first the single line labeled as the initiator in Figure 5.1. Simple manipulations of a line cannot produce a fractal. We can extend it, bend it, close it upon itself, and produce an infinite number of shapes, some of which are the Euclidean forms so familiar to us from K–12 mathematics (rectangles, trapezoids, circles, sine waves, etc.) without producing a fractal form. The generator is the required building block for a fractal form. The generator parts are Euclidean; in this case a "Y" has three parts, all straight lines. Building a fractal form requires using the generator in a recursive process that involves a repetitive action, in this case replacing each arm of the "Y" with yet another "Y." Leafless trees clearly exhibit fractal forms similar to forms shown in Figure 5.1. The figure reveals two important fractal traits: 1) fractal forms are made of parts similar to the whole in some way, and 2) fractal forms appear similar when viewed at different scales. Certainly, the branching nature is apparent as a similarity through all parts. Further, if we have no reference scale, it could be difficult to tell whether we are observing a seedling from a few feet away or an immense tree from a distance by looking at an object similar to that depicted in the more complex form of Figure 5.1.

The pattern in Figure 5.1 is imminently applicable to education because it provides a reasonable portrayal of change produced in the brain during learning. Leamnson (1999) was the first writer to broadly encourage college teachers to recognize learning as the building and stabilizing of synaptic connections and developing of neurological networks. Given a normal, healthy human brain, efforts to learn will produce branching neural networks that give us increased skills and developed thinking abilities. Prolonged effort and practice eventually provide abilities that separate expert from novice and an uneducated person from an intellectual. Teaching, like any skill, produces a complex neural network through prolonged study and practice. In fact, complex networks need to be developed before high-order thinking tasks can be successfully handled (Iannaccone & Khokha, 1996). We might consider the simple form in Figure 5.1 as representing the neural network of our students and the more complex form representing that of a professor. However, even the more complex network of Figure 5.1 is an oversimplification. Real neural networks possess much greater density, grow in three dimensions, and the branched interconnected forms themselves are interfolded (Iannaccone & Khokha, 1996). Learning produces fractal networks that are astounding in complexity and incredible in functionality. Further, the network is merely circuitry. When the circuits are active—when an electrical impulse involved in a thought in a single area triggers impulses in other areas with different sequences and in varied intensities—the electrical cascades represent a chaotic pattern with astounding possibilities. When viewed in this way, it is easy to see why the human brain is truly capable of infinite thinking with countless variations.

We now close in on part C of the ABCs of fractal thinking. The two qualities we have considered—fractal forms made of parts similar to the whole (A) and fractal forms appearing similar when viewed at different scales (B)—are still insufficient to define a fractal. Some Euclidean forms also meet these criteria. Consider a cube made of 1-inch cubic building blocks 10 blocks wide, 10 blocks high, and 10 blocks deep. Although the cube is made of parts similar to the whole, and the form appears similar when viewed at different scales, it is a Euclidean form. It lacks a fractal's signature trait: (C) a fractal form's dimensions change depending on the instrument used in the measure. In the cube example, no matter what size ruler we use to measure it, an edge will remain 10 inches long, the area of a face will remain a constant 100 square inches, and the volume will remain 1,000 cubic inches. This results because Euclidean forms are smooth and their dimensions have fixed quantities of length, width, and height. In contrast, fractal forms are rough rather than smooth, and their dimensions change in accord with the resolution of the instrument that measures them.

Consider what happens when we try to measure a fractal form, such as the length (L) of a seacoast between two points. A land-sea interface is just a line—an irregular continuous line that is perhaps as simple as any fractal form can be. If we have a map of the seacoast (see Figure 5.2), we can use a divider as a measuring tool. We can set the divider at a known width (r) and march the divider along the coastline from starting point to end point. We sum the number of divider steps (N) between the two points, multiply this sum by r, to arrive at a length (L) of the coastline. However, if we set the divider at a markedly shorter width, repeat the measure, and total that number of divider widths, the process reveals a markedly longer coastline than the former length we derived. If we go to larger maps that show more resolution, the coastline grows with every effort to measure it in increasing detail. A very small divider width (e.g., r equal about the size of a sand grain) applied along an actual coastline (rather than a scaled map) would capture such detail that the result would be essentially an infinitely long coastline. Unlike the cube edge, there is no "right answer" of seacoast length as a unique number. The harder we try to measure it, the bigger it gets.

Although many may intuit that a very crooked line (like a coastline) measured at first crudely and then more precisely might display an increase in length, intuition alone would not suspect the strength of the relationship between r and L. The points generated by each (r, L) pair generated from

FIGURE 5.2
Measuring a Fractal Form

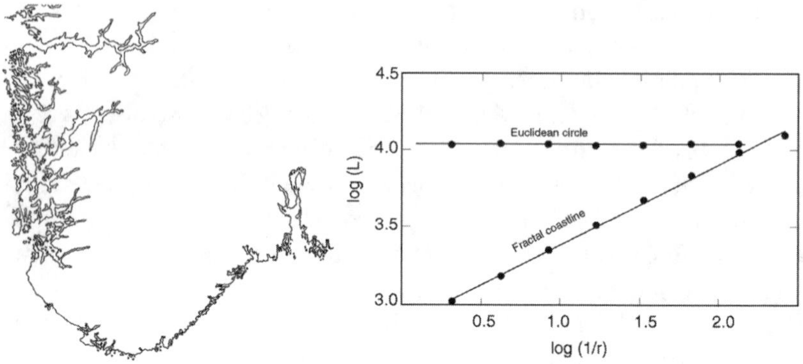

Note. Modified from examples in Feder (1988). Left, a map of part of a coastline in Norway. Right, the graph of change in coastline length (L) that results from multiple measures of the coastline by dividers set at different widths (r). The length of the coastline increases in a highly ordered manner as the feature is measured multiple times with dividers set at shorter spaces for increasingly greater resolution. This results in a plot of log (1/r) versus log (L) that describes a line with a steep slope (graph, lower). In contrast, Euclidean forms like circumferences of circles have a constant length (L) that changes little when measured with dividers set at varying widths of r. The slope of that plot of log (1/r) versus log (L) describes a line of markedly less slope (graph, upper).

multiple measures taken at different divider widths, if graphed through appropriate scaling, will plot neatly along the same straight line (as in Figure 5.2). The pairs are often plotted with an ordinate, log (L), and abscissa log (1/r). While a fractal form does not have a simple length, it has a characteristic quality termed the *fractal dimension,* which can be expressed by a single number associated with the slope of line: log (L)/log (1/r). Multiple measures taken along a true fractal form produce (r, L) pairs that plot on a best-fit line with a pronounced slope. Multiple measures made on Euclidean forms (e.g., the length of the circumference of a circle) will reveal very little change in length with measures taken at different divider settings. The resultant line fit through (r, L) pairs shows little slope.

Fractals not only describe geometric forms of physical objects, they also describe particular patterns in time (Nuhfer, 2005d). Rainfalls, floods, earthquakes, tsunamis, sediment accumulations, and volcanoes act mostly through fractal patterns in time. These patterns also possess the same ABC qualities. By becoming aware of these three concepts—the ABCs of fractal thinking—any educator can begin gaining insights of value to higher education.

Previous Work

Because the brain employs fractal neural networks (Iannaccone & Khokha, 1996), it is likely that most human knowledge and activity exhibit some fractal qualities. In 1987, a bestselling book took the mathematics specialties of chaos theory and fractal geometry and introduced their relevance to laypersons (Gleick, 1987). More reference books quickly followed, as others saw applicability of fractal thinking to business, science, and social science, but little awareness has yet spread to education. A few workers made brief mention of fractals in association with higher education and drew general connections between their practice and fractal properties. Duffy and Jones (1995) use "fractal" to describe their perception that their "Rhythms of the Semester" (p. xvi) could be seen at scales other than the semester, but they may have applied "fractal" to a non-fractal pattern (Nuhfer, 2005d). Wright (2001), summarizing institutional accreditation, writes, "All of this reminds me of fractals, which I first encountered about five years ago in a book by Margaret J. Wheatley called *Leadership and the New Science*" (p. 50). Cutright (2006) also cites Wheatley's work when examining applicability of chaos theory to the administrative realm of planning in higher education.

We introduced our fractal model for higher education in 2002 at the PacPair Conference in Hawaii (Nuhfer, Chambers, & Heckler, 2002). Two well-received pre-conference workshops at the 2002 and 2003 American Association for Higher Education (AAHE) assessment conferences followed (Nuhfer & Pletsch, 2002, 2003), which generated awareness in a number of assessment directors. Because assessment was both a relatively new and rapidly developing profession within higher education, the AAHE assessment conferences brought together educators from diverse institutions who were unusually receptive to new visions and who sought interconnections. The losses of the AAHE assessment conference and of AAHE itself were setbacks for higher education, and nothing comparable has yet replaced either. The Lilly Conference in Oxford, Ohio, hosted fractal workshops in 2004 and 2005. Several disciplinary organizations, colleges, and universities hosted invited workshops as result of the introductions at conferences. The Boot Camp for Profs® program evolved into a systematic, integrated development program based on fractal thinking. Since 2003, the *National Teaching and Learning Forum* has featured more than 15 articles on application of fractal thinking to faculty development and higher education.

The Value of Unifying Concepts

The value of unifying concepts is less about unique discoveries than about their effects in making dispersed information more relevant and accessible.

For example, the unifying concept of plate tectonics in geology did not accompany a specific discovery involving rocks, ore deposits, field geology, geochemistry, geophysics, oceanography, seismology, vulcanology, stratigraphy, and so on. Each of these specialties contributed knowledge and made impressive discoveries without any unifying theory. However, once plate tectonics made obvious the connections among these specialties, it greatly expedited understanding. In a short time, freshman students understood more about how the Earth worked from one course than their predecessor professors understood with a graduate degree. This, in turn, produced scientists equipped with more powerful models for deeper understanding, and certainly permitted newer discoveries in all these specialty areas at a faster rate than was previously possible. The concept had a profound effect from the level of individual scholar to an entire disciplinary profession. This effect across scales is a fractal trait and exemplary of the power enacted by a new concept.

In higher education, rich knowledge acquired in development of particular pedagogies, learning styles, levels of thinking, evaluation, assessment, course design, curriculum design, specialty education in disciplines, education designed for humans in different developmental stages, use of technology, and the like remains possible without any unifying theory, but these specialties remain largely unconnected. As a result, faculty who seek to develop better practice are similar to new geology students of the 1950s. Development of competence and professional philosophy requires long study and practice in consulting disparate specialty literature. Even when this literature is drawn together in various teaching improvement books, the narrative discloses little connectivity between content presented in separate chapters.

In higher education, a recent unifying concept relates teaching, learning, and thinking to brain function. Leamnson (1999) tied research on adult learning to brain neurology in a well-integrated, usable resource for the general college teacher. Zull (2002) followed with a book of similar focus that stressed brain neurology and portrayed particular learning style activities arising from particular regions of the brain. Learning style preferences almost certainly result from preferential development of particular neural networks. Both these books consider maturation of the brain, which explains why child learners and college students think differently and require different teaching approaches. One holistic way to consider education is to examine the brain's neurological development in response to teaching, learning, and thinking. Fractal thinking extends this consideration to include the fractal qualities of the brain together with the fractal qualities found within the performance, products, and practices generated from the brain.

Douglas Reimondo Robertson, assistant provost and director of the Professional and Organizational Development Center at Northern Kentucky University, achieved an early awareness about the applicability of fractals and chaos theory to higher education. He has been able to use fractal thinking to good advantage in his work in faculty, instructional, curricular, and organizational development. He writes,

> The fact that "fractal thinking" provides insights that have already been discerned, such as the necessity of multiple measures . . . is not what it contributes in my mind. I think that its value is that it is a part of a whole perspective (paradigm, worldview, frame of reference, assumptive world, way of constructing reality . . . pick your phrase), which, once integrated, provides insight after insight, effective practice after effective practice. It is not a single concept. It is an integrated whole conception of reality. There is an economy to embracing it. Rather than lugging around a bunch of loosely integrated insights . . . one simply looks through this one lens and effective insights and practices come to one in one novel situation after another. For example, once I understand fractals and attractors, then I understand that when I walk into class on the first day, not only do I have the opportunity to create and support new and desirable patterns and forces, but I know that other patterns and forces already exist that will support or compete with my desired patterns and forces for the outcome of each moment of my course . . . (personal communication, February 23, 2006)

Discussion and Sample Applications

Faculty Evaluation

The topic of faculty evaluation, particularly through use of student evaluations, creates a huge volume of literature. By 1988, more than 1,300 articles existed (Cashin, 1988), and more than double that number exists today. How is it possible, after so many studies, that the topic still generates impassioned arguments and counterarguments instead of widespread acceptance and skillful application of the findings? Sometimes we yet even hear or read "Good teaching is so complex that you can't really evaluate it."

If this statement were true, we could not evaluate any other learned proficiency. Attempts to evaluate proficiency are, without exception, efforts to characterize specific parts of an individual's neural network. Proficiency in any discipline—accounting, chemistry, engineering, philosophy, theatre, or college teaching—each requires the individual to build an expert's neural network through study and practice. These networks are fractal, and proficiency is the expression of such a network in action. Because we cannot observe the networks directly, the only way to evaluate proficiency is through measuring well-chosen products and actions of such networks.

Fractal thinking even helps in considering what constitutes "multiple measures." Some consider "multiple" as different means of measurement, as in paper and pencil self-report and direct observation rather than the number of items within a single instrument. However, 10 different questions about a single topic given on a paper and pencil instrument really tap 10 different areas of the brain, much as different divider widths sample unique parts of a coastline. Thus, responses to different items truly qualify as multiple measures of a neural network, and this chapter considers multiple measures in that sense.

A lesson taken from the coastline example reveals that single measures cannot characterize even the simplest fractal form. Experts in evaluation invariably recommend that evaluators use multiple measures (Arreola, 2000; Theall, Abrami, & Mets, 2001). However, practitioners often ignore expertise, and nowhere is the gap between expertise and practice larger than in the use of student ratings to evaluate faculty. Robert Leamnson describes the prevalent application.

> Over 25 years I was evaluated by more than 100 groups of students. For about 18 of those years, I participated in annual reviews of my departmental colleagues and in those of all Arts and Science departments at the college level. The methods were virtually invariable. Whenever a rating form had a global question, it alone was considered and all else simply ignored! If, in the real world, you put a global question on the rating form . . . the global question is the end-all and be-all—the alpha and the omega. (personal communication, November, 27, 2005)

Fractal thinking provides a stronger argument against this practice than even a reasoned appeal to authoritative recommendation based on dominant, well-established statistical trends. It addresses the concrete impossibility of using single measures to characterize fractal forms. Just as there will never be a "magic divider" to divine the true length of the coastline, there will never be a "magic item" and likely not even a single "magic form" that will allow us to divine the neural network of a teacher.

Could this perhaps support a pessimist's argument of teaching being too complex to describe? The answer is no. We recall (a bit of fractal thinking now!) that multiple measures allowed us to derive the fractal dimension of a coastline. The fact that we could not measure a unique length did not preclude our characterizing it in such a way that we could begin to understand it and to compare it with other coastlines. With a bit of additional fractal thinking, we will realize that established precedents exist in which selected multiple measures prove capable of characterizing specific neural networks. Perhaps the best-known precedent is the Myers-Briggs Type Indicator®. This tool takes between 93 and 125 measures in order to characterize dominant personality types. It has proven itself over many years to be reliable and valid. Another demonstrable success involving multiple measures is the Kolb Learning Style Inventory (Smith & Kolb, 1986). Both diagnostic tools use multiple items carefully selected to trigger responses from different networks of the brain involved in choices, and the results provide good characterization of the neural network being investigated. Although Myers, Briggs, and Kolb recognized that they needed a minimum number of measures, they lacked the unifying concept to explain *why* they could not diagnose types with only a few items.

How many measures do we need? A perceptive reader might note, "Look, we could characterize the fractal coastline in Figure 5.2 with just three good measurements needed to establish a line fit—why not three for a neural network?" The answer is that we are not characterizing a neural network that is remotely so simple as a coastline. The second is that networks we must characterize for faculty evaluation are not one system, but several that are interconnected. This is akin to the network involved in personality type coexisting and interconnected with those of learning style and intelligence type. The third is that established precedents for diagnosing such types seem to require several score of measures for each. The neural network that a professor develops is much larger and more complex than the networks characterized by these inventory types. In fact, it includes them. For the same reason we cannot derive personality or learning style types by single questions, we cannot know or evaluate instructional proficiency by the prevalent, yet hapless, practice of using a single global response item. My estimate is that we need close to 200 measures from students to be confident that we understand an instructor's teaching effectiveness from just the students' point of view. This would include about 150 or more items from a knowledge survey, about 40 to 60 formative items, and 3 to 5 summative global items (Nuhfer, 2005b).

Understanding the Controversy

Failure to appreciate the capacity of complex neural networks leads to a kind of Euclidean thinking that envisions topical knowledge as akin to the set volume of a cube is probably one of the worst side effects of establishing expertise. It erupts whenever a person accepts that current knowledge and prevailing interpretations constitute all worth knowing about a topic. The massive literature of student evaluations contributed to such a view. For many years, the research on student evaluations focused on teaching traits with an expected link to cognitive learning. Feldman (1986) is a significant exception. When reports such as Ambady and Rosenthal's (1993) "thin slice" studies determined that students' ratings for teachers after watching 30 seconds of silent content-free video were highly consistent ($r = 0.76$) with end-of-semester ratings, some scholars reacted by attacking the importance and credibility of the findings. When scholarship on the relationship between physical appearance and success in the workplace extended into study of the relationship between physical appearance and its influence on student ratings (Hamermesh & Parker, 2005), some scholars were livid. They openly speculated that the researchers themselves were physically unattractive, had records of low student evaluations (or both), or had some personal motivation to publish such research in order to deprecate student evaluations. Paradoxically, affective networks of experts produced a hostile reaction against the confirmation of the strength of affective relationships!

Fractal thinking anticipates the physical attractiveness and the thin slice results because both address first-impression phenomena. First impressions establish generators in the minds of students. Generators have overwhelming power in determining the final form, and the character of such generators should influence the nature of the neural network produced as a result of taking a course. Far from deprecating student evaluations, the studies confirmed the power of affective first impressions and revealed the astonishing speed with which such generators form. If improved student satisfaction follows from enacting the first class well dressed and operating in accord with one's highest aspirations and teaching philosophy, this is critically valuable information. A fractal thinker understands why such a first impression should have such a powerful effect.

Fractal thinkers also perceive why the vehement criticism should occur. The solid documentation of student ratings' relationship to cognitive factors led to countering individuals' reports of other influences as anecdotal myths and misbeliefs (Boice, 1990). This generated the expected aggrieved reactions (Fish, 2005; Trout, 1997) because networks built during establishment of professional identities and practiced philosophies carry affective components. Euclidean thinking senses that new findings threaten to displace old paradigms (i.e., "both interpretations cannot fit into the same cube"). However, fractal thinking senses that new findings do not displace old findings so much as they expand awareness (i.e., "there is more to this coastline than we thought"). From challenges like the coastline problem, fractal thinkers expect to find a number of significant correlations among student learning, student satisfaction, and many cognitive and affective factors. They expect that the more we look, the more we will find.

New unifying concepts are powerful as change agents in expert learners because they enable new generators to build by assimilating the vast existing resources of knowledge and skills. This produces major reorganizations that permit expanded ways of thinking. The effects we noted in the discipline of geology from plate tectonics and in the expanded awareness described by Robertson with regard to faculty, instructional, curricular, and organizational development are important case examples.

Evaluating Students and Assessment of Learning

Let's first contrast evaluation with assessment. The common use of these terms as interchangeable synonyms differs in the ways higher education uses them, although there is just enough inconsistency in the latter to create confusion. In formal use, *evaluation* examines an individual's capabilities and progress. Tools such as tests and grades, projects, theses, self-evaluation, references, and work performance ratings are common tools for evaluation of individuals. Evaluation of individuals may also include affective traits such as enthusiasm, reliability, and integrity. *Assessment* focuses on units such as a class, a course, a departmental curriculum, or an institution rather than on an individual. In assessment, we work mostly with aggregate data. Aggregate affective traits, such as general morale, may be included. Some confusing exceptions occur in terms such as *self- assessment,* which has established precedent as applicable to individuals (Loacker, 2000) and a unit's *self-assessment report,* which is clearly a report based on aggregate reflection. Assessment of student learning outcomes focuses primarily on the aggregate work being done, instead of on evaluation of individual instructors who promote it or individual students who do it.

We often hear that we should teach in a variety of ways and come at the same material from many directions. Good teaching practices encourage students' use of many senses (visually, auditory, kinesthetic) or address several poles of Kolb Learning Styles (such as confronting one topic through reading, writing, drawing, and arguing). We less often hear about incorporating diversity into our evaluative methods. When evaluating students' learning, keep in mind that the neural network in question is fractal and more complex than most imagine. Thus, the more measures made and the greater the variety of approaches taken (within reason), the better. If students truly meet a learning goal, they can demonstrate learning through a variety of outcomes. A course that evaluates learning based only on multiple-choice tests likely is sampling too little of the neural network involved in the desired learning and perhaps too much of the network developed in short-answer test-taking skill. A mix of in-class short-answer and take-home reflective writing tests, projects, and assignments is better than a single kind of measure. Fractal thinkers tend to teach and assess with multiple means and to create parts of a course that have similarity consistent to the whole.

Many distinguished teachers believe their tests to be direct measures of students' knowledge. Such belief stems from picturing attempts to measure knowledge as akin to measuring a cube edge rather than a coastline. If the problem of measuring knowledge were as simple as measuring the dimensions of a cube, there would be no challenge at all to creating reliable tests. When we realize we are trying to measure a fractal neural network, we realize that even the best tests, including standardized tests such as the Force Concept Inventory of physics or the Geoscience Concept Inventory of the Earth sciences, are merely samples of the complex network. Creating a reliable test, confirmed by reliability estimates (0.0 expresses no reliability; 1.0 expresses perfect reliability) (Jacobs & Chase, 1992), is challenging. A very good faculty-made test usually has a reliability of about 0.6 to 0.7. Raoul Arreola, a well-respected psychometrician, estimates that the average faculty-made test has a reliability of about 0.2 to 0.3 (personal communication, April 14, 2005).

The literature of assessment talks about "direct" and" indirect" measures of student learning (Maki, 2004), but in reality all practical measures are indirect. The only true direct measure would require observing the extent of the neural network in the brain, which we see is beset by the same problem as measuring the length of a coastline. Even then, we would only be measuring the wiring. Understanding the function of the network would involve recording infinite possible sequences and combinations when the wiring is live and current flowing between synapses. Direct assessment of learning becomes an engagement in measuring the infinite, a task that is clearly impossible to accomplish. Instead, we have to deduce the neural network indirectly through examining what the particular neural network of the brain does.

The language of assessment provides two useful terms: *goals* and *outcomes.* A goal is a generally descriptive statement about desirable qualities that might typify proficiency. For example, one goal for proficient chemistry students should be to understand the nature of science and its methods. For proficient professors, one goal should be to understand the content of their disciplines and the frameworks of knowing within them. However, a goal in itself provides nothing measurable. We need the student and the professor to do something to demonstrate they can meet the goal. That "something" is an outcome, which yields some measurable product that demonstrates a skilled action. Here are five outcomes through which the chemistry student might demonstrate science literacy.

1) Consider a cookbook and an introductory textbook on nutrition. Distinguish which is technology and which is science, and justify your answer.
2) The can containing the soda on your desk is made of aluminum. The can has a really bad attitude! Which statement can be resolved through science and why?
3) Marie Curie discovered radium. Mark Twain wrote Tom Sawyer. If neither Curie nor Twain had been born, what would we likely know about radium and Huck Finn? What does this show about how the reasoning in science differs from that of another discipline, such as literature?
4) Turn to Figure X on page number Y, and explain the methods of science required to produce that figure.
5) If you wanted to see whether a job applicant understood science, create a question or challenge through which you might deduce such understanding, and explain why it is a suitable challenge.

Any teacher's fractal neural network can create limitless measurable outcomes that are nevertheless narrowly restricted to one goal statement. Thus, practical assessment of a curriculum requires that the faculty focus on a limited number of goals and outcomes and then publish these as guides for students.

All regional accreditation groups have chosen assessment of student learning outcomes as the primary focus of accreditation review. By now, some readers have probably realized that evaluation and assessment of student learning are also attempts to characterize fractal neural networks and are not surprised to hear about the need for multiple measures from experts in assessment (Banta, Lund, Black, & Oblander, 1996; Maki, 2004).

Knowledge surveys (Nuhfer & Knipp, 2003) are a fractal thinker's assessment tool because they provide a large number of measures focused on learning outcomes. They are not tests, but address more content than tests can practically sample, and they furnish numerical data amenable to the same numerical analyses as tests. A knowledge survey with about 200 items can be completed in about 30 minutes. A knowledge survey is also a type of student evaluation, and the literature of student evaluations applies in the understanding of knowledge surveys. The tool thus furnishes information about a neural network that summative student evaluations and tests cannot capture.

It is perhaps the most useful of assessment tools for "closing the assessment loop" through readily supplying the data that targets areas for improvements and for tracking the results of changes (Wirth, Perkins, & Nuhfer, 2005).

Holistic Faculty Development Versus Remediation

The development I initially learned is analogous to emergency room treatment: faculty member injured by student evaluations→diagnose the problem→recommend treatment options for content clarity and improved pedagogical engagement→patch up the faculty member's damaged confidence and send back to the classroom→follow up. Such development is remedial and centers on content and pedagogical delivery. Through experience, I learned that content knowledge and proficiency in multiple pedagogies are less than a third of what a successful faculty member really needs to succeed. Although we developers should provide emergency room treatment when required, faculty who enjoy more holistic development are involved in the equivalent of preventive medicine. They are less likely to need emergency

FIGURE 5.3

A Fractal Generator for Faculty Development

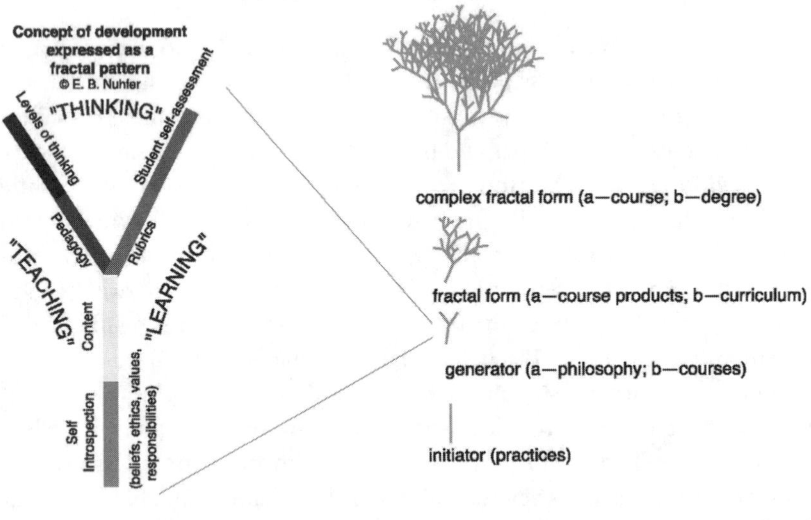

Note. From Nuhfer (2003b, 2003c). A fractal generator for faculty development showing six critical components needed for successful practice. The right side shows the place of the generator in forming an individual's products (a) and the same generator extended to a unit's (department, college/university) products (b). A strong teaching philosophy should reflect awareness of all six components of the generator.

rooms. Fractal thinking provides a way to formulate a holistic development program. Successful teaching results from learning and experience that produces an effective neural network. Fractal thinkers ask, "What constitutes a good generator that can develop into such a network?" If we can provide that generator early in a faculty member's career, it should have positive formative power akin to that of first impressions. For years, I asked the question, "What development best serves faculty?" and I asked that question without fractal awareness. Finally, in 2001, I recognized that system I was beginning to design involved awareness of patterns across scales and that these had the same qualities as the fractal nature of rocks, landforms, and sediment layers I'd studied 12 years earlier. In retrospect, this particular "Aha!" moment had some admittedly "Well, duh . . ." qualities because it took a dozen years before the particular synapses I'd developed doing science finally connected with those produced doing faculty development. The connection finally did boot the obvious into my awareness. Figure 5.3 encapsulates a generator suitable for holistic development that resulted.

An obvious product by which one might assess the state of a faculty member's development is a sophisticated philosophy (Nuhfer, Krest, & Handelsman, 2003). A sophisticated teaching philosophy should reveal awareness of the full generator. The written philosophy is a critical document that is constantly growing and undergoing refinement as the neural network produced in our own continued learning grows more complex and more capable. Here the traits of a fractal form's parts being similar to the whole and the forms appearing similar when viewed at different scales become important. Our practices should stem from that philosophy, and so should our course products and the final learning outcomes of the courses. If fractal thinking is involved in construction of a course, the parts of the course should be similar to the generator. An individual who reads a syllabus or final examination should be able to discern important aspects of the writer's teaching philosophy. Likewise, each of us is part of something larger. We are in the business of providing education through curricula and degrees, and not in simply providing training through single courses. Thus, our philosophy must include awareness of our place within the larger effort, such that our efforts at the level of individual lesson, course design, and so on are always conscious of how our course contributes to the student's greater education as a major and a degree recipient from an institution (Nuhfer & Adkison, 2003). The most important aspect, self-introspection, rests at the base of Figure 5.3. It is heavily affective in nature (Nuhfer, 2004a; 2005a), including what some would call the heart and soul of a teacher. We have elsewhere addressed the fractal nature of other components and products such as the following:

- Content (Nuhfer, 2003a; Nuhfer, Leonard, & Akersten, 2004)
- Evaluating content (Nuhfer, 2005c, 2005f)
- High-level thinking (Nuhfer & Pavelich, 2001, 2002)
- Rubrics (Nuhfer, 2004b)
- The role of the affective domain (Nuhfer, 2004a, 2005a)
- Teaching philosophies (Nuhfer & Adkison, 2003; Nuhfer, Krest, & Handelsman, 2003)
- Temporal qualities of teaching, learning, and thinking (Nuhfer, 2005d, 2005e)

If you have made some connections now between fractals and your own awareness of higher education, you have made more progress in about 30 minutes than my brain made in more than a decade. Take this awareness into your practice. Start to think in scales and patterns as you look at efforts of individuals and units across your campus. Consider (A) whether these may be more successful if efforts at small scales are similar to the desired whole, and (B) seek to invest in those efforts that show similarity even though enacted at different scales. Finally, (C) consider whether problems have solutions best met through Euclidean or fractal thinking. Pay attention especially to those that seem to grow the more people study them.

References

Ambady, N., & Rosenthal, R. (1993, March). Half a minute: Predicting teacher evaluations from thin slices of nonverbal behavior and physical attractiveness. *Journal of Personality and Social Psychology, 64*(3), 431–441.

Arreola, R. A. (2000). *Developing a comprehensive faculty evaluation system: A handbook for college faculty and administrators on designing and operating a comprehensive faculty evaluation system* (2nd ed.). Bolton, MA: Anker.

Banta, T. W., Lund, J. P., Black, K. E., & Oblander, F. W. (1996). *Assessment in practice: Putting principles to work on college campuses.* San Francisco, CA: Jossey-Bass.

Boice, R. (1990). Countering common misbeliefs about student evaluations of teaching. *Teaching Excellence, 2*(2).

Cashin, W. E. (1988). *Student ratings of teaching: A summary of the research* (Idea Paper No. 20). Manhattan, KS: Kansas State University, Center for Faculty Evaluation and Development.

Cutright, M. (2006). A different way to approach the future: Using chaos theory to improve planning. In S. Chadwick-Blossey & D. R. Robertson (Eds.), *To improve the academy: Vol. 24. Resources for faculty, instructional, and organizational development* (pp. 44–61). Bolton, MA: Anker.

Duffy, D. K., & Jones, J. W. (1995). *Teaching within the rhythms of the semester.* San Francisco, CA: Jossey-Bass.

Feder, J. (1988). *Fractals.* New York, NY: Plenum Press.

Feldman, K. A. (1986). The perceived instructional effectiveness of college teachers as related to their personality and attitudinal characteristics: A review and synthesis. *Research in Higher Education, 24*(2), 139–213.

Fish, S. (2005, February 4). Who's in charge here? Retrieved May 30, 2006, from *The Chronicle of Higher Education* web site: http://chronicle.com/jobs/2005/02/2005020401c.htm

Gleick, J. (1987). *Chaos: Making a new science.* New York, NY: Penguin Books.

Hamermesh, D. S., & Parker, A. M. (2005, August). Beauty in the classroom: Instructors' pulchritude and putative pedagogical productivity. *Economics of Education Review, 24*(4), 369–376.

Iannaccone, P. M., & Khokha, M. (Eds.). (1996). *Fractal geometry in biological systems: An analytical approach.* Boca Raton, FL: CRC Press.

Jacobs, L. C., & Chase, C. I. (1992). *Developing and using tests effectively: A guide for faculty.* San Francisco, CA: Jossey-Bass.

Leamnson, R. (1999). *Thinking about teaching and learning: Developing habits of learning with first year college and university students.* Sterling, VA: Stylus.

Liebovitch, L. S. (1998). *Fractals and chaos simplified for the life sciences.* New York, NY: Oxford University Press.

Loacker, G. (Ed.). (2000). *Self assessment at Alverno College.* Milwaukee, WI: Alverno College.

Maki, P. L. (2004). *Assessing for learning: Building a sustainable commitment across the institution.* Sterling, VA: Stylus.

Mandelbrot, B. B. (1982). *The fractal geometry of nature.* New York, NY: W. H. Freeman.

Nuhfer, E. B. (2003a). Content coverage, courses, and controversy part 1: Developing in fractal patterns V. *National Teaching and Learning Forum, 13*(1), 8–10.

Nuhfer, E. B. (2003b). Developing in fractal patterns I: Moving beyond diagnoses, evaluations, and fixes. *National Teaching and Learning Forum, 12*(2), 7–9.

Nuhfer, E. B. (2003c). Developing in fractal patterns II: A tour of the generator. *National Teaching and Learning Forum, 12*(4), 9–11.

Nuhfer, E. B. (2004a). Fractal thoughts on the forbidden affective in teaching evaluation and high level thinking: Educating in fractal patterns X. *National Teaching and Learning Forum, 14*(1), 9–11.

Nuhfer, E. B. (2004b). Why rubrics? Educating in fractal patterns IX. *National Teaching and Learning Forum, 13*(6), 9–11.

Nuhfer, E. B. (2005a). DeBono's red hat on Krathwohl's head: Irrational means to rational ends—more fractal thoughts on the forbidden affective: Educating in fractal patterns XIII. *National Teaching and Learning Forum, 14*(5), 7–11.

Nuhfer, E. B. (2005b). *A fractal thinker looks at student evaluations.* Retrieved May 30, 2006, from the Idaho State University, Center for Teaching and Learning web site: www.isu.edu/ctl/facultydev/extras/MeaningEvalsfract_files/MeaningEvalsfract.htm

Nuhfer, E. B. (2005c). Fractal views on good testing practices: Educating in fractal patterns XII. *National Teaching and Learning Forum, 14*(4), 9–11.

Nuhfer, E. B. (2005d). Perceiving education's temporal temperaments (part A–patterns): Educating in fractal patterns XIV. *National Teaching and Learning Forum, 14*(6), 7–10.

Nuhfer, E. B. (2005e). Perceiving education's temporal temperaments (part B–age, order, duration, frequency, rate, and magnitude): Educating in fractal patterns XIV. *National Teaching and Learning Forum, 15*(1), 8–11.

Nuhfer, E. B. (2005f). Tests as anchors that wobble: Understanding imperfect correlations in educational measurements: Educating in fractal patterns XI. *National Teaching and Learning Forum, 14*(2), 8–11.

Nuhfer, E. B., & Adkison, S. (2003). Unit level development: Teaching philosophies at the unit level: Educating in fractal patterns IV. *National Teaching and Learning Forum, 12*(6), 4–7.

Nuhfer, E. B., Chambers, F., & Heckler. (2002, June). *Teaching in fractal patterns: Recursive connections of assessment, individual faculty development, and unit level development.* Paper presented at the Pacific Planning, Assessment, and Institutional Research Conference, Honolulu, HI.

Nuhfer, E. B., & Knipp, D. (2003). The knowledge survey: a tool for all reasons. In C. M. Wehlburg & S. Chadwick-Blossey (Eds.), *To improve the academy: Vol. 21. Resources for faculty, instructional, and organizational development* (pp. 59–78). Bolton, MA: Anker. Addenda available electronically. Retrieved May 30, 2006, from the Idaho State University, Center for Teaching and Learning web site: www.isu.edu/ctl/facultydev/ADDENDUM.htm

Nuhfer, E. B., Krest, M., & Handelsman, M. (2003). A guide for composing teaching philosophies: Developing in fractal patterns III. *National Teaching and Learning Forum, 12*(5), 10–11.

Nuhfer, E. B., Leonard, L., & Akersten, S. (2004). Content coverage, courses, and controversy part 2: Developing in fractal patterns VI. *National Teaching and Learning Forum, 13*(2), 8–11.

Nuhfer, E. B., & Pavelich, M. (2001). Levels of thinking and educational outcomes. *National Teaching and Learning Forum, 11*(1), 5–8.

Nuhfer, E. B., & Pavelich, M. (2002). Using what we know to promote high level thinking outcomes. *National Teaching and Learning Forum, 11*(3), 6–8.

Nuhfer, E. B., & Pletsch, C. (2002, June). *Educating in fractal patterns: Linking development, instruction, and assessment from the individual to unit levels.* Pre-conference workshop presented at the American Association for Higher Education assessment conference, Boston, MA.

Nuhfer, E. B., & Pletsch, C. (2003, June). *Harnessing the power of fractal thinking in education, assessment, and faculty development.* Pre-conference workshop presented at the American Association for Higher Education assessment conference, Seattle, WA.

Smith, D. M., & Kolb, D. A. (1986). *The user's guide for the learning-style inventory: A manual for teachers and trainers.* Boston, MA: McBer.

Theall, M., Abrami, P. C., & Mets, L. M. (Eds.). (2001). *New directions for institutional research: No. 109. The student ratings debate: Are they valid? How can we best use them?* San Francisco, CA: Jossey-Bass.

Trout, P. A. (1997, September/October). What the numbers mean: Providing a context for numerical student evaluations of courses. *Change, 29*(5), 24–30.

Wheatley M. J. (1992). *Leadership and the new science: Learning about organization from an orderly universe.* San Francisco, CA: Berrett-Koehler.

Wirth, K. R., Perkins, D., & Nuhfer, E. B. (2005). Knowledge surveys: A tool for assessing learning, courses, and programs [Abstract]. *Geological Society of America Annual Meetings Program with Abstracts, 37*(7), 119.

Wright, B. (2001). Accreditation where credit is due. In L. Suskie (Ed.), *Assessment to promote deep learning: Insight from AAHE's 2000 and 1999 assessment conferences* (pp. 49–58). Sterling, VA: Stylus.

Zull, J. E. (2002). *The art of changing the brain: Enriching the practice of teaching by exploring the biology of learning.* Sterling, VA: Stylus.

Section III

Educational Development and the Scholarship of Teaching and Learning

6

Toward a Scholarship of Teaching and Learning in Educational Development

Peter Felten
Elon University

Alan Kalish
The Ohio State University

Allison Pingree
Vanderbilt University

Kathryn M. Plank
The Ohio State University

Educational development traditionally has been a practice-based field. We propose that as a profession we adopt the methods of the scholarship of teaching and learning (SoTL), so often shared with our clients, in order to look through a scholarly lens at the outcomes of our own practice. Using SoTL approaches in our work would deepen the research literature in our field and improve the effectiveness of decisions we make about where to spend limited time and resources. In this chapter, we explore what it might mean for individual developers, and for our professional community, to apply SoTL methods to our practice.

Educational development (ED) is a profession dedicated to helping colleges and universities function effectively as teaching and learning communities. This field includes all the areas for which we often name it: faculty development; TA development; instructional, academic, and organizational development. We have chosen the descriptor *educational development* rather than any of these other, perhaps more familiar names for the field, because we believe it is the broadest, most inclusive of the available terms. ED professionals work in a range of contexts, from teaching support units to professional development committees. Choosing to name the whole after a part is alienating to those who work in other ways. Although the term *educational development* is much more common in the UK, Canada, and Australia than the US, we hope it will be adopted more widely as a move to include all of our colleagues within our community.

As a part of this work, especially our work with individual faculty members, many educational developers have recently advocated for and supported a wide range of practices that fall under the rubric of the scholarship of teaching and learning (SoTL) (McKinney, 2004; Schroeder, 2005). Indeed, many teaching centers see SoTL as a central part of their philosophy and offerings. This is so common that in seeking to identify where SoTL is supported within colleges and universities, Huber and Hutchings (2005) identify teaching centers as a "place for good work" (p. 84). Despite this growing engagement with SoTL, however, developers have not done much to use this model to study *our own work as developers*. In this chapter, we explore what it might mean to do this kind of work. What might it involve and why should we consider doing it? What challenges and opportunities are inherent in pursuing SoTL in ED? In what ways might SoTL in ED draw on, and adapt, frameworks already established through SoTL itself? And what possible future directions emerge through all of these considerations?

SoTL in ED: What and Why?

Educational development has been a growing field for the last 50 years or so. However, for most of that time it has been a practice-based discipline with little in the way of systematic study of its range, its activities, or especially its outcomes. This is not to say that our practice is uninformed by research; in fact, one could make the claim that ED professionals are among the prime scholars of university pedagogies and certainly are major consumers and disseminators of educational research in higher education. But such engagement with educational research is parallel to what Richlin (1993) and Shulman (2000) call "scholarly teaching" as differentiated from the "scholarship of teaching." In their terms, scholarly teaching takes into account the work of others in deciding how to teach, whereas scholarship of teaching engages in structured inquiry into the outcomes of one's teaching practice. In similar fashion, many educational developers already perform "scholarly development" by basing their practice on the scholarly literature, but far fewer engage in a scholarship *of* teaching and learning *in* development by gathering data on the outcomes of their own work. We believe that our profession would be significantly enhanced if more of us began to apply SoTL methods to our professional practice—conducting systematic and public inquiry about the learning that emerges from practice.

To be more specific, what we know now about the work of educational development comes mainly from a few studies that survey the field, a great deal of local program assessment, and a strong tradition of sharing best practices. Broad studies over time (Centra, 1976; Chism & Szabo, 1996; Eble & McKeachie, 1985; Erickson, 1986; Hellyer & Boschmann, 1993) have offered important ways to outline the evolution and scope of educational development as an emerging field. Most recently, in *Creating the Future of Faculty Development,* Sorcinelli, Austin, Eddy, and Beach (2006) offer a review of current goals and practices, based on several earlier works and a survey of practitioners. As with previous surveys of the field, Sorcinelli et al. focus on the big picture, the range of practice at many institutions.

At the other end of the spectrum from these broad studies of the profession is program assessment. Most teaching support units regularly collect and analyze data in order to assess their usefulness to their constituencies. However, this analysis is not usually shared beyond the administrative hierarchy of that program. As educational developers, we also have a long and valuable tradition of sharing programs and ideas for practice. The POD publication *To Improve the Academy,* for example, offers many descriptive pieces on best practices, and the annual POD conference provides a rich array of practice-based sessions.

These kinds of study—broad surveys of the field, individual program review and assessment, and best practices—are important and useful. They help us understand and describe our work at both the global and local levels. But something is missing: systematic, evidence-based study and publication by practitioners of the outcomes of their practice. This is the same gap that SoTL fills in classroom teaching—the gap between individual practice and higher education research, between anecdotal sharing of best practices and publication of evidence-based scholarship, between individual evaluation of teaching effectiveness and a collective understanding and analysis of learning outcomes. We propose that we adopt the methods of SoTL, which we so often share with our clients, and look through that scholarly lens at our own practice. In so doing, we would be pursuing the same purposes Lee Shulman (2000) outlines for doing SoTL overall: 1) *professionalism*—recognizing "the inherent obligations and opportunities associated with becoming a professional scholar/educator" (p. 49); 2) *pragmatism*—assuring "that one's work as an educator is constantly improving and meeting its objectives and its responsibilities to students" (p. 49); and 3) *policy*—providing "the capacity to respond to the legitimate questions" (p. 49) of outside constituents about the quality and value of the work being done.

All three of Shulman's reasons align with the broader goals of the educational development community. In fact, defining the professionalism of ED is the second of the four core goals of the current *POD Network Strategic Plan* (2005): "to define what professionalization means in the context of POD." In adopting this goal, POD's governing committee identified the same need to recognize and fulfill the "obligations and opportunities associated with becoming a professional" that Shulman identified. Most of the objectives and strategies listed in the plan to meet this goal would be advanced by creating a rich body of scholarship analyzing the learning outcomes of our practice. Such work would serve the pragmatic function of informing our decisions about where best to spend our limited time and resources to achieve our professional mission of helping our colleges and universities function effectively as teaching and learning communities. Finally, Shulman's definition of policy describes a central need of the field of ED: to explain and justify our work as a scholarly area deserving respect in an academic world where such prestige is generally granted to disciplinary research.

Defining SoTL

So what, more specifically, would doing the SoTL of ED entail? Hutchings (2000, pp. 4–5) describes a taxonomy of questions for SoTL that also could provide a useful model for the SoTL of ED:

- What works?
- What is?
- Visions of the possible
- Formulating a new conceptual framework for shaping thought about practice

Moreover, while SoTL practice varies considerably across disciplines and institutional contexts (Huber & Hutchings, 2005), all SoTL projects share at least three common components (Hutchings & Shulman, 1999/2004):

- SoTL centers on *inquiry* into learning *in a specific context.*
- SoTL practitioners conduct inquiries by collecting and analyzing evidence—in other words, SoTL is *evidence-based.*
- SoTL, like all forms of scholarship, involves the *public sharing and critique* of both the process and the products of inquiry, and in following ethical standards in doing so.

What follows is a further exploration of how Hutchings's taxonomy, as well as these three components, introduce challenges and opportunities for educational developers attempting to conduct SoTL in ED.

Inquiry

Most educational developers, as well as our constituents, can quickly think of big questions we have about work in our field: Do the clients we work with become better teachers? Do their students learn more? Such ungainly questions can stymie research, particularly for busy people who have little time for research in the first place. This difficulty is not unique to ED. Many SoTL practitioners struggle to move from interesting but overly broad questions to more manageable but still significant lines of inquiry.

To help faculty new to SoTL focus on questions that are both answerable and evidence based, Georgetown University's Crossroads Online Institute (hosted by the Center for New Designs in Learning and Scholarship) uses a case study linked to a simple but powerful visual. The case explains how Curtis Bennett, a Carnegie scholar, narrowed his inquiry from vague questions about how students think mathematically to more discrete and evidence-based subquestions about the processes students take to learn, and the ways class activities promote mathematical thinking. Bennett found that his subquestions not only were more "doable" as research projects, but also that the results from these focused inquiries provided considerable insight into his larger concerns about mathematical thinking. Figure 6.1, which accompanies Bennett's case, illustrates the connections between overarching questions and progressively more narrow lines of inquiry linked to evidence.

This hierarchy breaks down a general question into component parts, which are further subdivided until specific questions can be tied directly to evidence of learning. The number of layers involved will depend on the nature of the questions and evidence; however, this process typically helps new SoTL practitioners move from broad but ill-defined "what works?" questions to more answerable "what is?" lines of inquiry.

FIGURE 6.1
Narrowing the Question

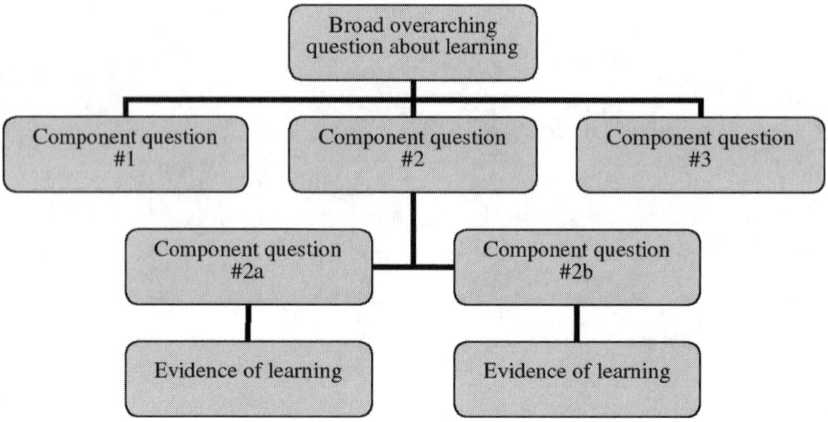

Note. Adapted from: Center for New Designs in Learning and Scholarship, Georgetown University. (n.d.). *Narrowing the questions: SoTL case studies.* Retrieved May 31, 2006, from http://cndls.georgetown.edu/sotl_module/intro2.html

What might SoTL in educational development look like in practice? If we follow this path, we might, for example, use SoTL approaches to explore the learning that results (or fails to result) from the Small Group Instructional Diagnosis (SGID). Many educational developers use variations on the SGID, a focus group process that gathers student feedback for faculty during a course. Although the SGID is a common tool, relatively little has been written about how it shapes faculty teaching or student learning; instead, articles have tended to offer a guide or step-by-step process approach for educational developers using this technique (Black, 1998; Clark & Redmond, 1982; Diamond, 2002; Millis, 2004; Snooks, Neely, & Williamson 2004).

Inquiries into the SGID might explore a range of possibilities along a hierarchy like the one pictured in Figure 6.2.

If we were to approach SGIDs by way of the first three questions in Hutchings's (2000) taxonomy, the lines of inquiry might include the following questions and issues:

- *What works?* What changes (if any) occur in faculty teaching practice as a result of the SGID process? To probe this question, an educational developer might conduct follow-up interviews with faculty to gather self-report data, and might also analyze course materials (syllabi, assignments,

FIGURE 6.2
Inquiry About SGIDs

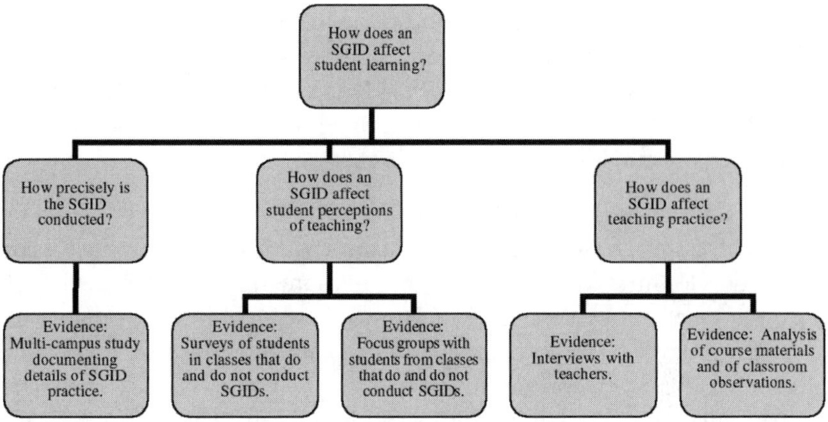

etc.) and conduct classroom observations (either live or on videotape) from before and after the SGID to look for evidence. Such an inquiry might begin with a relatively small sample, since the data gathering and analysis would be intensive. The pilot study then might be used to define the questions and methods for a larger inquiry, perhaps involving educational developers on multiple campuses.

- *What is?* Educational developers might document SGID practices at a variety of institutions and in a variety of teaching contexts (such as large lecture classes, small seminars, laboratories, or online courses). By collecting specific evidence of the ways SGIDs are conducted, within and across institutional contexts (e.g., How does the educational developer prepare for an SGID? What questions are asked of students? How is the class session conducted? Does the developer drive the discussion toward consensus? How is the student feedback compiled and presented to the instructor?), we might go beyond more generic descriptions into more precise distinctions and variations, and thus to further insights on our individual and collective practice.
- *Visions of the possible.* How is the SGID transformed if trained students facilitate the process? An inquiry into this question might gather evidence from the faculty and students participating in the SGID (e.g., What perceptions about SGIDs do students and instructors hold before,

during, and after we do them? How do those perceptions impact the effectiveness of the consultation practice? What changes in those perceptions occur when a student versus a developer facilitates the process?) and also from the student facilitator and the educational developer who trained that student. Observations, interviews, document analysis, and surveys all might provide useful evidence. Findings from this inquiry could open new paths both to educational development practice and to research on student empowerment.

A similar line of inquiry (which emerged in a discussion at a recent POD conference session) following the same taxonomy, this time focusing on educational development workshops, might look something like Figure 6.3. The big questions of our profession (e.g., How does student learning change as a result of our workshops? Our consultations?) are essential to ask, yet essentially impossible to answer on our own. Using SoTL methods to investigate these subquestions can help us grapple with difficult issues in ways that are manageable for both individual and collaborative groups of developers. An SoTL approach, of course, might not be capable of answering all our questions, and we should be wary of pursuing lines of research simply because evidence is available. This approach is not without risks, but the potential of SoTL for educational development, like more traditional SoTL, is transformational: "The scholarship of teaching and learning might then be defined as scholarship undertaken in the name of change, with one measure of its success being its impact on thought and practice" (Hutchings, 2000, p. 8).

FIGURE 6.3
Inquiry About ED Workshops

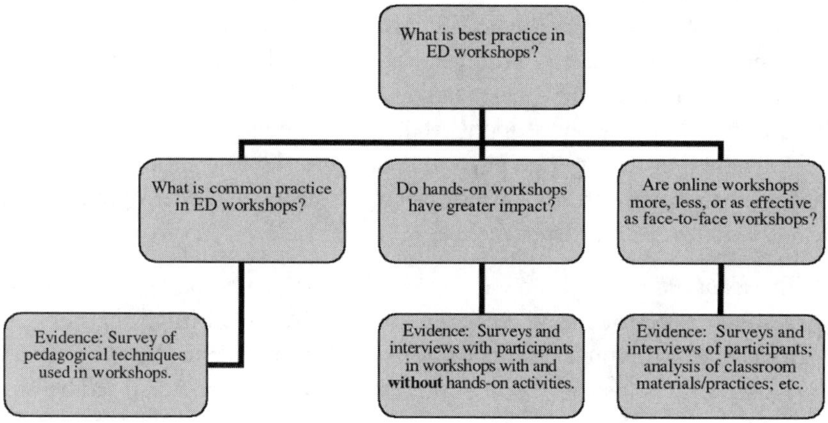

Methods and Evidence

In gathering the evidence necessary to answer our questions, educational developers will most likely face challenges not unlike those faced by faculty practicing SoTL in the disciplines. Like the vast majority of faculty, most educational developers are *not* trained as educational researchers. The coauthors of this chapter are an illustrative although not representative sample of educational developers: Three of us have earned a Ph.D. in English, and one in history. How might scholars from the humanities research these questions? What could they contribute to the SoTL of ED? What could they adapt or adopt from other traditions? In *Disciplinary Styles in Scholarship of Teaching and Learning*, Huber and Morreale (2002) provide many examples of specific disciplinary approaches to SoTL to demonstrate "the virtue of keeping an open mind when looking at the disciplines" (p. 21). They argue that these "very divisions, which some find disturbing, can be sources of strength for the scholarship of teaching and learning" (p. 21). Likewise, educational developers need to take advantage of our disciplinary training and to be open to adapting research methods from other fields (Hutchings, 2000). Over time, a common set of research methods might emerge among the educational development SoTL community; however, we always should cultivate the disciplinary richness of our profession since that will provide new perspectives and approaches to exploring our work (Huber & Hutchings, 2005).

In addition, like many faculty who practice SoTL, most educational developers also will *not* have large sample sizes or ample direct evidence for our studies. Rather than abandoning our inquiries, however, we can adopt the classroom research approach advocated by Cross and Steadman (1996), a typical move in SoTL. As Huber and Hutchings (2005) argue, a small sample can be enlightening if the right question is asked, the evidence is collected systematically, and the analysis is rigorous. Similarly, multiple streams of indirect evidence can be helpful when considering questions that are difficult to answer outside of an experimental lab. Indeed, trying to find the holy grail of evidence (large sample, direct evidence, clean data, etc.) can lead us astray—either by taking our focus off the point of our inquiry (to something answerable but not meaningful) or by pushing us to use research methods far outside our disciplinary training.

An added challenge for the SoTL of ED is that, while SoTL seems to assume some level of continuous contact with students, that longitude may be difficult to achieve for educational developers. Someone may come to just one workshop or do just one consultation over the course of several years. How would we track and study learning in that much more limited context?

For example, how many consultations would we need to do with the same person or even same set or genre of people (e.g., tenure-track faculty in the humanities) to draw any meaningful conclusions? Cohorts or working groups might offer a more robust opportunity for study—we could see how they change over the course of the cohort and then at a later point. But the wide variations in number of people and consistency of contact could pose an obstacle to drawing many solid conclusions.

With this challenge also comes an opportunity, however. In the SoTL of ED, the "students" whose learning we would study are reflective professionals who have a vested interest in the outcomes of the work and are able to provide analysis as well as data. The SoTL of ED may require transforming the role of the "subject" into someone who collaborates in the larger inquiry. In other words, some of the instructors with whom we work may want to be active co-investigators in projects where we study the ED intervention while they, in turn, investigate the learning outcomes for their students. Even if this parallel model is not used, the professional judgment and reflection of college and university faculty provides us with a very rich source of data. Huber and Hutchings (2005) consider how graduate students can contribute to and be developed by participation in traditional SoTL research; in a similar vein, we contend that partnering with clients (graduate student or faculty) in our SoTL in ED inquiries likely will enhance both the research outcomes and the professional development of all involved.

This is new territory, however, so educational developers will need to be aware of how such relationships might facilitate (or obstruct) SoTL in ED. Through all this, educational developers—like any SoTL practitioners—should

- Focus on questions about learning that most interest and motivate us.
- Define clearly the goals, terms, and methods of our inquiry.
- Collect the best evidence available (though it may be fuzzier than we'd like), relying on research methods that we are trained to use.
- Whenever possible, collect multiple streams of evidence so we can approach a question from multiple perspectives (if several fuzzy pieces of evidence seem to converge, then maybe we're on to something!).
- Go public with our entire research process—inquiry, methods, evidence, *and* conclusions.
- Recognize the limits of our individual inquiries, and rely on the community of educational developers to build collaborative projects and to reach conclusions that span multiple campuses.

These procedures and methods should, we believe, lead to useful, structured inquiries into the work of ED.

Ethics

Sharing our work publicly with this kind of scholarship introduces many ethical considerations. The SoTL of ED makes public detailed information about instructors and possibly students, so there is the potential to do harm. Scholars must comply with the standards of human subjects research. Educational developers should work together with their institutional review boards to clarify expectations and procedures for ensuring that our subjects are protected from harm.

Ethical considerations for SoTL in ED go further, however. Because this kind of research is rooted in practice, it needs to address not just research ethics, but professional ethics as well. For educational developers, the POD Ethical Guidelines (which are reproduced in this volume) outline these ethics. A challenge of SoTL in ED is to conduct research and share the results publicly while still adhering to principles of practice in those guidelines, such as "maintain appropriate boundaries in the relationship, avoid exploiting the relationship in any way, and be clear with themselves and their clients about their specific role" and "protect all privileged information, obtaining informed consent from clients before using or referring publicly to client cases in such a way that the client could be identified" (Professional and Organizational Development Network, 2002).

This challenge is similar to that faced by any instructor conducting SoTL. Just as a faculty member conducting SoTL plays a dual role as both teacher and researcher, an educational developer plays a dual role in conducting SoTL in ED, which complicates the ethical questions involved. For example, standard practice for human subjects research requires consent from the subjects. But in the client/consultant relationship, what would this consent look like? When would we ask for it? How would it affect both our research and our practice if we ask for consent when we first meet a client, before providing any services at all? What impact would asking for consent part way through an ongoing consultative relationship have? And how can we guarantee that a client feels free to say no? We may not like to think that there are power dynamics in our relationships with our clients, but there are, so we must consider how power and perceptions of power might affect the granting of consent.

In addition to protecting the client, we must also think about how we can ensure that our research does not impair our practice. Our work with clients depends on establishing trust. Will using them as research subjects affect that trust? Will it make us less able to provide service? That is, might the SoTL research process not only consume our precious time but also sap our ability to adapt to client needs? To be effective in consultations, for instance, consultants need to be flexible, interactive, and improvisational. How might we codify, structure, track, and evaluate *those* kinds of qualities? Put another way, how might we rigorously study and understand those kinds of interactions (and the learning that ensues from them) without draining or overlooking their core vitality?

In *Ethics of Inquiry: Issues in the Scholarship of Teaching and Learning,* Pat Hutchings (2002) uses case studies to explore questions like these as they pertain to traditional SoTL. She reassures us that "there's no single right way to resolve the ethical dilemmas that arise when investigating classroom practice; indeed, the most important resource may be awareness and reflection" (p. 4). Likewise, there are no simple answers to these questions for SoTL in ED. We can borrow models and strategies from related disciplines, but awareness, reflection, and discussion with our peers is essential. Just as it was suggested earlier that collaboration with peers is one way to broaden the scope of SoTL in ED projects, ongoing discussion of the ethical issues involved also can help us create and refine community standards of practice.

The POD Ethical Guidelines describe educational developers as having "a unique opportunity and a special responsibility to contribute to the improvement of the quality of teaching and learning in higher education." Perhaps a final ethical question to consider is whether or not part of that responsibility is to be as scholarly as possible in the work we do. That is, while there are ethical dilemmas in conducting such research, there may be a bigger dilemma if we do *not.* SoTL in ED may complicate our roles and our practice, but it may also inform them, enhance them, and in the long run, help us better fulfill our mission to improve the quality of teaching and learning.

Looking to the Future

Educational developers can and should advance our practice and extend our scholarship by applying SoTL to our own work. By doing so, we will be doing as Lee Shulman (2000) suggests—recognizing and fulfilling the "inherent obligations and opportunities associated with becoming a professional" (p. 49) in our discipline. ED is a part of the larger field of higher education, where professions and professionalism are regularly defined and judged by scholarly standards. We believe that SoTL in ED, in turn, will build our "capacity to respond to . . . legitimate questions" (Shulman, 2000, p. 49) about the quality and value of our work, highlighting it as a scholarly area deserving respect in academe. Such work can do more than address anxieties about prestige. Expanding the research literature on ED practices can improve greatly the effectiveness of decisions about where to spend limited time and resources. This should improve our ability to achieve our professional mission of helping our colleges and universities to function effectively as teaching and learning communities.

Of course, our exploration leads to more questions than we can answer here. If and as the profession of educational development does adopt the SoTL model, we also will need to address the following issues (and many others):

- What are the intersections between the core components of our practice and our institutional contexts? Sorcinelli et al.'s (2006) survey identifies these core components: individual consultations, orientations, workshops and programs, grants and awards, resources and publications, special services. Do all components of practice work equally well in all institutional contexts? Which best practices transcend institutional type, and which ones need to be honed more finely?
- How will SoTL in ED be supported and rewarded? Many questions about rewards and incentives have emerged for faculty doing SoTL (Huber, 2004). How might similar issues apply to educational developers? What is the appropriate trade-off for ED professionals between *doing* our practice and *researching* our practice? Are those two in opposition, or should they be integrated? How does SoTL in ED align with *our* reward structures—within our field, at our local institutions, and in our own personal development as professionals? Do we, like traditional SoTL, need to be advocating for new or revised systems to evaluate and recognize our scholarly work?
- Should SoTL in ED be built on a collaborative foundation? Randy Bass recently raised important questions about the value of individual SoTL research (Bernstein & Bass, 2005). Although welcoming all levels of SoTL practice, Bass calls for "an entirely different developmental model" (p. 42) that involves groups inquiring jointly into common questions. This, Bass contends, might permit SoTL to answer essential questions that are difficult to address through individual research alone. Educational development has a strong professional history of cooperation and sharing.

How might we leverage this tradition to create a new model of SoTL research that will produce knowledge capable of transforming both our individual practice and our profession?

These questions are beyond the scope of this chapter; indeed, they are beyond the ability of any member of our profession to answer alone. However, ED has a long tradition of sharing effort and working in community. As we go forward, we are confident that with awareness, reflection, and discussion in community, these questions—and the many others we have not yet identified—can be explored to the benefit of all.

References

Bernstein, D., & Bass, R. (2005, July/August). The scholarship of teaching and learning. *Academe, 91*(4), 37–43.

Black, B. (1998). Using the SGID method for a variety of purposes. In M. Kaplan & D. Lieberman (Eds.), *To improve the academy: Vol. 17. Resources for faculty, instructional, and organizational development* (pp. 245–262). Stillwater, OK: New Forums Press.

Centra, J. A. (1976). *Faculty development practices in U.S. colleges and universities.* Princeton, NJ: Educational Testing Service.

Chism, N. V. N., & Szabo, B. (1996). Who uses faculty development services? In L. Richlin & D. DeZure (Eds.), *To improve the academy: Vol. 15. Resources for faculty, instructional, and organizational development* (pp. 115–128). Stillwater, OK: New Forums Press.

Clark, D. J., & Redmond, M. (1982). *Small group instructional diagnosis: Final report.* Seattle, WA: University of Washington, Department of Biology Education. (ERIC Document Reproduction Service No. ED217954)

Cross, K. P., & Steadman, M. H. (1996). *Classroom research: Implementing the scholarship of teaching.* San Francisco, CA: Jossey-Bass.

Diamond, N. A. (2002). Small group instructional diagnosis: Tapping student perceptions of teaching. In K. H. Gillespie, L. R. Hilsen, & E. C. Wadsworth (Eds.), *A guide to faculty development: Practical advice, examples, and resources* (pp. 82–91). Bolton, MA: Anker.

Eble, K. E., & McKeachie, W. J. (1985). *Improving undergraduate education through faculty development: An analysis of effective programs and practices.* San Francisco, CA: Jossey-Bass.

Erickson, G. (1986). A survey of faculty development practices. In M. Svinicki, J. Kurfiss, & J. Stone (Eds.), *To improve the academy: Vol. 5. Resources for faculty, instructional, and organizational development* (pp. 182–196). Stillwater, OK: New Forums Press.

Hellyer, S., & Boschmann, E. (1993). Faculty development programs: A perspective. In D. L. Wright & J. P. Lunde (Eds.), *To improve the academy: Vol. 12. Resources for faculty, instructional, and organizational development* (pp. 217–224). Stillwater, OK: New Forums Press.

Huber, M. T. (2004). *Balancing acts: The scholarship of teaching and learning in academic careers.* Sterling, VA: Stylus.

Huber, M. T., & Hutchings, P. (2005). *The advancement of learning: Building the teaching commons.* San Francisco, CA: Jossey-Bass.

Huber, M. T., & Morreale, S. P. (Eds.). (2002). *Disciplinary styles in the scholarship of teaching and learning: Exploring common ground.* Washington, DC: American Association for Higher Education.

Hutchings, P. (2000). Introduction: Approaching the scholarship of teaching and learning. In P. Hutchings (Ed.), *Opening lines: Approaches to the scholarship of teaching and learning* (pp. 1–10). Menlo Park, CA: Carnegie Foundation for the Advancement of Teaching.

Hutchings, P. (Ed.). (2002). *Ethics of inquiry: Issues in the scholarship of teaching and learning.* Menlo Park, CA: Carnegie Foundation for the Advancement of Teaching.

Hutchings, P., & Shulman, L. S. (2004). The scholarship of teaching: New elaborations, new developments. In L. S. Shulman, *Teaching as community property: Essays on higher education* (pp. 145–154). San Francisco, CA: Jossey-Bass. (Original work published 1999)

McKinney, K. (2004). The scholarship of teaching and learning: Past lessons, current challenges, and future visions. In C. M. Wehlburg & S. Chadwick-Blossey (Eds.), *To improve the academy: Vol. 22. Resources for faculty, instructional, and organizational development* (pp. 3–19). Bolton, MA: Anker.

Millis, B. J. (2004). A versatile interactive focus group protocol for qualitative assessments. In C. M. Wehlburg & S. Chadwick-Blossey (Eds.), *To improve the academy: Vol. 22. Resources for faculty, instructional, and organizational development* (pp. 125–141). Bolton, MA: Anker.

Professional and Organizational Development Network in Higher Education. (2002). *Ethical guidelines for educational developers.* Retrieved June 2, 2006, from http://podnetwork.org/development/ethicalguidelines.htm

Professional and Organizational Development Network in Higher Education. (2005). *The POD Network strategic plan 2005.* Retrieved June 2, 2006, from www.podnetwork.org/pdf/PODplan.pdf

Richlin, L. (Ed.). (1993). *New directions for teaching and learning: No. 54. Preparing faculty for the new conceptions of scholarship.* San Francisco, CA: Jossey-Bass.

Schroeder, C. M. (2005). Evidence of the transformational dimensions of the scholarship of teaching and learning: Faculty development through the eyes of SoTL scholars. In S. Chadwick-Blossey & D. R. Robertson (Eds.), *To improve the academy: Vol. 23. Resources for faculty, instructional, and organizational development* (pp. 47–71). Bolton, MA: Anker.

Shulman, L. S. (2000, April). From Minsk to Pinsk: Why a scholarship of teaching and learning? *Journal of the Scholarship of Teaching and Learning, 1*(1), 48–52.

Snooks, M. K., Neely, S. E., & Williamson, K. M. (2004). From SGID and GIFT to BBQ: Streamlining midterm student evaluation to improve teaching and learning. In C. M. Wehlburg & S. Chadwick-Blossey (Eds.), *To improve the academy: Vol. 22. Resources for faculty, instructional, and organizational development* (pp. 110–124). Bolton, MA: Anker.

Sorcinelli, M. D., Austin, A. E., Eddy, P. L., & Beach, A. L. (2006). *Creating the future of faculty development: Learning from the past, understanding the present.* Bolton, MA: Anker.

7

Faculty Development Through Student Learning Initiatives: Lessons Learned

Nancy Simpson, Jean Layne,
Adalet Baris Gunersel, Blake Godkin, Jeff Froyd
Texas A&M University

A project aimed at improving student learning while facilitating the professional development of faculty participants in the area of teaching has yielded a rich collection of data. In addition to providing critical information about how faculty members think, the project has broadened our thinking regarding the link between student learning initiatives and faculty development. The project has also increased our understanding of the interests of faculty members who are not typically clients of faculty development centers and motivated thinking on how to serve the professional development goals of this group.

How do faculty members' beliefs and practices in the area of teaching and learning change as a result of their involvement in a project intended to improve student learning and teaching? This question has captured our attention as faculty developers on the research team for Writing for Assessment and Learning in the Natural and Mathematical Sciences (WALS), as we seek to understand the professional development of faculty members as teachers. The process of answering this question has refocused our attention on motivations and prior knowledge of the faculty members with whom we work. This chapter describes our methodology, initial findings, and lessons learned from this investigation, and their impact on our work as faculty developers. We begin by describing the motivation and activities of the project and the methodology for interviews with faculty participants. We then present findings from the interviews and conclude with a description of how what we learned has influenced the direction and activities of the project.

Project Description

Motivation for WALS

In 2003, a team of science faculty members and faculty developers at Texas A&M University received National Science Foundation funding for Writing for Assessment and Learning in the Natural and Mathematical Sciences, a project that uses Calibrated Peer Review™ (http://cpr.molsci.ucla.edu/), to create and evaluate student writing assignments in biology, mathematics, and physics. WALS was designed to address three needs: the need for assessment tools that yield information about the kind of learning valued by mathematics and science faculty members, the need for faculty-driven inquiry into questions about learning and teaching, and the need for students to write in order to refine their communication and thinking specific to particular disciplines.

The need for assessment tools. Mathematics and science learning that emphasizes conceptual understanding and promotes critical thinking and communication skills is central to producing a scientifically literate workforce and citizenry. The way we assess learning is the most powerful signal that we send to students about what is important (Wiggins, 1990). Measures that give insight into student thinking are needed—both to communicate to students that it is their ability to think like scientists that is valued and to provide information for the improvement of teaching methods. And, since faculty members reasonably seek evidence that a change from more traditional teaching methods will lead to better student learning, lack of adequate assessment hinders the widespread adoption of inquiry-based, active-learning teaching methods (Guskey, 2002; Wright et al., 1998).

The need for faculty-driven inquiry. Adequate assessment methods and tools are necessary—but not sufficient—for the improvement of student learning. Devotion of faculty time and intellectual energy to careful analysis of assessment is also required. While there is a need for assessment methods that can show *what* students have learned, even more pressing is the need for faculty members to investigate questions about optimal conditions under which students acquire deep conceptual understanding and develop habits of disciplinary thinking. As Cross and Steadman (1996) write in the introduction to their book *Classroom Research,* "Just as students must be actively engaged in formulating their own learning questions and thinking critically about them, so teachers must be actively engaged in formulating their own questions about learning and the impact of their teaching upon it" (p. 2).

The need for students to write. Not only is it important for students to learn to write, but writing is, in itself, an effective learning tool. Well-crafted writing assignments promote active reading and critical thinking (Lowman,

1996), and student writing gives a clearer picture of what students have learned than short answer or machine-scored multiple-choice exams (Elbow, 1997). Recognizing this, the university implemented writing-intensive course requirements, and WALS is motivated in part by the need to provide support for faculty members seeking to offer writing-intensive courses.

WALS Activities

Thirteen faculty members (four from mathematics, four from biology, and five from physics) participated in the project during 2003–2004, motivated both by their desire to have their students do more writing and by the provision of two weeks of summer support from the WALS grant. The initial activity was a two- and one-half-day workshop during which faculty learned to author and administer writing assignments using Calibrated Peer Review™ (CPR). CPR, a tool designed by a team of chemists from the University of California–Los Angeles with support from the National Science Foundation, requires significant faculty time in assignment authoring. However, because the assignments are peer graded and the whole process is computer managed, relatively little faculty time is needed in administration and grading. This makes it possible to implement writing assignments in large classes without adding significantly to grading time.

During the introductory workshop, faculty members met in three departmental teams to discuss the kinds of questions that would be appropriate for CPR assignments, and spent the majority of their time creating assignments that they would implement during either the fall or spring semester. Throughout the year, they met as a group and as departmental teams to share successes as well as to discuss the challenges involved with implementation. At the end of the academic year, they participated in an all-day retreat/workshop during which they analyzed samples of student writing to gain insight into the learning that the students were (or were not) able to demonstrate through their writing. The format of this analysis is described in a later section of this chapter.

How Faculty Members Were Initially Thinking About Thinking and Learning

Our evaluation of WALS addressed the question "How do faculty beliefs and practices change as result of their involvement with this project?" To provide a baseline from which to measure change, we interviewed faculty, using the stimulated recall method, then recorded, analyzed, and coded the interviews. This section describes the methodology and its implementation.

The stimulated recall method was first introduced by Bloom (1956), who used the videotape or audiotape of a class period to help the interviewee (usually the teacher of the class) remember and report his or her thoughts. For the WALS project, we videotaped faculty participants during a regular class period. We then interviewed them, using segments of the videotape to stimulate their recollection of what was happening and what they were thinking during the class. We audiotaped, transcribed, and analyzed all the interviews for their content (Clark & Peterson, 1986).

With stimulated recall, researchers can select interview segments in different ways. One approach is to watch the tape ahead of time, identify critical moments, and use them during the interview. We believed that using this approach would insert too much of our own thinking into the interview since we would be the ones deciding which incidents were important and which were not. Because the objective of these interviews was to obtain a picture of the current state of faculty thinking, we chose instead an approach that minimized the effect of our own beliefs and that could be kept consistent for all interviewees. At the beginning of each interview, the interviewer showed professors a few minutes of the beginning of the class to help them remember that specific class period. The interviewer then fast-forwarded to a two- to five-minute segment within each ten-minute interval. The segments were randomly selected by the interviewer unless the faculty member indicated a place on the tape where he or she wished to pause and make comments. After each of these segments the interviewer asked questions.

Since the purpose of the interview was to get the thoughts, beliefs, and practices of the professors, the interviewer used open-ended questions such as "What were you thinking at this moment?" and "What were you thinking about the students' understanding of the material?" The interviewer followed up with probing questions such as "Can you tell me more about that?" "How often does that happen?" "Why do you think that happened?" and "Why did you think that?" In order to better understand professors' pedagogical practices, the interviewer asked questions such as "How often do you use that strategy?" "How often do students ask questions?" or "What do you do when you encounter that problem?" In addition, after the initial three-minute segment, the interviewer asked the goals for that class period and at the end, the interviewer asked whether the goals had been accomplished.

We transcribed and coded the interviews. Rather than begin with a particular framework, we chose to allow the themes to emerge from the data (Strauss & Corbin, 1998). We each read the first several transcripts together and observed recurring themes and categories of professor statements, keeping in mind our research question: "What are the current teaching/learning beliefs and practices of these professors?" To keep our work consistent through all the transcripts, we kept notes about what we meant by each category. After completing six transcripts we refined the categories and finished coding the interviews. The interviews are the primary source of data for the findings that are presented in the next section.

Project Findings

Four categories of comments emerged from our analysis: 1) pedagogical practices, 2) personal practical theories, 3) assumptions about students, and 4) pedagogical content knowledge. While a comprehensive discussion of what participants said is beyond the scope of this chapter, the following briefly describes each category to anchor the lessons learned that are presented in the final section of this chapter.

Pedagogical Practices

We categorized participant descriptions of the methods they use to communicate content knowledge and to facilitate student learning as *pedagogical practices,* including descriptions of use of lecture, questioning, examples, and demonstrations. Faculty participants generally began by recalling what they were doing on the particular segment of videotape they had just viewed, then elaborating with descriptions of other strategies that they use in the classroom. Understanding how faculty describe their teaching practices at the outset of the project serves several purposes. First, while the ultimate goal of faculty development is improving student learning, it is not often easy to directly attribute increases in student learning to faculty development programs. What is possible, however, is to look for changes in teaching practices. This collection of faculty descriptions included in *pedagogical practices* gives us a baseline from which to identify change. Second, this category helps us identify what new strategies we might suggest to enhance current practice. Finally, since faculty members do not always find it easy to articulate their beliefs about teaching and learning, knowing *how* they teach allows us to infer beliefs that drive their practice. Many educational researchers suggest that faculty choose to teach in certain ways because of their beliefs about teaching and learning (Cothran et al., 2005). Ernest (1989, as cited in Cothran et al., 2005) suggests that beliefs impact what teachers select for content and how they deliver the content. Further, according to Grasha (1996), personal assumptions about teaching and learning "play an important role in how we design and implement a variety of classroom processes" and "help to guide and direct our actions in the classroom" (p. 101). The following interview excerpts illustrate some pedagogical practices.

> This is the pulling-teeth stage now. It's like, "How can I get them to get the answer without me just telling it to them? . . . I was thinking "I don't want to just give them the answer, but what questions can I ask to draw the answer out of them?"

> So, in the lecture, I have demonstrations . . . which I consider very important in introductory physics lectures . . . that's what physics is all about, I think.

> There was a time many years ago when I believed that I could sort of read their expressions. And if I got a lot of blank stares, I slowed down, I gave more examples, I provided more explanation. . . . I'm having more difficulty these days, . . . I'm seeing more deadpan expressions. There seems to be less overt signals, at least that I recognize, which tell me confusion or comprehension. I don't know what I'm missing.

Personal Practical Theories

While part of our understanding of faculty beliefs about teaching and learning is derived from their descriptions of how they teach, some faculty participants were explicit about what they believe about teaching and learning. We categorized these statements as *personal practical theories.* Such theories are "formed through experience and reflection, include images of teaching and learning, the roles of teachers and students, and the purposes of and methods for content instruction" (Gess-Newsome, Southerland, Johnston, & Woodbury, 2003, p. 758). They "both shape and constrain teachers' interactions with reform" (Gess-Newsome et al., 2003, p. 758), forming the filter through which new information is evaluated, internalized, and acted upon.

The identification of personal practical theories is critical to projects like WALS for several reasons. First, faculty members may not have articulated these theories often—or ever. Leaving these theories invisible makes them more difficult to identify and track for the purpose of professional development (Sanders & McCutcheon, 1986). Second, by identifying personal practical theories and examining them in light of the learning literature, we begin to get an idea of what the faculty participants already know about the learning process that is supported—or not—by cognitive science. Third, we gain insight into how faculty members are filtering and processing their experiences with students as well as their experiences in informal/formal faculty development opportunities. We give a few examples of these theories in the next paragraph.

When speaking of the language barrier between him and the students, one faculty participant commented, "Repetition. That's the cure for a lot of things. Do things over and over and over again, with different approaches, maybe with different words that mean the same things." About encouraging his students to ask questions, a participant said, "I can tell by the questions I'm getting where they are, what they're understanding, what they're missing." Another participant commented that in order to have an effective class, "you've got to engage students early on."

Assumptions About Students

In addition to descriptions of teaching practices and of beliefs about teaching and learning, faculty participants shared their assumptions about student ability and motivation and about their expectations of or about students. We included these statements in the category *assumptions about students.* All educators meet their learners with certain beliefs about teaching and learning (Leamnson, 1999), and these beliefs are affected and modified by beliefs about the learners themselves. Because of this, we believe it is important to understand the beliefs, expectations, and assumptions faculty have about students. We know that the potential impact of these assumptions is significant. Rosenthal and Jacobson's (1968, as cited in Bamburg, 1994) "Pygmalion in the Classroom" research began a series of research projects regarding the effect of teacher expectations on students. Douglas (1964) and Mackler (1969) found that

> Teachers' expectations about student achievement can be affected by factors having little or nothing to do with his or her ability, and yet these expectations can determine the level of achievement by confining learning opportunities to those available in one's track. (as qtd. in Bamburg, 1994, p. 7)

Tauber (1998) describes the Pygmalion Effect as "the idea that one's expectations about a person can eventually lead that person to behave and achieve in ways to confirm those expectations" (p. 3). It is possible that faculty participants' beliefs about their students affect the way in which they communicate with their students and artificially limit their choice of pedagogies.

We want to identify recurring assumptions of faculty participants and observe how these assumptions impact their teaching and evolve through the WALS experience. Does involvement in a project such as WALS lead faculty participants to question their assumptions or to inquire systematically about the underlying causes of student behavior? Our interviews have given us not only a baseline from which to gauge growth, but also a point of departure for motivating faculty classroom research. For example, one faculty member's comment suggested a testable hypothesis for a scholarly investigation:

> Typically—I may be a little cynical—I anticipate that most students haven't had to think much in math classes before. Coming into my freshman math class, coming out of high school, I expect them not to think much about what they had done. So it's kind of a new experience for them.

Other participants communicated beliefs about student fragility and shyness or about their study habits. Again, these could be tested in order to affirm or disprove an assumption about students.

> I think that students are a lot more fragile than they should be. And most of them don't enjoy arguing and give and take.

> They tend to be, on the whole, somewhat of a quiet class. Sometimes I think it's because they aren't really sure of what's going on, or what I'm trying to get at, or something like that.

> I get a lot more questions when homework is due. The reason is, of course, they usually do the homework the night before it's due. And they don't look at the course except when homework is due.

Pedagogical Content Knowledge

The final category that emerged from our analysis is *pedagogical content knowledge.* Shulman (1987) uses this term to describe the knowledge that faculty members need about the teaching of their discipline. Manouchehri (1996) describes pedagogical content knowledge as "how to represent specific topics or issues in ways that are appropriate to the diverse abilities and interests of learners" (p. 7). Bransford, Brown, and Cocking (2000) observe that

> Expert teachers know the structure of their disciplines, and this knowledge provides them with cognitive roadmaps that guide the assignments they give students, the assessments they use to gauge students' progress, and the questions they ask in the give and take of classroom life. (p. 155)

While only a few of the faculty participants made statements that could be identified as pedagogical content knowledge, we believe that is important to identify and build on even the beginning of this kind of expertise in teaching. For example, one building block for pedagogical content knowledge is the recognition that particular concepts in the disciplines are difficult for students to grasp, and several of our professors made statements in this regard. For example, a physics professor observed,

> . . . the class that we taped . . . is the hardest class of the entire semester in terms of comprehension . . . it's because we're talking about internal rotational motion which is just a harder concept to grasp for them than translational motion. People are familiar with that because they drive the car, they walk, and the concepts of that type of motion are much easier to grasp for students than this internal rotational motion. It's also complicated because of the mathematical language that we use for describing it; you know the different parameters are not the parameters that people use in every day life. . . . People, I guess, have a much easier approach to something like velocity, because they are seeing it on their dashboard in the car all the time.

Pace and Middendorf (2004) provide a faculty development model that builds on this kind of knowledge in their work on "decoding the disciplines," and these initial interviews indicate that this model could be a productive approach with faculty involved in WALS.

Understanding what college faculty know—and how they know it—about the teaching of their discipline is important for faculty developers. Faculty often do not recognize that the insights gained from years of experience constitute a particular kind of expertise, and therefore they do not see it as something worth sharing with others. But, while the experiences of individual faculty members may not lead to disciplinary teaching theory, the combined experiences of many faculty could in fact lead to significant understanding about how to facilitate learning in a particular discipline. Faculty developers are ideally situated to hear these stories and to look for the patterns and connections that advance understanding of teaching and learning in that discipline.

Lessons Learned and Future Work

We turn now to a discussion of what we learned from this analysis and how it is informing our continued work. As previously stated, faculty members who decided to become involved in this project were motivated primarily by their desire to include more writing assignments in their courses and by the incentive of two weeks of summer salary. In this regard, they were unlike most of the faculty with whom we have worked in the past: They were not primarily motivated by a desire to improve their teaching or to engage in scholarly inquiry about their students' learning. While we knew this, we were not prepared for the challenges we encountered throughout the year as we attempted to engage these faculty members in discussion of articles and book chapters from the learning literature. In contrast to other groups of faculty who had found this material both interesting and useful, WALS faculty participants did not. Reading the transcripts of the stimulated recall interviews with participating faculty members helped us understand why this was the case. Our interviews gave us a better understanding of the knowledge, beliefs, values, and questions of faculty participants as "learners," and provided insights into how we might better promote their growth as scholars of learning and teaching. Specifically, we learned that faculty members are highly motivated by the content of their courses and that they are unsure whether their students are learning what they hope or expect them to learn. In the paragraphs that follow, we elaborate on these two points and describe the steps the research team has taken or will take in response.

First, we recognized that participating faculty members are passionate about their respective disciplines. Whether mathematics, physics, or biology, they love the concepts and thinking processes of their field and believe strongly that it is important for students to learn these disciplines. When asked about learning goals, they almost always described content and concepts. The interview transcripts were filled with enthusiastic descriptions of the substance of what they were teaching.

We built on this knowledge of our audience to develop the agenda for the retreat at the end of 2003–2004 where we introduced Anderson and Krathwohl's (2001) revision of Bloom's taxonomy. Specifically, since we were by this time well aware that it was "knowledge of critical content in the discipline" that was of primary value to participating faculty members, we developed the workshop around the "knowledge dimension" (p. 46). After describing factual knowledge, conceptual knowledge, procedural knowledge, and metacognitive knowledge, we asked the faculty participants to consider one of their CPR assignments and write down what knowledge in each category would be required for student success on the assignment. Participants then worked in disciplinary teams to analyze sample student writing and look for evidence of each type of knowledge. The level of faculty engagement with this exercise indicated that this particular analytic tool was a useful one. The template for this analysis is shown in Table 7.1.

TABLE 7.1

The WALS Faculty's Template for Analyzing Student Writing

	Expectations (What did students need to know in order to be successful?)	Evidence Exhibited (What did students know and what is the evidence?)	Evidence Missing or Erroneous (What did students not know and what is the evidence?)
Factual Knowledge			
Conceptual Knowledge			
Procedural Knowledge			
Metacognitive Knowledge			

Note. Based on Anderson and Krathwohl (2001).

Second, while participating faculty were highly motivated to have their students "get" the content, they frequently expressed uncertainty that their students *were* learning—or if they are not learning, why not. Such uncertainty can either interfere with improvement of teaching and learning practices (by leaving faculty with a sense of discouragement regarding student learning outcomes) or be a catalyst for that improvement (by presenting questions worthy of investigation). Teaching is a complex activity that "involves more than simply behavior but thoughts, interpretations, choices, values, and commitments as well" (Sanders & McCutcheon, 1986, p. 51). Lack of certainty about student understanding can lead to efforts to gain insight into the difficulties students may be having with the concepts, and we wanted to support these efforts.

The uncertainty about whether students were "getting it" pointed to the importance of analyzing student outcomes using CPR data; that is, we needed to provide participating faculty members with concrete data from which to make their conclusions about student learning. During summer and fall 2005, we began this kind of analysis, using data from the classes of two WALS professors. In one case, the outcomes were encouraging, showing increases in student ability to write about the content of the course. In the other case, the outcomes were, on the surface, discouraging. The students did not improve in their ability to write in the language of the particular discipline involved.

But what appears to be bad news is, in fact, a catalyst for more careful investigation of what it is that makes this kind of writing so difficult for students. A particularly challenging element of teaching is that faculty members, who are longtime "expert" learners in their disciplines, may have forgotten what "novices" most need in order to make learning advances in the discipline. A next step is to work through the steps of the "decoding the disciplines" model (Pace & Middendorf, 2004) with not only the particular professor involved, but also the others in the project. We believe that this will lead to beneficial redesign or refinement of the CPR assignments and to more satisfactory student performance.

From a learning standpoint, one of the benefits of both the campus commitment to writing intensive courses and our work with CPR is the explicit linkage of the writing process to the learning process. Students' efforts to articulate their disciplinary thinking confronts both students and faculty members with tangible evidence of confusion, misconceptions, lack of clarity, and so on. And it gives faculty greater insight into what is right as well as wrong with student conceptualizations. Our next step is to continue the quantitative and qualitative analysis of student outcomes using data from CPR in order to capitalize on the writing of the students.

Our experience with this project has given us fresh appreciation for the importance of understanding the conceptions of learning and teaching that faculty bring to faculty development opportunities, in particular to those offered in connection with student learning initiatives. The stimulated recall method is time intensive, but it yielded a wealth of information and insight into the thinking of faculty participants about a variety of issues related to learning and teaching. We encourage any faculty development unit looking to gain a richer understanding of the population they serve to utilize this methodology and to compare data with those from our project and other campuses.

Note

This material is based on work supported by the National Science Foundation under grant number DUE–0243209.

References

Anderson, L. W., & Krathwohl, D. R. (Eds.). (2001). *A taxonomy for learning, teaching, and assessing: A revision of Bloom's taxonomy of educational objectives.* New York, NY: Longman.

Bamburg, J. D. (1994). *Raising expectations to improve student learning.* Naperville, IL: North Central Regional Educational Laboratory.

Bloom, B. S. (Ed.). (1956). *Taxonomy of educational objectives, handbook 1: Cognitive domain.* New York, NY: Longman.

Bransford, J. D., Brown, A. L., & Cocking, R. R. (Eds.). (2000). *How people learn: Brain, mind, experience, and school* (Expanded ed.). Washington, DC: National Academy Press.

Clark, C. M., & Peterson, P. L. (1986). Teachers' thought processes. In M. C. Wittrock (Ed.), *Handbook of research on teaching* (3rd ed., pp. 255–296.). New York, NY: Macmillan.

Cothran, D. J., Kulinna, P. H., Banville, D., Choi, E., Amade-Escot, C., MacPhail, A., et al. (2005, June). A cross-cultural investigation of the use of teaching styles. *Research Quarterly for Exercise and Sport, 76*(2), 193–201.

Cross, K. P., & Steadman, M. H. (1996). *Classroom research: Implementing the scholarship of teaching.* San Francisco, CA: Jossey-Bass.

Elbow, P. (1997). High stakes and low stakes in assigning and responding to writing. In M. D. Sorcinelli & P. Elbow (Eds.), *New directions for teaching and learning: No. 69. Writing to learn: Strategies for assigning and responding to writing across the disciplines* (pp. 5–13). San Francisco, CA: Jossey-Bass.

Gess-Newsome, J., Southerland, S. A., Johnston, A., & Woodbury, S. (2003, Fall). Educational reform, personal practical theories, and dissatisfaction: The anatomy of change in college science teaching. *American Educational Research Journal, 40*(3), 731–767.

Grasha, A. F. (1996). *Teaching with style: A practical guide to enhancing learning by understanding teaching and learning styles.* Pittsburgh, PA: Alliance.

Guskey, T. R. (2002, August). Professional development and teacher change. *Teachers and Teaching: Theory and Practice, 8*(3), 381–391.

Leamnson, R. (1999). *Thinking about teaching and learning: Developing habits of learning with first year college and university students.* Sterling, VA: Stylus.

Lowman, J. (1996). Assignments that promote and integrate learning. In R. J. Menges, M. Weimer, & Associates, *Teaching on solid ground: Using scholarship to improve practice* (pp. 203–232). San Francisco, CA: Jossey-Bass.

Manouchehri, A. (1996, October). *Theory and practice: Implications for mathematics teacher education programs.* Paper presented at the annual forum of the Association of Independent Liberal Arts Colleges for Teacher Education, Atlanta, GA.

Pace, D., & Middendorf, J. (Eds.). (2004). *New directions for teaching and learning: No. 98. Decoding the disciplines: Helping students learn disciplinary ways of thinking.* San Francisco, CA: Jossey-Bass.

Sanders, D. P., & McCutcheon, G. (1986, Fall). The development of practical theories of teaching. *Journal of Curriculum and Supervision, 2*(1), 40–67.

Shulman, L. S. (1987, Spring). Knowledge and teaching: Foundations of new reform. *Harvard Educational Review, 57*(1), 1–21.

Strauss, A., & Corbin, J. (1998). *Basics of qualitative research: Techniques and procedures for developing grounded theory* (2nd ed.). Thousand Oaks, CA: Sage.

Tauber, R. T. (1998). *Good or bad, what teachers expect from students they generally get!* Washington, DC: ERIC Clearinghouse on Teaching and Teacher Education. (ERIC Document Reproduction Service No. ED426985)

Wiggins, G. (1990). The truth may make you feel free, but the test may keep you imprisoned: Toward assessment worthy of the liberal arts. *AAHE Assessment Forum,* 17–31.

Wright, J. C., Millar, S. B., Koscuik, S. A., Penberthy, D. L., Williams, P. H., & Wampold, B. E. (1998, August). A novel strategy for assessing the effects of curriculum reform on student competence. *Journal of Chemical Education, 75*(8), 986–992.

8

Action Research for Instructional Improvement: Using Data to Enhance Student Learning at Your Institution

Constance E. Cook, Mary Wright, Christopher O'Neal
University of Michigan

Action research is a powerful tool that can be used by teaching centers to improve teaching and learning. This chapter describes an action research project conducted at the Center for Research on Learning and Teaching at the University of Michigan. The project concerns retention and attrition in science gateway courses, with particular attention given to the role of the teaching assistant. This chapter concludes with a discussion of six principles for teaching center staff who wish to conduct their own action research projects.

The role of most teaching centers at universities across the country is to improve teaching and student learning by creating a culture of pedagogical excellence, responding to instructors' needs, and advancing teaching and learning through new initiatives (Sorcinelli, Austin, Eddy, & Beach, 2006). In this chapter, we document one useful approach to enhance student learning through a methodology called *action research.* Coined by psychologist Kurt Lewin (1948/1997), action research (or action inquiry) generally refers to any research that is used as the basis and motivation for reform. Sorcinelli et al., in their discussion of the "evolution" of faculty development, describe a move from the 1950's and 1960's Age of the Scholar (emphasizing support for faculty research) to today's Age of the Learner (supporting effective pedagogy and scholarship of teaching and learning) and tomorrow's Age of the Network, in which faculty and developer roles expand and collaboration becomes key to success. An action research approach is ideally situated for contemporary faculty development activities as it emphasizes collaboration and supports student learning through data-driven investigation.

The Center for Research on Learning and Teaching (CRLT) at the University of Michigan illustrates the path of one teaching center to an action research approach. CRLT was established in 1962, and as its name implies, research was its primary focus for its first decades. In the 1980s, CRLT's emphasis moved to a mix of research and service to faculty, and by the 1990s, its focus was mostly on programmatic faculty development in response to the provost's mandate that teaching improvement was important and faculty development was the way to achieve it. This emphasis implies that there was no research at all, which was not the case; evaluation research was a regular part of the service CRLT provided. What the center rarely did, however, was initiate major research projects that went beyond investigation of a single course or curriculum.

In this new age, CRLT has broadened its own focus to embrace more of its research roots. We augment our faculty development programs with periodic research projects, and the research improves our programming. Our research usually is done at the request of academic leaders, especially deans, and it informs and improves the services we provide for them, as well as instructors' practice, curricula, and institutional cultures. This type of research is a form of inquiry termed *action research,* and it is a powerful tool by which teaching centers can improve instruction.

Lewin (1948/1997) described action research as a process, or a "spiral of steps each of which is composed of a cycle of planning, action, and fact-finding about the result of the action" (p. 146). Organizational action research is not new to higher education. Using evaluation research to inform institutional change in higher education has been around since the master planning movement of the 1960s (Halstead, 1974; St. John, McKinney, & Tuttle, in press). Since that time, action research has been used as a democratization method by which various constituencies can be brought into the change process (Armstrong & Moore, 2004; Benson & Harkavy, 1996; Park, 1999), an experiential tool to engage learners (Geltner, 1993; Krogh, 2001; Zuelke & Nichols, 1995), and a process to conduct classroom research (Cross & Steadman, 1996; Schön, 1983, 1987). There are many variants of action research, such as participatory action research, cooperative inquiry, empowerment research, community-based research, and feminist research (Reason, 1999; Small, 1995; Strand, Marullo, Cutforth, Stoecker, & Donohue, 2003).

There are several reasons why teaching centers are ideally suited to do action research. First, their institutional perspective is advantageous for this type of inquiry. While the organizational structure of teaching centers varies widely, most are central units with a broad mandate for change and the capacity to have an institution-wide perspective, not one rooted in a single school or college (Sorcinelli et al., 2006; Wright & O'Neill, 1995). This perspective can inform directors about the issues of concern to academic administration. Furthermore, the institutional position of a teaching center means that the staff know what data are available and are likely to be able to get permission to access it. Additionally, teaching centers, particularly larger ones, often are involved in evaluation projects, which means that data are near at hand and evaluation of action plans is efficacious (Wright & O'Neill, 1995).

Second, teaching center professional staff typically have the academic and professional backgrounds needed to conduct effective action research. Many have doctorates (Gillespie, 2001), and the action researcher's role as "catalyst" or "resource" (rather than "expert") parallels many consultants' approaches to their professional practice (Brinko, 1997; Stringer, 1999).

Finally, teaching centers are service organizations and their mission is to implement good ideas for improving teaching and learning on campus. When they analyze data and conclude that improvement is necessary and action needs to be taken, they already are positioned to use the data to implement an action plan, then evaluate its results. They can begin work on improving programs and services right away and are connected to campus faculty who are likely to agree to be early adopters of teaching innovations.

The most common type of teaching center-based action research is the solicitation of student opinions about a course through Small Group Instructional Diagnosis or evaluation and the use of that feedback to improve the course (Nyquist & Wulff, 1988; Seldin, 1997). However, action research that extends beyond the individual classroom appears to be rare. Key exceptions include action research on graduate students' career goals in order to plan professional development programs (Bellows & Weissinger, 2005), use of student feedback to assess and revise departmental curricula (Black, 1998), initiatives to enhance students' writing and study skills (Zuber-Skerritt, 1992), and other projects that fall under the heading of assessment of student learning or the scholarship of teaching and learning. Additionally, the Center for Instructional Development and Research at the University of Washington has collected data on departments, such as grade distributions, class size, student ratings, and TA training, and has used that data to help departments identify needs and effect improvements (J. Nyquist, personal communication, October 1996).

In spite of the many advantages that teaching centers have in conducting action research, these centers also face special challenges. Because they are service units, it is hard for professional staff to find time to do research that involves gathering data. Also, teaching center budgets are dependent on the decisions of academic administrators, so it is important to be collaborative and helpful, not adversarial and critical. Furthermore, teaching center programs and services are rarely mandatory. Faculty use them because of their perceived value, so it is vital for a center to maintain a positive image on campus as a place that supports faculty and the academic units. To engage in behavior that alienates it from its faculty constituency would be self-defeating. These issues echo questions raised in action research that address politically charged problems and engagement of multiple constituencies (Polanyi & Cockburn, 2003). Other questions raised in the action research literature that are relevant to teaching center staff who conduct such inquiries include

- How do researchers manage tensions among their multiple roles as change agent, researcher, consultant, ally, and evaluator (Chesler, 1990; Elden, 1981)?
- How do researchers manage tensions between themselves and organization members about the interpretation of research, needed interventions, and how or whether to communicate results (Bishop, 1994; Greenwood & Levin, 1998; Israel, Schurman, & Hugentobler, 1992)?

Despite these challenges, teaching centers have much to gain from engaging in action research. In the following sections, to describe what we have learned about how to effectively conduct action research in a teaching center, we first present one case study to illustrate the process. We begin by situating CRLT's action research project within the national problem of retention in the sciences. We then describe the steps we took to engage in the action research project on the local level; that is, our work with three large science departments at the University of Michigan. Action research typically involves three key steps: planning, acting on findings, and reflection (Lewin, 1948/1997; Zuber-Skerritt, 1992), and we note our process in each of these stages. Finally, based on our experiences and the challenges noted earlier in the action research literature, we recommend six principles for conducting effective action research in a teaching center. Table 8.1 integrates the action research stages, our recommendations for teaching centers that wish to conduct action research stages, and what CRLT did in its study of undergraduate attrition in the sciences.

The National Problem

Nationally, retention in science has become a matter of real importance as educational institutions try to slow the sizable flow of undergraduates out of scientific fields (Campbell, Jolly, Hoey, & Perlman, 2002; National Science Foundation, 2003; Strenta, Elliot, Adair, Matier, & Scott, 1994). For two decades, the National Science Foundation (NSF) has been especially active in addressing attrition through a series of grants, workshops, publications, conferences, and other interventions designed to improve science retention at US universities. In 2004, the Government Accounting Office reported that NSF and 12 other federal agencies spent $2.8 billion on programs intended to increase the number of students pursuing studies in science, technology, engineering, and

TABLE 8.1
CRLT Action Research Stages, Principles, and Steps

Action Research Stage	Principles to Guide Action Research in a Teaching Center	What CRLT Did in the Study of Student Attrition in the Sciences
Planning	1) Focus on research that is central to a teaching center's mission	1) Undertook a study central to CRLT's mission of promoting a university culture that values teaching and supports learning environments in which diverse students can excel
	2) Shape the action research project so it answers questions of national importance while also being relevant and specific to local problems	2) Designed a study that responded to local needs (task force report and departments' goals), as well the national problem of retention in the sciences
	3) Obtain the buy-in of both the administrators motivating the study and the faculty and units that are the subject of study	3) Met with dean and departments to gain support for study
Acting	4) Communicate the results of the study in a way that generates support for improvements without alienating the individual units or people who will have to implement those improvements	4) Presented results of study to departments and engaged in collaborative strategizing
	5) Enhance credibility for the project by modifying the teaching center's own programs and practice when research findings indicate a need	5) Made improvements to CRLT's TA training programs
Reflecting	6) Stay involved in the change process after research is complete to facilitate, guide, and evaluate reforms	6) Developed action research principles, worked with departments to enact changes, and planned for future evaluation of reforms

mathematics (Selingo, 2005). Attrition in the sciences is especially problematic in the undergraduate years because approximately 40% of the students who come to college intending to major in the sciences ultimately decide to major in something else (Astin & Astin, 1993; Seymour & Hewitt, 1997; Strenta, et al.). Many of those who leave the sciences are capable students with the aptitude to do well in science (Montgomery & Groat, 1998; Seymour & Hewitt, 1997; Tobias, 1990), and the attrition problem is particularly acute for women and people of color (Astin & Astin, 1993; Holstrom, Gaddy, Van Horne, & Zimmerman, 1997; Seymour, 2001; Xie & Shauman, 2003).

Not much literature exists on the role of teaching assistants in attrition or retention, and the literature that does exist reports that the TA is not an important factor (Seymour & Hewitt, 1997). Nonetheless, most undergraduate science, technology, engineering, and math majors are educated at research universities that employ large numbers of TAs in science courses (National Science Board, 2004). Students in the sciences often depend more on TAs to help them to learn basic concepts than do students in disciplines outside the sciences, especially because students find it more difficult to learn from science faculty and also because science faculty delegate more teaching responsibility to TAs (Seymour & Hewitt, 1997; Seymour, Melton, Wiese & Pedersen-Gallegos, 2005).

CRLT Research Project

The CRLT action research project grew out of the experience of the University of Michigan Task Force on Testing and Training Prospective Graduate Student Instructors (Cook et al., 2002). The task force was composed of a group of academic leaders from the major undergraduate schools at the University of Michigan: the College of Literature, Science, and the Arts, and the College of Engineering. It was convened to consider how to improve the training of TAs, particularly those who were teaching in the sciences. Lacking relevant data, the task force suggested that CRLT begin an action research project to gather relevant data for future decision-making.

Planning the Action Research Project

Attrition in the sciences is especially likely in the first two years of college (Seymour & Hewitt, 1997), so CRLT's research focused on the part of the leaky pipeline known as the gateway course. The gateway course is the initial college course in the sciences taken by a first- or second-year student who has studied science in high school and expects to major in science in college. After the institutional review board approved the study, CRLT surveyed more than 3,600 undergraduate students in the gateway courses for prospective science majors. The survey was distributed immediately following the completion of the survey course, and questions concerned students' intention to major in the sciences both before and after they enrolled in the course, as well as reasons for this decision and their views on their TAs. The high response rate (73%) is likely attributable to a small set of prizes offered to students taking the survey. To supplement survey data, we gathered information from the registrar on student grades in these classes and any additional courses they took in the sciences in two subsequent semesters. We also collected data on the science TAs: demographic characteristics, number of terms as University of Michigan graduate students and as TAs, undergraduate English language background, and end-of-term student ratings. Additionally, we examined the TA training programs in each of the departments.

Acting on Research Findings

This project generated three main findings that were especially relevant to the task force's initial questions.

- Most TAs in Michigan's science departments performed very well. Only a very small percentage of TAs could be classified as "problematic."
- Lab climate was one of the most important factors influencing students' plans to stay in or leave the sciences. Other factors that played a role in their decisions were their course grades, their math grades, and what they learned about careers.
- Retention of students in Michigan science programs was high, but still worrisome when considered in the long term, especially for female students.

This research project eventually led to reforms in the training of science TAs at the University of Michigan. The research findings were presented to chairs in the three departments surveyed, and CRLT staff collaboratively strategized with them on implications for their TA training programs and curricula. As a result of these discussions, two departments are revising their introductory courses significantly, two departments are implementing new evaluation and support systems for TAs (one department already had an effective system in place), and all three departments developed greater awareness of the impact of TAs on student performance and retention. We have recently initiated a follow-up study in one of the departments to assess the impact of their TA training and course reforms.

Reflecting

CRLT was a constant partner in this change and continues to be active in helping departments institute and evaluate these reforms. However, like much action research, this project was politically charged and required careful navigation by the center in order to emerge from the research project with allies in the departments instead of enemies. In the following section, we discuss six principles that we feel were key to our project's success.

Principle 1: Focus on research that is central to a teaching center's mission. Teaching centers are busy, often overcommitted, places. Because of their unique position on campus as an interface between students, faculty, departments, and administrators, they are also susceptible to mission creep. For a center to commit resources and staff to an action research project, that initiative must support a center's core mission. For CRLT, our central purpose is to "promote a University culture that values and rewards teaching, respects and supports individual differences among learners, and encourages the creation of learning environments in which diverse students can learn and excel."

This action research project on the TA's role in attrition and retention in the sciences was an excellent fit with this mission. While the research was enormously time-consuming for CRLT, we saw it as a *project* that could have a great impact on teaching and learning, especially through better TA training, and it even would support the center's multicultural mission by positively impacting science enrollments of underrepresented groups.

Principle 2: Shape the action research project so it answers questions of national importance while also being relevant and specific to local problems. This principle may seem counterintuitive to centers struggling to improve teaching and learning on their own campuses. However, there are a number of reasons to focus on national issues. First, the more teaching centers are connected to reform at the national level, the more they will be seen as legitimate players in shaping higher education. When tasked with investigating TA training in the sciences at the university, CRLT decided to focus on science student retention as one key measure of TA effectiveness. This decision has added prestige and exposure for the center through presentations of the research at national forums. That exposure has led to more willingness to engage with the center on these issues at the campus level. Second, faculty are immersed in their own departmental cultures and attuned to issues that are highlighted by their disciplines at the national level (Gouldner, 1957). By choosing to focus on student retention in the sciences as one measure of TA effectiveness, CRLT was focusing on an issue of real concern in the sciences. Department administrators, previously unexcited about a project on TA training, became very engaged with issues of student retention.

Principle 3: Obtain the buy-in of both the administrators motivating the study and the faculty and units that are the subject of study. Because the university's task force highlighted the dearth of data to inform its report, the need for a research project on the role of TAs was clear (Cook et al., 2002). That catalyst was very helpful in paving the way for the CRLT research project. Furthermore, we were fortunate to have a new dean in Michigan's liberal arts college who was eager to improve teaching and learning and who was willing to put his authority behind actions designed to accomplish those objectives. He is not a scientist and wanted to know more about the science instruction provided by his college, so he saw this research project as a way to inform himself. It is important to note that without his interest and support, the research could not have gone forward.

However, for this research project to succeed, the support of the dean and each of the chairs and associate chairs from the involved departments was necessary. We decided to meet individually with each department's administrators to stress that the survey data analysis on their departments was going to each of them directly (rather than going to the dean first) so they could decide independently what improvements and interventions might be helpful. Not surprisingly, some individual instructors and departments were not eager to have us collect data on their students and TAs. A fourth department opted out of the study altogether. We should note that due to the success of this initial research project, the dean is now working with the chair of this department to do a similar study of its TAs.

Once general buy-in to the project was achieved, CRLT worked with key faculty in the departments to determine the relevant gateway courses for study and agree on the research design. We worked with the departments until we gained their trust and finally agreed on specific courses and specific protocols for the research. This step was crucial for performing the research, but it also helped prime the departments to act on the research findings.

Principle 4: Communicate the results of the study in a way that generates support for improvements without alienating the individual units or people who will have to implement those improvements. Although the dean had supported the study and the department chairs and faculty helped to create the questionnaire, only CRLT was involved in data analysis and decisions about how to report the results. We began by giving aggregate results to the dean and associate deans. In these reports we did not release specifics about the strengths and weaknesses of the departments. Next, we met individually with representatives from each department and presented both aggregate results and their specific departmental results. Strengths were emphasized and weaknesses candidly discussed, along with our suggestions for improvement. This respect for the authority of the department chairs helped to create a safe space for the chairs to initiate their own changes to TA training. Toward the end of the action research project, the dean asked about the departmental data and wanted information about the receptivity of the departments to curricular reform and TA training improvements. In our communications to the dean we emphasized the responsiveness of the departments and the substantial investment in training and curricular reform being undertaken there (one department allocated more than $250,000 to the reforms suggested by our study).

Principle 5: Enhance credibility for the project by modifying the teaching center's own programs and practice when research findings indicate a need. Although many of the implications of our research fell within the purview of the science departments, CRLT also made a commitment to examining its own TA training programs. Our survey data showed that a special concern for undergraduates was communication with the TA, and student communication problems were named for both English-educated and non-English-educated TAs. First, we presented aggregate results to the university's English Language Institute, which together with CRLT, helps coordinate the training for new TAs educated abroad in a non-English medium. Many of the international TAs communicated very well, thanks to a variety of factors: careful screening of graduate students during the admissions process, workshops and courses offered by the English Language Institute and CRLT, and more rigorous testing of TAs' English classroom competency before they were assigned to the classroom. However, at the meeting we were able to strategize about how to enhance the training even further, such as by creating stronger early feedback and support systems for TAs after they enter the classroom.

Second, we focused on CRLT's training program for all TAs. Prior to the initiation of the study, recommendations of the Task Force on Testing and Training Prospective Graduate Student Instructors included two improvements to enhance the communication skills of all TAs, domestic and international (Cook et al., 2002). The first improvement was an individual practice teaching session (sometimes called micro-teaching) for every TA who attended the CRLT's central orientation. For two hours, all the TAs were divided into groups of six, each group with a trained instructional consultant. Each TA presented to the group a five-minute lesson in his or her own field and then received feedback on his or her teaching from the consultant and other TAs. Prior to the study, this portion of CRLT's TA orientation was optional, but findings of our research study confirmed the necessity of making this experience mandatory for all attendees. Given the hundreds of TAs who attend the University of Michigan TA orientations, this was a labor-intensive initiative, but the TAs reported it was the best part of the orientation and made them more confident as they began teaching classes. We were then able to recommend this practice to departments that hold their own TA training programs.

The second improvement to orientation was the addition of a one-hour interactive session on communication strategies. It describes and models ways to organize classes, use visual aids, and create interactivity among students. It also presents information about Michigan undergraduates in terms of academic background, social background, variations in learning styles, and patterns of intellectual development, to give TAs a good sense of the extent of diversity they will find in the classroom. Many TA developers know that because orientation programs have limited time, decisions about what to include in these programs can be difficult. However, because of the study's findings on TA undergraduate communication, we confirmed that this was a highly valuable part of the orientation that should be maintained.

Indeed, a follow-up formal evaluation of these elements in CRLT's TA evaluation confirmed that practice teaching and the session on communication strategies were valuable additions. Respondents reported that the sessions had a favorable impact on their sense of preparation for teaching at the university and their abilities to give effective presentations, teach a diverse group of students, create a positive classroom climate, use active learning methods, plan a lesson, and give feedback to students about what they are learning.

Principle 6: Stay involved in the change process after research is complete to facilitate, guide, and evaluate reforms. Although all the science departments had well-established TA training programs separate from CRLT's own orientation, it was clear from the student survey responses that there was considerable variation between departments in the effectiveness of their students' learning experiences. Students had rated some departments' TAs highly and qualitative comments did not suggest that there be substantial changes in training. For other departments, the message was less favorable. Students especially criticized some TAs for poor communication skills and unclear or problematic grading systems. CRLT offered to provide the new practice teaching and communications modules for TAs to future departmental training programs, but it was important to find interventions that would improve instruction during the upcoming fall term.

To supplement their own training, two of the departments decided to initiate an early evaluation of TAs, asking students to fill out instructor ratings early in the semester so that problematic instructors could be identified quickly and the departments, along with CRLT staff, could offer support to those TAs and help them improve their teaching over the course of the semester. One department went so far as to arrange a follow-up training session for all TAs during one day of fall break so that all new instructors, not just those identified as problematic, could receive additional training. Another department arranged to have graduate student mentors, or advanced TAs hired to assist with TA development in the departments, consult with TAs who were struggling.

Based on the data from the survey of students, two departments determined that the problems with gateway courses went deeper than TA instruction and could be attributed to the nature of the courses themselves. One of those departments immediately embarked on a costly and time-consuming curricular reform effort that involved multiple instructors and all of its gateway courses. Another department has recently begun the effort to revise and improve its course offerings.

As noted by Lewin (1948/1997), a complete action research cycle involves not only action but also "fact-finding about the result of the action" (p. 146). For the interventions in all three departments, CRLT provided assistance; for example, overseeing some of the early evaluation, offering instruction at the follow-up training sessions, and providing benchmark data for the course revisions. A good action research project involves evaluation of the changes, and that, too, will be a CRLT responsibility.

Conclusion

At CRLT, we learned a great deal from our action research. We learned that our own TA orientation could be improved, and we had the data to guide that improvement process. We learned that the dean and his department chairs are eager to improve instruction and welcome data that offer advice about how to do so. We also learned that our offers of assistance with the interventions were as important as the data. The departments lack the capacity to initiate all these changes on their own without assistance. So we provided some of the staffing for the reform efforts. Perhaps the biggest lesson for us at CRLT was the power of data. We operate in a university that prides itself on research excellence, and we found that our carefully designed research project, producing high-quality data, was an effective way to get the attention of faculty and administrators and accomplish teaching improvement objectives.

References

Armstrong, F., & Moore, M. (2004). Action research: Developing inclusive practice and transforming cultures. In F. Armstrong & M. Moore (Eds.), *Action research for inclusive education: Changing places, changing practices, changing minds* (pp. 1–16). London, England: RoutledgeFalmer.

Astin, A. W., & Astin, H. S. (1993). *Undergraduate science education: The impact of different college environments on the educational pipeline in the sciences.* Los Angeles, CA: University of California–Los Angeles, Higher Education Research Institute.

Bellows, L., & Weissinger, E. (2005). Assessing the academic and professional development needs of graduate students. In S. Chadwick-Blossey & D. R. Robertson (Eds.), *To improve the academy: Vol. 23. Resources for faculty, instructional, and organizational development* (pp. 267–283). Bolton, MA: Anker.

Benson, L., & Harkavy, I. (1996, June). Communal participatory action research as a strategy for improving universities and the social sciences: Penn's work with the West Philadelphia Improvement Corps as a case study. *Educational Policy, 10*(2), 202–222.

Bishop, R. (1994). Initiating empowering research. *New Zealand Journal of Educational Studies, 29*(1), 175–188.

Black, B. (1998). Using the SGID method for a variety of purposes. In M. Kaplan & D. Lieberman (Eds.), *To improve the academy: Vol. 17. Resources for faculty, instructional, and organizational development* (pp. 245–262). Stillwater, OK: New Forums Press.

Brinko, K. T. (1997). The interactions of teaching improvement. In K. T. Brinko & R. J. Menges (Eds.), *Practically speaking: A sourcebook for instructional consultants in higher education* (pp. 3–8). Stillwater, OK: New Forums Press.

Campbell, P. B., Jolly, E., Hoey, L., & Perlman, L. K. (2002). *Upping the numbers: Using research-based decision making to increase diversity in the quantitative disciplines.* Newton, MA: Education Development Center, Inc.

Chesler, M. A. (1990). Action research in the voluntary sector: A case study of scholar-activist roles in health care settings. In S. A. Wheelan, E. A. Pepitone, & V. Abt (Eds.), *Advances in field theory* (pp. 265–280). Newbury Park, CA: Sage.

Cook, C., Gerson, J., Godfrey, J., Kerner, N., Larsen-Freeman, D., Mullane, E., et al. (2002). *Report of the Task Force on Testing and Training Prospective GSIs.* Ann Arbor, MI: University of Michigan.

Cross, K. P., & Steadman, M. H. (1996). *Classroom research: Implementing the scholarship of teaching.* San Francisco, CA: Jossey-Bass.

Elden, M. (1981). Sharing the research work: Participative research and its role demands. In P. Reason & J. Rowan (Eds.), *Human inquiry: A sourcebook of new paradigm research* (pp. 261–266). Chichester, England: John Wiley & Sons.

Geltner, B. B. (1993, October). *Collaborative action research: A critical component in the preparation of effective leaders and learners.* Paper presented at the annual meeting of the University Council for Educational Administration, Houston, TX.

Gillespie, K. (2001, October). *Marketplace reality and our dreams of the profession.* Paper presented at the 26th annual conference of the Professional and Organizational Development Network in Higher Education, St. Louis, MO.

Gouldner, A. W. (1957, December). Cosmopolitans and locals: Toward an analysis of latent social roles. *Administrative Science Quarterly, 2*(3), 281–306.

Greenwood, D. J., & Levin, M. (1998). *Introduction to action research: Social research for social change.* Thousand Oaks, CA: Sage.

Halstead, D. K. (1974). *Statewide planning in higher education.* Washington, DC: U.S. Government Printing Office.

Holstrom, E. I., Gaddy, C. D., Van Horne, V. V., & Zimmerman, C. M. (1997). *Best and brightest: Education and career paths of top science and engineering students.* Washington, DC: Commission on Professionals in Science and Technology.

Israel, B. A., Schurman, S. J., & Hugentobler, M. K. (1992, March). Conducting action research: Relationships between organization members and researchers. *Journal of Applied Behavioral Science, 28*(1), 74–101.

Krogh, L. (2001, March). *Action research as action learning as action research as action learning . . . at multiple levels in adult education.* Paper presented at the 4th annual conference of the Australian Vocational Education and Training Research Association, Adelaide, Australia.

Lewin, K. (1997). *Resolving social conflicts.* Washington, DC: American Psychological Association. (Original work published 1948)

Montgomery, S. M., & Groat, L. N. (1998). *Student learning styles and their implications for teaching* (CRLT Occasional Paper No. 10). Ann Arbor, MI: Center for Research on Learning and Teaching, University of Michigan.

National Science Board. (2004). *Science and engineering indicators, 2004* (NSB 04–01). Arlington, VA: National Science Foundation, Division of Science Resource Statistics.

National Science Foundation, Division of Science Resources Statistics. (2003). *Women, minorities, and persons with disabilities in science and engineering: 2002* (NSF 03–312). Arlington, VA: Author.

Nyquist, J. D., & Wulff, D. H. (1988). Consultation using a research perspective. In E. C. Wadsworth, L. Hilsen, & M. A. Shea (Eds.), *A handbook for new practitioners* (pp. 81–88). Stillwater, OK: New Forums Press.

Park, P. (1999, June). People, knowledge, and change in participatory research. *Management Learning, 30*(2), 141–157.

Polanyi, M., & Cockburn, L. (2003, Summer). Opportunities and pitfalls of community-based research: A case study. *Michigan Journal of Community Service Learning, 9*(3), 16–25.

Reason, P. (1999, June). Integrating action and reflection through co-operative inquiry. *Management Learning, 30*(2), 207–226.

Schön, D. A. (1983). *The reflective practitioner: How professionals think in action.* New York, NY: Basic Books.

Schön, D. A. (1987). *Educating the reflective practitioner.* San Francisco, CA: Jossey-Bass.

Seldin, P. (1997). Using student feedback to improve teaching. In D. DeZure & M. Kaplan (Eds.), *To improve the academy: Vol. 16. Resources for faculty, instructional, and organizational development* (pp. 335–345). Stillwater, OK: New Forums Press.

Selingo, J. (2005, October 14). *U.S. spends billions to encourage math and science students, but it's unclear if programs work, report says.* Retrieved June 16, 2006, from http://chronicle.com/daily/2005/10/2005101402n.htm

Seymour, E. (2001). Tracking the processes of change in US undergraduate education in science, mathematics, engineering and technology. *Science Education, 86*, 79–105.

Seymour, E., & Hewitt, N. M. (1997). *Talking about leaving: Why undergraduates leave the sciences.* Boulder, CO: Westview Press.

Seymour, E., with Melton, G., Wiese, D. J., & Pedersen-Gallegos, L. (2005). *Partners in innovation: Teaching assistants in college science courses.* Lanham, MD: Rowman & Littlefield.

Small, S. A. (1995, November). Action-oriented research: Models and methods. *Journal of Marriage and the Family, 57*(4), 941–955.

Sorcinelli, M. D., Austin, A. E., Eddy, P. L., & Beach, A. L. (2006). *Creating the future of faculty development: Learning from the past, understanding the present.* Bolton, MA: Anker.

St. John, E. P., McKinney, J., & Tuttle, T. (in press). Using action inquiry to address critical challenges. In E. P. St. John & M. Wilkerson (Eds.), *New directions for institutional research: Improving academic success: Reframing persistence research.* San Francisco, CA: Jossey-Bass.

Strand, K., Marullo, S., Cutforth, N., Stoecker, R., & Donohue, P. (2003, Summer). Principles of best practice for community-based research. *Michigan Journal of Community Service Learning, 9*(3), 5–15.

Strenta, A. C., Elliot, R., Adair, R., Matier, M., & Scott, J. (1994, October). Choosing and leaving science in highly selective institutions. *Research in Higher Education, 35*(5), 513–547.

Stringer, E. T. (1999). *Action research* (2nd ed.). Thousand Oaks, CA: Sage.

Tobias, S. (1990). *They're not dumb, they're different: Stalking the second tier.* Tucson, AZ: Research Corporation.

Wright, W. A., & O'Neill, W. M. (1995). Teaching improvement practices: International perspectives. In W. A. Wright & Associates, *Teaching improvement practices: Successful strategies for higher education* (pp. 1–57). Bolton, MA: Anker.

Xie, Y., & Shauman, K. A. (2003). *Women in science: Career processes and outcomes.* Cambridge, MA: Harvard University Press.

Zuber-Skerritt, O. (1992). *Action research in higher education: Examples and reflections.* London, England: Kogan Page.

Zuelke, D. C., & Nichols, T. M. (1995, November). *Collaborative school climate action research for school improvement: Part II.* Paper presented at the annual meeting of the Mid-South Education Research Association, Biloxi, MS.

9

Moving From the Scholarship of Teaching and Learning to Educational Research: An Example From Engineering

Ruth A. Streveler
Purdue University

Maura Borrego
Virginia Polytechnic Institute and State University

Karl A. Smith
University of Minnesota

In The Advancement of Learning, *Huber and Hutchings (2005) state that the "scholarship of teaching and learning . . . is about producing knowledge that is available for others to use and build on" (p. 27). Can viewing the scholarship of teaching and learning (SoTL) as an educational research activity help make SoTL findings more available and easier to build on? This chapter describes a program that prepared engineering faculty to conduct rigorous research in engineering education. Project evaluation revealed that engineering faculty had difficulty making some of the paradigm shifts that were presented in the project.*

The late Ernest Boyer (1990) introduced the scholarship of teaching as one of four interdependent dimensions of scholarship, with the scholarships of discovery, integration, and application rounding out the quartet. In the years since this work was published, the scholarship of teaching (now more commonly called the scholarship of teaching and learning, or SoTL) has taken hold, and the promotion of SoTL is often a major activity of faculty development centers (Sorcinelli, Austin, Eddy, & Beach, 2006).

Involvement in SoTL usually begins with faculty's interest in how students in their own classrooms are learning (Huber & Hutchings, 2005), and the purpose of SoTL is to improve learning by improving teaching (Boyer, 1990). Thus SoTL tends to be very personal and situated in one person's classroom. The very personal nature of SoTL might lead to context-specific results that could be difficult to generalize and apply to broader settings. In some disciplines, this may diminish the perceived impact or significance of results.

Recently, there have been calls for increasing the impact of SoTL results. Faculty have been urged to "go meta" with their studies and to look at broader questions of how students learn that go beyond the specifics of their individual classrooms (Hutchings & Shulman, 1999; Schroeder, 2005). But what does "going meta" really mean? And what models can we provide to faculty to help them do this?

In engineering education, as in most disciplines, the majority of studies to this point have been classroom and curriculum focused. Several factors now point to the readiness of the engineering discipline to move from SoTL into the realm of engineering education research (Gabriele, 2005). Colleges of engineering have recently created new engineering education departments (Haghighi, 2005), and the premiere American journal in this field, the *Journal of Engineering Education,* has developed more stringent publication criteria (Felder, Sheppard, & Smith, 2005). In order to support more rigorous studies in engineering education, the Center for the Advancement of Scholarship in Engineering Education was founded by the National Academy of Engineering, and the American Society for Engineering Education will sponsor a year of dialogue about scholarship in engineering education in 2006.

This chapter describes a program in engineering education that may be useful both as a mechanism to further the discussion of SoTL, and as a model that could be applicable to disciplines other than engineering.

Conducting Rigorous Research in Engineering Education

Project Description

The focus for this chapter is Conducting Rigorous Research in Engineering Education: Creating a Community of Practice, or the RREE project. The RREE project was funded by the National Science Foundation for three years to prepare three cohorts of 20 engineering faculty to conduct rigorous engineering education research. Each yearlong experience began with a summer workshop and was followed by each participant conducting a systematic engineering education research project throughout the year. The projects were often small scale and informal. However, they were intended to assist in building engineering education research capabilities.

Faculty participants came from institutions across the US and were required to apply to the RREE project. Participants paid for their travel to the RREE project site, but all other expenses, such as lodging, meals, and materials, were covered by the RREE budget. In 2004, selection was made on a first-come, first-served basis. About 80 engineering faculty applied to be part of the RREE project during the week the application was posted to the project web site.

Due to the demand for participation, more stringent criteria for selection were created in 2005. Participants in 2005 were selected based on three criteria: 1) readiness to participate (including past involvement in engineering education conferences and projects, and the strength of research questions submitted as part of their application), 2) the broader impact of participation (as evidenced by their role as a national or campus change agent, and their local and/or national involvement with groups who are underrepresented in engineering), and 3) the degree of support for engineering education research on their campus (based on the strength of a letter of support from their dean or department head, and campus policies that support engineering education research). Two project coordinators independently scored each application. Even with these stringent criteria, about 45 engineering faculty applied to be part of the 2005 RREE project.

The National Science Foundation funded the RREE project as a mechanism to prepare current engineering faculty to be part of this move. The RREE project provided preparation, guidance, and a community as part of a yearlong experience for engineering faculty. Following acceptance, participation began with an intense workshop experience, a five-day summer workshop held each year from 2004–2006.

The learning objectives of the summer workshop were:

- List and briefly describe important principles about how students learn, and especially how students learn engineering
- List and briefly describe common methods used in education research
- Read and interpret education research articles to inform an engineering education
- Conduct informal or formal education research at their respective campuses

An assumption of the RREE project was that in order to increase the rigor of engineering education research, engineering practitioners needed to learn the literature, methods, and paradigms of educational research. This project provided a structure and mechanism for preparing faculty to conduct rigorous engineering education research through a collaboration of engineering educators, faculty developers, and learning scientists.

- *Engineering educators,* the American Society for Engineering Education, the lead on this project
- *Faculty developers* in higher education, the Professional and Organizational Network in Higher Education
- *Learning scientists,* specifically the Education in the Professions Division of the American Educational Research Association

The executive committee, whose 10 members represented each of the three collaborating organizations, designed the RREE project workshops and follow-up activities, and selected facilitators from each organization. In 2004, the first year of the project, the committee chose to emphasize theories of student learning with the intention of helping participants apply educational research to improve their teaching. In the following two years, however, the focus shifted to conducting, not just using, the research, which was the real objective of the RREE project. To redesign the workshop accordingly, the executive committee decided to focus on three issues: 1) the paradigm shifts engineering faculty needed to make to conduct educational research (versus engineering research), 2) the knowledge and skills they needed, and 3) the best format for the training.

Paradigm shifts. Engineers use a consistent, implicit theoretical framework anchored in the laws of nature and a standardized methodology to conduct disciplinary research. Since they need not choose a theoretical or methodological perspective, they are typically unaware that research in other disciplines—among them, education—offer and in fact require choices among potentially useful approaches. Engineers are also highly practical. Those in the 2004 cohort were mostly interested in personal, classroom-based assessments of the teaching methods they were already using, with the hope of documenting that their methods "worked."

The redesigned workshop tackled paradigm shifts explicitly on the first day by emphasizing three distinctions. The first difference highlighted was between engineering research, which takes a standardized approach, and education research, which requires selecting an appropriate theoretical framework and methodology. The second key distinction made was between assessment, which finds out "what kind of" and "how much" learning, and research, which pursues "why" and "how" the learning comes about (Paulsen, 2001). The engineers in this project seemed more comfortable with the former than the latter. The final comparison explained were the differences among the levels of teaching rigor, as summarized in Table 9.1. Hutchings and Shulman (1999) propose the first three levels—excellent teaching, scholarly teaching, and the scholarship of teaching—and the RREE Executive Committee added the fourth: rigorous research in engineering education.

Cognitive apprenticeship. During the remaining four days, the workshop became a cognitive apprenticeship (Brown, Collins, & Duguid, 1989; Collins, Brown, & Newman, 1989). Facilitators modeled the steps of the educational research process—developing good research questions, choosing an appropriate theoretical framework, and selecting methods and measurements—using examples out of engineering education. Then the participants worked in self-selected groups with similar research questions to develop a poster of the research design they planned to follow during the upcoming academic

TABLE 9.1

Levels of Rigor in Inquiry About Teaching and Learning

Level of Inquiry	**Attributes of That Level**
Level 1: Excellent Teaching	Involves the use of good content and teaching methods
Level 2: Scholarly Teaching	Involves good content and methods *and* classroom assessment and evidence gathering, informed by best practice and best knowledge, inviting of collaboration and review
Level 3: Scholarship of Teaching	Is public and open to critique and evaluation, is in a form that others can build on, involves question-asking, inquiry, and investigation, particularly about student learning
Level 4: Rigorous Research in Engineering Education	Also is public, open to critique, and involves asking questions about student learning, but it includes a few unique components: 1) Beginning with a *research* question, not an *assessment* question. Assessment questions deal with the "what" or "how much" of learning, while research questions focus on the "why" or "how" of learning (Paulsen, 2001). 2) Tying the question to learning, pedagogical, or social theory and interpreting the results of the research in light of theory and thereby allowing research to build theory and yield significant findings. For example, studies about teaching thermodynamics can be redesigned to become studies, based on cognitive theory, which can help explain why certain concepts in thermodynamics are so difficult to learn. 3) Paying careful attention to design of the study and the methods used, adding validity, reliability, and impact to the findings.

year. Both the workshop facilitators and fellow participants provided feedback on the posters. The grant provided modest funding for the research projects and for research mentors to advise participants on their research design and/or analysis.

Assessment of the 2004 and 2005 Workshops

The RREE grant was assessed every year using multiple strategies. The first strategy was a survey of the participations' satisfaction with various aspects of the five-day summer workshop. Table 9.2 displays the questions as well as the results from the 2004 and 2005 cohorts. While the average scores are quite similar overall, they differ appreciably on the goal attainment items that reflect the different foci of the two years. The 2004 engineers appraised their mastery of learning principles more highly than did the 2005 group, and this latter cohort considered their understanding of educational research methods stronger than did the former group.

The second assessment strategy was a pre-participation and post-participation survey of perceived knowledge gains. Table 9.3 shows the pre- and post-differences for the 2004 and 2005 cohorts, and they too reflect the change in emphasis from year to year. On most of the content familiarity items, the 2005 cohort reported greater gains, but not on most of the "more specific content knowledge" items, which the 2004 group learned just from acquiring familiarity with the literature. The results on the final question, which ask about one's comfort level designing education research, predictably favored the 2005 group.

An analysis of participant research journals, the third assessment strategy, revealed a shift from teaching to research issues from 2004 to 2005, and about a quarter of the 2005 entries addressed topics at the more rigorous, research-oriented end of the continuum shown earlier in Table 9.1.

The richest data, however, emerged from the fourth assessment strategy: evaluator observations of the 2005 workshop group discussions. How participants understood the generalizability of research studies reflected their appreciation of the distinction between SoTL and rigorous educational research. On the first day of the workshop they had disagreements, with some engineers contending that if research couldn't be generalized, it couldn't be good. Reflecting her discipline's approach to experimentation, one participant asked her discussion group, "If you do something in your classroom, isn't it automatically generalizable?"

TABLE 9.2

Ratings Results: Participant Feedback, 2004 Versus 2005

	2004	2005
General Workshop Satisfaction		
Scale: Excellent = 5 through Poor = 1		
How would you rate the quality of the following:		
Organization	4.28	4.55
Comfort (room, temperature, food)	4.67	4.27
Appropriateness of schedule pacing	4.08	4.25
Program		
Scale: Excellent = 5 through Poor = 1		
How would you rate the quality of the following:		
Overall importance of topics	4.49	4.49
Quality of content	4.38	4.32
Opportunities to be actively engaged	4.67	4.66
Organization of sessions	4.08	4.49
Communication skills of presenters	4.64	4.52
Amount of time allocated for planning work	4.33	4.23
Opportunities to interact with other participants	4.69	4.84
Opportunities to get feedback from experts/facilitators	4.26	4.36
Goal Attainment		
Scale: 5 = To a great extent through 1 = Not at all		
To what extent do you think the following workshop goals were achieved:		
Participants will be able to list and briefly describe important principles about how students learn and especially how students learn engineering	4.10	3.73
Participants will be able to list and briefly describe common methods used in educational research	3.87	4.15
Participants will be able to read and interpret educational research articles	3.97	3.97
Participants will be able to conduct informal or formal educational research at their respective campuses	3.79	3.98
Participants will be able to use the results of educational research to improve their curricula and/or teaching methods	3.87	N/A

TABLE 9.3

Self-Reported Post-Knowledge and Gains: 2004–2005 Cohort Results on Comparable Items

Item	Gain 2004	Gain 2005
Content Familiarity		
Scale: 5 = Know a lot through 1 = Know very little		
How would you rate your knowledge of the following:		
How engineering research and educational research differ	0.41	1.16
Designing research questions with educational issues in mind	1.36	1.18
Quantitative research methods in educational settings	0.97	1.07
Qualitative research methods in educational settings	0.74	0.79
Understanding educational studies	0.82	0.97
Applying educational studies	0.69	0.79
Venues for presenting results of educational research (journals and conferences)	1.08	0.85
More Specific Content Knowledge		
Scale: 5 = Can define well through 1 = Cannot define at all		
How familiar are you with the following terms or names:		
Cognitive apprenticeship	2.33	1.88
Epistemology	1.21	1.24
Construct validity	1.36	1.12
Design experiment	0.38	0.35
Mental models	1.36	0.74
Self-Reported Knowledge (open-ended)		
Scale: 5 = Can answer well through 1 = Cannot answer at all		
How well can you answer the following questions:		
What are standards for "rigorous research" in the STEM disciplines?	2.36	2.42
What do you see as the relationship between theory and measurement in educational research?	1.51	1.53
Describe the differences among experimental, relational, and descriptive studies.	1.56	1.25
Thoughts on Leaving		
Scale: 5 = Very comfortable through 1 = Not at all comfortable		
How comfortable do you now feel about designing educational research studies?	0.83	0.99

The following day, several individuals indicated understanding and acceptance of generalizability as an important goal of rigorous educational research. When the groups were asked to identify the characteristics of a good research question, they listed attributes including generalizability, "universal significance," contribution to society, and the ability to generate more questions. The facilitator then asked the groups to clarify the meaning of *significance.* They volunteered interpretations such as personal significance, passion, publication, and relevance to "something bigger."

By the end of the workshop, participants were still considering generalizability. When the facilitator introduced qualitative research methods, one participant asked how the focus on understanding a specific setting related to the need for generalizability stressed earlier in the week. During the final poster presentations, another participant explained his motivation for involving participants from three universities in his research project. He explained that, in his case, the small class sizes at each of the institutions limited the potential generalizability of his research, but combining studies would make his results more applicable to a variety of settings.

The participants also displayed resistance to the idea of choosing a theoretical framework and measurements—again, issues that engineers do not have to grapple with in their disciplinary research.

Conclusion

It may be useful to think of faculty participation in the teaching and learning process as a continuum with excellent teaching at one end and rigorous educational research on the other. Additionally, faculty developers may want to think about how to prepare interested faculty to venture into the realm of educational research, perhaps to "go meta" with their modest SoTL research.

When developing programs to help faculty move toward educational research, we should keep in mind the paradigm differences between disciplinary research and educational research. Facilitating paradigm shifts may be as (or more) important to making the transition to educational researcher as is obtaining the requisite knowledge and skills. Our experience with the RREE project has shown that paradigm shifts are difficult for faculty to make, and it takes time to understand the design and decision-making steps involved in educational research that may be unnecessary in other disciplines. Therefore, programs that prepare faculty to make this transition need to be long term. A few hours or a few days is too short a time period for faculty to assimilate these changes.

Lastly, we hope to spur discussions about new directions for SoTL. While respecting the value of the personal studies usually conducted in SoTL, we suggest that some faculty may be interested in conducting research that can yield findings useful to educational or learning theory. This kind of work can involve truly interdisciplinary collaborations, with disciplinary experts informing the work of learning scientists, and learning scientists informing the work of disciplinary experts.

Note

We wish to thank the National Science Foundation for supporting this work through grant number DUE–0341127, which funds Conducting Rigorous Research in Engineering Education: Creating a Community of Practice, also called the RREE project. We also thank Dr. Norman Fortenberry, of the National Academy of Engineering's Center for the Advancement of Scholarship in Engineering Education, for his partnership in this project. Special thanks goes to the RREE Executive Committee who jointly developed the "SoTL to educational research" model at the June 11, 2005, executive committee meeting. In addition to authors Streveler and Smith, the RREE Executive Committee members who were part of this discussion are Robin Adams, Nancy Chism, George B. Forsythe, Frank Huband, Marcia Mentkowksi, Ron Miller, and Marilla Svinicki. Appreciation goes to Debra Fowler, who assisted with evaluation of the RREE in 2004, and Maura Borrego, who contributed to the 2005 evaluation and who also helped to create the SoTL to educational research model. Our thanks also go to Mary Deane Sorcinelli, who is a member of the RREE Executive Committee, but who was not able to attend the June 11, 2005, meeting.

References

Boyer, E. L. (1990). *Scholarship reconsidered: Priorities of the professoriate.* Princeton, NJ: Carnegie Foundation for the Advancement of Teaching.

Brown, J. S., Collins, A., & Duguid, P. (1989, January/February). Situated cognition and the culture of learning. *Educational Researcher, 18*(1), 32–42.

Collins, A., Brown, J. S., & Newman, S. E. (1989). Cognitive apprenticeship: Teaching and crafts of reading, writing, and mathematics. In L. B. Resnick (Ed.), *Knowing, learning, and instruction: Essays in honor of Robert Glaser* (pp. 453–494). Hillsdale, NJ: Lawrence Erlbaum.

Felder, R. M., Sheppard, S. D., & Smith, K. A. (2005, January). Guest editor's foreword: A new journal for a field in transition. *Journal of Engineering Education, 94*(1), 7–10.

Gabriele, G. A. (2005, July). Guest editorial: Advancing engineering education in a flattened world. *Journal of Engineering Education, 94*(3), 285–286.

Haghighi, K. (2005, October). Guest editorial: Quiet no longer: Birth of a new discipline. *Journal of Engineering Education, 94*(4), 351–353.

Huber, M. T., & Hutchings, P. (2005). *The advancement of learning: Building the teaching commons.* San Francisco, CA: Jossey-Bass.

Hutchings, P., & Shulman, L. S. (1999, September/October). The scholarship of teaching: New elaborations, new developments. *Change, 31*(5), 10–15.

Paulsen, M. P. (2001). The relationship between research and the scholarship of teaching. In C. Kreber (Ed.), *New directions for teaching and learning: No. 86. Scholarship revisited: Perspectives on the scholarship of teaching* (pp. 19–29). San Francisco, CA: Jossey-Bass.

Schroeder, C. M. (2005, October). *Going "meta" with SoTL: Research-based frameworks as the missing link.* Paper presented at the 30th annual conference of the Professional and Organizational Development Network in Higher Education, Milwaukee, WI.

Sorcinelli, M. D., Austin, A. E., Eddy, P. L., & Beach, A. L. (2006). *Creating the future of faculty development: Learning from the past, understanding the present.* Bolton, MA: Anker.

Section IV

Instructional and Curricular Development

10

Structuring Complex Cooperative Learning Activities in 50-Minute Classes

Barbara J. Millis
University of Nevada-Reno

Given the power of learning-centered teaching, faculty can be coached to structure cooperative activities wisely and well, even within 50-minute class periods where there is a perception that complex group work is difficult. In addition to giving some basic advice on team formation and classroom management, this chapter provides examples of five complex cooperative learning structures—Jigsaw, Send-a-Problem, Cooperative Debates, Guided Reciprocal Peer Questioning, and Bingo—that can be conducted within 50-minute classes. The specific literature-based examples are complemented by examples in a variety of other disciplines, making them seem doable to more faculty.

As Bob Dylan sang so hauntingly in the 1960s, "The Times They Are A-Changin'." Even in academia, where change is notoriously slow, faculty members are becoming increasingly aware, particularly with the broadening pool of incoming students, that business as usual will not result in significant learning gains. Barr and Tagg's (1995) influential *Change* magazine article, "From Teaching to Learning—A New Paradigm for Undergraduate Education," started a healthy movement toward rethinking the nature of teaching and learning. Subsequent books such as Weimer's (2002) *Learner-Centered Teaching* and Fink's (2003) *Creating Significant Learning Experiences*, as well as numerous articles, provided useful models and convincing research. Bransford, Brown, and Cocking's (2000) *How People Learn* made it difficult for even the most lecture-committed faculty member to ignore research with clear implications for a more learning-centered basis of teaching. In fact, Finkel (2000) concludes, "Educational research over the past twenty-five years has established beyond a doubt a simple fact: What is transmitted to students through lecturing is simply not retained for any significant length of time" (p. 3).

Execution, however, remains a key issue for faculty developers and the faculty they support. Even faculty committed philosophically to the new paradigms often lack the know-how to successfully adapt teaching techniques and classroom management practices that can lead to more learning-oriented approaches, particularly in content-driven courses that meet only during 50-minute class periods.

Faculty, however, can learn to use learning-centered approaches—particularly group work—if they can adopt a philosophical framework that allows for flexibility in the specific techniques employed.

Cooperative learning can provide a philosophical framework with clearly defined tenets, such as individual accountability (no undifferentiated "group grades" or social loafing) and positive interdependence (students have vested reasons to work together), that faculty can combine with virtually any other known pedagogy. Cases, for example, can be adapted to a cooperative format (Millis, 1994). Approaches such as the double entry journal, popularized by the writing across the curriculum movement, can be modified to include peer sharing and coaching as students read and discuss one another's products rather than watching them stuffed into a teacher's briefcase. Cooperative learning philosophies and practices also mesh beautifully with the research on how people learn and deep learning (Millis, 2002). Classroom assessment, problem-based learning, and academic games can all be enhanced through a cooperative approach. Technology and cooperative learning are natural partners, thanks to email, web-based teaching, and course management packages such as Blackboard or WebCT. Not surprisingly, virtual team performance requires many of the attributes of well-conducted classroom cooperative learning: attention to planning, executing, rewarding the tasks, and care in structuring individual accountability and mutual interdependence.

For faculty fearful of losing control if they relinquish the podium, cooperative learning components that focus on classroom management can be reassuring. Group processing, for example, provides approaches used by both students and faculty to help groups function well. Attention to group-based social skills such as leadership and group facilitation offer concrete ways to structure class experiences.

Team Formation and Classroom Management

If faculty do not normally use group work in their classes, the faculty developer needs to coach them in effective team formation. Teachers should select the teams based on criteria suitable for the assignment, aiming for heterogeneity on as many levels as possible. In an adult education children's literature class, for example, teams might deliberately contain an English major (for content knowledge), a male (for gender balance), and a person with children (for "real-world" experience). Streuling (2004) purposefully distributes students with poor attitudes toward group work among the various teams to "defuse" (p. 136) their impact.

If purposeful selection is unnecessary or too time consuming, then random selection is the next option. Encourage faculty not to let students self-select their own team members because they usually select friends who look like and think like themselves and who often fall into traditional roles. Student self-selection is the number one reason teams fail. In one study, 155 students surveyed claimed in a 2:1 ratio that their worst group work experiences were with self-formed groups and their best ones were with instructor-formed groups (Feichtner & Davis, 1984–85). Other studies in the cooperative learning literature generally support this finding. If groups or teams are to be used over the course of a semester, then it is important to keep them together long enough to go through the expected group dynamic process. Tuckman (1965) and Tuckman and Jensen (1977) have identified these phases as forming, storming, norming, and performing (later versions of Tuckman's work refer to adjourning). Stein and Hurd (2000) remind us that working in teams is a developmental process that is aided by "an atmosphere of openness and reason" and by clearly defined "goals, procedures, and expectations" (p. 20). Weimer's (2002) work on learner-centered teaching also emphasizes the importance of a developmental approach that moves students from "dependent, passive, often not confident . . . to autonomous, motivated, responsible, empowered learner[s]" (p. 167).

Felder and Brent (1994) recommend that faculty forming teams should "avoid groups in which women and minority students are outnumbered." They argue against forming teams with one woman and two or three men, applying the same rule to minorities. Having taught for nine years at a service academy where women and minorities typically have strong voices, I usually ask the students in question how they feel about this issue.

Because roles are critically important in many activities, I typically form groups of four and have students distribute playing cards among team members. Thus, each team (aces, twos, threes, fours) consists of four members with the four suits, making it easy to assign roles or tasks when necessary (Millis & Cottell, 1998).

The Transition to More Sophisticated Learning-Centered Approaches

As faculty developers, we can coach faculty in these classroom management approaches and watch them successfully try, even in large classes, well-known, relatively simple cooperative approaches such as think-pair-share (Lyman, 1981). We can even exult in their adaptation and skillful use of so-called clickers (classroom response systems). But the transformation toward learning-centered teaching often remains stagnant at this point, particularly in 50-minute classes. Without adequate coaching to provide models and instill confidence, faculty rarely use more complex cooperative approaches, particularly in 50-minute class periods where the tacit assumption appears to be that there is insufficient time. Nothing, however, is further from the truth.

Specific Examples of Complex Cooperative Learning Approaches Used in 50-Minute Classes

This chapter will briefly describe how to sequence complex cooperative learning activities in 50-minute classes using five examples from a literature course that can be adapted to a range of other disciplines. Suggestions for adaptations follow the literature-based explanation. The cooperative learning examples include 1) Jigsaw based on homework on literature characters completed using a graphic organizer, 2) Send-a-Problem based on open-ended literature questions (e.g., Why does Hamlet treat Ophelia as he does?), 3) Cooperative Debate based on four teams focused on two questions (Pro/Con: Should Antigone have buried her brother? and Pro/Con: Should Creon be impeached for poor leadership?), 4) Guided Reciprocal Peer Questioning (structured group work based on Allison King's Question Stems), and 5) Bingo, a game used as a review for exams.

Jigsaw

Jigsaw is particularly useful for problem-solving activities that require students to confront complex, challenging topics involving multiple pieces of information necessary for final, overall mastery. In this activity, each member of a cooperative learning team assumes responsibility for a specific part of a problem.

They are responsible for more than just mastering or knowing their part. As "specialists," they must also be able to teach it to their fellow teammates. Thus, working together, the group merges the various portions to solve the "puzzle." If carefully structured, the full sequence of a Jigsaw can occur within 50-minutes.

With works of literature having four strong characters such as *Antigone* (Creon, Antigone, Haemon, Ismene), *Hamlet* (Gertrude, Claudius, Laertes, Hamlet), or *Charlottte's Web* (Charlotte, Wilbur, Fern, Templeton), I use a graphic organizer to focus each student's homework assignment and the follow-on class work in the expert teams. For example, with *Charlotte's Web,* I assign each person in a four-person cooperative learning "home" team one of the characters based on playing card suits. The hearts in each team, for example, focus on Charlotte, the diamonds on Wilbur, the clubs on Fern, and the spades on Templeton.

Each student receives a graphic organizer (see Figure 10.1). As homework, students write in the center block the name of their assigned character. They write on the four spokes the four traits that best describe their character. In the evidence boxes, based on what is known in literature as "close textual reading," they provide support for the traits they chose by citing things the characters do or say, or things that are said about them, giving page numbers for each example.

FIGURE 10.1

Sample Graphic Organizer

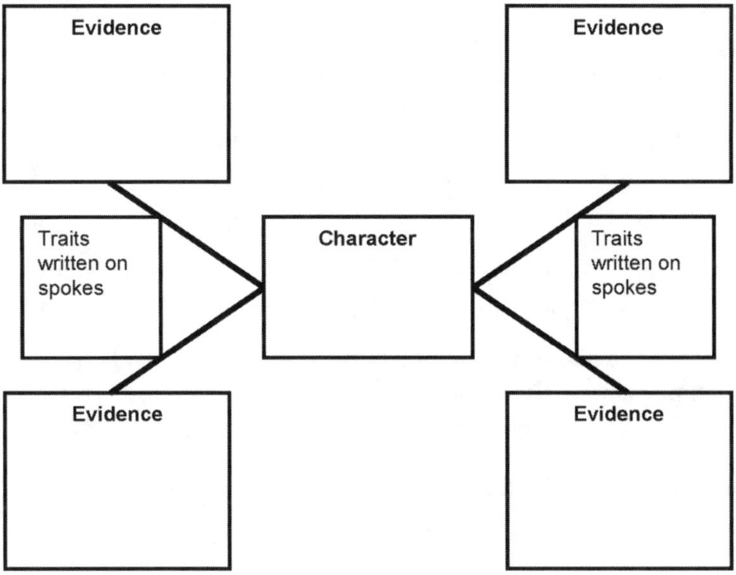

When students come to class with their completed graphic organizers, the hearts from each team assemble in an expert team to review each graphic organizer on Charlotte. They select the four best traits and the best textual evidence to support their decision, creating another graphic organizer synthesizing their ideas. Similarly, expert groups are completing new synthesizing graphic organizers for Wilbur, Fern, and Templeton. The students then return to their home teams, where each in turn teaches their character by sharing their newly created graphic organizer.

Students receive pass-fail points counting toward a criterion-referenced grading scheme for the graphic organizer they brought to class (their homework), but I don't grade their in-class work. I do, however, carefully monitor both expert and home groups to be certain that they remain on task and on target with the content they will share.

The learning that occurs in 50 minutes is enormous. In the expert teams, students are working at the highest levels of Bloom's (1956) taxonomy, evaluating each person's contribution and synthesizing to create a new graphic organizer. In a revised version of Bloom's taxonomy (Anderson & Krathwohl, 2001), "create" is the highest level of learning. In the home teams, students are teaching other students, a practice research suggests leads to deep learning because it capitalizes on the power of peer tutoring (Fantuzzo, Dimeff, & Fox, 1989; Fantuzzo, Riggio, Connelly, & Dimeff, 1989). This in-depth approach to learning can be contrasted with a superficial alternative where a teacher says, "OK class. You have all read *Charlotte's Web*, so please form groups and discuss the characters."

Jigsaw is remarkably versatile and thus useful even in large classes: The home teams remain the same size, usually composed of four students, but several expert teams can look at the same piece of the puzzle. Three expert teams of four to six students, for example, could look at Charlotte, another three teams could focus on Wilbur, and so on.

Examples of Jigsaw in other disciplines are

- Psychology: Underpinnings of childhood moral development (cognition, social, emotional, biological)
- Botany: The major plant groups (nonvascular land plants; seedless vascular plants; vascular plants with "naked seeds" [gymnosperms]; vascular plants with flowers and protected seeds [angiosperms]
- History: Causes of the American Civil War (economic, political, social)
- Anthropology: Branches of the discipline (cultural, linguistic, physical, archeology)

- Biochemistry: Polymers of carbon (carbohydrates, lipids, proteins)
- Accounting: Four methods of depreciation (straight line, units of production, sum of the year's digits, double declining balance)
- Engineering: Designing a solar hot water system (collecting the solar energy, transferring the solar energy to the hot water, storing the hot water, controlling the operation of the system, incorporating safety considerations into the design) (A. Gates, personal communication, August 10, 2005)
- Pharmacy: cholinesterase inhibitors used to treat Alzheimer's (Donepezil, Tacrine, Rivastigmine, Galantamine).

Send-a-Problem

The Send-a-Problem structure gives students the opportunity to identify or focus on their own issues or problems and to participate in a carefully structured problem-solving process in the context of community. Like Jigsaw, if carefully structured, the process can be completed—including reports—within a 50-minute class period.

To initiate Send-a-Problem, instructors have at hand a list of problems or issues. The instructor can identify the issues, but students have far more investment in the Send-a-Problem activity if they have direct input. I use Send a-Problem in literature classes to pose thought-provoking, open-ended questions. Teams, for example, tackle complex interpretations of characters in a short story such as *Theft* by Joyce Carol Oates: What do we learn about Marya in the opening pages? What can we deduce about her character/personality? How does Marya feel about herself? How do we know? How are Marya and Imogene Skillman different? In what ways are Marya and Imogene Skillman similar? Explain what kinds of thefts are occurring in the novel.

I bring to class file folders (large envelopes can also be used) with one of the above questions posted on each one. I announce the activity and its time limits. I then distribute the folders, one per team. In large classes, several teams can work simultaneously on the same problems with the caveat that the teams cannot be seated close together. Because of the three steps discussed next, they need to be spaced so that teams have three different problems to address.

The activity proceeds in three carefully structured steps. First, each team discusses its particular problem and generates within the given timeframe as many solutions as possible. The solutions, recorded on a sheet of paper, are placed in the folder. Second, the folders are then passed clockwise to another team, which does not open the folder. Reading the problem or issue from the front of the folder, they follow an identical procedure and brainstorm solutions, adding their recorded conclusions to the folder. Third, the folders are passed again, but in this case, the third team opens the folder and reviews the ideas/solutions generated by the other two teams. They can add additional ideas of their own or consolidate those already suggested by the two other teams. Their primary task, however, is to synthesize the best ideas from all three groups in order to reach the most viable conclusion.

Each step is carefully timed. Instructors need to make judgment calls about the total time allotment. Send-a-Problem can be used successfully as a brainstorming activity with each team "blitzing" through as many solutions as possible within a narrow time limit such as four minutes per step. By allotting more time for the discussion and expecting well-crafted mini-essays as responses, I use the structure within a 50-minute class period as a vehicle for meaningful discussion, thoughtful synthesis and evaluation, and creative problem solving. Like Jigsaw, students are working at the highest levels of Bloom's (1956) taxonomy because the final step requires both evaluation and synthesis.

Group reports provide useful closure. If classes are large, precluding a report from every team, two approaches are possible if students have playing cards. In the first case, the teacher draws a card, such as the five of clubs, and asks the person holding it to offer the team's report. The instructor continues drawing cards and hearing reports until class time is over (or until students tire of the responses). Alternatively, the teacher can use a reporting approach called Three Stay, One Stray.

The Three Stay, One Stray structure described by Kagan (1992) requires the easy identification of a team member who will become the group's spokesperson. After the problem-solving discussions are complete, I allow time within the teams for peer coaching so that any team member can give the team's report, an important step to promote accountability. I then call on one of the suits, such as the diamonds, to designate which student from each team will "stray." That is, one student from each group rotates to an adjoining team to give the report. In large classes, the order of rotation must be clear. Playing cards work particularly well because the aces know to rotate to the twos, the jacks to the queens, and so forth.

These designated students, who are welcomed as visitors, share with the new team the results of their original groups' discussion, giving proposed solutions to problems or summarizing discussions.

Three Stay, One Stray offers a low-threat forum where students can exchange ideas and build social skills such as asking probing questions. It also offers students the opportunity to learn by teaching. Placing the report-out responsibility on the students reinforces the valuable conception that knowledge resides within the learning community, not just with the "authority figure" instructor. Perhaps its greatest value lies in its efficiency. For example, instead of 10 sequential 5-minute reports to the entire class (50 minutes, plus transition time), individual students are simultaneously giving 5-minute reports throughout the room. I usually have the students rotate twice, making two reports, because teams then get exposure to more ideas and the reporter has rehearsal time.

Virtually all disciplines lend themselves to problem-solving activities where many heads are better than one. Here are some examples.

- Medicine: What things would a clinician need to know before considering a diagnosis of Attention-Deficit Disorder/AIDS/Alzheimer's?
- Art: What features would an art historian look for to authenticate an original Rembrandt/Renoir/Klee?
- Religion: Discuss the ramifications and possible solutions for issues facing the Catholic church today (challenges to papal authority, pedophilia, the declining priesthood, etc.).
- History: Outline the various claims to territory of the cattleman, the farmers, and the Native Americans.
- Geography: Explain the effects of linguistic diversity on European unity. What makes the Balkan region unique as compared to other shatter belts? Discuss the relationship between the pattern of landforms and cultural diversity in Eastern Europe (K. Hart, personal communication, July 30, 1999).

The Send-a-Problem concept does not need to be limited to issues only. In place of the folders, geologists can pass around rocks needing identification, paralegal instructors can have teams fill out worksheets on various legal books, and ESL or language teachers can have teams caption various cartoons using the target language.

Cooperative Debates

In my English literature class studying *Antigone*, I establish teams of four to five students to examine two key questions relevant to the play: Pro/Con: Should Antigone have buried her brother? and Pro/Con: Should Creon be impeached for poor leadership?

Students draw slips of paper to determine their teams. This random approach allows students to interact with a variety of classmates and ensures that the highest achieving students do not self-select each other, thus skewing the debate results.

As homework, each student reads the play closely and gathers support for their team's perspective. I give students class time to compare their notes and work on preparing the best possible arguments. I expect students to contribute evidence from the play based on their close textual reading as well as any other insights into the issues, such as concepts gleaned from class discussions and from an earlier guest lecturer speaking on justice and legality.

I carefully explain the ground rules to the students. Because I want all the team members to be prepared to debate and to understand the material well enough to present their side, I determine each team's spokesperson at random just before the debate begins. Thus, the teams are potentially only as strong as their weakest member, a situation that results in a lot of peer coaching and genuine learning. The spokespersons have four minutes to present their sides. I then allow each team four minutes to prepare a rebuttal. In the second round, the teams choose their own spokesperson. The rebuttals last three minutes. Then, the students who are observing the debate (the half of the class assigned to the other debate topic) vote to determine which side has made the most convincing argument. The second pair of teams then follow the same procedure for their debate on the second question.

The 50-minute class period provides a perfect setting for these highly animated, hotly contested cooperative debates. Best of all, students clearly do their homework, coming to class with an in-depth knowledge of the literary work and the issues surrounding both these questions.

Almost all disciplines have key issues that lend themselves well to debate.

- Computer science: Blackboard or WebCT platforms?
- History: Should the US have dropped the second bomb on Nagasaki?
- Biology: To clone or not to clone?
- Economics: Should the US adopt a flat rate income tax system?

Guided Reciprocal Peer Questioning

Developed and researched by King (1990, 1992, 1995), this activity helps students to generate task-specific questions that can then be answered within a cooperative team. Guided Reciprocal Peer Questioning empowers students to take charge of their own learning—to generate their own critical questions—through structured practice.

To initiate this activity, I give each student a copy of King's question stems (see Appendix 10.1) and ask them to email me three to five authentic questions (ones they truly want to discuss) on a given work of literature such as Gwendolyn Brooks's *Maud Martha*. These question stems, based on Bloom's (1956) taxonomy, challenge students to move beyond dualistic thinking by forming questions such as "What are the strengths and weaknesses of . . . ?" I provide specific examples to help students understand the process of generating effective questions.

Students bring their questions to class and use them in their cooperative teams. I assign four roles through the playing cards in each group: discussion leader, recorder, reporter, and time keeper. The team leader poses one of the specific questions he or she has written to which the other team members respond. Since the questions do not have a single right answer, reflective discussion follows. Each student in turn offers a question for the team to discuss, preferably using a different stem. The recorders in each team capture the question posed and the gist of the discussion. About 20 minutes before the close of class, I ask the teams to review their recorders' notes and to determine the question—and the subsequent discussion—that led to the most productive insights. Because my writing-based literature classes are typically small, I ask each team (usually four to five teams composed of four students each) to succinctly share their best question and discussion. In larger classes, instructors might want to share a few randomly selected reports, but then have all of them emailed for later posting to a web page or for distribution to students through email or course management systems such as WebCT or Blackboard.

This activity lends itself to virtually any discipline. The possibilities are seemingly endless. King (1995) notes that she and her colleagues throughout California have used the question stems with subjects as diverse as anthropology, biology, business accounting, history, mathematics, psychology, research methods, and teacher education. The more often students practice this activity, the higher the quality of the questions, particularly if the instructor has conscientiously provided feedback on the quality of the questions, reinforcing those that promote higher order thinking. Davis (1993) reminds us that

> [Good thinking] is learned by practice—by thinking—under the guidance and criticism of an effective mentor, presumably a teacher who is also a "good thinker" and who understands thinking processes. Above all, thinking involves asking questions—sometimes new questions about old questions in the search for new answers. (p. 234)

Bingo

Bingo offers a game format easy to adapt to many teaching needs. Bingo sheets can be created using the "Table" option on most word processing packages. Alternatively, Sugar (1998), of the Game Group, has developed a set of reusable materials for a variation of Bingo called QUIZO. Bingo, often classified as a "frame game" or a "matrix game" is easily adapted to virtually any teaching scenario. When carefully structured and paced, the game can be played successfully in 50-minute class periods.

I use Bingo to get students to review material for the midterm or final examination. I coach them on designing and submitting appropriate questions, an ongoing process throughout the semester or half semester.

Most students need to be coached on question writing. Learning to pose viable, cogent questions is a valuable skill. For example, a Nobel prize-winning physicist, Isidor Rabi, credits his mother with prompting him to value the questions he asked above the answers he gave. When he returned from school, she would never ask him what he learned that day. Instead, she would ask, "What good questions did you ask today?" (Barell, 1988, qtd. in Costa & O'Leary, 1992, p. 59). Students tend to make their questions too rigid for the Bingo format. They need to allow for some wiggle room (e.g., not, "Name the characters in Ernest Gaines's *A Lesson Before Dying*," but "Name three important characters in *A Lesson Before Dying*").

I have students submit two types of questions: factual ones, that I can use to speed up play, and open-ended ones, which result in in-depth learning. The student who submits the question becomes the "arbitrator" of acceptable answers, not me. Thus, students post questions to a web page in the following format:

Type of Question: Factual

The Question:	Define plagiarism
Student's Name:	John Doe
The Answer:	To steal or pass off the words or ideas of another as one's own, without crediting the source.
Source:	*Student Handbook*, p. 77.

I carefully review all the questions, returning for revision any that are inappropriate. Before the game, I add any significant questions that will help students learn critical material. I then rank order the questions within the two categories (factual and open-ended) so that the most valuable questions will occur early in the play.

To use the questions during play, I enlarge the fonts to prepare transparencies or to project slides. At the top appears the question and the person submitting it. Space between the student's name and the answer that follows it allows the answer to be easily covered or added later in a PowerPoint slide.

I purchase needed supplies: Skittles or M&Ms for the markers (seasonal markers can be candy corn or Valentine hearts), and candy bars—large and snack sizes—for the prizes (healthier prize alternatives are bags of pretzels, cocoa packets, ballpoint pens, etc.).

To play the game, I pair students, forming a trio if there are an uneven number of participants. Although most students know the object of Bingo (five markers in a row in any direction) and the rules of play, it is important to explain the procedures so that anyone unfamiliar with Bingo will not feel compromised or inept. Each pair receives markers and two-colored worksheets (as an example, green for the factual; gold for the higher-level open-ended questions) where they record their answers and if they were right or wrong. They can also note the space where the marker is to go. A worksheet, which is abbreviated here, looks like this:

Factual Questions

Pair or trio (responding to a question about William Faulkner's *A Rose for Emily*):

Answer	Right or Wrong?	Space
1) rat poison	Right	B2
2)		

The teacher then poses the questions in sequence within each category, giving sufficient time based on their complexity. To make the game participant-centered and to allow students to receive feedback on the viability and fairness of their questions, I have the student who submitted the question call "time" and then decide what alternative answers are acceptable.

Pairs with correct answers place a marker on the designated square (e.g., B3 or G1). The square is determined by having the pairs in turn draw a Scrabble tile or a homemade variation (B, I, N, G, O) and roll a die (they roll again if a six emerges or teachers can purchase ten-sided die with only five numbers at novelty shops).

Pacing is very important in a 50-minute class period. The factual questions speed up play and the higher-order thinking questions, as indicated earlier, lead to valuable discussions. I can typically ask 25 factual questions and 12 open-ended ones, but the number will depend on the depth of the open-ended responses and the skill of the student "arbiters." Thus, always mindful of the clock, a savvy Bingo facilitator will offer frequent open-ended questions for their learning value but speed up play with factual questions. To facilitate this process, I have the stacks of sorted transparencies on either side of an overhead projector. Teachers comfortable with computer projections can toggle between the two types of questions.

The first pair (often there will be ties) to cover five contiguous squares in any direction declares "Bingo." After the two (or sometimes three) students select a prize, they then clear their board and continue playing until the time period ends. In a 50-minute class period, it is theoretically possible for every pair to become "winners."

There are many reasons to use a Bingo game format. Because students submit in advance questions for which they are responsible, they are far more likely to read and reflect on the desired material. Furthermore, the very process of framing questions and later receiving feedback on their value, efficacy, and fairness encourages students to concentrate on learning useful information and skills. Bingo also has assessment value: The worksheets completed by student pairs during play offer teachers valuable insights into what students know and don't know. They also uncover important misconceptions that might be addressed on other occasions.

Useful in virtually any discipline, Bingo games keep students actively engaged with the material, thus increasing the likelihood of their remembering it. As Rodgers and Starrett (2005) state, "If we as educators can find a way to tap into the power of games to deeply engage students, we will have found a truly exciting tool for teaching and learning" (p. 11). Enthusiastic and energetic, students often high-five each other when they get a correct answer. They listen attentively to the answers and suddenly care about the material. Best of all, Bingo games build collegiality. The pairs who work together develop personal bonds and the whole-group discussions over the open-ended questions allow students to engage in meaningful conversations that would likely not occur in less structured settings.

Conclusion

Good teaching, as faculty developers know, is not simply a grab bag of techniques. One of our key responsibilities is helping faculty to appreciate and capitalize on the complexity and richness of teaching and learning, particularly within a learning-centered context. One way to do this is to frame specific techniques such as the ones discussed here—Jigsaw, Send-a-Problem, Cooperative Debates, Guided Reciprocal Peer Questioning, and Bingo—within the context of sequencing activities with an emphasis on cooperative learning during face-to-face class time, even in brief 50-minute periods.

References

Anderson, L. W., & Krathwohl, D. R. (Eds.). (2001). *A taxonomy for learning, teaching, and assessing: A revision of Bloom's taxonomy of educational objectives.* New York, NY: Longman.

Barr, R. B., & Tagg, J. (1995, November/December). From teaching to learning—A new paradigm for undergraduate education. *Change, 27*(6), 12–25.

Bloom, B. S. (Ed.). (1956). *Taxonomy of educational objectives: Handbook 1. Cognitive domain.* New York, NY: Longman.

Bransford, J. D., Brown, A. L., & Cocking, R. R. (Eds.). (2000). *How people learn: Brain, mind, experience, and school* (Expanded ed.). Washington, DC: National Academies Press.

Costa, A. L., & O'Leary, P. W. (1992). Co-cognition: The cooperative development of the intellect. In J. Davidson & T. Worsham (Eds.), *Enhancing thinking through cooperative learning* (pp. 41–65). New York, NY: Teachers College Press.

Davis, J. R. (1993). *Better teaching, more learning: Strategies for success in postsecondary settings.* Phoenix, AZ: American Council on Education/Oryx Press.

Fantuzzo, J. W., Dimeff, L. A., & Fox, S. L. (1989). Reciprocal peer tutoring: A multimodal assessment of effectiveness with college students. *Teaching of Psychology, 16*(3), 133–135.

Fantuzzo, J. W., Riggio, R. E., Connelly, S., & Dimeff, L. A. (1989). Effects of reciprocal peer tutoring on academic achievement and psychological adjustment: A component analysis. *Journal of Educational Psychology, 81*(2), 173–177.

Feichtner, S. B., & Davis, E. A. (1984–85). Why some groups fail: A survey of students' experiences with learning groups. *Organizational Behavior Teaching Review, 9*(4), 58–71.

Felder, R. M., & Brent, R. (1994). *Cooperative learning in technical courses: Procedures, pitfalls, and payoffs.* Retrieved June 16, 2006, from the North Carolina State University web site: www.ncsu.edu/felder-public/Papers/Coopreport.html#IssuesAndAnswers

Fink, L. D. (2003). *Creating significant learning experiences: An integrated approach to designing college courses.* San Francisco, CA: Jossey-Bass.

Finkel, D. L. (2000). *Teaching with your mouth shut.* Portsmouth, NH: Boynton/Cook.

Kagan, S. (1992). *Cooperative learning.* San Juan Capistrano, CA: Kagan Cooperative Learning.

King, A. (1989, October). Effects of self-questioning training on college students' comprehension of lectures. *Contemporary Educational Psychology, 14*(4), 366–381.

King, A. (1990, Winter). Enhancing peer interaction and learning in the classroom through reciprocal questioning. *American Educational Research Journal, 27*(4), 664–687.

King, A. (1992). Promoting active learning and collaborative learning in business administration classes. In T. J. Frecka (Ed.), *Critical thinking, interactive learning, and technology: Reaching for excellence in business education* (pp. 158–173). Chicago, IL: Arthur Andersen Foundation.

King, A. (1994). Autonomy and question asking: The role of personal control in guided student-generated questioning. *Learning and Individual Differences, 6*(2), 162–185.

King, A. (1995, Winter). Guided peer questioning: A cooperative learning approach to critical thinking. *Cooperative learning and college teaching, 5*(2), 15–19.

Lyman, F. (1981). The responsive classroom discussion: The inclusion of all students. In A. S. Anderson (Ed.), *Mainstreaming digest* (pp. 109–113). College Park, MD: College of Education, University of Maryland.

Millis, B. J. (1994). Conducting cooperative cases. In E. C. Wadsworth (Ed.), *To improve the academy: Vol. 13. Resources for faculty, instructional, and organizational development* (pp. 309–328). Stillwater, OK: New Forums Press.

Millis, B. J. (2002). *Enhancing learning—and more!—through cooperative learning* (IDEA Paper No. 38). Retrieved June 16, 2006, from the Kansas State University, IDEA Center web site: www.idea.ksu.edu/papers/Idea_Paper_38.pdf

Millis, B. J., & Cottell, P. G., Jr. (1998). *Cooperative learning for higher education faculty.* Phoenix, AZ: American Council on Education/Oryx Press.

Rodgers, M. L., & Starrett, D. A. (2005, October). Is it time to get in the game? *National Teaching & Learning Forum, 14*(6), 10–11.

Stein, R. F., & Hurd, S. (2000). *Using student teams in the classroom: A faculty guide.* Bolton, MA: Anker.

Streuling, G. F. (2004). Overcoming initial mistakes when using small groups. In L. K. Michaelsen, A. B. Knight, & L. D. Fink (Eds.), *Team-based learning: A transformative use of small groups in college teaching* (pp. 133–143). Sterling, VA: Stylus.

Sugar, S. (1998). *Games that teach: Experiential activities for reinforcing learning.* San Francisco, CA: Pfeiffer.

Tuckman, B. W. (1965). Developmental sequence in small groups. *Psychological Bulletin, 63*(6), 384–399.

Tuckman, B. W., & Jensen, M. A. C. (1977). Stages of small-group development revisited. *Group and Organizational Studies, 2*(4), 419–427.

Weimer, M. (2002). *Learner-centered teaching: Five key changes to practice.* San Francisco, CA: Jossey-Bass.

Appendix 10.1
Guiding Critical Thinking

Generic Questions	**Specific Thinking Processes Induced**
Explain why ____. (Explain how ____.)	analysis
What would happen if ____?	prediction/hypothesizing
What is the nature of ____?	analysis
What are the strengths and weaknesses of ____?	analysis/inferencing
What is the difference between ___ and ___?	comparison-contrast
Why is ____ happening?	analysis/inferencing
What is a new example of ____?	application
How could ____ be used to ____?	application
What are the implications of ____?	analysis/inferencing
What is ____ analogous to?	identification/creation of analogies and metaphors
How does ___ effect ____?	analysis of relationship (cause-effect)
How does ___ tie in with what we learned before?	activation of prior knowledge
Why is ____ important?	analysis of significance
How are ____ and ____ similar?	comparison-contrast
How does ____ apply to everyday life?	application—to the real world
What is a counterargument for ____?	rebuttal to argument
What is the best ____, and why?	evaluation and provision of evidence
What is the solution to the problem of ____?	synthesis of ideas
Compare ____ and ____ with regard to.	comparison-contrast and evaluation based on criteria
What do you think causes ____? Why?	analysis of relationship (cause-effect)

Do you agree or disagree with this statement: ____? What evidence is there to support your answer?	evaluation and provision of evidence
What is another way to look at ____?	taking other perspectives
What does ____ mean?	comprehension
Describe ____ in your own words.	comprehension
Summarize ____ in your own words.	comprehension

Note. Adapted from King (1989, 1992, & 1994).

11

"Heritage Rocks": Principles and Best Practices of Effective Intercultural Teaching and Learning

Peter Frederick, Mary James
Heritage University

This portrayal of the intercultural teaching/learning culture and classroom stories at one fully multicultural institution, Heritage University, itself reflecting many diverse "heritages," provides a glimpse into the faces of the future of higher education in America. We offer several examples and a synthesis of the principles and best practices of effective intercultural teaching and learning, with the intention of helping other institutions move intercultural education from the margins to the "center," thereby preparing both teachers and learners for effective intercultural learning and living in the 21st century.

> Do something the first day of class to establish an inclusive and interactive tone for the class. . . . Know your story and your students' stories.
>
> —Faculty member

> Students don't care what you know as much as they need to know you care and respect them and their cultures.
>
> —Faculty member

> I like the cultural sensitivity here. As a new student, I feel welcome and can be who I am. I can concentrate on education.
>
> —Student

> There were several different cultures in the class, and I felt mine was right up there with everyone else's. Because of the final project, I was

> able to embrace myself as a person, open up to other people, and learn from their cultures and mine.
>
> —Student

Under a full moon in the midst of harvested hops fields and apple orchards, it is an early evening in mid-November. Mary has invited Peter to teach some African-American history and culture to her Communication 305 course. Comm. 305 (and 105 for new students), together known as the "Heritage Core," is a combined intensive writing and cultural awareness course required of all students. Typical of this Hispanic-serving, multicultural institution on the Yakama Nation Indian reservation in central Washington, in the class are the faces of the future: seven Latinos/Latinas, themselves a mixture of *Espana y Indios;* two Yakama Natives; three with mixed Native American heritages; four ethnically blended white Euro-Americans; and one Pacific Islander.

Knowing Mary's success helping Heritage students understand and value their own and other cultures, Peter asks the students (think-pair-share) to "take a moment of reflection and write down the one or two most essential things you have learned about intercultural communication in the course so far." As they reflect on the task and talk with someone nearby, Peter readies a video clip of an inspiring black women's gospel chorus group, "Sojourner" from Indiana University's "Ancestral Spirits." After only 10 minutes, we debrief the student reflections. With an energy akin to gospel music, the students "rock" with stunning insights, comments, and personal stories. With surprising unanimity, they state (in our words) the following essential principles of intercultural awareness, understanding, and communication.

- That racial prejudice is brought about by ignorance and by fears of the unknown, fears of those different from oneself.
- That students, like all people, are limited by their fears and by their ethnocentric points of view, but that this is fixable with knowledge and intercultural contact.
- That they have learned to see, appreciate, and respect the diverse cultures and cultural context of others and to value the uniqueness of those cultures.
- That they also see and understand the universal commonalities of the human condition across cultural differences; they value both uniqueness *and* universality.
- That more and more Americans, including many in that class, are both struggling with and celebrating their blended, bi- or tri-cultural ethnicity

and identities. Which of us does not live in and negotiate at least two worlds within us?

- That it is important not to reduce persons to their ethnic or racial identity because all of us have multiple cultural identities (including also gender, socioeconomic status, age, religion, region, race, sexuality, ableness, etc.).

Against this background of impressive understanding, the class then listens to two exuberant black gospel songs of praise, thanksgiving, and hope, responding with feelings, thoughts, their own stories, then making two more crucial intercultural points.

- That despite experiencing histories of oppression and victimization, all social groups have found in their cultural traditions courageous and creative means of achieving self-empowering dignity, such as the affirmations of gospel.
- That staying stuck in a victimization view—by whites or by people of color—ennobles none of us. Hope in the human spirit and in cross-cultural understanding and interaction, as Tatum argues (1997), is essential.

Purpose, Context, and Approach

What kind of teaching leads to such admirable intercultural understanding? This chapter is intended to convey a portrait of the essential principles and best practices of effective intercultural teaching and learning in a multicultural university whose student profile reflects the changing class, cultural, and color composition of the United States. Heritage University was founded by Dr. Kathleen Ross in 1982 with the mission of providing "quality, accessible higher education to multicultural populations which have been educationally isolated" (Heritage University, 2004, p. 2). Undergraduate Heritage students are 54% Hispanic (mostly Mexican American farm worker families), 12% Native, 31% white, and 3% African American and Asian, percentages that reflect the demographics of the Yakima Valley. In different proportions, they also increasingly reflect the changing demographics of the nation, including increasing numbers of blended ethnicities. With an average age of 31, 70% of the students are women, most of whom are working poor; many are single parents and English language learners.

Heritage University is therefore a multicultural laboratory—and perhaps a model—of intercultural education. One of our general education learning outcomes specifies four competencies for working and living in a multicultural society. One of six key characteristics (and assessment criterion) of the effective faculty member is one who actively values and celebrates the diverse cultures represented by our students. These goals and criteria, as education professor Pam Root said in a recent faculty workshop, are "not just articulated but also actualized in practice." Data from the 2004 National Survey of Student Engagement (NSSE), based on student self-reporting, shows that entering freshman at Heritage, largely because they come from majority single-ethnicity high schools, scored half as high as other Hispanic-serving institutions on items such as "understanding people of other racial and ethnic backgrounds," "had serious conversations with students of a different race or ethnicity than your own," and "worked with other students on projects during class." Seniors, by contrast, scored *four* times higher than freshmen in each of these areas. The Heritage senior results exceeded that of other Hispanic-serving institutions as well as predominately white institutions in the NSSE sample.

The university mission specifically encourages intercultural engagement not only across cultures on campus but also in "grass-roots community involvement" aimed at the "special needs of multicultural and rural or isolated constituencies" (Heritage University, 2004, p. 3); that is, the Native, Hispanic, Filipino, Japanese, and Anglo cultures of the valley. Virtually every Heritage student completes at least one service-learning project and most do several projects. NSSE data confirm high scores on "contributing to the welfare of your community." A required community-based assignment in Comm. 105 and 305 sets the tone, and service-learning continues across all disciplines and professional programs, as we shall see.

Concern for others starts on campus. Heritage faculty encourage students to work with support partners and in study groups, teaching each other and helping with missed work. Student support for each other's learning is an essential part of the Heritage culture, especially given the frequency of challenges students face with extensive work schedules, single parenthood, car breakdowns, sick children, and family addictions. Students also create their own groups. Mary Anne Quahapama, a Yakama woman and recent graduate, reported that "the only way I made it through" statistics was "six of us stayed around after class and talked about what we did and didn't understand." Guided by the university motto "Knowledge Brings Us Together," there is an almost total absence of competition among students.

As reflected by the student response to Peter's question in Mary's Comm. 305 class, Heritage students come to know the university mission, celebrate it, and thoroughly expect to be engaged in intercultural contact and learning in almost every class. This chapter describes several faculty strategies for intercultural student learning that achieve these goals across the disciplines—in the arts and sciences as well as professional programs. Our title, with its intended double meaning, comes from a t-shirt that Heritage business students, with obvious pride, recently designed and sold. The shirt, intermixing on a black background white and red images of the Heritage logo, diverse student faces, and rock star Jimi Hendrix, is headed by the words "HERITAGE ROCKS."

Some definitions may be helpful. We define the term *multicultural* as a descriptor of the changing population of the nation's classrooms, and the term *intercultural* as the actual dynamic, difficult interactions among multiple diverse students in those classrooms. Aware of the literature on intercultural education (e.g., Adams, Bell, & Griffin, 1997; Border & Chism, 1992; Frederick, 1995; Millem, Chang, & Antonio, 2005; Ouellett, 2005; Tatum, 1997), we conclude that the principles and best practices of effective intercultural learning and teaching are virtually identical to the principles and best practices of *any* effective teaching and learning, but that the slight differences are instructive. Neither of us is an educational researcher, although Peter has been an active faculty developer and higher education consultant for 30 years, and Mary headed the Academic Skills Center at Heritage for 15 years. We are both primarily teachers, Mary in English and communication, Peter in history and American cultural studies.

Our research approach is humanistic, qualitative, naturalistic inquiry (Creswell, 1998; Lincoln & Guba, 1985). As opposed to empirical positivist paradigms, naturalistic inquiry emphasizes holistic, ethnographic realities rooted in natural contexts featuring the real-life experiences and stories of participants—that is, our Heritage colleagues and students. We are ourselves part of that context and we interact with others naturally every day, grounding our study on classroom research and other forms of feedback from students, informal classroom observations, qualitative surveys, workshops, and our colleagues' stories of teaching and learning. Our conversations occur in one-to-one, in-depth interviews and in casual meetings in hallways, college paths, and in the cafeteria—that is, in naturalistic ways. In diverse settings we have essentially asked the same basic questions: What's working best to help your students' learning? What's hindering their learning? In what ways did the intercultural mix of students matter? Would you tell a story about a recent intercultural moment in one of your classes?

Intercultural Learning in a Storytelling Culture

We recently heard such a story from Steve Camerer, a writing and reading teacher working with English language learners in the pre-college program.

When asked what, in his experience, worked best to help his students' learning, he thought for a while, then said, "Understand where they are coming from—their histories, cultures, even pop culture—and bring it into class." Then he told a story about the day he was teaching students how to paraphrase a passage.

> I had asked them to pick a song of their choice and paraphrase it. I was used to a 40%–50% success rate in accurate, well-written paraphrasing, but with this one I had an 80%–90% success rate. They wrote about something that meant something to them.

Thus, Steve went right to the heart of a crucial principle of learning: Connect learning goals with students' inner worlds. Shulman (1999) has written,

> we now understand that learning is a <u>dual</u> process in which . . . the inside beliefs and understandings must come out, and only then can something outside get in. . . . The first influence on learning is [what's] already inside the learner. (p. 12)

Heritage teachers intentionally focus learning on what we know about our students. We teach on Yakama Nation lands in the shadow of sacred Mt. Adams (*Pahto*). Five generations of English-speaking, white migrants blend with three generations of Mexican and Asian migrant labor families, all living among native people who have been here "since time immemorial." From this convergence of peoples, Heritage inherits a storytelling culture. President Ross, whose field is intercultural education, leads an effort to capture and transform this shared inheritance of storytelling traditions. The intent is to translate informal oral memories into a formal learning methodology for integrating knowledge and experience. At monthly breakfasts sponsored by the president, staff and faculty tell stories about family backgrounds, migration routes, work experiences, and significant people who drive the different and similar challenges, fears, hopes, and aspirations in their lives. The annual retreat for faculty and staff features life stories by members of the Heritage community, and faculty workshops often examine the role of stories in learning by connecting student lives with important course goals.

This use of classroom stories is consistent with the growing body of literature on the role of emotions in learning and its inextricable connection with the intellect. Building on the work of Kolb (1983), Damasio (1994), and LeDoux (1996), Zull (2002) has shown that deep learning depends on the interplay of affect and cognition in which learners process information first in the inner (limbic) emotional centers of the brain and then make reasoned connections and meaning in the cognitive, integrative centers of the outer cortex (Zull, 2002). Stories, Zull says, "engage all parts of the brain" (p. 228), which makes them key to accessing emotions where "learning is deepest" (p. 228). Therefore, he says, "you can see the value of stories for the teacher. We should tell stories, create stories, and repeat stories; and we should ask our students to do the same" (p. 228).

At Heritage, we base storytelling not only on Zull and others (Coles, 1989; Schank, 1990; Witherell & Noddings, 1991) but also on the Native American medicine wheel, a model for holistic learning integrating mental, emotional, physical, and spiritual dimensions of the self and therefore of learning (Frederick, 1991). Stories are an essential part of Comm. 305 (and 105), designed in 1999 as the centerpiece of the curriculum by a campus team headed by President Ross, Provost Sneh Veena, Mary James, and other faculty members. Students begin the course with short writing on what they already know about their own cultures' norms and values, then do a storytelling group activity in which students choose one of four animals with which they identify. Each of the animals (rabbit, eagle, turtle, or coyote) has cultural significance in the major American ethnic cultures represented in the class. Finally, students then break up into their respective "animal" groups to discuss the reasons for their choice and make a matrix of the comparisons and contrasts between their animal's characteristics and those of the other three. In the debriefing, students introduce themselves through their animal stories and present their matrices. The follow-up writing assignment draws out intercultural communication concepts of stereotyping, in-group and out-group, and the importance of seeing similarities and differences across and within groups.

The course continues emphasizing the journey from ethnocentricity to empathy through readings, class discussions, examination of the internal and external aspects of cultures, and service-learning projects. In addition to frequent writing assignments, students make cultural identity collages or drawings and share the stories with their service-learning groups. They choose mentors who help them deepen their understanding of career, family background, personal self-identity, and another culture. Guest speakers from the major cultures in the Yakima Valley present their personal journeys, telling of barriers experienced and conquered. Inspired by a talk by Miguel Puente, director of the College Assistance for Migrants Program and a Heritage core instructor, one student wrote, "I realized I have two contradictory cultures living inside me: a majority culture (Mexican in Mexico) and a minority culture (Mexican in the United States). All non-white immigrants living in the United States have to contend with being an 'other.'"

"Hearing each other's voices," Mary says, "we all grow." Student voices testify to their feelings/thoughts about the class. A young Euro-American student said, "Before enrolling in this class, I didn't care to understand others and their cultures; I was very ethnocentric. But I have started to look at things differently over the last two months." A self-identified "Mexican" wrote that he came into the class with feelings of inadequacy and "hate," but learned that "culture and identity are filters for how we see the world, and that I myself who had felt a victim of discrimination was also criminal because I unconsciously created [prejudice] in my own small world." Most students describe these kinds of transformations in themselves: "This class has really opened my eyes to my own biases. I have had to reexamine my perceptions of others" and "This class has taught me to be more observant in how I treat others and how my reactions to other cultures need to be more empathetic."

Peter's approach to American history survey courses, starting with Native cultures and the Spanish in Mexico and the southwest (in contrast to the usual New England-centered approach), also uses student stories as a way of exploring cultures and connecting student lives to historical content and themes. For example, in teaching about agriculture-based cultures, he asks students first to tell stories from their own experience about what land-owning farmers and farm workers most need, want, and fear. Within minutes, the board is filled with a rich, detailed socioeconomic and human set of facts and concepts about agriculture, bringing textbook pages alive with meaning derived from the students' own farm labor, land-owning, and land-losing life experiences.

In both surveys and advanced courses about Native and Mexican American history, Peter, like Mary, uses student stories to explore their various multiple identities. A recent class on the Native American boarding school experience led to an intense discussion of the costs and benefits of assimilation and the many variations of student bicultural identities. We also look at the blurred meaning of "borders," both metaphorical and real, in American history. Students tell stories about the meaning of *la frontera* in their lives. What does a border mean to Mexicans, whose young nation after independence in 1821 once included all of the southwest from California and Texas to Oregon, and whose rights were once promised protection by the Treaty of Guadalupe Hidalgo in 1848? What does a border line mean to the Apache and Tohono O'odham of the southwest, or the Lummi, Ojibwe, Blackfeet, and Mohawk tribes along the Canadian-American border of the North, or to the Yakama with guaranteed treaty rights from 1855 to hunt and fish "in all the usual and accustomed places"?

Informed by these wider explorations of borders and *mestizahe* blended ethnicities in all cultures, including various hyphenated Euro-Americans, students tell stories about their families. Each course concludes with training in conducting oral history interviews as part of writing a family history and making a poster presentation. The pride in their projects is palpable. "I thought it was awesome putting... items that represented my parents on the poster, and they were excited helping me with the project." The assignment respects the importance of extended families in Native and Mexican American traditions. It also helps many students connect not only with family and the larger themes of American history, but also with themselves. A Native woman explains,

> Because of this challenging final project, I was able to embrace myself as a Native person and open up to other people and learn from their historical memories. I was afraid at first, thinking I would personally defeat myself and back out of the project, solely because I hated my past. But when I listened to another person tell their story, and learned of their struggles, their memories of overcoming adversity, I realized that I was not alone. I felt more confident about the person I am becoming and how to use the past as a tool and learning experience.

Engaging Diverse Students in Diverse Disciplines and Professional Programs

Learning insights such as these happen as a result of intercultural engagement across all disciplines and professional programs. In the humanities, Loren Schmidt, chair of English and humanities, works with students to produce a literary magazine, *Pahto's Shadow,* which is posted online and distributed throughout the Valley. Heritage arts professors hold an Arts Day at the end of each semester in which students exhibit paintings, masks, and ceramic pieces, read poetry, perform multicultural dances, sing, and perform dramatic scenes, the casting intentionally race and gender blind. Thus, in *Sara Crewe,* an English story, the characters were all played by Latinos/Latinas, while in *Spirit of Hispania*, a series of Mexican folktales, most characters were white. *Cinderella: The World's Favorite Fairy Tale* presented the story from the point of view of different cultures. The Chinese Cinderella was played by a Swede, the Russian by a Latina, and the Native American by an African-American Nez Perce with multi-ethnic sisters. The witch was a willing white male.

As theatre instructor Linda Walker explains, "Through drama a participant learns about other cultures, not about what they eat, but how individuals perceive and deal with self, life, and the human condition on a daily basis. They learn what it's like to be someone else," thus gaining cultural understanding. In addition, as Levine and Cureton (1998) and many others have discovered, students break down cultural barriers when engaged together in common tasks, whether in theater, choral groups, or athletic teams. A white adjunct teacher who has lived on the Yakama reservation her entire life, Linda uses creative, improvisational process drama courses to help students develop language skills, interpersonal understanding, and the ability to analyze character and social history. All drama, she says, "is listening to what the other person is saying." Theatre helps students overcome shyness and gain "a sense of inner value and self-worth," Linda points out. "I didn't know I could do this" and "I learned a lot about myself" are comments she hears most frequently. "I lost my shyness," one said, "not totally, but I feel better about myself." And another said the drama class "gave me the opportunity to work in skills I didn't know I had."

Confidence building, combined with a tough, entrepreneurial approach, is at the heart of the business program. As business chair Len Black puts it, when the goal is to educate confident business professionals, "traditional methods do not work with nontraditional students." Teaching is done through real-world projects. The most recent among many joint faculty and student entrepreneurial ventures is the Peruvian purple potato, a heart healthy, nutrient-filled potato (actually purple) developed with local farmers and marketed through Costco. Len's "tough love" teaching methods are both rigorous and nurturing. A former businessman in both Mexico and the Philippines and fluent in Spanish, he understands the worlds his students come from. So does Charro Cruz, a Filipino American, who helped design the Heritage Rocks t-shirt. He knows how "to get students hooked" on his enthusiastic passion for business by bringing in analogies and examples from their daily lives—relationships, pop culture, advertisements, and adversity. Len tells them that their lives, filled with unpredictability, are manageable—just like the world of business. "Know yourself and your vision," he says, "know business principles, know opportunities, know the nature of the world, and you will be in the 20% of the business world that succeeds and not the 80% that doesn't." Recently, two of his students were hired as managers at Macy's, chosen in a highly competitive process from among thousands of applicants.

Students blossom as a result of their participation in the Students in Free Enterprise (SIFE) club, an energetic, entrepreneurial student group that won regional and placed high in two national SIFE competitions. SIFE students have brought motivational speakers to campus, taught other college and local high school student clubs how to raise money, produced a business news program on local public access TV, raised funds to buy materials for Moonjar, an effective way of teaching the ethics of money management and business to seventh graders, and worked with local farmers, the USDA, and retail outlets to develop alternate uses of the land, such as growing the Peruvian purple potato. Such programs benefit not only the community but also students. "I was quiet when I came," a Latina student said, "but I had to give presentations in class, then at conferences, and now to business leaders. Heritage built my confidence."

Social work students are engaged in hands-on learning in local community social agencies, such as neighborhood after-school programs, residential treatment centers, and the mental health clinics and social service agencies of the local Farm Workers Clinic and Yakama Tribal government. The program's core principles include social and economic justice, populations at risk, and an ecological perspective, as well as such standard topics as social stratification, cultural diversity, and conflict resolution strategies. Social work instructor Miguel Juarez, who received his bachelor's degree from Heritage, engages his students in service-learning because he is aware that as a lifelong citizen of mostly Hispanic nearby Sunnyside, he has to be a "model for students" not only of appropriate social worker behaviors but also of commitment to his community. Social work chair Ray Bending, a Pima native, involves students in community activities addressing the needs of the elders in culturally sensitive ways. As an elder himself, Ray says, "I share my experience with students." He also encourages colleagues to "hear their [students'] voices."

Kirstin James, teaching introductory sociology, uses repeatable classroom rituals that guarantee that each student's voice is heard in every class. To begin, each student checks in and talks about an observation, idea, story, or feeling related to the course, followed by a small group exercise that experientially conveys a sociological principle, followed by the discussion of a related reading. Class concludes with in-class journal writing and a reflective closure in which the whole group synthesizes the learning from that class. On the night Peter observed her class, six students, their turn to "bring something about you, your values, your culture," presented moving stories of family, relationships, spiritual beliefs, parenting, and recovery from addiction. Most were accompanied by music, photos, and deep feelings.

Nursing instructor Georgette Kerr applies Paulo Freire to nursing education, eschewing lecturing for interactive, democratic, concept-driven, culturally inclusive, community-based teaching methods. The mostly female students in the nursing program are active in local hospitals, the Farm Workers Clinic, and other community health intervention agencies. Sandra Wells, chair of the nursing program, explains, "We specifically teach students ways of being aware of cultural as well as other aspects of the social identity of patients without reducing patients to a race or ethnicity." In examining the intercultural dimensions of health, nursing students are encouraged to incorporate Native, Latino/Latina, and Asian traditional methods of healing into their clinical practice. Yoder (1997) says, "It is critical that nursing faculty examine their teaching approaches and develop effective teaching strategies for ethnically diverse students who are being educated to provide care for today's multicultural population" (p. 77). This advice is especially applicable for practitioners in a valley cursed by high rates of diabetes, obesity, and other diseases caused in part by the decline in salmon and other traditional foods.

Engaged, Intercultural Learning in the Sciences and Science Education

Responding to these health realities, mathematics instructor Tana Knudson has devised culturally informed teaching strategies using local examples to help her students feel more comfortable going to the board to solve problems and make presentations. Tana teaches both statistics and calculus to her mostly female, multicultural students by having them keep careful calculations of weight losses and gains during a specified time of attending to a diet and exercise program. In a 2004 statistics class, she gave students articles from a featured newspaper series on multiculturalism in the valley, including the human genome finding that genetically humans are 99.9% alike. That fact alone led to lively discussions in student groups assigned to analyze the many statistics in the article.

Biology, botany, and natural resource science students regularly work in the field. Aided by a NASA grant, they use satellite imagery to identify and address problems with ecological resources on Yakama reservation lands, in particular to preserve shrub steppe native flora in the highlands of Mt. Adams and Mt. Rainier. In summer 2004, led by Dean Jim Falco, 12 students (equally divided among Hispanics, Native Americans, and Euro-Americans) spent the summer in the field working with NASA equipment, the National Park Service, and Yakama Nation elders on this project. The team developed a new approach to characterize mixed vegetation to significantly improve the management of natural resources.

Chemistry professor Eric Leber wants his students to "pursue science-related questions in uncharted territory outside the confines/constraints of a lab book" in order to solve real-world problems with hands-on practical experiences using knowledge of chemistry. In the EcoVino program, working with vineyards and wineries in the Yakima Valley, he and his students have developed processes of turning the more than 50,000 tons of winery wastes from grape seeds, skins, and stems in eastern Washington into usable products such as animal feeds, antioxidants, soaps, fuels, paper, and bioplastics.

Part Blackfeet and Chata, Apanakhi Buckley, who teaches multicultural education and science teaching methods, has a huge commitment to her own as well as her students' civic engagement. "I love seeing my students teaching out in the community. It is one way I feel effective." As a pre-student teaching experience, her students design and teach an after-school curriculum for elementary age youngsters in Safe Haven, a neighborhood center in a tough gang area of Toppenish. When lack of funds threatened to close Safe Haven, Apanakhi both lobbied to keep it open and launched a new program at a school in Wapato, a nearby community whose population is 70% Latino, Native, and Filipino. Apanakhi's students do not just plan tutoring exercises for English and math skills but also design full curricula for science and health units. As Apanakhi describes in "Tipi Technology," her science education students learn how to teach principles of structural engineering, mathematics, and physics (convections, insulation, cohesion of water molecules) by working in groups to build a tipi over twice their height (Buckley, 2000). The task requires applying not only western science but also an understanding of traditional Native world views. "Multicultural science," she says, "suggests that our understanding of the world may be illuminated if we are willing to admit more than one truth" (p. 17).

Heritage science and education students also work in partnership with the local Toppenish Tribal School, strengthening young peoples' own understanding by teaching science concepts and providing role models for Indian youth. Jessica Sutterlict, a Winnebago Santee Dakota environmental science and botany student, visited the Tribal School to teach about native plants and their medicinal value, bringing examples from her field work for students to examine. In physics, Heritage students have taught principles of evaporation, condensation, and structural engineering by helping Tribal School students build a sweat lodge for healing rituals. As environmental science professor Pat Falco says in her Tennessee drawl, "we teach the science and bring in Yakama elders to teach the traditions." Science faculty members teach students not just to "hear it," but also to "see it, say it, do it, do it in groups."

Summary Reflections on Effective Intercultural Teaching and Learning

What have we said here? A summary of the Heritage principles and best practices for intercultural education mentioned in this chapter would go something like this:

- Start where students are, and make connections with their lives, work, families, cultures, religious traditions, developmental concerns, and career aspirations.
- Use student stories to affirm their voices, honor their backgrounds, and connect their prior experiences and previous understandings with core course concepts and desired learning outcomes.
- Use interactive, active, collaborative, student-centered learning methods that encourage students to construct meaning themselves.
- Immerse students in hands-on, closely supervised, constructivist activities typical of the discipline, practiced and assessed over and over again ("time on task").
- Involve students in civic engagement, service-learning, and problem-based, even entrepreneurial inquiry, research projects in their own local communities and natural field sites.
- Build student self-confidence and motivation by providing opportunities for success, by giving prompt and thorough feedback on their work, and by showing genuine concern about their academic progress.
- Be challenging and supportive (tough love), hold realistically high expectations, and use study groups and other interventions, especially for at-risk students.
- Do not be afraid of emotions. Teach to both minds and hearts. Honor the affective, inner life (the heart) and rigorous critical thinking (the head), and understand the relationship among cognitive, affective, and even spiritual learning.
- Teach important new concepts at least two or three different ways, and provide frequent opportunities for meta-cognitive reflection, integration, and synthesis.

- Establish classroom rituals and guidelines, and develop active listening and other interpersonal skills to make classrooms safe for discussion, disagreement, and multiple perspectives, all of which lead to deeper intercultural understanding.
- Respect students both individually and culturally by seeing—truly seeing, hearing, and honoring—who they are holistically.

Except for perhaps the last two points, how is this list specifically about good *intercultural* practices? Are not these principles and practices the same as the seven principles of good practice (Chickering & Gamson, 1987) as updated by Bransford, Brown, and Cocking (2000), Zull (2002), and many other cognitive science and educational researchers on learning? Are not, then, the principles and best practices of effective intercultural education virtually the same as for *any* effective learning?

Consider, as one example, the "pedagogical suggestions" made by Warren (1998–99), a national leader in diversity education. In her article on "Class in the Classroom," Warren cites several principles to enhance learning for students "regardless of their background" (p. 2): being explicit about classroom norms and expectations; knowing one's students; varying learning strategies to include collaboration and group work; using examples from class (and we would add cultural) perspectives; and being a model in accepting differences. But are not Warren's superb set of suggestions virtually identical to good educational practices in general?

The "virtually" qualifier is instructive, especially given the rapidly changing cultural faces of the future of American higher education. What is most distinctive—and instructive—about Heritage is its effectiveness with its multicultural students. We suggest three intersecting reasons, each having to do with context. First, Heritage's institutional mission holds "cultural pluralism within our own and other communities" and the "honoring of each person's human dignity and potential" as core values, not just in rhetoric but in daily practice (Heritage University, 2004, p. 3). Valuing and practicing intercultural learning pervades everyday activities, in class and out. Second, that practice happens not only in required program courses such as Multicultural Education, Managing Business Diversity, Cultural Diversity and Social Justice, and Comm. 305, but also, as we have seen, in most courses across the disciplines and professional programs at Heritage. Third, the student population itself is so thoroughly diverse, making the pervasive intercultural learning richer and more meaningful.

Because intercultural teaching and learning is extremely challenging as well as pervasive, Heritage faculty members are constantly learning from each other. With so many at-risk, multicultural, often marginalized students at the center of institutional attention, the Center for Intercultural Learning and Teaching, which we facilitate, is synonymous with the institution itself. The entire university is, in fact, a "center" for intercultural learning and teaching, where the margins have moved to the center, a pattern likely to follow throughout American higher education. The examples of effective intercultural learning and teaching we have described are illuminating, for the diverse multicultural faces at Heritage University today increasingly will be the faces in other institutions tomorrow and for decades to come.

References

Adams, M., Bell, L. A., & Griffin, P. (Eds.). (1997). *Teaching for diversity and social justice: A sourcebook.* New York, NY: Routledge.

Border, L. L. B., & Chism, N. V. N. (Eds.). (1992). *New directions for teaching and learning: No. 49. Teaching for diversity.* San Francisco, CA: Jossey-Bass.

Bransford, J. D., Brown, A. L., & Cocking, R. R. (Eds.). (2000). *How people learn: Brain, mind, experience, and school* (Expanded ed.). Washington, DC: National Academies Press.

Buckley, A. (2000, Spring). Tipi technology. *Teaching Tolerance, 17,* 14–17.

Chickering, A. W., & Gamson, Z. F. (1987, June). Seven principles for good practice in undergraduate education. *AAHE Bulletin, 39*(7), 3–7.

Coles, R. (1989). *The call of stories: Teaching and the moral imagination.* Boston, MA: Houghton Mifflin.

Creswell, J. W. (1998). *Qualitative inquiry and research design: Choosing among five traditions.* Thousand Oaks, CA: Sage.

Damasio, A. R. (1994). *Descartes' error: Emotion, reason, and the human brain.* New York, NY: G. P. Putnam.

Frederick, P. (1995, Summer). Walking on eggs: Mastering the dreaded diversity discussion. *College Teaching, 43*(3), 83–92.

Frederick, P. J. (1991). The medicine wheel: Emotions and connections in the classroom. In K. J. Zahorski (Ed.), *To improve the academy: Vol. 10. Resources for student, faculty, and institutional development* (pp. 197–214). Stillwater, OK: New Forums Press.

Heritage University. (2004). *Heritage University catalog, 2004–2006.* (2004). Toppenish, WA: Author.

Kolb, D. A. (1984). *Experiential learning: Experience as the source of learning and development.* Upper Saddle River, NJ: Prentice Hall.

LeDoux, J. (1996). *The emotional brain: The mysterious underpinnings of emotional life.* New York, NY: Touchstone.

Levine, A., & Cureton J. S. (1998). *When hope and fear collide: A portrait of today's college student.* San Francisco, CA: Jossey-Bass.

Lincoln, Y. S., & Guba, E. G. (1985). *Naturalistic inquiry.* Newbury Park, CA: Sage.

Millem, J. F., Chang, M. J., & Antonio, A. L. (2005). *Making diversity work on campus: A research-based perspective.* Washington, DC: Association of American Colleges and Universities.

National Survey of Student Engagement. (2004). *Student engagement: Pathways to collegiate success.* Bloomington, IN: Center for Postsecondary Research, Indiana University Bloomington.

Ouellett, M. L. (Ed.). (2005). *Teaching inclusively: Resources for course, department, and institutional change in higher education.* Stillwater, OK: New Forums Press.

Schank, R. C. (1990). *Tell me a story: Narrative and intelligence.* Evanston, IL: Northwestern University Press.

Shulman, L. S. (1999, July/August). Taking learning seriously. *Change, 31*(4), 10–17.

Tatum, B. D. (1997). *"Why are all the black kids sitting together in the cafeteria?" and other conversations about race.* New York, NY: Basic Books.

Warren, L. (1998–99). Class in the classroom. *Essays on Teaching Excellence, 10*(2).

Witherell, C., & Noddings, N. (Ed.). (1991). *Stories lives tell: Narrative and dialogue in education.* New York, NY: Teachers College Press.

Yoder, M. K. (1997, Fall). The consequences of a generic approach to teaching nursing in a multicultural world. *Journal of Cultural Diversity, 4*(3), 77–82.

Zull, J. E. (2002). *The art of changing the brain: Enriching the practice of teaching by exploring the biology of learning.* Sterling, VA: Stylus.

12

How Do You Handle This Situation? Responses by Faculty in Great Britain and the United States to Workshops on the Ethics of Teaching

Miriam Rosalyn Diamond
Northwestern University

Faculty in the United States and Great Britain took part in workshops exploring educational ethics. Participants articulated concerns about balancing approachability with fairness, cross-cultural communication, conveying standards to students, and academic integrity. Responses to the session were positive, and both groups indicated an interest in continuing discourse on the topic. The groups differed on specific issues of interest, as well as feedback on the session. Some of these appear to be culturally influenced. Overall, this workshop presents a model for providing faculty with the opportunity to examine and formulate direction when dealing with ethical issues related to teaching.

> You are asked to provide a graduate school recommendation on behalf of a student who did not perform well in your subject area. You hear that some learners were offended by a comment you made in class. You run into a few members of your course through an off-campus community group to which you belong. A student asks for extra time on a test, but cannot verify having a disability. What do you do?

Professors in the United States do not always receive extensive preparation for their roles as instructors. While such training is much more standard in Great Britain, formal discussions on recognizing and effectively dealing with ethical dilemmas related to teaching are not commonplace. Yet professors in both countries frequently face predicaments in interactions with students that call for reflection and judgment when responding, and which may have broader reaching implications beyond the immediate situation.

What types of ethical issues arise in teaching? Are faculty concerned about these issues? How can an exploration of ethics foster reflection, enhance professional development, and facilitate optimal ways of dealing with the situation? What is the response of academics to this type of exploration? What differences and similarities are there in holding discussions on this issue in different cultures?

This chapter describes an approach used to foster discussion on ethical matters involved in university teaching in both the United States and Great Britain. In response to cultural differences, some variation in the specific topics addressed in each setting was introduced. The facilitator collected faculty responses at the conclusion of the seminars.

Defining Ethics in Teaching

The word *ethics* originates from the Greek *ethos,* meaning character. Ethics can be viewed as a moral code. People also refer to ethics as an incentive system for choosing among behaviors, based on ideas of right and wrong. Synonyms include *belief, conduct, conscience, convention, criteria, decency, goodness, honor, integrity, principles, standards,* and *value.* Ray (1996) points out that the meaning of ethics may range from theoretical inquiry into what is "good" for the community to a more applied discourse of concrete expectations and consequences. Contemporary uses of the term tend to stress actions and outcomes rather than the ideas and motivations behind them.

Articulating ethics provides a guideline or foundation that can inform behavior and decision-making. Ethical statements may be particularly useful for people who need to deal with complex situations while under pressure to contend with several different and competing demands.

Many professional fields have developed codes of ethics. Among these is the American Association of University Professors' (1987) "Statement on Professional Ethics." This report states,

> As teachers, professors encourage the free pursuit of learning in their students. They hold before them the best scholarly and ethical standards of their discipline. Professors demonstrate respect for students as individuals and adhere to their proper roles as intellectual guides and counselors. Professors make every reasonable effort to foster

> honest academic conduct and to ensure that their evaluations of students reflect each student's true merit. They respect the confidential nature of the relationship between professor and student. They avoid any exploitation, harassment, or discriminatory treatment of students. They acknowledge significant academic or scholarly assistance from them. They protect their academic freedom.

Issues arise even where there are efforts to establish standards for ethical behavior. Some have their origin in faculty actions such as taking advantage of student work, using class time to promote unrelated causes, and making analogies that students may find offensive. Multiple relationships between professors and students as well as unclear interpersonal boundaries can set the stage for inappropriate interactions, exploitation, and harassment (Callahan, 1982 ; Klein, 2006). Other concerns—including academic dishonesty, attempts to manipulate the grading process, intolerance of others' perspectives, and erratic behavior—may arise from student conduct, thereby calling for professors to formulate a response.

Brown and Krager (1985, p. 405) applied a counseling psychology taxonomy to faculty ethical practices. Categories include *autonomy* (such as tolerance of student perspectives that differ from the professor's), *nonmaleficence* (as in differentiating personal viewpoints from facts), *beneficence* (e.g., varying teaching methodologies to suit individual student needs), *justice* (e.g., providing equitable time and opportunity to all students), and *fidelity* (e.g., accessibility outside of class time).

Braxton and Bayer (1999) surveyed more than 1,000 professors regarding what they saw as unsuitable conduct by their colleagues. Respondents' statements fell into seven categories, including being condescending to students, having inappropriate interactions with students, being unprepared to teach, having inconsistent grading policies, unreliability, not communicating course-related information to students, and refusing to participate in education-related activities such as advising.

Undergraduates at several universities identified similar behaviors as being problematic. In one study, 50 respondents articulated which faculty actions they found most objectionable (Johnston, 2004). Most frequently cited were arriving to class late, failing to keep office hours as stated, insulting students, disregarding email messages, making no effort to become acquainted with students, and not adhering to the course syllabus. In another investigation, students ranked specific behaviors according to the level of ethical appropriateness or inappropriateness (Kuther, 2003). Given a list of 25 actions, the greatest ethical violations from the learners' perspectives were teaching while under the influence of drugs or alcohol, publicly shaming students, and violating student confidentiality. Accepting valuable presents from students caused greater concern than low-cost gifts.

These actions on the part of faculty can, in turn, promote unethical practices on the part of students. Wilson (1982) maintains that ethical matters are often the result of unequal distribution of power in education. He stresses student vulnerability, reliance on good grades, lack of learner input in shaping curriculum, and unclear performance expectations in classes as some of the conditions that contribute to learner misconduct. Difficulties can also arise from low student engagement and meaningless coursework. Kuther (2003) addresses the issue of faculty responsibility and accountability by saying

> Professors must be cognizant of student expectations and should begin to reflect on their behavior both in and out of the classroom. It appears that professors hold not merely a professional obligation to their students, but a moral one as well. (p. 159)

Worsfold (2002) adds that instructors should "realize the need to be inside ethics" (p. 42); to devote themselves to mindfully working through ways of dealing with ethical dilemmas, rather than simply responding in a way that seems to be most convenient at the moment. If educators are encouraged to articulate and maintain a code of behavior, he notes,

> Ethical consistency builds a sense of dependability on the part of those making the moral decisions; ethical consistency develops trust between those making the moral decisions and those affected by those decisions; ethical consistency saves those making moral decisions from the process of ever renewing their moral stance each time they are confronted by having to address a moral dilemma; ethical consistency allows its practitioners a sense of moral integrity in their morality. (p. 44)

Can faculty be supported in an effort to define and identify constructive codes of behavior regarding interactions with students? A number of experts have considered this matter.

Fostering Exploration of Ethics Among Faculty

Despite the fact that issues arise, ethics is often overlooked as a subject explicitly addressed in the training of instructors. One explanation of this situation is that "college teaching [is often] not recognized as a distinct profession"

(Klein, 2006). Additionally, the autonomous nature of education can cause incidents involving ethical decision-making and actions to go undisclosed outside the classroom or office where they occur (Svinicki, 1999). A review of sample faculty teaching center curricula in both the United Kingdom and the United States reveals workshops dealing with student academic dishonesty as well as diversity in the classroom, but few, if any, sessions explicitly devoted to the development of ethical behavior on the part of instructors.

Callahan (1982) argues that colleges should go beyond simply developing a code of behavior: They should develop programs and events to promote open discourse regarding ethical concerns, expectations, and implications. Such discussions can promote awareness and reflection among all members of the academic community. Larger questions about the role of the university and the goals of the faculty can be examined and articulated in this light.

De Russey (2003) suggests institutions show their commitment to fostering ethical behavior by providing annual reports on programming provided in this area. Trustees can promote, even require, attendance at programs to spur members of the academy to realize high standards of behavior. Case-based workshops for new, experienced, and future professors are among the programming De Russey recommends.

Another example of such programming is Worsfold's (2002) session for novice teachers. The goal of this gathering is to foster reflection on the role of ethics in the lives of attendees, with particular focus on their work as educators. He does this by directing participants to describe difficult situations they have faced in teaching. He urges them to consider what differentiates an ethical predicament from other types of concerns. Group members then discuss their own ethical codes and how these play out in all aspects of their lives. Finally, Worsfold asks the instructors to look at the importance and types of principles that affect instruction.

Some universities have introduced creative techniques to foster awareness of ethical issues among faculty. "A Question of Academic Ethics" is a board game developed for adjunct faculty at the University of Maryland (Sugar & Willet, 1994). In this activity, facilitators provide teams of participants with case studies and ask them to choose among multiple-choice responses. The facilitators then award points based on the predetermined appropriateness of each option. Topics include textbook selection, grading policies, and copyright laws. In post-workshop surveys, nearly 90% of the participants reported an increased awareness of ethical considerations related to course development. Clemson University uses a similar game in training biology teaching assistants (Haag, Christopher, Cummings, Dickey, & Gilder, 1999).

Games like these help faculty focus on specific types of situations they may face. However, given the many variables operating simultaneously, it is often difficult to determine that one and only one course of action is always the most correct or appropriate. Open-ended scenarios can foster unrestricted deliberations that can move in myriad directions, without concern about getting points for the "right answer." For instance, the vignette in which a student offers his or her professor a gift may lead to discussions about classmate perception of favoritism, expressions of apprehension about students trying to "buy" grades, conversations on whether faculty-student contact can differ during and after the term, debates about whether the nature and value of the gift should be a factor for consideration, or an opportunity to call attention to cultural diversity as it plays out in the meaning of gift-giving for students from different backgrounds. Given few constraints, each conversation can follow the interests, concerns, experiences, and perspectives of the particular group attending.

Furthermore, it is more valuable for participants to develop a set of principles that will guide them when issues arise than to merely generate or memorize one response to each of the situations provided in the workshop and be unprepared when faced with dissimilar situations. While all aspects of faculty life have implications for ethical behavior, there are so many issues involving teaching and interactions with students that it is worthwhile to conduct a session primarily emphasizing this realm of conduct.

The Ethics of Teaching Workshop

History and Development

As the literature indicates, it is prudent for instructors to examine ethical concerns and articulate their moral codes in relation to genuine situations that may arise. A group setting provides an ideal environment in which to foster deliberation and discourse. In response to these considerations, an instructional developer created a scenario-based ethics of teaching workshop.

The workshop, "Ethics and Teaching: Tools for Addressing Dilemmas," has its origins in a program created for teaching assistants (Diamond, 2002, 2003). Faculty conveyed an interest in having an opportunity to address these issues as well. The initial session was then adapted for professionals with a more experienced and sophisticated perspective on instruction, as well as greater accountability for their work.

This session provided time usually not available for faculty to contribute to and draw on group wisdom in considering alternative actions and possible implications. The prime objective of this workshop was to foster group exploration into ethical quandaries that faculty commonly face in their interactions with students. Through discussion and sharing, the aims were to develop increased sensitivity to ethical concerns that arise in the educational realm on a regular basis. This was done by increasing professors' understanding about what constitutes such a dilemma, promoting insight into the many underlying issues involved in these situations, and encouraging participants to share perspectives on the range and implications of possible courses of action. Other goals included identifying principles to guide and give instructors a foundation for developing their own standards for behavior, and to increase their awareness of resources available to support them in dealing with these issues. Participants also had the opportunity to share their own experiences and quandaries and the means they have developed to address concerns.

The philosophy behind this exercise is that there often are several ways to respond to ethical dilemmas. However, it is important to be aware of implications and possible consequences of various actions. Through the personalization of situations, reflection, exchange of ideas, experiences with peers, and brainstorming, the workshop leader encouraged participants to note how seemingly simple circumstances warrant thoughtful, and often prepared, action on their part.

Workshop Format

This workshop was offered as a half-day session in the United Kingdom to 21 faculty in a large urban university. The facilitator expanded it to a day-long program as part of a multi-day conference for state university faculty in the United States. Twenty-eight faculty members participated in this meeting. In both sessions, participation was voluntary and included faculty from a variety of disciplines (including allied health professions, communications, computer science, engineering, English, management, marketing, mathematics, psychology) with varying amounts of teaching experience. In Britain, the workshop was held on a university campus. Teaching center staff publicized the program via a flyer and email notification circulated to faculty, and those interested preregistered for the program. In the United States, this session was one of four concurrent sessions offered at the conference. Conference organizers provided information electronically prior to the event and requested preregistration.

The heart of this workshop was discussion and sharing. Participants formed groups of three with colleagues from other disciplines whom they did not previously know well. Each group addressed two unique scenarios based on predicaments often faced by instructors. The facilitator had collected these scenarios through personal teaching experience and discussions with instructors (see Appendix 12.1 for examples). The descriptions of these dilemmas were short (a few sentences), rather than detailed cases. The intent was to provide enough specificity to convey the (potential) predicament, yet remain general enough to encourage each participant to draw on their own background, current circumstances, the context of their campuses and student population, and the perspective they brought into reading and interpreting the situations. In addition, the objective of this exercise was to focus on discussion, rather than reading and understanding the details of a case. As in real life, faculty do not know all the details, motivations, and circumstances when interacting with students. As Fisch (1996) notes,

> Brevity requires that material be left out, forcing participants to speculate on the precipitating causes of problems, the historical precedents, and a multitude of other factors that mimic circumstances that we face in real life. As a result, they jump into the discussion, literally making themselves, their emotions, and their responses part of it. Furthermore, by being succinct in our discussion kickoff we allow maximum time for participant interaction, the essential aspect of the session. (p. 92)

For each scenario, participants read the dilemma, collectively identified the core issues at hand, worked together to brainstorm possible responses to the event, and decided as a group what course of action they would most likely pursue. This was emphasized over the decision they "should" take, as there may be several appropriate ways to address each matter. In addition, contextual factors such as energy available, time constraints, other job demands, and additional considerations often influence the actions one is likely to take. If time permitted, they did the same with the second predicament.

Following small group discussions, each group presented their dilemmas to all the participants. They disclosed the key influences they thought were operating in each situation and described the response they chose, as well as the justification for this choice. Some role-played the scenario and possible responses. The entire group was encouraged to respond by asking questions of the presenters. These questions usually added insights or drew on personal experiences in similar situations (e.g., "Have you thought about..." or "Why did you rule out... as an option?"). They also built on perspectives and implications that may have been lacking in the suggested course of action. Questions had the power to open up discussion, where comments had the possibility of closing it down.

After wrapping up discussion, the facilitator presented the group with questions designed to encourage reflection on the dimensions of Professionalism, Reliability, Open-mindedness, and Fairness (PROF) as related to ethical decision-making (see Appendix 12.2). Questions included: Are you clear about your role and responsibilities? Do you know when and where to refer students who need help beyond your area of expertise? Are you comfortable communicating what you can and cannot do for students? The facilitator then provided a list of campus offices (developed in collaboration with local contacts) that could assist in addressing dilemmas. This list included campus mediation services, tutoring offices, and departments for students with disabilities.

Because of the extra time allotted, the US group also participated in a fishbowl-style role-play regarding the "gray area" of faculty-student interactions: How to deal with distraught, demanding students asking for extra help from an instructor who is under pressure to meet other professional and personal obligations. One dyad would role-play the situation, followed by a group discussion identifying the approaches observers and presenters found most effective. Similar situations were role-played repeatedly by different participants to demonstrate variations and options in addressing the same issues. In the next portion of the program, the group brainstormed, drafted, and shared lesson plans for addressing disciplinary ethical issues with students in their own classes.

At the conclusion of the program, all participants replied to two open-ended questions: What is the most useful idea you got from this session? and What questions do you now have on this topic?

Participant Reactions

In both countries, faculty were eager to discuss these scenarios and related issues. The comments and questions raised by each scenario provoked extensive debate and deliberation, with people sharing related circumstances they personally faced. They chose to focus on a number of issues, including the balance between being accessible to students while maintaining impartiality and fairness, sensitivity to diverse cultural backgrounds, the responsibility faculty have in dealing with student prejudices, clearly conveying expectations to students, and addressing suspected academic dishonesty.

Participants at the American conference were asked how they define ethics. They described it as "a system of actions and responses [involving] integrity and fairness." According to the participants, ethics involves a "balance of care and justice in decision-making," "adhering to university standards," and "doing least harm." They spoke about "behaving rightly" to benefit the "greater good" while maintaining "professional standards." Their definition of ethics included "modeling behavior for students" and developing "value-driven decision-making."

While nearly all participants completed the questionnaire at the end of the session, in both workshops some chose to answer only one of the two questions. Table 12.1 shows what workshop attendees found most valuable in the program. The British faculty found the overall guidelines to be the most useful aspect. One participant appreciated "the top ten tips for Ethical Teaching—really useful session. Allowed me to feel more confident about my role as a lecturer and that my concerns are the same as many others in the group." The second most commonly cited highlight was the direction they received for addressing specific dilemmas. For example, one participant reported that a suggestion to "tell the student who asks a question 'I don't know,' to look it up, and report back to class next time" was most helpful.

TABLE 12.1

What Participants Found Most Useful in the Session

Category	**UK Responses** (n = 19)	**US Responses** (n = 26)	**Overall** (n = 45)
General guidelines for addressing ethical dilemmas	37%	11.5%	22.5%
Direction for dealing with specific issues	21%	23%	22.5%
Sharing and hearing colleagues' perspectives	16%	—	7%
Reflecting on dilemmas	10%	—	4%
Teaching approaches modeled/articulated	—	53%	31%
Appreciation for topic complexity	—	9 %	4%
Other	16%	3.5%	9%

A number of the British professors indicated that participating in the discourse and having an opportunity to reflect were the most enlightening features of the session. For example, one found it "Very interesting to hear other people's viewpoints—using colleagues more as a sounding board."

The American cohort's responses varied somewhat from their British peers. More than one-half of this group stated that the most helpful feature of the session was inspiration for introducing ethics in their own classrooms. They developed this motivation in part from the modeling of approaches used in the workshop and in part from a discussion specifically on this topic. One workshop member valued the following aspects: "the pedagogical entertainment value of 'role playing.' The phrase 'impression management' was very helpful for it gives me a term/a name to use in class when I address questions of ethics and personal choices in class."

Like their European counterparts, about one-fifth of this group indicated that suggestions for dealing with particular situations came in handy. For instance, as a result of the discussion, one professor is now planning "To post a solution set when I know I'll be behind in returning student papers." The general principles, as in "developing accountability, responsibility, personal choices," assumed third position in the most commonly cited useful feature in the American session.

While none of the Americans acknowledged the discussion process in itself to be the most valuable aspect, some did acknowledge having gained insight into the complexity of ethical issues. One participant benefited from "The idea that there are many more technical considerations out there in the profession than I had previously imagined," while another learned that "Ethics is much more complex than one thinks."

Table 12.2 illustrates questions participants felt the workshop raised or left unanswered. More than one-third of the British group said the workshop produced additional questions pertaining to particular incidents, such as cases of plagiarism by peers, receiving specific kinds of gifts from students, and faculty who date their students despite being told that it is inappropriate. Some wanted more information on general ethical issues, including concerns arising out of the increased use of technology in education. The same number of participants in this workshop also desired more information and resources, including books and web sites, on the theory behind ethical awareness and behavior. In comparison, the largest group of American responses to this item pertained to obtaining more general information. One raised the question of "How to promote a culture of ethical behavior in the professoriate."

TABLE 12.2

Questions Raised by and/or Remaining After the Session

Category	**UK Responses** (n = 20)	**US Responses** (n = 25)	**Overall** (n = 45)
Ways to address specific situations	35%	16%	24%
More on general issues	25%	24%	24%
Additional references /theoretical constructs	25%	16%	20%
Ways to instruct students on ethics	—	12%	7%
No questions at this time	15%	20%	18%
Other/feedback	0%	12%	7%

Although about one-fifth of this group stated they had no further questions, some did have particular situations in mind, such as one participant who wondered how to support students who have emotional difficulties without "feeling like I'm 'passing the buck' to a counseling center." This category was tied in frequency of responses with those who wanted more theory and references. Because fostering discussions on ethics in their classes was touched on in the American group, a number of participants wanted more direction in this area. Other responses included general faculty conduct, such as the propriety of requiring students to buy a textbook one has written, what to do about "incentives" provided by publishers for choosing their products, and the obligations of faculty engaged in extensive consulting or small businesses on the side.

Discussion

The ethics workshop engaged experienced faculty in exploration and discussion of important situations and concerns frequently raised in the teaching process. There were some interesting commonalities and discrepancies in the topics discussed, as well as the ways in which the American and British groups responded to the sessions.

Similarities Between Countries

Both sets of participants were eager to discuss diversity and the way these dynamics play out in their classrooms. American and British faculty chose to spend a good deal of time talking about how their actions and comments are perceived by students from different cultures.

In their written comments on the session, more than one-fifth of attendees in both workshops indicated that they gained direction for addressing specific situations which they had experienced. In both sessions, about one-quarter of respondents found that the session led to further questions about dealing with ethical issues in general. Several of the American and British faculty stated they were interested in spending more time examining theories of ethical behavior, as well as receiving more references on the topic. At the end of each session, nearly one-fifth indicated that all their questions had been answered. There were members of both groups who desired continuing discussions on ethics at their campuses and intended to develop formats for doing so.

While there were commonalities in how the groups responded to the session, there were also some dissimilarities. Some of these appear to be based in cultural-institutional differences, others reflected variations in the material addressed.

Differences Between the Groups

The process of writing and grading examinations in the United Kingdom is very highly regulated. The standard is for external examiners to validate the way faculty scored and tallied each student's work. Therefore, concerns around student negotiation of re-grades and grade changes do not present the same challenges they do in the US. The discussion among British faculty seemed more focused on navigating the balance between being accessible to and maintaining their objectivity. Perhaps this is in part the result of working in a system that institutionalizes objectivity and fairness. In response to the question about what aspects of the session were most valuable, some British participants mentioned the usefulness of the very act of discussing and debating issues with peers.

The topic of grading commanded a lot of discussion on the part of the US cohort. The topic of group work—assigning, facilitating, mediating, and grading—was emphasized more among the Americans. There may be greater use of graded group assignments in this culture. These activities raise a number of concerns unique to this kind of task.

While most of the Americans seemed to appreciate the discussion component of the workshop, none of them identified that in itself as a major contributor to their knowledge. This could be because they were more outcome- than process-oriented, and more focused on the application to their own situations. It is also possible that British education and culture in general place a greater emphasis on the intrinsic value of argument and discourse.

Unlike their British colleagues, some participants in the American session stated they gained an appreciation of the complexity of the subject as a result of participating in the workshop. Also, the longer American workshop allowed for a discussion on addressing disciplinary ethics with students. Many participants found this topic most useful, and several wanted to pursue it further.

These comments help illuminate the ways in which interested faculty perceive ethical concerns. They also provide information about the ways in which they respond to the opportunity for exploration and discussion of these matters. Additional research can inform future projects aimed at increasing awareness and constructive response to issues on the part of instructors.

Recommendations for Future Research

There is virtually no data available about the long-term effects of ethics training on behavior. Does participation in a program like this lead to better-informed, more confident instructors who make more prudent decisions when facing complex interactions with students? Longitudinal studies would be useful in tracking the session's influence on faculty decision-making and actions. One way to do this is through questionnaires presented one semester or academic year following the workshop to investigate if and how participants implemented guidelines developed during the session. One set of questionnaires could go to participants, another to a matched set of professors (similar disciplines, years of experience, etc.) who did not attend the program. Responses by the two groups could then be compared.

One could begin to measure the workshop's effect by asking attendees to complete pre- and post-workshop surveys regarding ways they approach situations that have ethical implications. Participants could respond to the post-workshop survey several months after the session to track actual changes in thought and behavior.

Another measure of the workshop's effectiveness would be student perceptions of classroom management and interactions. Researchers could survey learners in classes with faculty workshop participants before and after training to note changes in their reported experiences. Similarly, investigators could tally the number of student complaints to departments such as affirmative action and deans' offices to identify if the introduction of programs of this type impacts the quantity of grievances filed.

Through studies like these, researchers can come to a more complete understanding of the impact of workshop participation on attitudes and actions.

Summary

Faculty in both the United States and the United Kingdom commonly face ethical predicaments related to their roles as teachers. Participants in a workshop bringing these concerns to the forefront responded positively to the program; indeed, participants seemed eager to discuss these issues and thankful for a forum to do so. This study demonstrates that such a program can be adapted to suit varying cultures and concerns. There were similarities and differences in how the two groups responded to the program, some of which were culturally influenced. As a result of the sessions, faculty articulated increased awareness and appreciation of the issues involved, as well as considerations to keep in mind when dealing with these situations.

References

American Association of University Professors. (1987). *Statement on professional ethics.* Retrieved June 17, 2006, from www.aaup.org/statements/Redbook/Rbethics.htm

Braxton, J. M., & Bayer, A. E. (1999). *Faculty misconduct in collegiate teaching.* Baltimore, MD: Johns Hopkins University Press.

Brown, R. D., & Krager, L. (1985). Ethical issues in graduate education: Faculty and student responsibilities. *Journal of Higher Education, 56*(4), 403–418.

Callahan, D. (1982, May/June). Should there be an academic code of ethics? *Journal of Higher Education, 53*(3), 335–344.

De Russy, C. (2003, September 19). Professional ethics begin on the college campus. *The Chronicle of Higher Education,* p. B20.

Diamond, M. R. (2002). Preparing TAs to respond to ethical dilemmas. In W. Davis, J. Smith, & R. Smith (Eds.), *Ready to teach: Graduate teaching assistants prepare for today and for tomorrow* (pp. 47–50). Stillwater, OK: New Forums Press.

Diamond, M. R. (2003). How would you handle this situation? Teaching assistant responses to an ethics workshop. *Journal of Graduate Teaching Assistant Development, 9*(2), 89–96.

Fisch, L. (1996). *New directions for teaching and learning: No. 66. Ethical dimensions of college and university teaching: Understanding and honoring the special relationship between teachers and students.* San Francisco, CA: Jossey-Bass.

Haag, M., Christopher, K., Cummings, J., Dickey, J., & Gilder, B. (1999). *Effective methods of training biology laboratory teaching assistants.* Retrieved June 17, 2006, from the University of Toronto, Department of Zoology web site: www.zoo.utoronto.ca/able/volumes/vol-21/22-haag.pdf

Johnston, K. (2004). *MSU thoughts on teaching #10: What undergraduates say are the most irritating faculty behaviors.* Retrieved June 26, 2006, from the Michigan State University, Teaching Assistant Program web site: http://tap.msu.edu/PDF/thoughts/tt10.pdf

Klein, J. (2006). A collegiate dilemma: The lack of formal training in ethics for professors. *Journal of College and Character,* 2. Retrieved June 17, 2006, from www.collegevalues.org/articles.cfm?a=1&id=1416

Kuther, T. L. (2003). A profile of the ethical professor: Student views. *College Teaching, 51*(4), 153–160.

Ray, T. T. (1996). Differentiating the related concepts of ethics, morality, law, and justice. In L. Fisch (Ed.), *New directions for teaching and learning: No. 66. Ethical dimensions of college and university teaching: Understanding and honoring the special relationship between teachers and students* (pp. 47–54). San Francisco, CA: Jossey-Bass.

Sugar, S. E., & Willet, C. A. (1994). The game of academic ethics: The partnering of a board game. In E. C. Wadsworth (Ed.), *To improve the academy: Vol. 13. Resources for faculty, instructional, and organizational development* (pp. 121–131). Stillwater, OK: New Forums Press.

Svinicki, M. (1999). Ethics in college teaching. In W. J. McKeachie, *Teaching tips: Strategies, research, and theory for college and university teachers* (10th ed., pp. 289–300). Boston, MA: Houghton Mifflin.

Wilson, E. K. (1982, May/June). Power, pretense, and piggybacking: Some ethical issues in teaching. *Journal of Higher Education, 53*(3), 268–281.

Worsfold, V. L. (2002). A workshop on the ethics of teaching. In W. Davis, J. Smith, & R. Smith (Eds.), *Ready to teach: Graduate teaching assistants prepare for today and for tomorrow* (pp. 41–46). Stillwater, OK: New Forums Press.

Appendix 12.1

Sample Dilemmas for Group Discussion

1) Your students have just completed their final examination for the class. After you collect the papers, a very upset group of students approaches you and tells you that the people sitting in front of them were passing notes and cheating throughout the entire test. You haven't observed any suspicious activity yourself. How do you proceed?

2) A student you taught two years ago approaches you asking for a letter of recommendation to graduate school. You recall that this student did not perform well in your class. Her attendance was poor, her grades mediocre at best. What do you tell her?

3) You have assigned student papers on a topic related to your area of research. One student comes up with an idea that had not occurred to you, and you feel that it would be a nice addition to the paper you are currently writing. How can you integrate it into your work?

4) You notice that some of your international students attend religious services the same place that you do. Your place of worship has a policy that members invite others to their homes who have nowhere to spend holiday meals. Every year, your family participates in this program by having some people over. This year, the coordinator asks if you will host some of your own students. What do you do?

5) As you are calculating final grades for the term, a student approaches you requesting a grade change. He is concerned that the C he is about to receive may jeopardize his scholarship. You would like to see him continue his studies. Consequently, you review his work, but cannot find justification for raising the grade. How should you address the situation?

6) You inherited a course rather close to the start of the semester and decided to stick with the previous instructor's choice of readings. In the middle of the term, you are approached by several students. They are upset by some of the readings, which they feel portray their ethnic culture inaccurately. They are afraid that classmates unfamiliar with their culture will get a biased and negative impression, and that this might promote prejudice. What can you do?

Appendix 12.2

PROF: Questions for Reflection

A professor should keep in mind the following qualities when addressing ethical concerns:

*P*rofessionalism
*R*eliability/accessibility
*O*pen-mindedness
*F*airness

Professionalism

- Do you project a professional demeanor at all times?
- Do you set a good example for your students?
- Do you cite student work appropriately in your own research?
- Are you clear about your role and responsibilities?
- Do you know when and where to refer students who need help beyond your area of expertise?
- Are you comfortable communicating what you can and cannot do for students?

Reliability/Accessibility

- Do you grade and return assignments in a timely manner, with sufficient feedback so students can learn from your comments?
- Are students clear about how their final grades will be determined?
- Are you available to help students?
- Do they feel comfortable approaching you with questions?

Open-mindedness

- Do students feel comfortable in your class?
- Do you create an atmosphere that is welcoming and safe for every student?
- Is your use of humor, metaphors, and so on unlikely to offend students?
- Do students know guidelines for appropriate interactions with their classmates?

Fairness

- Do students know how their work is being evaluated?
- Is it apparent that your grading is fair and that you apply the same standards (including opportunities for make-ups and extra credit) for all?
- Are your expectations for academic honesty clear and the consequences of dishonesty spelled out?
- Are you familiar with the university's guidelines regarding accommodations for students with disabilities?

13

In the Eye of the Storm: Students' Perceptions of Helpful Faculty Actions Following a Collective Tragedy

Therese A. Huston
Seattle University

Michele DiPietro
Carnegie Mellon University

On occasion, our campus communities are shaken by national tragedies such as Hurricane Katrina and the terrorist attacks of September 11, 2001, or by local tragedies such as the murder of a faculty member or student. Because these are unusual circumstances, faculty are often initially confused about how to respond, and later have little or no sense of how effective their actions have been (DiPietro, 2003). This chapter investigates the most common instructor responses following a tragedy and which of those responses students find most helpful. Implications for faculty and faculty developers are discussed.

Campus communities deal with tragedy on both the national and local level. In the past decade, students and faculty across the country have struggled with the implications of the destruction brought about by Hurricane Katrina, the 9/11 terrorist attacks, the Columbine shootings, and Matthew Shepard's brutal beating and death. Even though these events were geographically localized, their impact has been far-reaching. In particular, following Hurricane Katrina, students from the affected colleges and universities were relocated in institutions across all 50 states, generating unpredicted ripples in campus dynamics everywhere (Mangan, 2005). There are also local tragedies that receive less national attention but still leave faculty, staff, and students feeling frightened, angry, and vulnerable. For example, in fall 2002, a student at the University of Arizona–Tucson killed three professors in the nursing school with an automatic weapon before killing himself (Rooney, 2002). Another disturbing example occurred at Gallaudet University, where two students were murdered in the same dormitory within a period of a few months (Guterman, 2001). Sadly, these are only a few of the violent losses that campuses have faced in recent years.

Tragedies and disasters have a strong emotional and cognitive impact on students, even if the students are not directly affected by the catastrophe (Honos-Webb, Sunwolf, Hart, & Scalise, 2006; Silver, Holman, McIntosh, Poulin, & Gil-Rivas, 2002). Many students in the Boston area, for example, who were not directly impacted by the 9/11 terrorist attacks, were nonetheless severely affected psychologically for two months or more following the attacks (Liverant, Hofmann, & Litz, 2004). Recognizing the distress caused by natural and man-made disasters, the American Psychiatric Association (n.d.) has provided mental health guidelines to help college students deal with the loss and disruption caused by such tragedies.

Given the widespread impact of such tragedies, how do most campuses respond? Many college and university administrations have created crisis response teams, either in anticipation of or in response to a collective tragedy (Asmussen & Creswell, 1995; Farrell, 2001). Campus officials also increase support for the members of their community; many schools issue campus-wide policies to give everyone time to grieve, and university officials often create venues for students, faculty, and staff to learn more about the threatening events or to cope with heightened stress levels (e.g., Hurst, 1999). Administrators also have access to published guidelines on how to prepare a crisis response team, itemized lists of things to say and do immediately following a security threat, and recommendations for ensuring prompt and effective communication (Larson, 1994; Paine & Sprague, 2000; Whiting, Tucker, & Whaley, 2004).

Although administrators have benchmarks to follow before, during, and after a crisis, faculty members receive precious little guidance as to what to say or do in their classrooms. As a noteworthy exception, the Center for Research on Teaching and Learning at the University of Michigan (2004) has consistently assumed a leadership role on this issue by providing timely guidelines for discussions of Hurricane Katrina, the December 2004 tsunami, the war on Iraq, and 9/11 on the "Publications and Links" page of their web site. Other exceptions we uncovered include the Faculty Center for Excellence in Teaching at Western Kentucky University (2000), which produced a booklet of short papers and reports on "Teaching and Learning in a Time of Crisis," and

Michigan State University Libraries (2005), which compiled a list of resources for doing research on hurricanes as a way to address the Katrina crisis as a course project.

Given that faculty represent the arm of the campus community that has the most day-to-day student contact, it is crucial that they receive the tools to best support students in the context of their classes. This includes deciding whether to address the tragic events, and if so, knowing some different ways to do so and the comparative value of those options.

The crisis literature for administrators does not define which events constitute a crisis warranting a response from the administration. It only advises that the crisis management plans be as flexible as possible to include emergencies as diverse as crimes, natural disasters, suicide, plant failures, riots, bomb threats, disease, and scandals, among others (Larson 1994; Siegel 1994).

In the same vein, we too resist an inevitably narrow treatment of tragic events. Instead, this chapter reports the results of a study designed to categorize instructor responses, or lack thereof, following one specific crisis, the terrorist attacks of September 11, 2001. The survey asked students to identify how their instructors responded to the attacks and to evaluate the usefulness of those actions. Even though the survey refers to a specific event, all the strategies listed and collected generalize to other catastrophes, so that the insights from this research are widely applicable.

Literature Review

Clinical researchers have examined psychological interventions to help people cope with the events of 9/11, but their reports have focused on recommendations for psychologists and mental health professionals. For example, one study found that college students who participated in a journal writing exercise or who listened to a story that addressed themes relevant to the terrorist attacks showed greater improvements and fewer signs of trauma than a control condition (Honos-Webb et al., 2006). Another study found that adults who took an active approach, such as getting involved in their community efforts to help others, felt less distressed by the attacks (Silver et al., 2002).

Few researchers, however, have directly examined faculty responses to a national crisis, and the only relevant research we were able to uncover was a faculty survey developed by DiPietro (2003). Faculty were asked to report what, if anything, they had done in class after the 9/11 attacks, the rationale for their response, and their perceptions of effectiveness. Three main themes emerged from that investigation.

- Faculty responded in many different ways. Even in this high-end, self-selected sample, where most people were eager to share what they had done, a number of instructors (11%) admitted that they did not address the attacks in class. When faculty did address the attacks directly, their responses ranged from quick, low-effort strategies (e.g., a minute of silence) to more lengthy, involved responses (e.g., incorporating the tragedy into the course topics or the final project).
- There was a general sense of confusion; some instructors were unsure about what their role should be. Other instructors, even though they felt a strong need to do something, were confused about what would be appropriate or advisable and, as a result, did nothing. Men and international instructors reported the most confusion.
- Some confusion persisted after the fact. Several instructors had no idea whether their actions had any impact. Likewise, some instructors who did nothing reported that even though it seemed like the best thing to do at the time (to foster a sense of normalcy), they later had no idea if that was indeed the best course of action.

These findings clearly reveal that faculty members need to be equipped with appropriate pedagogical tools, well in advance of tragic events.

Method

Sample

A sample of 2,000 students from a private, medium-size university was selected from the enrollment database by randomly generating the names of 400 students from each of the following five groups: first-year students, sophomores, juniors, seniors, and master's/Ph.D. students. Students completed the online survey voluntarily and were offered a lottery incentive: Two randomly drawn respondents from each group won a $50 gift certificate toward purchases on Amazon.com.

Instrument

The survey was an online adaptation of an instructor survey (DiPietro, 2003), and most questions were simply modified to address students' perspectives. For instance, the original question "How many academic classes were you *teaching* in September 2001?" was changed to "How many academic classes were you *taking* in September 2001?"

We administered the online survey using SurveyMonkey, a survey administration and data collection service. The survey included nine questions about demographics and academics, the last of which asked how many courses the student was taking in September 2001. For each course, the respondent answered six questions concerning the instructor-led activities following September 11 (see Appendix 13.1 for the complete survey).

Procedure

Each student received a brief email message in March 2002 inviting him or her to participate. The initial invitation included a link that took respondents to the online consent form. The software monitored which students had completed the survey to ensure that they could only complete the survey once. Two names were randomly drawn from each class for the online gift certificates, and prizes were awarded via email.

The results were calculated in terms of the number of reports (e.g., the number of reports in which faculty teaching labs offered extensions, led discussions, etc.). Helpfulness was only coded for the first two courses that each student reported because incrementally fewer and fewer students ranked the helpfulness of their third, fourth, and fifth courses.

Results and Discussion

Respondents

A total of 484 respondents (24.2% of the original 2,000 students in the sample) completed the survey. Table 13.1 provides a breakdown of respondents by gender, year in school, and academic discipline. An equal number of men and women completed the survey, but this was surprising because the student body at this institution for the 2001–2002 academic year was 65% male and 35% female. Either females were over-represented in the original sample of 2,000 students, or a greater proportion of females were interested in the survey or the lottery prize. Table 13.1 also shows the proportion of respondents by academic discipline. Overall, the response rates were representative of the relative distribution of students across schools. For example, the engineering school had the highest response rate (26.4%), but engineering is also the largest school at the institution, with 23.6% of all students in 2001–2002. In summary, the survey data represent first-year students through graduate students, a variety of academic disciplines, and equal numbers of men and women.

TABLE 13.1

Demographic Characteristics of Participants (N = 484)

Gender	n	%
Male	243	50%
Female	242	50%
Year in School		
First year	123	25%
Sophomore	116	24%
Junior	82	17%
Senior	90	19%
Master's or Ph.D.	73	15%
Academic Discipline		
Fine arts	85	18%
Engineering	128	26%
Sciences and computer science	106	22%
Humanities and social sciences	90	19%
Business and public policy	69	14%
Other*	6	1%

* Includes enrolled students who had not yet declared their majors or students who were taking classes but were not working toward a specified degree.

Responses to the Attacks

Courses where the attacks were addressed. Students reported taking an average of 4.43 classes on September 11, 2001, ranging from one class to five classes, with a median of five classes. As shown in the first row of Table 13.2, the majority of the reports came from small lecture (< 50 students), large lecture (> = 50 students), and discussion classes.

According to the students, only 62% of their instructors addressed the attacks, and the remaining 38% of their instructors failed to mention the attacks in class at all. Students indicated that faculty were more likely to mention the attacks in some types of courses than others: most frequently in discussion and studio courses (in 78% of discussion courses and 73% of studios) and least frequently in large lecture and project classes (53% and 46%, respectively).

It is not surprising that the terrorist attacks were addressed more frequently in discussion and studio courses, where enrollments are typically smaller and classes are usually structured with a relatively high degree of faculty-student interaction. Using the same reasoning, one might have predicted that faculty would be less likely to mention the attacks in lecture halls with 50 students or more because faculty are less likely to know their students (particularly in the second week of classes, which is when the tragedy occurred for this campus). Faculty in large lectures may also have experienced more confusion about their roles with respect to the attacks, and DiPietro (2003) found that faculty who felt confused often said nothing about the attacks.

The fact that the attacks were mentioned least frequently in project courses was surprising because students usually receive individualized faculty attention around a group or individual project in such courses. One would predict a relatively high level of faculty-student interaction, much like discussion or studio courses. The project courses reported in this survey, however, varied dramatically in size, ranging from very small courses (i.e., one student in a drama thesis course) to relatively large team-based courses (i.e., an information systems course with more than 80 students). The size of the course could predict whether instructors addressed the attacks. It could also be that faculty (and perhaps students) in project courses were more focused on a specific product or outcome, so the tendency might have been to "get back to work" rather than linger on the terrorist attacks.

Fortunately, only eight students (1.7%) reported that none of their instructors addressed the terrorist attacks. Five of these students were freshmen or sophomores taking four to five classes each, predominantly in science, mathematics, and business.

Frequency of responses. When faculty addressed the terrorist attacks, what kinds of comments did they make, and what kinds of activities did they lead? The survey provided 14 possible responses based on DiPietro's (2003) faculty survey. Table 13.2 presents the frequency of responses organized by different types of courses. Students reported that the most common response (Response A, 31% of the instructors) was to communicate a two-part message—that the class needed to go on with the material despite the attacks but there would be additional opportunities to review the material down the road. The second most common response (Response E, 23%) was to excuse students from class or to offer an extension on an assignment. Faculty who addressed the attacks in class typically addressed them in multiple ways, so the total for each column in Table 13.2 exceeds 100%. For example, faculty who asked if family and friends were affected (Response M) were also likely to lead a brief discussion in class (Response G).

TABLE 13.2

Types of Instructor Responses Across Different Types of Courses

Instructor Response	Discussion N = 342	Small Lecture N = 338	Large Lecture N = 674	Lab N = 81	Studio N = 157	Project N = 87	Total N = 1679
No Response	22%	38%	47%	37%	27%	54%	38%
Types of Responses							
A	38%	31%	26%	36%	46%	18%	31%
B	13%	13%	15%	15%	9%	9%	13%
C	5%	5%	5%	4%	8%	2%	5%
D	12%	12%	9%	12%	23%	5%	11%
E	20%	24%	22%	25%	32%	13%	23%
F	14%	14%	9%	12%	25%	8%	13%
G	24%	22%	14%	14%	49%	7%	20%
H	12%	11%	6%	5%	17%	8%	10%
I	10%	11%	8%	6%	11%	6%	9%
J	1%	1%	0%	1%	2%	1%	1%
K	2%	1%	1%	0%	1%	0%	2%
L	12%	7%	6%	5%	13%	5%	8%
M	35%	17%	8%	10%	36%	23%	19%
N	6%	4%	3%	5%	4%	3%	5%

Key to Instructor Responses

A) Acknowledged that the class needs to go on with the material but reassured the class that if students were too distressed to process the material that there would be other opportunities to review it down the road
B) Acknowledged that the attacks had occurred and said that the class needs to go on, with no mention of opportunities for review or extra help
C) One minute of silence
D) Mentioned counseling services
E) Excused students/offered extensions if assignments were due
F) Offered to talk privately with anyone who might want to
G) Had a brief discussion in class
H) Devoted the whole first class after the attacks to discussion
I) Incorporated the event into the lesson plan/curriculum
J) Decided to do a project as a class (i.e., quilt, fence painting, etc.)
K) Read a passage from an inspirational book
L) Mentioned ways that people can help (i.e., gave out phone numbers for the Red Cross or charities, talked about the benefits of donating blood, etc.)
M) Asked students if their families and friends were physically affected
N) Other ___ (write-in) ____

Table 13.2 shows that some responses were more common in certain types of courses. For example, students reported that instructors led brief discussions about the attacks (Response G) in studio classes more frequently than in other types of classes. In fact, brief discussions were reported in 49% of studio courses but in only 24% of traditional "discussion courses." One possible reason that discussions occurred with such high frequency in studio courses, most common in the fine arts (art, drama, architecture, etc.), is that the dean of the College of Fine Arts contacted all department chairs immediately following the attacks and encouraged faculty to be responsive to their students. To our knowledge, no other dean coordinated such efforts.

Likewise, certain responses were reported with less frequency for some classroom environments. For example, only 8% of the students in large lectures indicated that their instructors asked if friends or family had been affected by the attacks (Response M), whereas 10%–36% of the students reported that instructors asked about their families in other types of classes. By definition, these large lecture classes have enrollments of 50 students or more, and faculty may have felt unnatural or awkward posing such a personal question to large groups.

Helpfulness of responses. When an instructor did not mention the attacks at all, students did not rate the helpfulness of this nonresponse, so there is little quantitative data to report. Some students offered comments about their instructor's lack of response, and their comments conveyed frustration, disappointment, or apathy, but few conveyed that "doing nothing" was helpful or even appropriate. The following are some sample comments from students whose instructors made no mention of the terrorist attacks.

> The instructor's ignoring of the events was terrible. People were panicking and he was acting like nothing happened.
>
> —Female sophomore in a small lecture music class

> My professor was a complete *** about the whole situation . . . not only did he fail to try to do anything positive related to the attack, he made us come in on a Saturday morning to make up the class period that we missed due to classes being cancelled on September 11.
>
> —Male graduate student, small lecture business class

> Very unhelpful. Showed little personal concern for the students.
>
> —Female senior, psychology discussion class

> The instructor appeared not to take the event seriously enough.
>
> —Male graduate student, small lecture engineering class

> The instructor didn't mention the tragedy at all and surprisingly didn't give a nice historical or informational perspective: something I was hoping a history teacher would explain.
>
> —Male first-year student, large lecture history class

> None—no room for discussion at all.
>
> —Female sophomore, large lecture chemistry class

> The lack of activity was not detrimental. It didn't matter to me whether the professor talked about it or not.
>
> —Male graduate student, project computer science course

When instructors did respond to the terrorist attacks, approximately two-thirds of the students evaluated the helpfulness of that response (66.4%). The 33.6% of students who did not rate the helpfulness of their instructor's actions may have lacked a clear sense of what did or did not help them cope with the events, or they may have been fatigued by the length of the survey. Table 13.3 lists students' helpfulness ratings for 14 instructor-led activities.

As revealed in Table 13.3, many students found most responses very helpful, with the exception of Response B, which we shall return to momentarily. For the other 13 possible responses, 69%–100% of the respondents thought that the instructor's efforts to address the attacks were quite helpful, regardless of whether the instructor's response required relatively little effort, such as asking for one minute of silence (Response C), or a great deal of effort and preparation, such as incorporating the event into the lesson plan or topics for the course (Response I). When instructors developed a class project related to the attacks, 100% of their students found such projects helpful, but the N for this response was small, with only two students (Response J). Some students indicated that their instructors' responses were not helpful, but at most, only 15% of the students found a response unhelpful or problematic (with the exception of Response B). The general conclusion from the students' perspective appears to be "do something, just about anything."

Several of the responses that students appreciated were consistent with the research on coping with highly stressful events. For example, 78% of the students found it very helpful when their instructor mentioned ways that people can support the rescue efforts: Instructors provided phone numbers for the Red Cross and other charities, informed students where they could donate blood, and the like. Taking action to address a problem is known as problem-focused coping and it is a relatively adaptive response to cataclysmic events, often more effective at reducing stress than simply venting or focusing on one's emotional reaction (Carver, Scheier, & Weintraub, 1989). Accordingly,

TABLE 13.3

Students' Perceptions of the Helpfulness of Instructor Responses

Instructor Response	Number of Reports Which Rated Helpfulness	Helpfulness Rating			
		Uncertain or N/A	Not Helpful	Somewhat Helpful	Very Helpful
A	174	11%	7%	11%	71%
B	54	17%	41%	6%	36%
C	32	3%	10%	7%	80%
D	66	15%	9%	7%	69%
E	150	8%	7%	16%	69%
F	86	12%	9%	8%	71%
G	140	9%	13%	9%	69%
H	77	6%	6%	4%	84%
I	73	7%	15%	6%	72%
J	2	0	0	0	100%
K	9	11%	11%	0	78%
L	45	14%	4%	4%	78%
M	115	15%	8%	8%	69%
N	29	10%	15%	13%	62%

Key to Instructor Responses

A) Acknowledged that the class needs to go on with the material but reassured the class that if students were too distressed to process the material that there would be other opportunities to review it down the road
B) Acknowledged that the attacks had occurred and said that the class needs to go on, with no mention of opportunities for review or extra help
C) One minute of silence
D) Mentioned counseling services
E) Excused students/offered extensions if assignments were due
F) Offered to talk privately with anyone who might want to
G) Had a brief discussion in class
H) Devoted the whole first class after the attacks to discussion
I) Incorporated the event into the lesson plan/curriculum
J) Decided to do a project as a class (i.e., quilt, fence painting, etc.)
K) Read a passage from an inspirational book
L) Mentioned ways that people can help (i.e., gave out phone numbers for the Red Cross or charities, talked about the benefits of donating blood, etc.)
M) Asked students if their families and friends were physically affected
N) Other ___ (write-in) ____

one national study found that people who were indirectly affected by the 9/11 attacks had lower levels of long-term stress when they took active, problem-focused approaches, which may explain why students benefited when instructors offered something concrete that they could do (Silver et al., 2002). Other potential responses addressed the cognitive load of a disaster. Recall that 69% of the students who were offered extensions or who were excused from class found this short-term break from their academic responsibilities to be very helpful. Although one might cynically interpret these numbers as students' general eagerness to postpone work whenever possible, cognitive and neuroscience research demonstrates that working memory capacity is reduced immediately following an acutely stressful experience (e.g., Arnsten, 1998; Newcomer et al., 1999). Since students would be less capable of learning new material in the initial wake of a collective tragedy, providing them with extensions or excusing them from class reduces their stress and allows them to produce work later that better reflects their normal abilities and study habits.

The one response that was clearly problematic, however, was Response B, which consisted of "acknowledging that the attacks had occurred and saying that the class needs to go on with no mention of opportunities for review or extra help." Relatively few students found this approach helpful (36%), and an almost equal number found this response unhelpful (41%). Some students explained that Response B was unhelpful because so little was done (e.g., "It wasn't really helpful because it was never really discussed"), and others found it unhelpful because students' needs were not addressed (e.g., "Very unhelpful—showed little personal concern for the students"). In contrast, most students found Response A very helpful (71%), which, like Response B, emphasized moving on with the material, but unlike Response B, recognized students' needs by offering to review material later.

Implications

Previous research found that faculty generally felt uncertain about their responses to the events of September 11 (DiPietro, 2003). The current study offers some reassuring clarity as to how faculty and faculty developers can be most effective following a collective tragedy.

Implications for Faculty

The first issue for faculty is deciding which events qualify as a collective crisis that should be addressed in the classroom. This was not one of our research questions, but we believe that several converging factors can help identify such events. Some events are likely to affect students because of their proximity (local campus events) or the sheer magnitude and scale (national events with wide media coverage). Other factors include a significant likelihood that the event will have a direct impact on students' families or social networks. Faculty should also consider the degree to which students are likely to identify with the victim(s) of the tragedy and feel like "vicarious victims" (which occurred with the 9/11 terrorist attacks and could also occur for members of a group targeted by a hate crime) (Wayment, 2004). Finally, instructors can pay attention to a variety of situational cues. Are the students mobilizing on campus (e.g., through vigils)? Do faculty themselves find it hard to go back to class after the event? In all these cases, our results indicate that from the students' perspective, it is best to do something. Students often complained when faculty did not mention the attacks at all, and they expressed gratitude when faculty acknowledged that something awful had occurred. Beyond acknowledging a tragic event, faculty would be well advised to take the extra step of recognizing that students are distressed and to show some extra support, such as offering to grant extensions for students who request them.

It is perhaps a surprising relief to learn that an instructor's response need not be complicated, time intensive, or even personalized. Students are likely to appreciate responses that require relatively little effort, such as taking a minute of silence or offering to review material later in the course, so faculty should not feel pressed into redesigning their courses. Faculty responses that required high levels of effort were also viewed as helpful, so those who wish to use the lens of their discipline to examine the events surrounding a tragedy are encouraged to do so. A repeated issue that appeared in students' comments was that they appreciated an instructor who responded in a unique and humane way, so faculty should not feel pressured to homogenize their responses.

Implications for Faculty Developers

The results suggest that faculty developers can play several roles in the wake of a collective tragedy. First, faculty developers can provide resources and leadership to deans and department chairs. We know that one dean, the dean of the College of Fine Arts, contacted all of his department chairs to encourage faculty to address the attacks and support students. Professors teaching studio courses in the fine arts responded more strongly than most of their peers by leading more discussions, offering more extensions, offering to talk privately with more students, and so on. Although these studio instructors might have been just as proactive and compassionate without their dean's leadership, faculty developers should note that deans and department chairs are the nexus of faculty action. Connecting these key personnel with the findings from this study, along with online resources such as those at the University of Michigan (Center for Research on Learning and Teaching, 2004), empowers administrators to help their faculty respond more effectively.

A second implication for faculty developers is that if time and resources are limited, as they are likely to be following a tragedy, it would be strategic to focus on schools or departments that offer a greater number of project courses or large lecture courses. Our results indicate that faculty in these two types of courses were the least likely to mention the attacks, which would suggest that they are the most likely to benefit from guidance on how to respond. Although a full class discussion may not suit these courses, some of the quick, low-effort activities might work well.

The third role for faculty developers is to reassure faculty after the fact that their actions were probably helpful to students, even if it was not clear in class. As DiPietro (2003) noted, many faculty were still unclear about whether their responses were helpful several weeks later. The good news is that many students found most instructor responses, with the one noted exception, to be very helpful.

Limitations

There are limitations to this research. First, the data were collected several months after the tragic event, so students' memories might have been prone to error. The survey was intentionally delayed for several reasons. First, students' high stress levels immediately following the attacks would have impaired their ability to judge the effectiveness of an activity (Lazarus & Lazarus, 1994; LeDoux, 1996; Liverant et al., 2004). Second, some instructors created final projects around the attacks, and students would not have completed such projects until the end of the course. Lastly, we were concerned that administering the survey too soon after the attacks might augment students' stress or emotional difficulty. Many students at this institution come from New York or New Jersey (22% of the undergraduate students for 2001–2002), and students across campus experienced the events of 9/11 quite personally.

A second limitation of this study is that the data were collected with respect to one tragic event that raised controversial issues of race, religion, cultural differences, and politics (to name a few), which could explain faculty hesitancy to mention the event in class. Faculty may be more likely to respond to other tragedies. However, as we observed with Hurricane Katrina and Matthew Shepard's death, traumatic events are often controversial. In that respect, faculty responses to the events of September 11 are likely to shed some light on how faculty navigate their way through other highly charged collective tragedies.

Conclusion

A crisis raises anxiety and confusion throughout an institution, and faculty are likely to be unsure about what to do in the classroom. As faculty developers, we can provide suggestions and resources to administrators, and we can offer instructors a variety of approaches so they feel more empowered and less paralyzed. Faculty will be relieved to learn that most responses, even the simplest recognition that it will take time to adjust, are helpful to students.

References

American Psychiatric Association. (n.d.). *Disasters: Mental health recommendations for students and colleges.* Retrieved June 17, 2006, from http://healthyminds.org/katrinatipsforcollege.cfm

Arnsten, A. F. T. (1998, June). The biology of being frazzled. *Science, 280*(5370), 1711–1712.

Asmussen, K. J., & Creswell, J. W. (1995, September/October). Campus response to a student gunman. *Journal of Higher Education, 66*(5), 575–596.

Carver, C. S., Scheier, M. F., & Weintraub, J. K. (1989). Assessing coping strategies: A theoretically based approach. *Journal of Personality and Social Psychology, 56*(2), 267–283.

Center for Research on Learning and Teaching, University of Michigan. (2004). *Publications and links.* Retrieved June 17, 2006, from the University of Michigan, Center for Research on Learning and Teaching web site: www.crlt.umich.edu/publinks/publinks.html

DiPietro, M. (2003). The day after: Faculty behavior in post-September 11, 2001, classes. In C. M. Wehlburg & S. Chadwick-Blossey (Eds.), *To improve the academy: Vol. 21. Resources for faculty, instructional, and organizational development* (pp. 21–39). Bolton, MA: Anker.

Faculty Center for Excellence in Teaching, Western Kentucky University. (2000). *Teaching and learning in a time of crisis.* Retrieved June 17, 2006, from the Western Kentucky University, Faculty Center for Excellence in Teaching web site: www.wku.edu/teaching/booklets/crisis.html

Farrell, E. F. (2001, December 21). Hedging against disaster. *The Chronicle of Higher Education*, p. A40.

Guterman, L. (2001, February 16). Student murdered in dormitory at Gallaudet University. *The Chronicle of Higher Education*, p. A49.

Honos-Webb, L., Sunwolf, Hart, S., & Scalise, J. T. (2006). How to help after national catastrophes: Findings following 9/11. *The Humanistic Psychologist, 34*(1), 75–97.

Hurst, J. C. (1999, July/August). The Matthew Shepard tragedy: Management of a crisis. *About Campus, 4*(3), 5–11.

Larson, W. A. (Ed.). (1994). *When crisis strikes on campus*. Washington, DC: Council for Advancement and Support of Education.

Lazarus, R. S., & Lazarus, B. N. (1994). *Passion and reason: Making sense of our emotions*. New York, NY: Oxford University Press.

LeDoux, J. (1996). *The emotional brain: The mysterious underpinnings of emotional life*. New York, NY: Touchstone.

Liverant, G. I., Hofmann, S. G., & Litz, B. T. (2004, June). Coping and anxiety in college students after the September 11th terrorist attacks. *Anxiety, Stress, & Coping, 17*(2), 127–139.

Mangan, K. S. (2005, November 25). "Katrina" students are in every state. *The Chronicle of Higher Education*, p. A45.

Michigan State University Libraries. (2005). *Hurricane Katrina: Research and resources*. Retrieved June 17, 2006, from the Michigan State University Libraries web site: www.lib.msu.edu/libinstr/katrina.htm

Newcomer, J. W., Selke, G., Melson, A. K., Hershey, T., Craft, S., Richards, K., et al. (1999, June). Decreased memory performance in healthy humans induced by stress-level cortisol treatment. *Archives of General Psychiatry, 56*(6), 527–533.

Paine, C., & Sprague, J. (2000). Crisis prevention and response: Is your school prepared? *Oregon School Study Council Bulletin, 43*(2), 1.

Rooney, M. (2002, November 8). Student kills three University of Arizona professors. *The Chronicle of Higher Education*, p. A12.

Siegel, D. (1994). *Campuses respond to violent tragedy*. Phoenix, AZ: American Council on Education/Oryx Press.

Silver, R. C., Holman, A., McIntosh, D. N., Poulin, M., & Gil-Rivas, V. (2002, September). Nationwide longitudinal study of psychological responses to September 11. *Journal of the American Medical Association, 288*(10), 1235–1244.

Wayment, H. A. (2004, April). It could have been me: Vicarious victims and disaster-focused distress. *Personality and Social Psychology Bulletin, 30*(4), 515–528.

Whiting, L. R., Tucker, M., & Whaley, S. R. (2004, June). *Level of preparedness for managing crisis communication on land grant campuses.* Paper presented at the annual conference of the Association for Communication Excellence in Agriculture, Natural Resources, and Life and Human Sciences, Lake Tahoe, NV.

Appendix 13.1

Survey Questions for Activities Following the September 11, 2001, Terrorist Attacks

1) Do you give Drs. Huston and DiPietro and their associates permission to present this work in written and oral form without further permission? Yes No
2) Gender: (1) Male (2) Female
3) College: *Colleges listed*
4) Major(s) or department in which you'll be getting a degree:
   Relevant departments listed for each college
5) Indicate your status as a student: (1) US citizen (2) International student
6) Class: (1) First-year student, (2) Sophomore, (3) Junior, (4) Senior, (5) Master's/Graduate student
7) Please check the boxes of any university-wide activities you attended after 9/11: (1) Prayer/candlelight vigil (evening of the attacks), (2) A Time to Learn: Professors Explain the Crisis, (3) Peace rally, (4) Other—please explain.
8) How effective do you think the university-wide activity(ies) was (were)?
9) How many academic classes were you taking in September 2001?
10) Please think of one of the courses you were taking in September 2001. What department offers this course?
11) What type of class was this? (You may select multiple answers): (1) Discussion, (2) Small lecture (< 50 students), (3) Large lecture (> = 50 students), (4) Lab, (5) Studio, (6) Recitation, (7) Project course
12) Did the professor or TA mention the 9/11 attacks in class or lead any activities related to them? Yes No
13) Please check the boxes next to anything that your professor did in this class that was related to 9/11. This is easier if you read all of the options before you begin selecting them. You may check more than one.
    See Key for Instructor Responses in Tables 13.2 and 13.3 for specific response items.
14) If you had a TA for this course, did the TA do anything in class to help the students? If so, what did he or she do? *Same list of activities A–N as in Question 13.*
15) How helpful or effective do you think the instructor's or the TA's activities were? If an activity was helpful, what made it helpful? If an activity was unhelpful, why didn't it help you?

Questions 10–15 were then repeated for each course that the student was taking in September 2001.

14

Sustaining the Undergraduate Seminar: On the Importance of Modeling and Giving Guidelines

Shelley Z. Reuter
Concordia University

Student-led discussion is a valuable means of involving students in the collaborative creation of knowledge. This activity becomes especially important in the seminar course where, either individually or in small groups, students lead their peers through a set of readings. Unfortunately, student-led discussions often focus more on summary than critical analysis, largely because seminar leaders, left to their own devices, do not know what a seminar should look like or how to lead one effectively. This chapter demonstrates that undergraduates can learn seminar leadership when provided with guidelines and opportunities to see the skill modeled.

Student-led discussion is a valuable means of actively involving students in the democratic and collaborative creation of knowledge. It also encourages class citizenship and collective responsibility for the learning process. One type of course in which student-led discussion becomes especially vital is the seminar, where students, either individually or in small groups, are expected to lead their peers through a set of weekly readings.

Unfortunately, student-led discussions do not always unfold as professors imagine or hope, so seminars can sometimes be lackluster and aimless, focusing more on summary than on analysis and insight. Perhaps part of the problem is our assumption as professors that at the university level students will somehow *just know* how to lead a seminar. Though we understand the importance and value of a class discussion (Brookfield & Preskill, 2005;

Parker, 2001), we often forget that facilitating one is ultimately a form of teaching and requires skill that has to be cultivated.

To help revive our student-led seminars, we might turn to the instructional development literature. There we will find an abundance of materials on leading effective discussions (see, for example Davis, 1993, especially Chapter 3; McKeachie, 1994, especially Chapter 4), but for the most part these resources tend to be directed at graduate teaching assistants and new professors. In addition, their emphasis is more likely to be on how to give effective presentations (Taylor, 1992; Taylor & Toews, 1999), how to structure (Knapper, Wilcox, & Weisberg, 1996) and improve discussion (Cashin & McKnight, 1986; Hollander, 2002), how to encourage participation (Reynolds & Stevenson, 2003; Weimer, 1990), and how to ask good, discussable questions (Bonwell & Eison, 1991; Rasmussen, 1984). Missing from these otherwise helpful resources are materials that concentrate on the unique context of a student-led seminar course—that is, information for professors who wish to show their students what a productive seminar looks like and how to lead one—though Steen, Bader, and Kubrin (1999) come close. This information is especially crucial for professors teaching upper-level undergraduates and even new graduate students whose prior university courses have mostly, and in some cases entirely, been of the large, impersonal lecture-theater variety.

Building on my experiences with teaching fourth-year undergraduate seminars in Contemporary Theories, Feminist Theories, Sociology of Knowledge, and Sociology of Health and Medicine, I have developed a set of step-by-step guidelines that I give to and model for my students. A work in progress over the past several years, I have found modeling these guidelines to be extremely effective for cultivating the skill of seminar leadership and for realizing my goals for teaching seminars, namely 1) having students gain knowledge (content and theory) about the topic of the seminar, 2) developing students' competency in critical thinking about texts and especially in analyzing complex arguments that authors make, and 3) fostering the leadership skills required of a seminar leader, including the ability to engage in intellectual discussion. While all these goals involve skills that must be taught and learned, this chapter will focus in depth on the third objective—the process of training students in seminar leadership.[1]

The following is a sample set of guidelines used in a Feminist Theories course in the 2005 winter term. I then describe the steps I take in reviewing the guidelines and modeling the seminar for students. The chapter ends with a brief analysis of potential pitfalls and solutions.

Step-by-Step Guidelines for Leading and Participating in Seminars

Each student will, with my help, facilitate one seminar discussion. I have no expectation that you will be an "expert" but only that you *generate discussion and guide the class* to important things to think and talk about.

Think of the seminar as a *group conversation* that depends on everybody participating. This assignment is not meant to be scary or make anybody look foolish. Rather, it is intended to be part of a collective effort to help each of you gain a deeper understanding of the readings. This will, in turn, help you write stronger papers in this course. The seminars are also designed to allow you to take responsibility for your own learning. Doing so will make this course a much more rewarding experience for all of us.

Steps for Seminar Leaders

Before Your Seminar

1) *Plan your seminar in advance.* Make an appointment to meet with me the week before your seminar so that I can make sure that what you've got planned is feasible and relevant and to give you an opportunity to ask any questions you may have. This meeting is worth 10% of your grade for this assignment.

2) *Prepare an agenda for your seminar and make enough copies for everyone in the class, including me.* This agenda should be a guide to what you intend to do in your seminar. It should not contain everything you plan to say, but only the *key points/issues/questions* you plan to address. It should not be more than one side of a page and should include a rough timeline for each component. This agenda will be included in the calculation of your overall grade for this assignment. A sample agenda will be provided.

During Your Seminar

I will lead the first two seminars. As I do so, we will discuss the assigned readings, but also the process of leading seminars. I will point out to you what I am doing as I lead the discussion as a way of modeling what I expect to see in your seminars. Briefly, your seminar should include the following:

1) *Synthesis.* Provide a *brief* overview of the content of the assigned readings. Synthesize the main concepts, key points, and important issues raised by the readings. Be sure to address the similarities, differences, and connections among the assigned readings, focusing in particular on the argument each author is making.

2) *Taking stock.* Have everyone in the class share their impressions and questions about the readings. Two options (you may think of other methods): You could ask your classmates to write down the most important idea they got from the readings, and then have them share this with a partner, then the whole group. Or you could go around the circle and ask each person to give her or his impression of the readings—that is, the arguments. The purpose of this step is to see if people have common perceptions of the readings and/or where the points of contention or difficulty lie. Allow time for discussion at this point.

Remaining Elements, Not Necessarily in This Order

1) *Critique.* Having heard your classmates' opinions, now do your own analysis of the arguments and ideas in the readings. Focus on the content and authors' assumptions rather than the form (i.e., language and style). Link the readings to ideas and issues raised in previous classes. Ask your classmates to evaluate which of the authors has a stronger argument, and why.

2) *Reflection.* Think about what you've learned from the readings, and what you took for granted before you read them. Think to yourselves, "This argument has changed the way I think about . . ." Compare your reflections with each other, and ask your classmates to share their reflections as well.

3) *Questions for discussion.* Ask your classmates to position themselves in relation to the arguments being made: "Would you align yourself with this belief? If not, what is your belief, and why?" Ask your classmates to consider the implications of the arguments: "If we take Author X's argument further, then it will mean that . . ." "This is a good idea because, or this idea is a problem because . . ." "If we accept Y's argument, then that means that Z's argument from three weeks ago is problematic because . . ." Ask any questions you can think of that might help your classmates think deeply about what is being argued in the readings.

Steps for Seminar Participants

There are three main components to your role as seminar participant.

1) *Reading.* To optimize your participation, you must have completed the assigned readings. In a 400-level theory course, simply scanning the pages will be insufficient to sustain your contributions in class. At the end of each seminar, I will introduce the following week's topic, so you will need to study the readings and consider them in relation to this introduction.

2) *Getting involved.* You should join in the discussion whenever you have something to contribute that will help us move the discussion/debate forward. Whatever points you make should be relevant to and supported by specific references to the readings.

3) *Reflection.* What you can expect as a participant:
   - You will be asked to comment on the readings.
   - You may be asked to write a "minute paper" at the beginning of the seminar on "the most important idea I got from the articles for today is . . ." Or you may be asked to reflect in some other way, or to share your ideas for discussion. The more thoroughly you do the readings, the better the seminar discussion is likely to be.
   - "Do unto others as you would have them do unto you." The success of a seminar is equally dependent on the seminar leadership and the seminar participation. If you want your classmates to be interested and actively involved when it's your turn to facilitate, you must be interested and actively involved in their seminars, too.

Note: It is acceptable from time to time to "pass" when asked a question, or to simply concur with an earlier point of view. However, be aware that repeatedly passing or agreeing with earlier comments without ever contributing anything new to the discussion may call into question your preparedness for the seminars and this in turn will impact your participation grade.

I look forward to our seminars!

Discussion

However helpful these seminar guidelines may be on their own, their real potential to be useful to seminar leaders is contingent upon three key factors. First, the professor must introduce the seminar topic in the class *before* it is to be taken up. I use the last part of each three-hour class for this. Although not ideal, in courses broken up into two meetings per week, it is possible to stagger the classes so that the new topic is introduced in the second class of the week, giving students the weekend to prepare for the seminar the following week. Defining key concepts and outlining the background and main ideas of the material they will be seeing the following week helps student seminar leaders and participants focus their reading, which in turn places them in a better position to actually discuss the material during the seminar.

The second key component is meeting with the seminar leader(s) a few days before their class to review their plans and answer their questions. Students often have questions about the seminar process as well as the readings, especially in a theory course that assigns primary texts, and will need the opportunity for clarification. It is also important to be available by email or phone for any last-minute concerns.

The third and perhaps most important element is modeling the first two seminars. By modeling I mean the following: I go to the first class early and set up the desks in a circle, so the students get an initial sense on that first day of what a seminar physically looks like. After the preliminaries and housekeeping that normally take place in the first week of a course, I like to launch directly into the seminar format immediately in the second week. I tell students on that first day that I will be providing them with seminar guidelines and leading the first two seminars beginning the following week, and that they only need to come to the next class prepared with the readings done. In this first meeting I also introduce them to the topic of our first formal seminar.

When we meet for the second class, I come with enough copies of the guidelines and a sample corresponding agenda that outlines (in point form) the key ideas in the readings, points of critique and analysis, and questions for discussion (see Appendix 14.1). I give the students a few minutes to read through the guidelines and then I go over them in more detail. Once each step has been explained and any questions have been answered, we examine the assigned readings step-by-step, following both the guidelines and the agenda I have given them. I draw their attention to what I will be looking for in the agenda, since it will be part of the evaluation of their seminar: Is the handout helpful and easy to follow? Does it give the class a clear and brief outline of what will happen in the seminar? Then, as we go along, I say things like,

"Okay, now I'm going to synthesize the readings. Note that I will be very brief, touching only on the highlights, and so on." I tell them that I assess how concise, focused, and on target their summary of the main points is. At this stage I also identify the central arguments of the readings and encourage them to focus on doing that in their summary.

Then we begin hearing from the other students. I will say, "Okay, let's take stock of people's sense of the readings" and ask them to write a minute paper about their initial impression of the arguments. Following this, I go around the circle and have students share what they wrote. (I point out that writing a minute paper is not a requirement of future seminars but an option to consider if the seminar leaders think it will be helpful for sparking discussion.) In this first seminar meeting, students do not yet know each other and giving them a moment to collect and write their thoughts seems to make it easier for them to then speak to the group. Discussion and reflection almost invariably take off from here, but if they are a less chatty group, I have discussion questions prepared (also included on the agenda).

Once students have expressed their own ideas about the readings, I summarize their comments, making links between them and adding any points of critique that may not have been raised but are important to consider. I also raise further questions for discussion and reflection as time permits. I conclude this first seminar by outlining for students the grading criteria (see Appendix 14.2) according to which their seminars (and participation) will be assessed, taking into consideration the relevance of the discussion and summary, the depth and creativity of the critical analysis, the kinds of discussion questions leaders raise, and the helpfulness of the agenda handout. I also emphasize that the leaders' role is to give the class things to think and talk about.

In short, I explain the steps outlined in the guidelines and model them at the same time. It is important to note that this first seminar will be unusually time-consuming and feel somewhat artificial due to its emphasis on the mechanics of leading a seminar. Thus it is necessary to limit the reading assignment for this first meeting to ensure that I have enough time to go through the different steps and to introduce the following week's topic. When I lead the second seminar, however, I do not spend time reviewing the guidelines again, except to point out which step I am at as I go along. At this point, the process always feels more natural because it focuses more on analysis and discussion of the assigned readings, and students are usually more at ease now that they have already experienced one seminar. In this second seminar I emphasize the critical analysis component, as well as the importance of making sure that the critical analysis is relevant to the readings, is creative, stimulates discussion, and explores the topic in depth. That said, the skill of seminar leadership is one that students develop over the course of the term. Modeling only two seminars does not magically transform them into expert facilitators, but it does give students much-needed direction and a place from which to begin from week to week.

Potential Pitfalls and Solutions

One problem that may arise is that the seminar leaders may not come prepared or not come at all for their meeting prior to their seminar. To avoid this, I stipulate that not showing up or coming completely unprepared will result in a loss of 1 point out of a possible 10 seminar points. In four years of using these guidelines, I have never had to actually levy this penalty. In my experience students are happy for the opportunity to check in with me before they "present."

Another potential problem is that students may not do the readings for the seminar, thereby causing the leaders' efforts to fall flat. However, I do not penalize seminar leaders if their classmates come unprepared. Therefore, going around the room to solicit students' opinions in the first two seminars is a very important step in the modeling process. This strategy makes it clear to students very quickly that they cannot be invisible and that they need to come to class prepared to discuss the material. It is also important to establish a positive sense of community in the class to allow students to see how dependent they are on each other to pull their own weight. In reality, students rarely come with none of the readings done. If I see the class as a whole is struggling to do all of the readings, I will reduce them accordingly.

A third potential problem is that the student-led seminar can go astray, in spite of the guidelines. It should be clarified that these guidelines are not meant to eliminate work for the professor but simply to make it easier for the professor to do the work. That is, instructors must still take an active role in the classroom and be prepared to steer discussion when it veers off track. Even though students will lead the seminar, the professor must clarify what he or she wants the class to take away from the meeting (e.g., understanding the arguments and certain implications) and work collaboratively with the student leaders to ensure that the class meets this objective. Guiding the class in reading critically is important (see Rovinescu 2005), as is asking well-timed, pointed questions about the arguments being discussed.

A final potential problem is that providing these seminar guidelines may send the message to leaders that they are to take a methodical cookie-cutter approach that does not deviate from any of the steps outlined. I tell students that their seminar does not necessarily have to follow the steps exactly but that it must simply contain all the elements I have identified. I encourage them to be creative and to add their own touch, and some do. However, I prefer they do not do so to the point of disregarding the guidelines and leading an uninspired discussion.

Conclusion

Since I began taking the time to actually tell and show my students how a seminar is conducted, the quality of discussion (and in turn students' writing) in these courses has improved significantly and has helped reduce students' anxiety about their role as seminar leaders. As one student wrote in a recent university course evaluation, this was "good preparation for future seminar classes," and as another put it, "I appreciated learning the skills of directing a seminar in an environment [in which] I felt safe/open to questioning and ideas." I recently solicited feedback about the guidelines and modeling specifically from students in my Sociology of Knowledge course (n = 15) and received positive appraisals: A score of 4.2 out of 5 on "The seminar guidelines will help me prepare to lead a seminar . . ."; 4.4 on "The first two seminars gave me a good idea of what a seminar should look like . . ."; and 4.3 on "I have a better sense of what is expected of me because of the seminar guidelines . . ."

Seminars are obviously much more effective and enjoyable when students come prepared and the class has a coherent plan of action. The steps outlined in this chapter help students develop such a plan. In addition, these guidelines allow both the students and me to focus on the content of their seminar rather than the structure—students in their preparation and analysis, and me in my assessment. When seminar leaders can go beyond merely summarizing the assigned readings to facilitating analysis, critique, and reflection, then the conditions are in place for all students to develop insight into the readings that they might not otherwise have. In turn, students' writing about the materials improves and deepens. The benefits of a productive student-led seminar are irrefutable, but they can elude us if we fail to show students exactly what a good seminar leader does.

Acknowledgments

I wish to thank Katherine Lagrandeur, Susan Wilcox, and the anonymous reviewers for their encouragement and suggestions. Laura DesRosiers was instrumental in doing the library research for this chapter. Eileen Bragg helped me to develop these guidelines and convinced me to share them in an instructional development workshop that we co-facilitated at Memorial University in 2003; her input, along with feedback from the workshop participants, played a crucial role in bringing this chapter to fruition. Finally, I am grateful to all my seminar students over the years for patiently, if unwittingly, helping me learn how best to help them learn.

Endnotes

1) Instructors must also take steps to support other goals. For example, in support of the goal of learning content, I introduce students to each topic the week before each seminar (see the "Discussion" section). I also spend time with students working on the identification and analysis of arguments by 1) examining a critical reading handout (see Rovinescu, 2005) at the beginning of the term, 2) providing students with questions to think about for the following week's seminar, and 3) giving a reaction paper assignment where students identify and react to some aspect(s) of the arguments being made. To support this assignment we read and compare two sample reaction papers—an A and a C paper—within the first two classes to illustrate the difference between summary and rigorous analysis (e.g., strengths, limits, links between, and implications of the arguments being made). Additionally, when modeling the seminar, I zero in on the main arguments of the assigned readings and lead the students through the process of critique. Taken together, these measures are useful for helping students learn to identify arguments and discuss them, both orally and in written form.

References

Bonwell, C. C., & Eison, J. A. (1991). *Active learning: Creating excitement in the classroom.* Washington, DC: George Washington University.

Brookfield, S. D., & Preskill, S. (2005). *Discussion as a way of teaching: Tools and techniques for democratic classrooms* (2nd ed.). San Francisco, CA: Jossey-Bass.

Cashin, W. E., & McKnight, P. C. (1986). *Improving discussions* (Idea Paper No. 15). Manhattan, KS: Kansas State University, Center for Faculty Evaluation and Development.

Davis, B. G. (1993). *Tools for teaching.* San Francisco, CA: Jossey-Bass.

Hollander, J. A. (2002, July). Learning to discuss: Strategies for improving the quality of class discussion. *Teaching Sociology, 30*(3), 317–327.

Knapper, C., Wilcox, S., & Weisberg, M. (1996). *Teaching students more: Discussion with more students.* Ontario, Canada: Queen's University, Instructional Development Centre.

McKeachie, W. J. (1994). *McKeachie's teaching tips: Strategies, research, and theory for college and university teachers* (9th ed.). Lexington, MA: D.C. Heath.

Parker, W. C. (2001, March). Classroom discussion: Models for leading seminars and deliberations. *Social Education, 65*(2), 111–115.

Rasmussen, R. V. (1984). Practical discussion techniques for instructors. *AACE Journal, 12*(2), 38–47.

Reynolds, G., with Stevenson, K. (2003). *Leading discussions: What every student (and lecturer) needs to know!* Retrieved June 18, 2006, from the Staffordshire University, Department of Sociology and Crime, Deviance, and Society web site: www.staffs.ac.uk/schools/humanities_and_soc_sciences/sociology/leaddiss.htm

Rovinescu, O. (2005). *Critical reading guide.* Quebec, Canada: Concordia University, Centre for Teaching and Learning Services.

Steen, S., Bader, C., & Kubrin, C. (1999, April). Rethinking the graduate seminar. *Teaching Sociology*, 27(2), 167–173.

Taylor, K. L., & Toews, S. V. M. (1999, July). Effective presentations: How can we learn from the experts? *Medical Teacher, 21*(4), 409–414.

Taylor, P. (1992). Improving graduate student seminar presentations through training. *Teaching of Psychology, 19*(4), 236–238.

Weimer, M. (1990). Successful participation strategies. In M. Weimer & R. A. Neff (Eds.), *Teaching college: Collected readings for the new instructor* (pp. 95–96). Madison, WI: Magna.

Appendix 14.1
Sample Agenda

Liberal Feminism

1) Synthesis (10–15 minutes)

Betty Friedan

- Housewives in despair, need more in their lives
- Equal access to college educations and full-time paid work

Joyce Trebilcot

- There shouldn't be separate sex roles based on psychological differences between women and men

Kathleen Jones

- Liberal feminist argument for inclusion of women in military is contradictory, shortsighted
- Inclusion of women in military will not change patriarchal values, nor will it mean equality for civilian women
- Women need access to positions of power; only then can women redefine what it is to be a full "citizen"

2) Taking stock (20–25 minutes)
   - Everyone's impressions, most important ideas, discussion

3) Critique and analysis (3–5 minutes)
   - Inequality and privilege
   - Affirmation of patriarchal values
   - Affirmation of capitalism

4) Reflect and discuss (remaining time)
   - In what respects and to what extent does liberal feminism challenge the social order (or not)?
   - Does liberal feminism continue to serve any purpose today?
   - How do we account for the recent craze over "housewife shows" (*Desperate Housewives, Wife Swap,* etc.)?
   - What does liberal feminism, especially Friedan's, mean for men today—that is, "househusbands"?
     Are these men headed down the same road that Friedan describes?

Appendix 14.2

Grading Criteria: Feminist Theories

Grading Criteria for Seminar Leadership

Outstanding				Inadequate
A (80+)	B (70–79)	C (60–69)	D (50–59)	F (49–)

Discussion is relevant to the week's readings	Discussion has little relevance
Topic is explored in depth	Superficial treatment of topic
Takes off from and builds on the readings, and external materials are used when relevant	Is strictly a summary of the readings
Engaging, creative, and encourages class discussion; raises new and interesting questions; gives group things to think and talk about	Does not encourage or enable class discussion
Handout is helpful, easy to follow, gives class a loose outline of what will happen	Handout has too much irrelevant information and doesn't help the group keep up

Remember: You don't have to be the "expert" on feminist theory, nor do you have to understand absolutely everything in the readings. But you do have to lead us in what we'll talk about. (It's okay to ask that we go over specific difficult bits!)

Grading Criteria for Preparation and Involvement in Discussion

- Attendance, coming to class on time
- Preparation for seminar (i.e., do the readings, come to class prepared to discuss the material)
- The quality of your contribution to the group; the extent to which you supply ideas that move others' learning forward
- Receptiveness to others' ideas and the extent to which you actively listen to what others have to say
- Your part in facilitating a community of learning

15

Teaching Business by Doing Business: An Interdisciplinary Faculty-Friendly Approach

Larry K. Michaelsen, Mary McCord
Central Missouri State University

This chapter describes the implementation of an interdisciplinary undergraduate curricular innovation in two different university settings. The Integrative Business Experience (IBE) requires students to enroll concurrently in three required core business courses and a practicum course in which they develop and operate a startup business (based on a real-money loan of up to $5,000) and carry out a hands-on community service project. This chapter also reports outcomes for students (including data from an assessment), examines the variables that minimize the difficulty of achieving cross-disciplinary integration in IBE, and suggests keys to enabling faculty-friendly integrative course designs in other settings.

Faculty at postsecondary institutions face an ongoing dilemma based on the fact that academia is organized around discipline-based academic courses and departments while "Simply put: life is interdisciplinary" (DeZure, 1999, p. 1). On the one hand, faculty are trained within disciplines and, as a result, are seldom academically equipped to teach interdisciplinary courses unless they engage in and incur the costs that typically accompany any form of team-teaching. These include the additional time required for jointly developing plans for both dealing with the course content and evaluating student performance (Eby, 2001) and adjusting to student needs as the course unfolds (Harris & Harvey, 2000). In addition, many members of teaching teams experience emotional costs that stem from learning to accommodate differences in each others' personalities (Robinson & Schaible, 1995; Vogler & Long, 2003) and teaching methods (Eby, 2001). On the other hand, studies report that interdisciplinary courses, teaching teams, or both produce a wide variety of benefits including revitalizing course material (Robinson & Schaible, 1995), creating new styles of teaching (Inch & McVarish, 2003), giving students access to "experts" (Ware & Gardner, 1978) whose input promotes understanding across disciplines (Bartlett, 2002), higher achievement, greater retention, improved interpersonal skills, and an increase in regard for positive interdependence (Johnson, Johnson, & Smith, 1991).

Although interdisciplinary learning initiatives are proliferating throughout higher education at an unprecedented rate (Creamer & Lattuca, 2005; DeZure, 1999), it would appear that the costs of team-taught and/or interdisciplinary courses are still perceived to outweigh their benefits. However, based on our experience, just the opposite can be true. The purposes of this chapter are to 1) describe an undergraduate curricular innovation called the Integrative Business Experience (IBE) that has proven to be faculty-friendly even though it is both highly interdisciplinary and team-taught, and 2) review the evidence that has led us to conclude that the benefits of IBE have far outweighed the costs in two very different university settings.

Background

In most undergraduate business programs, students have four types of required coursework. During their freshman and sophomore years, they must complete a university core curriculum (a broad-based set of general education requirements) and a pre-business core (courses in economics, statistics, computers, business communications, and mathematics). In their junior year, they must complete a set of core courses that focus on four or five key business functions (finance, information systems, legal studies, management, and marketing). For the remainder of their junior year and in their senior year, students complete the coursework in their major and minor fields of study and conclude by taking a required capstone course.

The curricular innovation reported in this chapter involves a change in the way in which students completed their junior-level core business requirements. Traditionally, they had enrolled in four or five (depending on the university) stand-alone lecture-oriented courses. Starting in spring 1995 at the University of Oklahoma and in spring 2004 at Central Missouri State University, students have had the opportunity to choose a program called the Integrative Business Experience (IBE) (see Figure 15.1). This program, which was inspired by MG101 at Bucknell University (see Miller, 1991), links students' work in three core courses to an intensive hands-on experience (see Figure 15.2). Thus, in contrast to the traditional activities of listening, taking notes, and demonstrating competence by taking multiple-choice exams, IBE students have the opportunity to 1) practice using basic business concepts and analytical tools to solve a wide range of unstructured problems, 2) receive an integrated exposure to concepts from three core business disciplines, and 3) develop interpersonal and group interaction skills in a work-like setting. IBE students gain experience by creating and managing two significant enterprises—an actual startup company (funded by a real-money bank loan of up to $5,000) and a hands-on community service project. They receive an integrated exposure to core business concepts as faculty deliver content instruction that is specifically sequenced to provide real-time conceptual support for managing students' business and service ventures. Students also have the opportunity to develop interpersonal and group problem-solving skills in both learning teams in the content courses (see Michaelsen, Knight, & Fink, 2004) and through their IBE company activities.

FIGURE 15.1
Traditional Versus IBE

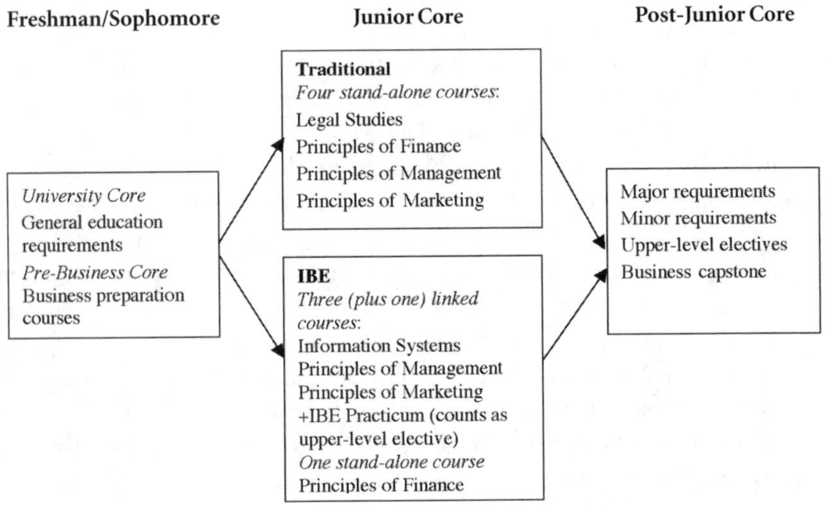

FIGURE 15.2

IBE Key Program Elements

Learning linked to experience. In one 16-week semester, students:

- Concurrently enroll in four courses—three required core business courses and an entrepreneurship/community service practicum
- Are responsible for mastering the content in the three required core business courses
- Are assigned to a permanent five- to seven-member learning team that is expected to complete projects and exams in all three core courses
- Are "employees" of a 20- to 35-member company (4 or 5 of the core course teams) that develops a business plan for:
  ~ A startup business venture
  ~ A hands-on community service project
- Obtain a real-money bank loan (up to $5,000) to finance their startup business
- Generate enough income to pay back their loan and finance their service project
- Prepare and present a company annual report

Team-Based Learning to ensure:

- Content coverage
- Time for emphasis on concept applications
- Development of effective student teams
- Development of interpersonal/group problem-solving skills

IBE Program Business and Service Outcomes

In many ways, IBE has been a resounding success. For example, the financial and community service performance of IBE companies has surpassed our wildest expectations. A total of 1,474 students have participated in IBE between the 1995 spring semester and the 2003 spring semester at the University of Oklahoma, where the program was originally developed as the Integrated Business Core, and between the 2004 spring semester and the 2005 fall semester at Central Missouri State University. These students have formed and managed 53 remarkably successful companies. In total:

- IBE student businesses have received $171,926 in loans (from a local bank) and have generated total revenue of $1,175,374 and total net profit of $671,789.

- More than 100 community service and/or voluntary nonprofit organizations have received $687,501 in direct financial support from the efforts of IBE student businesses, and 22,352 hours of community service from IBE-organized activities.

IBE's Impact on Students: Formal Assessment

Both formal and informal data from students at the University of Oklahoma strongly suggest that the experience has had a profound positive effect on many aspects of their learning. The formal data were collected during class from 8 of the 10 sections of the Policy/Strategy capstone course (see Figure 15.1 shown earlier) in the final week of the 2001spring semester. Students in these courses were all graduating seniors and, as a result, had completed their junior-core requirements 18 months to 2 years earlier. Further, since it was not a required track, we had the basis for a natural experiment on the impact of IBE.

We deliberately hid our intent to assess the impact of IBE in two ways. One was that there was no mention of IBE until a block of demographic questions at the very end of the questionnaire. The other was that the study was largely double blind in the sense that most of the instructors who administered the questionnaires used to collect the data for the study were unaware of its connection assessing the impact of IBE.

In all, 274 students (i.e., virtually all those who were present on the day the questionnaire was administered) completed the questionnaire. All but 23 of the respondents completed the question indicating whether or not they had participated in IBE. Thus, the responses of 251 students were usable. Of these, 201 had completed the junior core in the traditional track and 50 had participated in IBE.

The questionnaire used in the study contained 26 questions. The first set of questions asked students to rate (on a 1–5 Likert scale) the extent to which their experience in junior-level core courses (Legal Environment of Business; Principles of Finance, Information Systems, Management, and Marketing) and upper-division courses beyond the junior core had enabled them to develop skills, understanding, or both in seven specific areas (see Table 15.1).

The next two questions were open-ended so that students could express in their own words what they felt had been the single most beneficial aspect of their undergraduate business degree program, as well as the greatest disappointment in helping them develop the skills and understandings needed to be successful in their career. Students' responses on these questions were coded into one of nine categories that were developed from reading through and comparing students' write-in responses.

The final nine questions asked about different aspects of students' background "to help us learn if our program is 'working' better for some groups than for others." The question that asked students whether they had been in IBE was included in this set of background questions.

Study Results

The results from the seven questions related to students' experience in the junior-level core and in the upper-division courses beyond the junior-level core are shown in Table 15.1. In general, the scores indicate that IBE students had recalled their educational experience in both the junior-level core and in the upper-division courses beyond the junior-level core more favorably than students who had taken the same courses on a stand-alone basis. Ratings for students who had been in IBE were higher on all seven questions about both the junior-level core and the upper-division courses beyond the junior-level core. In addition, five of the seven differences between traditional and IBE students with respect to the junior-level core and four of the seven differences with respect to the upper-division courses beyond the junior-level core were significant beyond the .05 level.

Overall, the results show a consistent pattern suggesting that participation in IBE is uniformly associated with more positive ratings of a wide variety of important and positive educational outcomes. Even though students had completed their junior-level requirements some 18 months to 2 years before completing the questionnaire, the data support two important and positive outcomes that appear to be directly related to having participated in IBE. One is that IBE predisposes students to recall their junior-level core as having contributed more to their overall educational experience in a variety of ways. The other, and even more important, outcome is that even though both groups were asked to report on their experience in the same courses beyond the junior core (see Figure 15.1 shown earlier), IBE students reported that they had gained more from upper-division major and minor coursework than their peers who completed the junior-core requirements by taking four stand-alone courses.

Students' Write-In Responses to the Open-Ended Questions

The pattern of write-in responses of traditional students was very different than that of IBE students on all three open-ended questions. Students' responses to the first open-ended question ("What has been the single most

TABLE 15.1

Questions and Result Summaries for Junior-Core Courses and Courses Beyond the Junior Core

Item		Junior-Core Course Results				Beyond the Core Results			
	Frame of reference for the Likert-type questions was "My overall experience in the junior core (questions 1–7*) or courses beyond the junior core (questions 8–14**) enabled me to . . ."	IBE Mean	Non-IBE Mean	IBE Minus Non-IBE	IBE Mean	Non-IBE Mean	IBE Minus Non-IBE	IBE Mean	Non-IBE Mean
1 & 8	Understand the core concepts well enough to be confident in my ability to function effectively in my subsequent courses and in the initial stages of my career	3.49	3.34	0.15	p<.23	3.92	3.62	0.31	p<.02
2 & 9	Go beyond the theory to the point that I clearly understood how the concepts would apply to workplace situations/problems	3.41	3.06	0.35	p<.02	3.74	3.55	0.19	p<.17
3 & 10	Understand how the concepts from different disciplines fit together to solve real-world problems	3.51	3.35	0.16	p<.24	3.96	3.60	0.36	p<.01
4 & 11	Understand the kinds of problems that are inherent in working with others	3.96	3.59	0.37	p<.01	4.26	3.83	0.43	p<.00
5 & 12	Experience solving the kinds of problems that I am likely to face in my future jobs	3.35	2.99	0.36	p<.02	3.70	3.52	0.18	p<.22
6 & 13	Develop skills I need to be able to work effectively with others	3.90	3.53	0.36	p<.02	4.08	3.85	0.23	p<.09
7 & 14	Experience the difficulties involved in translating theory into action	3.45	3.14	0.31	p<.03	3.84	3.50	0.34	p<.02

*Answers for questions 1–7 reflect students' perceptions at least 18 months to 2 years after their actual experience. Also, ratings from IBE and traditional students are subject to the influence (mostly negative) of the Finance 3303 which is part of the required core coursework but was taken as a stand-alone course for both groups.

**Both IBE and non-IBE students go into the same upper-division courses. As a result, these questions and responses reflect how participation in IBE was related to students' perceptions of their experience in the courses that followed IBE (i.e., mostly courses in their major).

beneficial aspect of your undergraduate business degree program?") showed three differences that were quite striking (see Table 15.2). First, almost 31% of the students who had completed the traditional junior core either left the question blank or made some sort of a negative comment. By contrast, only 4% of the former IBE students left the question blank and none gave a negative comment. Second, only one student in the non-IBE group wrote a positive comment specific to the junior core (she commented on the positive influence of the Marketing Principles instructor in helping her to decide on a major), while 50% of the former IBE students specifically mentioned their participation in IBE as being the single most beneficial aspect of their undergraduate business degree program. Third, 10% of the students who completed the junior-core requirements by taking the four stand-alone courses identified "good teaching" (often citing one or more specific teachers by name) as the single most beneficial aspect of their undergraduate business program. By contrast, "good teaching" was not even mentioned by former IBE students.

TABLE 15.2
Most Beneficial Aspect of Students' Degree Program

Non-IBE		**IBE**		**Responses Coding Category**
n	%	n	%	
49	24.4%	2	4.0%	Left question blank
13	6.5%		0.0%	Gave *negative* (e.g., "absolutely nothing," "you must be kidding")
1	0.5%	25	50.0%	Something *specifically* related to junior core and/or named IBE
31	15.4%	7	14.0%	Group work/teamwork
52	25.9%	11	22.0%	Post-junior core (e.g., "field project," "working with cases," "capstone")
20	10.0%		0.0%	Specific mention of one or more good teachers
10	5.0%	2	4.0%	Extracurricular (e.g., leadership program, clubs, placement)
14	7.0%	1	2.0%	Concepts learned/skills gained (e.g., "business knowledge," "computer skills")
11	5.5%	2	4.0%	Other (e.g., "friendships," "learned how to learn," "gained self-discipline")

Except for one common theme, students' write-in comments on the second open-ended question ("What aspect of your undergraduate program has been the greatest disappointment with respect to helping you develop the skills and understandings you will need in your chosen career?") were also quite different for traditional and IBE students. The only common theme was "bad teaching": more than 30% for both groups, with more than one-half of the complaints focusing on the junior-core courses (see Table 15.3).

TABLE 15.3

Students' Greatest Disappointment in Personal Outcomes From Degree Program

Non-IBE		**IBE**		**Responses Coding Category**
n	%	n	%	
47	23.4%	4	8.0%	Left question blank
3	1.5%		0.0%	Undifferentiated negative (e.g., "everything," "too many to list")
14	7.0%	8	16.0%	Bad teaching in and/or philosophy of Finance 3303
21	10.4%	1	2.0%	Bad teaching in and/or philosophy of other junior core
26	12.9%	7	14.0%	Bad teaching (post-junior core and/or general)
7	3.5%	1	2.0%	Group work/teamwork in post-junior core
33	16.4%	15	30.0%	Too little "real-world" focus (more experience and/or assignments)
17	8.5%	3	6.0%	Irrelevant coursework
33	16.4%	11	22.0%	Other (e.g., "enrollment," "program inadequacies," "outdated courses")

Again, the differences between traditional and IBE students seem to be concentrated in three areas. First, a much higher proportion of traditional students either left the question blank or wrote in an undifferentiated negative than was the case for IBE students. Second, although both groups voiced concerns about the teaching and or philosophy of the junior-core courses, the focus of their comments was quite different. Both groups had concerns about the Principles of Finance course, but a much higher percentage of IBE students listed it as their greatest disappointment than was the case for traditional students (16% versus 7%). On the other hand, 10.4% of the traditional students wrote in comments about one or more of the stand-alone junior-core courses as compared to the one student (2%) who was clearly disappointed in the teaching in IBE ("The IBE teachers didn't teach"). Finally, although students who had participated in IBE reported having had a higher degree of "real-world" focus in both their junior core and in their subsequent courses (see items 7 and 14 in Table 15.1 shown earlier), a much higher percentage wrote that "too little real-world focus" was their greatest disappointment than was the case for traditional students (30% versus 16.4%).

Informal Assessment: Comments From Students' Program Portfolios

The second school involved in the study is Central Missouri State University (CMSU), a mid-size, regional, teaching-oriented school, with a population of 16,000. Since the IBE program had only been in operation at CMSU for three semesters when this chapter was written, we had no opportunity to conduct a formal assessment of its impact like the one at the University of Oklahoma. However, comments from a program portfolio (graded pass-fail) that students are required to create for prospective employers provide persuasive evidence supporting the same kinds of outcomes that occurred at the University of Oklahoma. Some of their comments are as follows:

> I feel that I learned more and got more experience in the IBE class than I have in any other school activity. I feel that I have a better understanding of myself and of other people. I am more willing to work in groups to accomplish goals. I would recommend taking the IBE class even if I wasn't a business major.

> Almost all of my learning experiences came from actually doing something or relating the topic to something that I already had knowledge of. For example, I can study for a test and make an "A." This does not mean that I learned the material, though; I will most likely forget it within the week. However, if I can physically do an action, it is easier to remember.

> I always thought that people would only help me if they could get some sort of benefit from it. After participating in my company, I have realized that is simply not true. Most people are willing to help with anything you could need. Being part of a non-profit organization really opened my eyes to this.

> I have learned one must take the good with the bad, the fun with the work, and at times, just complete frustration. The ability to manage all these feelings and moods is what makes a student a leader in a class and potentially a leader in the business world.

> This experience has not only taught me the course material, or how to start and run a business, but also it has taught me a lot about myself. I am a very hard worker and always strive for success. I have also learned that I care about other people and their own opinions. I have also discovered that I learn best from trial and error and hands-on experience.

> Overall the IBE experience has been one of the best I've had since I have been in college. Just learning about the key factors of running a business and growing along the side of your peer was an experience within itself. I have earned a greater respect for those who have tried, but sometimes have failed and also those peers that have now become my friends.
>
> Being in IBE was a one of a kind experience and I would recommend it to every business major. I learned things about myself, interacting with others, and had my first hands on business experience.
>
> I've learned that I tend to take control on my side of things and don't let others help me. Had I gotten someone to help me, maybe things could have gone faster and better. My interaction with others has changed greatly over the course of the semester.
>
> I was complimented on my presentation, but learned bankers are much more pessimistic than optimistic. The numbers I showed them were for a "best case" scenario, and they expanded my knowledge for the future by explaining the reasons to use a "worst case" instead . . .
>
> The service project was a great experience raising money for such a good organization. It has taught me important areas such as ethics, communication, and working with others as a member of a team.
>
> I have learned a lot about myself from this class. I have learned now that people need incentive or need a drive to succeed. For me a drive is money and will always be money, but in this class we didn't make a profit, so we couldn't pay our employees with money. We had to energize our members to sell without incentives.
>
> IBE has opened a gateway into a different learning style for me and it has also helped in the learning aspects of my other courses that I am taking and will take. If I had to go back and choose to do IBE, I would make the same choice and not change a thing.

Many of the comments indicate that students were learning a great deal about themselves as well as developing the knowledge of business concepts and work-related skills. IBE is often a student's first opportunity to assess their abilities in a setting that approximates the kinds of situations they will face when they graduate and enter the workforce.

Discussion

Data from the formal study at the University of Oklahoma clearly support two very important conclusions with respect to the impact of IBE. First, students who participated in IBE perceived that the knowledge and skills they had gained from their junior-core courses were greater than was the case for non-IBE students. Second, even though they were enrolled in exactly the same post-core courses as the students who took the four stand-alone junior-core courses, IBE students appear to have gained more from and had a more positive experience in their *subsequent* courses. They were more confident in their understanding of course concepts, how concepts from different disciplines fit together, the problems inherent in working with others, and how to translate theory into action. In addition, the student comments from CMSU strongly suggest that the IBE experience enables students to learn much about themselves as well.

Although any conclusions about students' attitudes require a degree of inference, data from literally every question in the entire questionnaire and from each of the student comments suggest that participation in IBE has a strong and lasting positive impact on students' attitudes. For example, one clear indicator is that IBE students' scores on all 14 questions that asked them to rate the understandings and skills they had gained from the junior core and from their subsequent coursework (see Table 15.1 shown earlier) were higher than the traditional group.

In our judgment, some of the data from the open-ended questions provide less direct but even more powerful evidence of IBE's positive impact on students' attitudes. For example, one general indicator is simply that a much higher number of non-IBE students were unwilling to put forth the effort to answer the open-ended questions than were former IBE students (see Tables 15.2 and 15.3 shown earlier). Another indicator is that, as a group, the students who were in the traditional junior core seem to have taken a far more negative slant in answering the open-ended questions. For example, when asked about the beneficial aspect of their undergraduate business degree program, six times as many in that group failed to provide any answer, and another 6.5% wrote in a negative comment, compared to 0% for the IBE group (see Tables 15.2 and 15.3). Further, in contrast to the traditional group, none of the former IBE students wrote in an undifferentiated negative on the question asking for students' greatest disappointment.

Probably the greatest strength of the study was the fact that the data were collected in a setting that was temporally and contextually removed from the junior core. This allowed us to be quite confident that the responses were largely unbiased with respect to the issues we wanted to study. On the other hand, because IBE was not a required program, we had no way of knowing how much of the differences reported by traditional versus IBE students were due to self-selection bias. To some extent, however, our concerns in this area were reduced by two factors. First, the ability level of the two groups (measured by GPAs at the time they entered the junior core) was identical. Second, although we know that two types of students were overrepresented, the impact would seem to be offsetting. One overrepresented group was students who were in the JCPenney Leadership Program. These students were all in the upper tier with respect to their academic performance. The other overrepresented group consisted of students in three potentially at-risk categories who were encouraged by academic counselors to enroll in IBE. These were students who were unsure they really wanted to major in business, students who thought they wanted a business degree but were unable to decide on a major, and students who were "on contract" because they had low GPAs.

The other major weakness in the study was that it was, at best, an interim report because the *real* test of the impact of IBE had not yet occurred. Even though the graduating seniors who were in IBE reported having gained more from both their junior-core and their subsequent courses, the real test will come when they actually go to work. Unfortunately, that study will have to come later.

Impact on Faculty

Benefits

The greatest benefit for faculty is a direct result of students' reactions to IBE. Teaching in a setting where the vast majority of students are growing both professionally and personally is truly rewarding. In many ways, it is a dream that just keeps coming true—sometimes in spite of the fact that, particularly in the early stages of the program, we were still trying to figure out how to take advantage of the powerful "teaching moments" that regularly and automatically occur as students are trying develop and implement their business and service ventures. Other benefits are less obvious but no less real. One is an ongoing opportunity to enrich students' understanding of the material being taught as a natural consequence of seeing it in a context that is both applied and automatically linked to ideas from other disciplines.

Another benefit is that IBE faculty have a great deal of flexibility in managing their teaching schedule. The core courses are scheduled for three consecutive hours on a Monday/Wednesday/Friday schedule, followed by an hour for the practicum during which students generally meet on their own to do company business. Prior to the start of the semester, we create a master calendar showing which blocks of time each faculty member will be meeting with students and can easily adjust the schedule to work around everything from lab availability or academic conferences to special family events that we would be hesitant to miss a class to attend. Further, when emergencies arise (e.g., illness), we can almost seamlessly adjust to meet our teaching needs without creating problems for either students or our own overall class schedule.

Costs

The major faculty cost associated with IBE is remarkably small and is primarily limited to the additional effort required in two areas during the first semester of teaching the course. One is that instead of following a sequence in their textbook, each instructor is required to resequence their *own* topics with the idea of covering topics "just-in-time" in relation to students' needs as they formulate and operate their businesses. The other is the cost of developing team assignments that produce information that can be used to meet company needs. For example, instead of having teams do market analysis for an existing business, the marketing instructors need to reframe the assignment so that teams are doing an analysis of a potential business for the students' own startup company. Another cost has been that the faculty team meets weekly (usually for about one-half hour) with a group consisting of a student advisor (who is paid a modest stipend) from each company to brief the faculty on students' progress, issues, and concerns. All these costs are, however, offset by the fact that the faculty effort required to supervise the practicum is less than would be required for a normal course in which they would be organizing and carrying out a teaching plan.

Conclusion

The overwhelmingly positive impact on students combined with the fact that the approach is faculty-friendly appears to be so unusual that it naturally leads to two questions: Why does it work so well? What can we learn from this example that might enable similar win-win outcomes in other situations?

In part, our answer to the first question is no different than the advice offered a number of years ago by Ward (1988), who maintained that the key is using projects in which students solve real-world problems, and by Pappas, Kiefer, and Levstik (1990), who argue that interdisciplinary/cross-curricular teaching should be organized around activities that promote and support the *active construction of meaning* for students. We have simply implemented those two ideas in a business school setting. There is nothing more "real world" for business students than getting a real-money loan and starting a business, and there is no better opportunity for constructing the meaning of core business concepts than trying to use them to run their own business. This, in fact, is the simple explanation of why IBE is so faculty-friendly. The experience is so compelling that as long as faculty have *individually* exposed students to the relevant concepts from the courses in a sequence that links them to the business and/or service activities of the practicum, integration of the concepts from different disciplines almost automatically occurs in *students'* heads. There is simply little or no need for the extremely difficult and time-consuming work that typically threatens the sustainability of interdisciplinary teaching efforts—close coordination of concepts by faculty members from different disciplines.

With respect to the second question, we strongly believe that our positive experience with interdisciplinary teaching can be replicated in other settings by following two key guidelines. The most important is building the interdisciplinary teaching effort around a situation or problem that is challenging, is focused on *doing*, and is truly "real life" for the *students.* The other is finding a group of faculty who clearly understand how their discipline relates to the situation or problem and who are willing to use a teaching approach that actively involves students in the construction of meaning (Michaelsen et al., 2004; Savin-Baden & Major, 2004).

References

Bartlett, T. (2002, May 10). Students become curricular guinea pigs. *The Chronicle of Higher Education,* p. A12.

Creamer, E. G., & Lattuca, L. R. (Eds.). (2005). *New directions for teaching and learning: No. 102. Advancing faculty learning through interdisciplinary collaboration.* San Francisco, CA: Jossey-Bass.

DeZure, D. (1999). *Interdisciplinary teaching and learning.* Retrieved June 19, 2006, from the College of Charleston, Center for Effective Teaching and Learning web site: www.cofc.edu/~cetl/Essays/InterdisciplinaryTeaching&Learning.htm

Eby, K. K. (2001, Summer/Fall). Teaching and learning from an interdisciplinary perspective. *Peer Review, 3–4*(4–1), 28–31.

Harris, C., & Harvey, A. N. C. (2000). Team teaching in adult higher education classrooms: Toward collaborative knowledge construction. In M-J. Eisen & E. J. Tisdell (Eds.), *New directions for adult and continuing education: No. 87. Team teaching and learning in adult education* (pp. 25–32). San Francisco, CA: Jossey-Bass.

Inch, S., & McVarish, J. (2003, February). Across the divide: Reflecting on university collaboration. *Reflective Practice, 4*(1), 3–10.

Johnson, D. W., Johnson, R. T., & Smith, K. A. (1991). *Cooperative learning: Increasing college faculty instructional productivity*. San Francisco, CA: Jossey-Bass.

Michaelsen, L. K., Knight, A. B. & Fink, L. D. (Eds.). (2004). *Team-based learning: A transformative use of small groups in college teaching*. Sterling, VA: Stylus.

Miller, J. A. (1991, May). Experiencing management: A comprehensive, "hands-on" model for the introductory undergraduate management course. *Journal of Management Education, 15*(2), 151–169.

Pappas, C. C., Kiefer, B. Z., & Levstik, L. S. (1990). *An integrated language perspective in the elementary school: Theory into action*. New York, NY: Longman.

Robinson, B., & Schaible, R. M. (1995, Spring). Collaborative teaching: Reaping the benefits. *College Teaching, 43*(2), 57–60.

Savin-Baden, M., & Major, C. H. (2004). *Foundations of problem-based learning*. London, England: Open University Press.

Vogler, K. E., & Long, E. (2003, September). Team teaching two sections of the same undergraduate course: A case study. *College Teaching, 51(*4), 122–126.

Ward, G. (1988). *I've got a project on . . .* Portsmouth, NH: Heinemann.

Ware, M. E., & Gardner, L. E. (1978, October). Team teaching introductory psychology as pedagogy and for faculty development. *Teaching of Psychology, 5*(3), 127–130.

Section V
Faculty Careers

16

The Scholarship of Civic Engagement: Defining, Documenting, and Evaluating Faculty Work

Robert G. Bringle, Julie A. Hatcher
Indiana University-Purdue University Indianapolis

Patti H. Clayton
North Carolina State University

Civic engagement, which is presented as teaching, research, and service in and with the community, presents new challenges for evaluating faculty work as part of the reappointment, promotion, and tenure process. The nature of service-learning, professional service, and participatory action research are examined as faculty work that can be scholarly (i.e., well informed) and the basis of scholarship (i.e., contributing to a knowledge base). As such, examples of evidence for documenting the work and issues associated with evaluating dossiers are presented.

Much of faculty work occurs on campus: teaching in classrooms, service to the university and discipline or profession, and research. However, each of these can also occur off campus when instructors deliver courses at remote sites, faculty provide professional services to the community (e.g., serving on boards, contributing to a government task force, consulting), and researchers collect data in communities. Figure 16.1 illustrates how community involvement is related to the traditional areas of faculty work. Although not part of this diagram, the intersection of teaching, research, and service in the community can occur when a faculty member designs and implements courses that use participatory action research. Community involvement can occur in all sectors of society (e.g., nonprofit, government, business) and has no geographic boundaries.

FIGURE 16.1
Community Engagement as Faculty Work

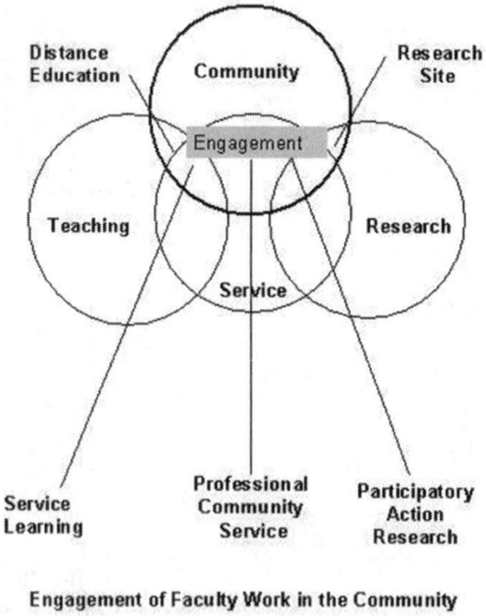

We differentiate between the terms *community involvement* and *civic engagement* in the following way: community involvement is defined primarily by location and includes faculty work that occurs in communities and in clinical settings either on or off campus. Civic engagement is a subset of community involvement and is defined by location as well as process (it occurs not only in but also *with* the community). According to this distinction, civic engagement develops partnerships that possess integrity and that emphasize participatory, collaborative, and democratic processes (e.g., design, implementation, assessment) that provide benefits to all constituencies and thus encompass service to the community. Civic engagement is consistent with many reinterpretations of community involvement that focus on the importance of reciprocity as a new model for these activities (e.g., Bringle, Games, & Malloy, 1999a; Kellogg Commission, 1999). This distinction between community involvement and civic engagement is consistent with Boyer's (1990) call for fundamental changes in the structure and behavior of the academy.

Furthermore, it is also consistent with Rice's (1996) observation that faculty work is moving from an emphasis on autonomous, individualistic work to collaborative, interdisciplinary work, and changing from the isolated character of higher education to a more public and democratic approach to academic work.

This chapter focuses on one set of implications from this shift in perspective to civic engagement: How should the scholarship of engagement be documented and reviewed as faculty work? Documenting and reviewing traditional research and classroom teaching are familiar territory for most academic institutions. In contrast, the nature of service-learning, professional service, and participatory action research (see Figure 16.1 shown earlier) are less familiar and may have unique qualities that warrant additional consideration as their scholarly nature is assessed. Each of these will be discussed as the basis for faculty work, scholarly work, and scholarship. We will begin with an overview of recent changes in the promotion and tenure process, followed by a discussion on defining and documenting service-learning, professional service, and participatory action research. In addition, issues related to evaluating dossiers, along with suggestions for faculty development and institutional change, will be offered.

Emergence of Civic Engagement From Outreach and Community Involvement

The manifestations of community involvement in higher education are remarkably varied. Faculty at many colleges and universities are involved in a range of community-based activities including cooperative extension, outreach, and continuing education programs; clinical and pre-professional programs; top-down administrative initiatives; centralized administrative-academic units with outreach missions; faculty professional service; student volunteer initiatives; economic and political outreach; applied research; and most recently, service-learning courses (Thomas, 1999). Because each of these activities can be situated within the traditional areas of academic work (i.e., teaching, research, service) they do not necessarily produce any tension toward change in defining, documenting, and evaluating faculty work. However, new interpretations of and innovative approaches to community involvement, in particular service-learning courses, have presented opportunities for both altering the ways that faculty work is valued and reinvigorating the public mission of higher education.

The emergence of civic engagement within higher education produces a dynamic tension on existing views of faculty work and can become a driver for a reexamination of traditional approaches for defining, documenting, and evaluating scholarship. The foundational work for considering new approaches to scholarship was put forth by Ernest Boyer (1990). He wrote extensively on the role of service, community, and values in education, and his later years focused on implications for faculty and higher education (Glassick, 1999). Boyer offered an expansion of the use of the term *scholarship* to encompass faculty work in four areas, including discovery, teaching, application, and integration (Boyer, 1990), and this was followed with an analysis of the attributes of scholarship that could apply to these more extensive types of faculty work (Glassick, Huber, & Maeroff, 1997).

Boyer (1996) promoted a new model for higher education in which "the academy must become a more vigorous partner in searching for answers to our most pressing social, civic, economic, and moral problems, and it must affirm its historic commitment to society" (pp. 19–20). Boyer's vision did not simply target a quantitative increase in existing outreach and community programs, but rather called for fundamental changes in the academy. Boyer (1994) noted that "what is needed is not just more programs, but a larger purpose, a larger sense of mission, a larger clarity of direction" (p. A48). Boyer (1994, 1996) added to his new vision a call for the "scholarship of engagement," which "means connecting the rich resources of the university to our most pressing social, civic, and ethical problems, to our children, to our schools, to our teachers, and to our cities" (Boyer, 1996, p. 19). We assert that Boyer very intentionally articulated "scholarship" as an aspiration for his vision because of a belief that engagement could and should have the same scholarly qualities that are characteristic of traditional research.

Although Boyer's view of the scholarship of engagement can be interpreted as an expansion of application, the scholarship of engagement can also be viewed as a new approach that reinterprets the nature not only of application but also of discovery, integration, and teaching (Bringle, Games, & Malloy, 1999b; Glassick, 1999; Rice, 2005). Many have built on Boyer's thinking and offered critical examinations that explore how community involvement can change the nature of faculty work, enhance student learning, better fulfill campus mission, influence strategic planning and assessment, and improve university-community relations (e.g., Boyer, 1994, 1996; Bringle et al., 1999a; Calleson, Jordan, & Seifer, 2005; Colby, Ehrlich, Beaumont, & Stephens, 2003; Edgerton, 1994; Harkavy & Puckett, 1994; O'Meara & Rice, 2005; Rice, 1996).

Promotion and Tenure as a Mechanism for Change

Checkoway (2001) noted that asking faculty to do one set of activities when other activities are being rewarded is "dysfunctional for the individual and the institution" (p. 135). The control of the promotion and tenure process is unevenly distributed across various constituencies on campus (e.g., chairs and deans, faculty, committees, presidents, boards of trustees, unions), and perceptions differ on who has pivotal or significant control. Regardless of the specific distribution of control on a campus, there is an opportunity to use its leverage points as mechanisms for developing understanding for a broader view of scholarship that is prompted by civic engagement. In addition, this provides an opportunity for developing the institutional capacity to honor through the advancement process some civic engagement activities as scholarly academic work and as scholarship. Our discussion will focus attention on the review of tenure-track faculty for reappointment, promotion, and tenure (RPT). This is critically important to the future of civic engagement as a new way of thinking about academic work because, as Plater (2004) notes,

> Regardless of the degree of prominence attached to civic engagement, in an era of diminishing resources and an increasing commitment to serve the public good, the aspirations for civic engagement and the support for faculty roles, rewards, and recognitions must be aligned with and proportionate to the institution's declared mission.

Thus, the RPT process can play a pivotal role in institutional transformation through the degree to which it reflects the evolving public mission on a campus.

Revising the RPT process can also improve the quality of both community involvement and civic engagement by driving change of other institutional processes that either support or deter faculty participation (e.g., hiring, annual review, faculty development, use of faculty time, institutional assessment, strategic planning). Plater (Plater, Chism, & Bringle, 2005) suggests that critical examinations of RPT must consider the particular roles of criteria (e.g., what is valued?), standards (e.g., what constitutes different levels of performance within the criteria?), and evidence (e.g., what is presented to determine level of performance?). Optimally, criteria and standards will be clearly articulated and aligned, and evidence will then be brought forward by candidates so that well-informed decisions can be made by reviewers. Unfortunately, even when criteria are clear, there can be disparate views (e.g., across ranks, across disciplines, across individual reviewers) of standards and the quality of evidence of faculty work that is expected, particularly for the non-traditional types of academic work involved in civic engagement.

Change is occurring in higher education around issues related to faculty work and its appraisal as scholarship in RPT (O'Meara & Rice, 2005). This change was aided when Glassick et al. (1997) delineated six qualities against which faculty work of all four types (i.e., discovery, teaching, integration, application) can be evaluated as scholarship. These six criteria include clear goals, adequate preparation, appropriate methods, significant results, effective communication and dissemination, and reflective critique. Similarly, Diamond and Adams (1993) identified six criteria for appraising scholarship, including discipline-related expertise, innovation, replicability, documentation, peer review, and significant impact. Both sets of criteria offer strong guidance for campuses to refine the RPT process.

Based on these analyses and the emergence of civic engagement, institutions of higher education have slowly begun to reexamine the structures, frameworks, and procedures for evaluating a broader range of faculty work as scholarly work (e.g., Bringle, Hatcher, Jones, & Plater, 2006; Brukardt, Holland, Percy, & Zimpher, 2004; Calleson, Jordan, et al., 2005; Committee on Institutional Cooperation, 2005; Driscoll & Lynton, 1999; Gelmon & Agre-Kippenhan, 2002; Michigan State University, 1996; O'Meara & Rice, 2005; Sandmann, Foster-Fishman, Lloyd, Rauhe, & Rosaen, 2000). In a recent study by O'Meara (2005), 2 out of 3 of the 729 chief academic officers surveyed reported that during the past 10 years, their institutions had changed mission and planning documents, amended faculty evaluation criteria, and provided incentive grants or developed flexible workload programs as a basis for a broader definition of scholarly work. Nevertheless, about only one-third of the chief academic officers observed increases in the scholarship of integration, student contact with faculty, and scholarship focused on civic engagement and professional service (O'Meara, 2005). The trajectory of these changes must continue, and administrative and faculty leaders must find ways to ensure that RPT reflects these changing views of scholarship.

Because higher education is still working to accommodate broader views of scholarship, especially those that result from civic engagement activities, the nature of service-learning, professional service, and participatory action research are examined as faculty work and the case is made that these activities can provide the basis for assessments that the work is scholarly (i.e., well informed) and scholarship (i.e., contributing to a knowledge base).

Civic Engagement: Service-Learning

Defining the Nature of the Pedagogy

Although not a new pedagogy (see Stanton, Giles, & Cruz, 1999), service-learning gained prominence during the 1990s due largely to the shift in focus of Campus Compact (www.compact.org) from cocurricular to curricular service, and developmental grants awarded by the Corporation for National and Community Service (www.nationalservice.org). *Service-learning* is defined as a

> Course-based, credit-bearing educational experience in which students participate in an organized service activity that meets identified community needs, and reflect on the service activity in such a way as to gain further understanding of course content, a broader appreciation of the discipline, and an enhanced sense of civic responsibility. (Bringle & Hatcher, 1995, p. 112)

Some campuses have adopted a broader definition that includes cocurricular or other activities, but in all cases service-learning must have an academic component that is connected to the service activities through structured reflection and must target both academic and civic learning outcomes.

Unlike many other forms of practice-based learning (e.g., cooperative education, extension service placements, field education, internships, practicum), service-learning is integrated into a course and has the intentional goal of developing civic skills and dispositions in students (Battistoni, 2002; Furco, 1996; Westheimer & Kahne, 2003). Unlike cocurricular community service programs (e.g., volunteer programs, community outreach, student service organizations), service-learning is academic work in which the community service activities are used as a "text" that is interpreted, analyzed, and related to the content of a course in ways that permit a formal evaluation of the academic learning outcomes (Furco, 1996). Academic credit is based on the documented learning that occurs as a result of structured reflection on the community service, not just for the service itself. Reflection activities can take a variety of forms, including journals, written assignments, group discussion, multimedia presentations, and reports to the community agency (Eyler, Giles, & Schmiede, 1996; Hatcher & Bringle, 1997). Effective reflection activities should clearly link the service experience to the learning objectives; be structured; occur regularly; provide feedback from the instructor; and include the opportunity to explore, clarify, and alter values (Hatcher & Bringle, 1997; Hatcher, Bringle, & Muthiah, 2004). In addition, high-quality service-learning classes demonstrate *reciprocity* between the campus and the community, between academics and service providers, between students and community representatives, with each giving and receiving, each teaching and learning, and each gaining new understanding of and respect for the other.

Although there is more to civic engagement than service-learning, the values, theories, and practice of service-learning can serve as a basis for informing and valuing professional service and participatory action research (see Figure 16.1 shown earlier) as civic engagement. As such, service-learning becomes an impetus for higher education to examine critically both the methods and goals of a broad range of community involvement activities (e.g., Boyer, 1994, 1996; Bringle et al., 1999a; Clayton & Ash, 2004; Colby et al., 2003; Harkavy & Puckett, 1994; Langseth & Plater, 2004; Rice, 1996; Zlotkowski, 2000).

Documenting Service-Learning as Teaching and Service

There is emerging consensus from multiple disciplinary perspectives regarding the qualities of good learning environments (Chickering & Gamson, 1987; Hatcher, 1997; Marchese, 1997; Pascarella & Terenzini, 1991), and well-designed service-learning courses will typically contain many of the components of effective learning environments for undergraduate students. Because service-learning heightens the role that students and communities can assume as constructors of knowledge, it reflects a paradigm shift in higher education from teaching to learning (Barr & Tagg, 1995). Service-learning also broadens the perspective on learning outcomes beyond rote learning of discipline-specific content. Research shows that service-learning students are likely to have increased contact with faculty (Eyler & Giles, 1999), interact and collaborate with others as they provide service (Eyler & Giles, 1999), engage in active learning at their service activity and through reflection activities, devote more time to coursework (Sax & Astin, 1997), participate in diverse ways of learning (Kolb, 1984), and develop more sophisticated ways of thinking about academic and civic matters (Ash, Clayton, & Atkinson, 2005). Service-learning not only encompasses "serving to learn," but also "learning to serve." To the degree that educators are concerned with developing civic education (Battistoni, 2002; Westheimer & Kahne, 2003), civic-minded professionals and graduates (Sullivan, 2005), and socially relevant knowledge (Altman, 1996), service-learning is a powerful pedagogy (Astin & Sax, 1998; Eyler, Giles, Stenson, & Gray, 2001; Sax & Astin, 1997).

This discussion provides an outline of the various ways in which service-learning instructors can demonstrate that what they are doing is not only good service-learning but also good teaching. Faculty who teach service-learning courses should be able to demonstrate in dossiers focused on teaching that, first and foremost, they designed learning opportunities that contain elements known to produce depth of understanding; that is, they are engaged in scholarly and well-informed teaching (Chickering & Gamson, 1987; Marchese, 1997). All pedagogies should be held to this standard, not just service-learning. An even higher standard is for faculty to offer evidence not only that their pedagogy conforms to good practice but also that their instruction resulted in the desired learning outcomes. This standard of evidence should be expected in order to demonstrate scholarly teaching, whether through service-learning or some other pedagogy (Huber & Hutchings, 2005). For example, Ash et al. (2005) found that structured, guided reflection in a service-learning course enhanced academic mastery, as well as the overall quality of thinking, when written products were independently assessed with a rubric. In addition, instructors of service-learning courses have the opportunity to demonstrate superior attainment of discipline-based educational objectives as well as civic outcomes (Ash et al., 2005; Eyler et al., 2001). This is the type of evidence that would be valued in a dossier to demonstrate excellence in teaching.

Instructors of service-learning courses can also demonstrate in their dossiers that their courses and students have had a positive impact on communities through service (e.g., through their students' community service). Often, through service-learning, faculty become professionally involved in a variety of ways at the community organization and this involvement can be documented as an important dimension of professional service. Additionally, service-learning instructors can provide evidence of having formed and maintained good working relationships with community partners that often have mutual benefits beyond the course (e.g., program development, grants). Again, this is not to say that service-learning courses should be held to a different standard than traditional instruction; rather, this set of outcomes illustrates the richness of evidence that can be presented by faculty documenting service-learning and demonstrates how service-learning raises the bar toward aspirations that should be held for documenting all types of teaching and learning.

When the faculty member's work and research on service-learning provides a basis for informing others about designing and implementing service-learning courses or increases understanding of teaching and learning in the discipline or campus-community partnerships, then it has the potential to be viewed as scholarship (i.e., scholarship of teaching and learning). As such, scholarship regarding service-learning contributes to scholarship on civic engagement.

Civic Engagement: Professional Service in and With the Community

Defining the Nature of Professional Service

Professional service is the least well understood area of faculty work and typically results in a perfunctory approach toward institutional work (e.g., committees) and disciplinary and professional work (e.g., roles and responsibilities in associations). However, professional service can also be the basis for scholarly academic work and scholarship. Lynton (1995) provides a conceptual analysis of how professional service can aspire to scholarship, and Driscoll and Lynton (1999) provide further details and examples to illustrate how faculty can present documentation for professional service as scholarship.

Lynton (1995) limits the scope of professional service (versus private or personal service) to activities that are grounded in and informed by the faculty member's disciplinary or professional knowledge. Thus, for example, a faculty member in physics who is active in professional service in the community should only present for administrative review those activities that are related to physics or science (e.g., serving on a government task force on nuclear safety), not other activities (e.g., activities in the community that are unrelated, per se, to disciplinary expertise). The guidebook *Service @ Indiana University* (Center for Public Service and Leadership, 1999) presents a broader view of potential knowledge bases and suggests that professional service can draw on three types of knowledge: 1) as a member of a discipline or professional organization, 2) as an educator (i.e., the faculty member may have special expertise on pedagogy that transcends the discipline), and 3) as a member of an institution (i.e., institutional knowledge can enable a faculty member to accomplish tasks for which others are less able). Because most campuses have not had discussions about the nature of professional service, there is little guidance for faculty to know what should and should not be documented for RPT review beyond denotative lists.

Professional service as civic engagement reflects an approach to working with communities that emphasizes significant contributions through democratic and participatory processes. Faculty regard themselves as social trustees of knowledge and their expertise is valued as a public good intended for public purposes (Sullivan, 2005). When the professional service not only draws on the faculty member's knowledge base (i.e., scholarly professional service) but also contributes to knowledge bases (e.g., disciplines, profession practice, interdisciplinary) and other communities of practice, then it has the potential to be viewed as scholarship (i.e., scholarship of professional service).

Documenting Professional Service as Civic Engagement

Professional service is poorly documented for a number of reasons. Fundamentally, it is underappreciated as faculty work, it is poorly understood, and it is typically not seen as warranting academic evaluation. Inadequate documentation is often limited to listing only assignments and roles (e.g., membership on a committee), with no indication of the nature and results of the work (e.g., level of activity, significance of accomplishments), with no evidence of the role of the particular faculty member (e.g., chair, key author of a new policy), with little or no external peer review (although typically there will be peer review from colleagues and the chair), and with no reflective statement about how the service activities are consistent with the faculty member's professional goals and other interests (e.g., why *these* service activities?). This is analogous to documenting teaching by simply providing evidence that classes were held and, for research, by simply providing evidence that data were collected. Even when professional service is a secondary area of consideration in the review process, there should be annotation of some (but not necessarily all) service activities that is in proportion to their nature and significance. If there is no significance to the aggregate of service activities, then it should be acknowledged by reviewers as "unsatisfactory service" or unsatisfactorily documented service.

Academic advancement for professional service, whether in the community, university, or discipline/profession, should not be based solely on "doing good" nor doing one's administrative job well. Whereas such claims may be appropriate for some awards and for annual reviews, they should not be the basis for academic promotion in the RPT process. At the least, documentation of significant professional service activities should demonstrate that they are well informed by good practice (i.e., scholarly service).

When professional service becomes more salient in a faculty member's work, particularly for the civically engaged scholar, then the documentation should be correspondingly more complete and rigorous. This must occur when the professional service activities are claimed to be scholarly. Key questions that distinguish good service activities from activities that approach scholarly status include "What is the compelling intellectual question?" (Sandmann et al., 2000) and "How have others learned from your good work?" Scholarly claims will be warranted for professional service when documentation presents 1) multiple forms of evidence about the impact of the activities; 2) clear evidence of the academic qualities of the work, including innovation (versus repetitive, routinized activities); 3) effective communication to relevant stakeholders, including academic audiences (i.e., academic publications); 4) peer review of the work, including academic peers from the discipline; 5) evidence of professional growth in the work; and 6) contributions to a knowledge base (Center for Public Service and Leadership, 1999). When the professional service is not just community involvement but also aspires to being civic engagement, then there should also be evidence that it has been conducted in a manner that is reciprocal and mutually beneficial to the community partners, and that the results of the service activities have been shared in multiple ways with diverse stakeholders.

Civic Engagement: Participatory Action Research

Defining the Nature of Participatory Action Research

Whether applied or basic, documenting research is familiar territory. Participatory action research is civically engaged research that involves collaboration between the campus and community to identify mutually beneficial outcomes of the research (Strand, Cutforth, Stoecker, Marullo, & Donohue, 2003). That is, the research is conducted in such a way that the academic participants benefit because it meets their scholarly interests (i.e., contributes to the academic knowledge base), and the community participants benefit because it meets their civic interests (e.g., informs action that promotes social justice and quality of life). To the degree that these motives and outcomes converge, the activities and the supporting partnership fulfill the expectations of civic engagement.

As a form of civic engagement, participatory action research is not just research in the community, but research *with* the community. As such, it democratizes knowledge and acknowledges different ways of knowing and different types of knowledge (Bender, 1997). In addition, those in the community are co-researchers who participate in the design, implementation, analysis, dissemination, and utilization of the research (Strand et al., 2003). Furthermore, to be scholarly (well informed), participatory action research requires not only that it produces meaningful results but also that the academic participant demonstrates how the work respects the context in which it takes place. When the research also contributes to the discipline or profession's knowledge base, improves the practices of participatory action research, or informs the academic community about how to undertake similar work, it then has the potential to be the basis of scholarship and part of the scholarship of engagement.

Documenting Participatory Action Research as Research and Service

In addition to traditional criteria for research (e.g., publications, peer review, grant funding, significance to the discipline), documenting participatory action research as scholarly, well-informed research and as scholarship, like documenting professional service in the community and service-learning, warrants some additional types of evidence. In all these cases, there is a broader collection of stakeholders (e.g., community partners) who can provide evidence beyond discipline-based or profession-based peers about the significance and impact of the research. The faculty member needs to demonstrate how the work has contributed to a body of knowledge not only for the discipline or profession (e.g., peer-reviewed publications) but also for the community (e.g., through effective communications that were appropriate for different audiences). Furthermore, documenting the nature of the partnerships that supported the work is integral.

Supporting Faculty Participation in Civic Engagement

Bringle et al. (2006) use Kolb's (1984) model as a framework for designing faculty development activities and campus interventions to support civic engagement: Concrete experiences provide a basis for observations and reflections, which lead to abstract conceptualizations that have new implications for action. Faculty are predisposed to abstract conceptualization and therefore can be receptive to workshops, lectures and conferences that discuss new models of teaching (e.g., service-learning) and research (e.g., participatory action research), and presentations by experts, all of which are aimed at broadening their views of scholarship. Similar interventions can target the gatekeepers for administrative review (e.g., chief academic officers, deans, chairs) and those who participate on RPT review committees.

Faculty are too often deterred from actively experimenting with civic engagement because of logistics (e.g., too little time, too much work) (see Abes, Jackson, & Jones, 2002), so institutions need to find resources that can be devoted to support faculty (e.g., student scholarships for assistance with engagement, seminars, release time) and opportunities through which faculty and departments can enhance engagement activities (e.g., course development grants, engaged department grants). Because many faculty also lack knowledge and experience with civic engagement (Abes et al., 2002), they can benefit from concrete experiences (e.g., immersions in service-learning activities, neighborhood tours, visits to community agencies) that demonstrate the potential for community involvement to enhance their teaching, research, and service. Abes et al. (2002) found that faculty also appreciate learning from colleagues in their discipline/profession or on their campus about how they have developed scholarship around civic engagement (e.g., through presentations of exemplary engagement on web sites and in newsletters, through on-campus poster displays, sponsoring trips to disciplinary conferences). These venues provide opportunities for faculty active in civic engagement to be reflective about their work (e.g., through writing articles, participating on panels). Clayton and Ash (2005) have articulated the value of reflection by faculty as part of an immersion service-learning activity to help faculty better understand the nature of service-learning and to bring the lens of reflective practice and scholarship to bear on their work: Just as critical reflection helps students generate, deepen, and document their learning and growth, it can also provide these same outcomes for faculty. Those focused on faculty development can play a key role in reaching these outcomes by structuring faculty development and other interventions accordingly.

Supporting Faculty in Documenting Civic Engagement

Once faculty have gained an understanding of civic engagement and have the confidence to embark on this type of work, attention should be given to documentation. Faculty can be coached on how best to present their good work in ways that respond to campus guidelines and to general criteria for scholarship (Calleson, Kauper-Brown, & Seifer, 2005). Workshops, one-on-one coaching, mock RPT reviews, and archiving successful dossiers can help faculty prepare dossiers that present the appropriate evidence in a persuasive manner. Understanding the various guidelines and models early in a faculty member's career can provide strategies for accumulating pertinent evidence (Committee on Institutional Cooperation, 2005; Driscoll & Lynton, 1999; Michigan State University, 1996), which can also be used for portfolios for awards, grant applications, and recognitions (Plater, 2004). An excellent dossier is one that educates readers from diverse backgrounds about the scholarly aspects of the work as sound academic work and creates advocates for the case.

Faculty development programs can also be designed to foster scholarship associated with service-learning and other aspects of civic engagement. Successful faculty learning communities support a group of faculty over the course of a year to explore a variety of topics and conduct scholarly work (e.g., Bringle, Games, Foos, Osgood, & Osborne, 2000; Rice & Stacey, 1997). A Boyer Scholars Faculty Development Program at Indiana University–Purdue

University Indianapolis involves six faculty in scholarship and research in their service-learning course. The Service-Learning Program at North Carolina State University seeks out and creates opportunities for experienced service-learning faculty to coauthor articles, present on conference panels, and conduct research in collaboration with program staff. These initiatives intentionally build a cohort of faculty with the explicit goal of advancing their scholarship associated with civic engagement.

Supporting Faculty in Evaluating Civic Engagement

As Rice (1996, 2005) notes, the trajectory of change for an expanded view of scholarship, including engaged scholarship, faces obstacles that are deeply ingrained. Cherwitz (2005) suggests that key obstacles include "inflexible administrative structures, historically embedded practices, status quo thinking, and inertia" (p. 49). Because the work is often interdisciplinary, team oriented, process oriented, and diffuse in impact across nontraditional constituencies (e.g., beyond the discipline), the academy is not well prepared to review its documentation, which impedes cultural change. Examining the three nontraditional areas of faculty work that form the core of civic engagement (i.e., service-learning, professional service in the community, participatory action research) highlights the similarities that they have with implicit and explicit views of what constitutes scholarship. However, inertia as well as active resistance inhibit expanding views of scholarship beyond the traditional but narrow prescriptive presumption that if it is not basic research published in one of the top-tier journals in the discipline, then it does not count. Changing RPT guidelines (Langseth & Plater, 2004), while important for the opportunity of discussing issues and for providing structural support for change, are incomplete and insufficient. Braxton, Luckey, and Helland (2002) conducted a national survey of faculty in four disciplines from five different types of institutions to determine the extent to which Boyer's (1990) four types of scholarly work had achieved structural, procedural, and incorporation institutionalization—stages of institutionalization with incorporation being the highest level. All four types of scholarship achieved structural institutionalization, but only teaching and discovery were perceived as receiving significant consideration in the workload of faculty (procedural), and only discovery was firmly engrained in the values of the institutions surveyed and in the support offered to faculty (incorporation). This suggests that the changes are slow and that more focused institutional work must be devoted to changing not just RPT guidelines but also the culture of a campus in order for scholars to be rewarded for dedicating themselves to civic engagement.

Thus, in addition to changing RPT guidelines, it is important to consider other interventions that can support change in the institutional culture regarding what is recognized as scholarship. Diamond and Adams (1993) identify the importance of executive leadership, faculty as advocates, policies, and broad faculty ownership as key components in producing institutional change. Executive leadership is important, and chief academic officers must provide leadership to promote change (Langseth & Plater, 2004; O'Meara, 2005). In addition, campuses are initiating change in other ways to support engaged scholarship (see campus case studies in Langseth & Plater, 2004, and O'Meara & Rice, 2005). Reexamination of mission statements and accreditation presents opportunities for campus deliberation.

Broadening discussion and exposure beyond current practitioners of civic engagement increases familiarity with and appreciation of the work among those least familiar with it (even if they do not do it), and helps prepare other faculty to understand how it can warrant claims of scholarly work and scholarship so that they can more effectively review dossiers. In addition, workshops and discussions can be directed at RPT committees (e.g., department, school, university), deans, and chairs about guidelines, changes in guidelines, and advising faculty about the guidelines. These can be complemented with presentations at new faculty orientation and in workshops for those preparing dossiers in ways that produce greater alignment among criteria, standards, and evidence.

The fundamental question that must be addressed across all campus interventions directed at structural and cultural change to the RPT process is "In what significant ways is the intellectual culture of your institution compatible and incompatible with programs that embrace civic engagement?" (Walshok, 2004). Answering that question candidly will provide guidance about designing campus-specific interventions to enhance the capacity to review dossiers and to support faculty work.

Summary

Cherwitz (2005) calls for academic engagement to result in a substantial shift in how we understand our purpose and how we conduct our work toward public purposes, public problem solving, and public participation in knowledge generation. Cherwitz suggests—as have many others in the past decade—that these changes will require radical rethinking of service, epistemology, and the organizational processes and structures used to effect change. The risk is that the traditions of higher education will be more successful in changing work done under the banner of civic engagement than civic engagement is in changing the work of the academy.

In spite of the widespread lack of institutionalization (Braxton et al., 2002; O'Meara, 2005), faculty are venturing into civic engagement in increasing numbers (Campus Compact, 2005). However, as Glassick et al. (1997) challenged higher education to adapt to a new, broader vision of faculty work and of scholarship, they concluded by noting that "courage" may be a requisite without sufficient institutional support.

> Scholars must gain confidence that through their courage to move beyond the ordinary they can enrich and further theoretical knowledge, strengthen practical applications of knowledge, and demonstrate new ways of looking at the connecting pints where different kinds of knowledge converge. (p. 66)

As laudable and important as courage may be, faculty should not be asked to undertake this work with only limited hope of recognition. Rather, as the result of deliberate campus work and commitments, faculty can be encouraged and supported in pursuing the scholarship of engagement, knowing that their good work will be honored as scholarly work. However, in absence of institutional work focused on criteria, standards, and evidence for civic engagement, the risk exists that is illustrated in a line from the movie *Amadeus:* "You are passionate, but you do not persuade" (Forsman, 1984).

Any discussion of RPT as it relates to faculty development activities designed to prepare faculty for engaged scholarship, its documentation, and its review, is necessarily embedded in a broader agenda (Bringle et al., 1999a; Gelmon & Agre-Kippenhan, 2002; Sandmann et al., 2000; Calleson, Kauper-Brown, et al., 2005). For most campuses, positioning civic engagement within this broader context is complicated by 1) the civic agenda being poorly defined, 2) service, and how it might be integrated with teaching and research, is too often not a high priority, 3) there is a lack of leadership for these initiatives, and 4) the civic agenda is perceived as too laden with values, which are often considered messy and too subjective to be a component of rigorous scholarship (Wellman, 1999). Thus, Walshok (1999) has proposed that each campus seriously consider the following questions:

- Are you asking faculty to account for the *public meaning and impact* of their scholarship beyond the discipline or profession?
- How is civic engagement presented as an *intellectual imperative*?

- How is the institution *intentionally* supporting faculty (e.g., enabling infrastructures) with an interest in civic engagement activities?

Broad campus discussions answering these questions coupled with dedicated executive leadership can contribute to producing a culture that supports, recognizes, and rewards a more inclusive view of scholarly work that will include civic engagement.

References

Abes, E. S., Jackson, G., & Jones, S. R. (2002, Fall). Factors that motivate and deter faculty use of service-learning. *Michigan Journal of Community Service Learning, 9*(1), 5–17.

Altman, I. (1996, April). Higher education and psychology in the millennium. *American Psychologist, 51*(4), 371–378.

Ash, S. L., Clayton, P. H., & Atkinson, M. P. (2005, Spring). Integrating reflection and assessment to capture and improve student learning. *Michigan Journal of Community Service Learning, 11*(2), 49–60.

Astin, A. W., & Sax, L. J. (1998, May/June). How undergraduates are affected by service participation. *Journal of College Student Development, 39*(3), 251–263.

Barr, R. B., & Tagg, J. (1995, November/December). From teaching to learning—A new paradigm for undergraduate education. *Change, 27*(6), 12–25.

Battistoni, R. (2002). *Civic engagement across the curriculum: A resource book for service-learning faculty in all disciplines*. Providence, RI: Campus Compact.

Bender, T. (1997). *Intellect and public life: Essays on the social history of academic intellectuals in the United States.* Baltimore, MD: Johns Hopkins University Press.

Boyer, E. L. (1990). *Scholarship reconsidered: Priorities of the professoriate.* Princeton, NJ: Carnegie Foundation for the Advancement of Teaching.

Boyer, E. L. (1994, March 9). Creating the new American college. *The Chronicle of Higher Education,* p. A48.

Boyer, E. L. (1996, Spring). The scholarship of engagement. *Journal of Public Service and Outreach, 1*(1), 11–20.

Braxton, J. W., Luckey, W., & Helland, P. (2002). *Institutionalizing a broader view of scholarship through Boyer's four domains* (ASHE-ERIC Higher Education Report, 29[2]). San Francisco, CA: Jossey-Bass.

Bringle, R. G., Games, R., Foos, C. L., Osgood, R., & Osborne, R. (2000, February). Faculty Fellows Program: Enhancing integrated professional development through community service. *American Behavioral Scientist, 43*(5), 882–894.

Bringle, R. G., Games, R., & Malloy, E. A. (Eds.). (1999a). *Colleges and universities as citizens.* Needham Heights, MA: Allyn & Bacon.

Bringle, R. G., Games, R., & Malloy, E. A. (1999b). Colleges and universities as citizens: Reflections. In R. G. Bringle, R. Games, & E. A. Malloy (Eds.), *Colleges and universities as citizens* (pp. 193–204). Needham Heights, MA: Allyn & Bacon.

Bringle, R. G., & Hatcher, J. A. (1995, Fall). A service-learning curriculum for faculty. *Michigan Journal of Community Service Learning, 2*(1), 112–122.

Bringle, R. G., Hatcher, J. A., Jones, S., & Plater, W. M. (2006). Sustaining civic engagement: Faculty development, roles, and rewards. *Metropolitan Universities Journal, 17*(1), 62–74.

Brukardt, M. J., Holland, B., Percy, S. L., & Zimpher, N. (2004). *Calling the question: Is higher education ready to commit to community engagement? A Wingspread statement.* Milwaukee, WI: University of Wisconsin–Milwaukee, Milwaukee Idea Office.

Calleson, D. C., Jordan, C., & Seifer, S. D. (2005, April). Community-engaged scholarship: Is faculty work in communities a true academic enterprise? *Academic Medicine, 80*(4), 317–321.

Calleson, D. C., Kauper-Brown, J., & Seifer, S. D. (2005). *Community-engaged scholarship toolkit.* Seattle, WA: Community-Campus Partnerships for Health.

Campus Compact. (2005). *Season of service.* Providence, RI: Campus Compact.

Center for Public Service and Leadership, Indiana University. (1999). *Service @ Indiana University: Defining, documenting, and evaluating.* Indianapolis, IN: Author.

Checkoway, B. (2001, March). Renewing the civic mission of the American research university. *Journal of Higher Education, 72*(2), 125–147.

Cherwitz, R. A. (2005, November/December). A new social compact demands real change: Connecting the university to the community. *Change, 37*(6), 48–49.

Chickering, A. W., & Gamson, Z. F. (1987, June). Seven principles for good practice in undergraduate education. *AAHE Bulletin, 39*(7), 3–7.

Clayton, P. H., & Ash, S. L. (2004, Fall). Shifts in perspective: Capitalizing on the counter-normative nature of service-learning. *Michigan Journal of Community Service Learning, 11*(1), 59–70.

Clayton, P. H., & Ash, S. L. (2005, September). Reflection as a key component in faculty development. *On the Horizon, 13*(3), 161–169.

Colby, A., Ehrlich, T., Beaumont, E., & Stephens, J. (2003). *Educating citizens: Preparing America's undergraduates for lives of moral and civic responsibility.* San Francisco, CA: Jossey-Bass.

Committee on Institutional Cooperation. (2005). *Resource guide and recommendations for defining and benchmarking engagement.* Champaign, IL: Author.

Diamond, R. M., & Adams, B. (Eds.). (1993). *New directions for higher education: No. 81. Recognizing faculty work: Reward systems for the year 2000.* San Francisco, CA: Jossey-Bass.

Driscoll, A., & Lynton, E. A. (1999). *Making outreach visible: A guide to documenting professional service and outreach.* Washington, DC: American Association for Higher Education.

Edgerton, R. (1994). The engaged campus: Organizing to serve society's needs. *AAHE Bulletin, 47*(1), 2–4.

Eyler, J., & Giles, D. E., Jr. (1999). *Where's the learning in service-learning?* San Francisco, CA: Jossey-Bass.

Eyler, J., Giles, D. E., Jr., & Schmiede, A. (1996). *A practitioner's guide to reflection in service-learning: Student voices and reflections.* Nashville, TN: Vanderbilt University.

Eyler, J., Giles, D. E., Jr., Stenson, C. M., & Gray, C. J. (2001). *At a glance: What we know about the effects of service-learning on college students, faculty, institutions, and communities, 1993–2000* (3rd ed.). Nashville, TN: Vanderbilt University.

Forsman, A. (Director). (1984). *Amadeus* [Motion picture]. United States: Warner Brothers.

Furco, A. (1996). Service-learning: A balanced approach to experiential education. In B. Taylor (Ed.), *Expanding boundaries: Serving and learning* (pp. 2–6). Washington, DC: Corporation for National Service.

Gelmon, S. G., & Agre-Kippenhaan, S. (2002, January). Promotion, tenure, and the engaged scholar: Keeping the scholarship of engagement in the review process. *AAHE Bulletin, 54*(5), 7–11.

Glassick, C. E. (1999). Ernest L. Boyer: Colleges and universities as citizens. In R. G. Bringle, R. Games, & E. A. Malloy (Eds.), *Universities and colleges as citizens* (pp. 17–30). Needham Heights, MA: Allyn & Bacon.

Glassick, C. E., Huber, M. T., & Maeroff, G. I. (1997). *Scholarship assessed: Evaluation of the professoriate.* San Francisco, CA: Jossey-Bass.

Harkavy, I., & Puckett, J. L. (1994, September). Lessons from Hull House for the contemporary urban university. *Social Science Review, 68*(3), 299–321.

Hatcher, J. A. (1997, June). *Classroom assessment techniques: Ways to improve teaching and learning in a service learning class.* Paper presented at the American Association for Higher Education Assessment Forum, Miami, FL.

Hatcher, J. A., & Bringle, R. G. (1997, Fall). Reflections: Bridging the gap between service and learning. *Journal of College Teaching, 45*(4), 153–158.

Hatcher, J. A., Bringle, R. G., & Muthiah, R. (2004, Fall). Designing effective reflection: What matters to service learning? *Michigan Journal of Community Service Learning, 11*(1), 38–46.

Huber, M. T., & Hutchings, P. (2005). *The advancement of learning: Building the teaching commons.* San Francisco, CA: Jossey-Bass.

Kellogg Commission on the Future of State and Land-Grant Universities. (1999). *Returning to our roots: The engaged institution.* Washington, DC: National Association of State Universities and Land-Grant Colleges.

Kolb, D. A. (1984). *Experiential learning: Experience as the source of learning and development.* Upper Saddle River, NJ: Prentice-Hall.

Langseth, M., & Plater, W. M. (Eds.). (2004). *Public work and the academy: An academic administrator's guide to civic engagement and service-learning.* Bolton, MA: Anker.

Lynton, E. A. (1995). *Making the case for professional service.* Washington, DC: American Association for Higher Education.

Marchese, T. J. (1997). The new conversations about learning: Insights from neuroscience and anthropology, cognitive studies, and work-place studies. In *Assessing impact: Evidence and action* (pp. 79–95). Washington, DC: American Association for Higher Education.

Michigan State University. (1996). *Points of distinction: A guidebook for planning and evaluating quality outreach* (Rev. ed.). East Lansing, MI: Michigan State University.

O'Meara, K. (2005). Effects of encouraging multiple forms of scholarship nationwide and across institutional types. In K. O'Meara & R. E. Rice, *Faculty priorities reconsidered: Rewarding multiple forms of scholarship* (pp. 255–289). San Francisco, CA: Jossey-Bass.

O'Meara, K., & Rice, R. E. (2005). *Faculty priorities reconsidered: Rewarding multiple forms of scholarship.* San Francisco, CA: Jossey-Bass.

Pascarella, E. T., & Terenzini, P. T. (1991). *How college affects students: Findings and insights from twenty years of research.* San Francisco, CA: Jossey-Bass.

Plater, W. M. (2004, June). *What recognitions and rewards should a campus create to promote civic engagement of students?* Paper presented at the Wingspread Conference, Racine, WI.

Plater, W. M., Chism, N. V. N., & Bringle, R. G. (2005, February). *Revising promotion and tenure guidelines.* Panel presented at the meeting of the American Association of State Colleges and Universities, San Diego, CA.

Rice, D., & Stacey, K. (1997). Small group dynamics as a catalyst for change: A faculty development model for academic service-learning. *Michigan Journal of Community Service Learning, 4*, 64–71.

Rice, R. E. (1996). *Making a place for the new American scholar* (New Pathways Working Paper Series No. 1). Washington, DC: American Association for Higher Education.

Rice, R. E. (2005). "Scholarship Reconsidered": History and context. In K. O'Meara & R. E. Rice, *Faculty priorities reconsidered: Rewarding multiple forms of scholarship* (pp. 17–31). San Francisco, CA: Jossey-Bass.

Sandmann, L. R., Foster-Fishman, P. G., Lloyd, J., Rauhe, W., & Rosaen, C. (2000, January/February). Managing critical tensions: How to strengthen the scholarship component of outreach. *Change, 32*(1), 44–52.

Sax, L. J., & Astin, A. W. (1997, Summer/Fall). The benefits of service: Evidence from undergraduates. *Educational Record, 78*(3–4), 25–32.

Stanton, T. K., Giles, D. E., Jr., & Cruz, N. I. (1999). *Service-learning: A movement's pioneers reflect on its origins, practice, and future.* San Francisco, CA: Jossey-Bass.

Strand, K., Marullo, S., Cutforth, N., Stoecker, R., & Donohue, P. (2003). *Community-based research and higher education: Principles and practices.* San Francisco, CA: Jossey-Bass.

Sullivan, W. M. (2005). *Work and integrity: The crisis and promise of professionalism in America* (2nd ed.). San Francisco, CA: Jossey-Bass.

Thomas, N. (1999). *The institution as a citizen: How colleges and universities enhance their civic roles* (Working Paper No. 22). Boston, MA: University of Massachusetts Boston, New England Resource Center for Higher Education.

Walshok, M. L. (1999). Strategies for building the infrastructure that supports the engaged campus. In R. G. Bringle, R. Games, & E. A. Malloy (Eds.), *Colleges and universities as citizens* (pp. 74–95). Needham Heights, MA: Allyn & Bacon.

Walshok, M. L. (2004, March). *It's not just about public service: The intellectual benefits of civic engagement.* Colloquium presented at Indiana University–Purdue University Indianapolis, Indianapolis, IN.

Wellman, J. V. (1999). *Contributing to the civic good: Assessing and accounting for the civic contributions of higher education.* Washington, DC: Institute for Higher Education Policy.

Westheimer, J., & Kahne, J. (2003, Winter). What kind of citizen? Political choices and educational goals. *Campus Compact Reader, 3*(3), 1–13.

Zlotkowski, E. (2000, Fall). Service-learning in the disciplines. *Michigan Journal of Community Service Learning* [Special issue], 61–67.

17

How Post-Tenure Review Can Support the Teaching Development of Senior Faculty

Mary Deane Sorcinelli, Mei-Yau Shih,
Mathew L. Ouellett, Marjory Stewart
University of Massachusetts-Amherst

A key question that campuses face as they develop and implement post-tenure review policies is how to blend the concepts of accountability and renewal. This chapter examines a faculty development initiative linked to a post-tenure review policy at a research-intensive university. It describes the goals, processes, and outcomes of a five-year study of the program, extending research on post-tenure review and its potential for positive faculty development.

As colleges and universities seek to renew curriculum, advance academic programs, and engage in innovations in teaching and student learning, they will need to rely on their mid-career and senior faculty. Amidst dwindling resources and a concurrent rise in adjunct and part-time faculty, institutions can no longer assume that new tenure-track faculty will be hired in numbers great enough to invigorate classrooms, laboratories, and research projects (Baldwin & Chronister, 2001). The vitality of institutions will depend to a large degree on the productive engagement of mid-career and senior faculty.

Institutions have not yet fully answered the question of how best to keep senior faculty vital and productive throughout their careers. There has been much attention given to identifying and supporting the needs of new and early career faculty (Rice, Sorcinelli & Austin, 2000; Sorcinelli, 2000). In contrast, much less research has focused on faculty whom the literature refers to as "tenured," "experienced," "seasoned," "mid-career," or "senior." While it is difficult to precisely define this group of faculty, we do know that senior faculty now represent higher education's largest faculty cohort (Finkelstein, 1993), with data suggesting that more than two-thirds of all full-time faculty are over the age of 50 and approximately 50% of full-time faculty hold the rank of associate or full professor (Bland & Bergquist, 1997).

In fact, when institutions, policymakers, and higher education associations have turned their attention to tenured faculty—their roles and responsibilities, performance evaluation, and long-term career development—they have focused more on assessing faculty performance rather than on nurturing faculty development (Walker, 2002). Over the past decade, two fundamental responses to concerns about tenured faculty have emerged: post-tenure review systems and senior faculty development initiatives. It should be noted that these two processes have rarely been linked to one another in any meaningful way. This study fills a gap in the literature by examining a faculty development initiative linked to a post-tenure review policy at a research-intensive university, presenting data that assesses the program's impact as part of a post-tenure review process.

Post-Tenure Review

In the past decade, due to demographic and economic pressures, state policymakers and higher education board members have urged institutions to initiate post-tenure review policies to ensure accountability for the quality of faculty teaching, research, and service. Collective bargaining agreements in more than 37 states have initiated mandates for the implementation of post-tenure review and evaluation of tenured faculty (Licata & Morreale, 2002).

Post-tenure review refers to a "systematic, comprehensive process, separate from the annual review, aimed specifically at assessing performance and/or nurturing faculty growth and development" (Licata & Morreale, 1997, p. 1), which can be embedded in either a summative or formative framework. As Licata and Morreale (1997) note, the summative framework uses the review to collect accurate and reliable information about past performance that is used to make a personnel decision. Specific actions are taken as a result of the review—either *reward* when the performance is above average or *remediation*, in the form of a professional development plan, when the performance is judged to be below average. In contrast, the formative framework outlines a review process that is developmental, and the outcome of such a review is the development of a professional growth plan that focuses on future career development. This framework is usually not connected to any personnel decision-making and, in some cases, only the faculty member sees the review.

Researchers have noted that while the philosophy of most post-tenure review policies is formative, nearly all have summative aspects and policies outlining actions to occur if the faculty member does not address deficiencies identified in a review (Licata & Morreale, 1999). A key question that campuses face as they develop and implement post-tenure review policies, then, is how to blend the concepts of accountability and renewal into a workable system (Alstete, 2000; Licata & Morreale, 1997).

Senior Faculty Development Programs

At the same time that a range of post-tenure review processes have been taking shape, institutions have increasingly recognized the need to provide opportunities for tenured faculty to address new teaching and learning challenges. Faculty members are facing instructional situations in which students may differ widely in their levels of interest and commitment, their preparation, their availability for course-related work, and their learning styles. The ethnic and social diversity in the classroom is also changing, as enrollments of women, multicultural, and minority students continue to increase. Many faculty have not learned to teach with technology and may require support and training to function optimally in a rapidly changing technological environment. In addition, faculty are being asked to assess student learning outcomes and study and document their own teaching (Sorcinelli, Austin, Eddy, & Beach, 2006).

Given dramatic changes in the teaching and learning landscape, what does research tell us about teaching vitality among experienced faculty? While studies support the presence of some unhappiness and malaise, overall they conclude that senior faculty devote considerable energy to teaching and student concerns. Studies further suggest that the effectiveness of tenured faculty as teachers is less related to time spent on teaching than to an enlargement of teaching styles and relationships with students (Karpiak, 1997; Romano, Hoesing, O'Donovan, & Weinsheimer, 2004).

Crawley (1995) surveyed 104 research universities to learn about faculty development programs available to senior faculty. Findings revealed a high level of support for traditional approaches to faculty development (e.g., sabbaticals, unpaid leaves), but suggested that faculty development approaches that expanded or created new roles and responsibilities for senior faculty were more limited. Our review of programs at teaching and learning centers confirmed Crawley's findings. While many centers provide programs and interest groups where faculty can share issues and concerns about teaching, fewer have programs designed specifically for tenured senior faculty. Of those that do, two faculty development models predominate. The first and more common model is the provision of individual funds to encourage renewal in teaching by tenured faculty (e.g., small grants to buy books, supplies, hire technical support, and fund travel to disciplinary and teaching conferences). The literature suggests that relatively modest grants can support the development of new course or program initiatives and also send a message that the institution values the engagement and new directions taken by tenured faculty (Baldwin, 2002; Finkelstein & LaCelle-Peterson, 1993).

Some campuses have developed programs that offer a second type of opportunity in which senior faculty join other senior colleagues in structured learning communities to learn and share ideas about teaching and learning. These programs have been designed in response to studies that suggest that faculty at mid-career and senior level experience isolation and desire opportunities to talk about teaching with colleagues (Bland & Bergquist, 1997; Karpiak, 1997, 2000). Both of these senior faculty development programs have documented positive outcomes in terms of the development of new skills in and attitudes about teaching, enhanced collegiality, awareness of teaching and learning styles and strategies, and gains in student learning (Blaisdell & Cox, 2004; Jackson & Simpson, 1993; Romano et al. 2004; Shih & Sorcinelli, 2000; Stassen & Sorcinelli 2001).

Linking Post-Tenure Review and Faculty Development

While senior faculty development programs have reported a number of positive outcomes, there has been little research into the outcomes of the different but related concepts of post-tenure review and faculty development. Studies focusing on the developmental aspects of post-tenure review offer differing perspectives. Some campuses have noted benefits such as improved faculty productivity, morale, and commitment to one's discipline (Goodman, 1994). The majority of studies on post-tenure review, however, reveal little impact on a faculty member's professional development (O'Meara, 2003, 2004; Wesson & Johnson, 1991). The problem is that many of these studies are limited to data obtained during the initial startup of the program, prior to the creation of any faculty development initiatives (Harrington, 2002; O'Meara 2003, 2004). Such studies also reveal that few institutions have actually created post-tenure review processes with any relationship to faculty development programs. In fact, a new study of faculty development programs in the United States and Canada found that post-tenure review was the issue for which faculty developers from all institutional types offered the fewest services and which they ranked as least important to address through their faculty development programs (Sorcinelli et al., 2006).

The post-tenure review and professional development process described in this chapter offers one model for how to link a post-tenure review process with faculty development in teaching, providing insight into the benefits of post-tenure review that joins performance review with the fostering of the continued professional development of tenured faculty. We also highlight several key features of this model. For example, unlike many other post-tenure processes (Alstete, 2000; Licata & Morreale, 2002), this initiative has the support of the administration and faculty, sparing it from being viewed as merely symbolic. It is framed in the context of renewal rather than remediation, supporting faculty with proven records as well as those whose teaching merits attention. Additionally, institutional funds are readily available to support a wide range of development initiatives. Finally, there has been a concerted effort to document and assess the outcomes of faculty development projects.

University of Massachusetts Post-Tenure Review

The practice of regular annual reviews based on an annual faculty report and peer review by personnel committees, chairs, and deans has been well established on the University of Massachusetts–Amherst campus. However, when the University of Massachusetts System mandated post-tenure review for all its campuses in 1999, the Amherst campus set about developing a periodic multi-year review (PMYR) of all faculty, with goals distinct from annual or major personnel reviews.

The goals of PMYR were twofold. First, the reviews were designed to allow faculty to overview their performance in a way that would inform evaluations, rewards, and academic planning. Second, reviews would allow for timely consultation, intervention, and assistance that would stimulate and encourage professional development. In adopting the PMYR policy, the university and the tenured faculty, represented by the Massachusetts Society of Professors (www.umass.edu/msp), wanted to address external concerns about accountability while fostering continued professional development.

In terms of process, a PMYR is conducted every seven years for all tenured faculty. The faculty member submits a current curriculum vita and brief statement of principle activities, goals and approaches, and new directions since the last promotion review or PMYR. The statement may include a request for development funds needed for that initiative or change in direction. This statement is reviewed by the department chair and personnel committee and then forwarded to the college dean. The administration and the union agreed to an annual allocation of development funds, primarily for the enhancement of research, to be awarded through the college dean. The administration and union also directed an annual allocation of funding for teaching development to the campus's teaching and learning center, the Center for Teaching (CFT).

The CFT formed a committee representing senior faculty, the union, chairs, and deans to collaboratively create the general outline for a program to be administered by the CFT following the post-tenure personnel process. To refine and implement this development program, the CFT staff named a highly regarded senior faculty member who had been involved in the development of the PMYR process to work with them on the project. The outcome of this process was the development of a grant program designed to provide individual incentives for teaching improvements (e.g., resources, individual consultation) as well as an opportunity for collegial conversation with fellow program participants through an annual luncheon and seminar. The following is a summary of the goals, processes, and outcomes of a five-year study on the program, with the hope of extending research on post-tenure review and its potential for positive faculty development.

Grants for Professional Development in Teaching (PMYR)

Licata and Morreale (1997, 2002) suggest that professional development should be a component of any post-tenure review process. Since the 1999–2000 academic year, the CFT has funded PMYR Grants for Professional Development in Teaching in conjunction with the university-wide PMYR program.

Goals of the Grants for Professional Development in Teaching Program

The goals for the Grants for Professional Development in Teaching program are to

- Provide PMYR participants with opportunities for professional growth and renewal in teaching

- Provide funding for instructional projects designed to enhance participants' courses and teaching methods, and their students' learning
- Provide support for participants as they apply new knowledge and techniques in their teaching
- Reinforce an instructional environment that honors and recognizes dedicated senior teaching scholars

Program Structure and Processes

The Grants for Professional Development in Teaching program provides funds to faculty members for improvements and innovations in instruction through a variety of approaches which include but are not limited to development and use of multimedia or other instructional technology; development of interdisciplinary teaching methods or projects; inclusion of diversity and multiculturalism into teaching; new approaches to the assessment of teaching and student learning; improvements in course design, content presentation, delivery styles, and effectiveness.

Immediately following the department/college PMYR review process, each PMYR participant receives a copy of the grant's call for proposals and relevant information regarding the application process. These letters are followed by an email or personal telephone call reminding faculty of the proposal deadline. To further encourage participation, one-on-one information sessions are offered to assist interested faculty in the application process. Proposals are reviewed and evaluated by a committee comprised of members of the CFT staff and faculty associates to the CFT. Grants of up to $3,000 are awarded to individual faculty and can be used for such resources as classroom materials, books, travel, equipment, or hiring a research assistant.

Each grant requires at least one consultation meeting with a member of the CFT staff, participation in one voluntary and confidential classroom assessment opportunity (e.g., collecting student feedback at mid-semester followed by a consultation with CFT staff), and submission of a feedback questionnaire/project self-evaluation report at the end of the grant period. Individual faculty retain full control of all teaching plans, assessment feedback, and information on teaching improvement collected by the center. Each awardee is also personally invited to participate in an end-of-year luncheon and seminar for grant participants. At the seminar, several awardees share their project outcomes, followed by discussions among senior faculty regarding course and teaching development goals, campus resources, benefits, and challenges.

Evaluation of the Grants for Professional Development in Teaching (PMYR)

During the 2004–2005 academic year, we conducted a formal evaluation of the Grants for Professional Development in Teaching program, collecting both quantitative and qualitative data from the first five years of the program (1999–2004). The data pool of participants (N = 98) represents a wide range of disciplines (n = 42) across eight out of nine schools and colleges. All participants had completed the post-tenure review in their department and college during the previous academic year and had applied for and received funds from the CFT's Grants for Professional Development in Teaching program. We summarized data by year, college, and project type (see Table 17.1 and Figures 17.1, 17.2, and 17.3). Information was also collected from self-evaluation reports at the end of the grant period (n = 49).

Findings

In reporting findings, we first examine the grant program from an institutional perspective, using quantitative data to determine the impact of the grant program in terms of participation and project type. Second, we use qualitative data collected through consultations and self-evaluation reports to explore the ways in which faculty who have recently undergone post-tenure review articulate their individual development needs and interests as a means of advancing their teaching.

Participation in the Program

Faculty participation by year. In Table 17.1, the number of eligible faculty represents those individuals who were scheduled to complete the PMYR review process at the department and college levels. The participation rate represents the percentage of eligible faculty who applied for and were awarded grants for professional development in teaching. As indicated, the proportion of eligible faculty participating in the program has risen dramatically since year one. Between 1999 and 2004, a total of 98 teaching grants have been awarded to faculty members undergoing the PMYR process. Perhaps more importantly, participation has risen from only 6 grants awarded after the 1999–2000 call for proposals to between 23 and 25 annual awards during the past three years of the program.

TABLE 17.1
Participation Rate by Year

	Number of Grant Recipients*	Number of Eligible Faculty**	Participation Rate
1999–2000	6	90	7%
2000–2001	20	73	27%
2001–2002	23	44	52%
2002–2003	25	50	50%
2003–2004	24	70	34%

*Up to 25 grants can be awarded annually.

**Those faculty members who were scheduled to complete the PMYR review process at the department and college levels.

FIGURE 17.1
Total Grant Recipients by School and College (N = 98)

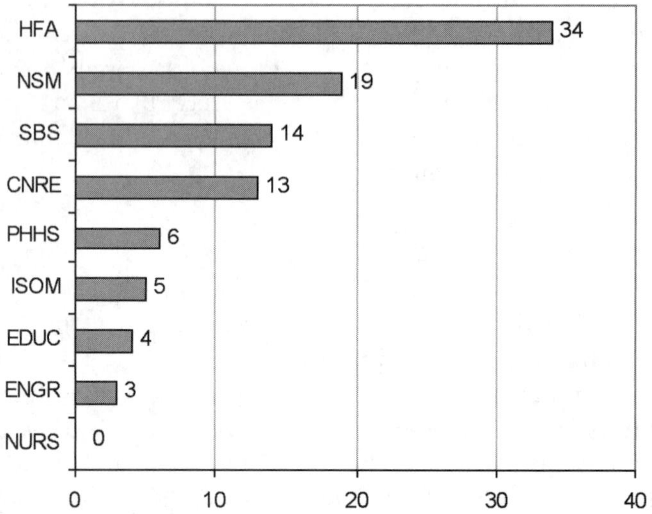

Key to Schools and Colleges

HFA: Humanities and Fine Arts
NSM: Natural Sciences and Mathematics
SBS: Social and Behavioral Sciences
CNRE: Natural Resources and the Environment
PHHS: Public Health and Health Sciences
ISOM: Isenberg School of Management
EDUC: Education
ENGR: Engineering
NURS: Nursing

Participants across schools and colleges. Over the five-year period of the study, awards have been widely distributed across schools and colleges as illustrated in Figure 17.1. A total of 98 faculty members undergoing the PMYR evaluation process in eight of the nine schools and colleges have participated in the CFT grants program.

Figure 17.2 outlines the percentage of faculty, by school and college, who participated based on the total number of faculty identified as PMYR eligible during the study period. The overall participation rate has ranged from 0% in the School of Nursing (NURS) to 75% in the School of Public Health and Human Services (PHHS). The average participation rate of the eight schools and colleges submitting grant applications was 34% over the five-year period.

FIGURE 17.2

Number of Grant Participants/Number of Eligible Faculty by School and College

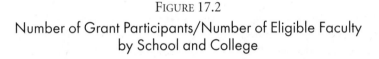

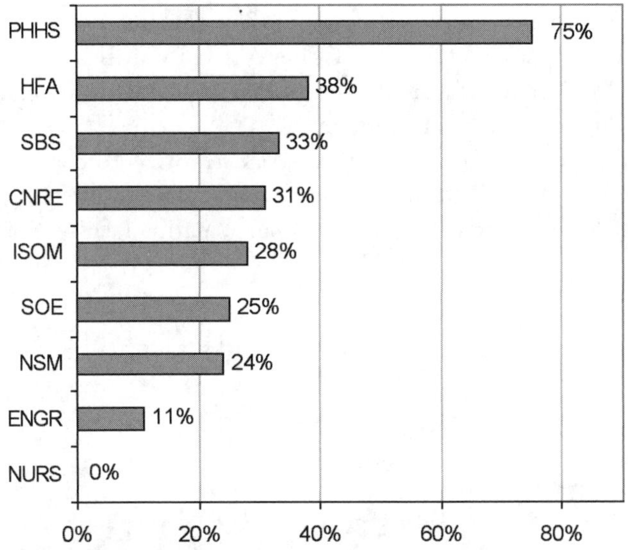

Key to Schools and Colleges

PHHS:	Public Health and Health Sciences
HFA:	Humanities and Fine Arts
SBS:	Social and Behavioral Sciences
CNRE:	Natural Resources and the Environment
ISOM:	Isenberg School of Management
SOE:	School of Education
NSM:	Natural Sciences and Mathematics
ENGR:	Engineering
NURS:	Nursing

We explored possible reasons for the lack of participation from faculty in the School of Nursing and the exceedingly high participation in the School of Public Health and Health Sciences. Analysis revealed that during the time period of the study, a number of senior faculty members in the School of Nursing elected to retire, thereby terminating their PMYR review and eligibility for teaching funds. This left only two eligible faculty during the study period, neither of whom chose to apply for the grant funding. In the case of PHHS, both the dean and department chairs personally encouraged each of their faculty to apply for the grant program, resulting in six out of eight eligible faculty applying for and awarded grants. Administrative encouragement for teaching development probably played a factor in the PHHS's high participation rate.

Another college, the College of Engineering (ENGR), had a significantly lower than average participation rate, averaging 11% over the period of the study, with only 3 of 28 eligible faculty applying for teaching grants. Upon further consultation with the dean of the college, it was clear that engineering faculty were strongly encouraged to focus their efforts on securing large grants from external sources in support of their research mandate. In contrast, the participation rate for the College of Humanities and Fine Arts (HFA) (38%) reflected a culture that encouraged the seeking of small, internal funds in support of teaching initiatives.

Scope of faculty development projects. We categorized the ways in which senior faculty self-identified their professional needs and interests, as illustrated in Figure 17.3. The vast majority of participating faculty (80%) chose

FIGURE 17.3
General Focus of Proposed Projects

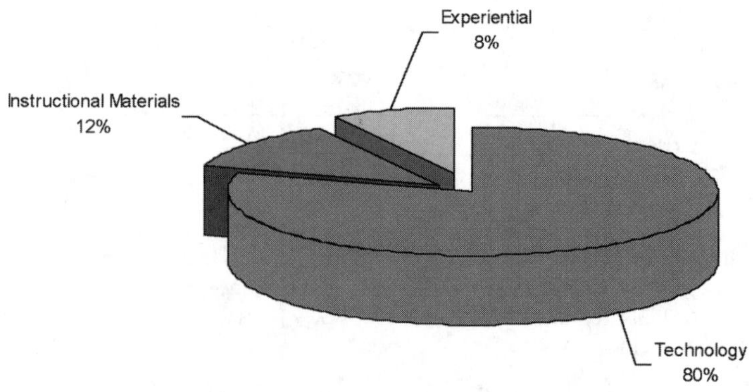

to experiment with new teaching techniques that incorporated learning technologies. Such projects included the development or update of course and departmental web sites, as well as the use of digitized materials, videos, and PowerPoint slides to improve classroom demonstrations and presentations. Another 12% of awards supported faculty development or redesign of courses or travel to teaching-related conferences to bring back new, fresh content and methods. The remaining 8% of awardees focused on teaching enhancements in the areas of experiential learning and other student-centered pedagogies. For example, one faculty member created a student-faculty partnership aimed at promoting social justice and cross-cultural understanding, integrating three related courses to create a series of interrelated learning opportunities that were student facilitated.

End of Project Year Faculty Self-Evaluation Report/Survey

Each year, a survey focusing on faculty self-reflection and evaluation is forwarded to the participants at the conclusion of the grant period. In this survey, faculty are asked to respond to a number of questions regarding their end-of-project self-evaluation. To date, 65 surveys (66%) have been received from the 98 participants from 1999–2004. For the purpose of this study, we focused on a qualitative, open-ended item—"What were the most positive effects of your project in terms of student learning and your own teaching? Any negative effects?"—and a global rating—"Rate the overall success of your project."

Faculty self-assessment of teaching practice. Almost all participants provided valuable feedback as to the status of individual projects and their perceptions of the impact of such projects on their teaching. Often highlighted was the design of "enriched" and more effective lectures. Faculty described their presentations as more well-thought-out and clearer, particularly through the use of technology such as PowerPoint. Comments such as "My lectures are now more logically structured," "I am convinced that this is the most effective way to deliver my lecture," and "I have incorporated [these strategies] into my other courses" were among the responses. Some faculty specifically identified experiencing a "transformation" or an improvement in their teaching practice through the use of active learning. For some, active learning was a result of the integration of technology into their teaching. Through personal response systems and online discussion, for example, participants reported having more tools for interacting with students in a more meaningful way. For others, active learning was evidenced by more student engagement in the classroom: "There is more interaction among students as they work together in class."

Faculty impressions of student learning. In open-ended comments, faculty also provided evidence of improved student learning. Some indicated that innovations elicited positive reactions from students, particularly in cases involving the integration of technology. One participant reported that the introduction of new technologies "reduced student frustration in learning course content," leaving them with a "real sense of achievement and confidence" the instructor had not witnessed before. Again, a number of the respondents also cited feedback from students reporting increased engagement in active learning through the use of online discussions, integrated video clips followed by class discussion, and "the addition of more frequent problem-solving activities."

Student impact and assessment. The integration of assessment strategies into the projects afforded students the opportunity to give their input. While all participants had at least 1 one-on-one consult with CFT staff, 20% also participated in formal midterm assessments of their teaching (Midterm Assessment Process, or MAP). The MAP provides a unique opportunity to collect feedback from students early in a course. A teaching consultant collects, synthesizes, and helps interpret feedback from students (through small group or survey) as well as identifies appropriate teaching suggestions. In their comments, faculty indicated that the MAP provided "useful information on students' perceptions of the course and what helps them learn" as well as concrete suggestions that allowed them to redirect their efforts to better accommodate and enhance student learning.

Overall faculty evaluation of project outcomes. Faculty were asked to rate the overall success of their project using a 5-point rating scale that ranged from "fair" at the lowest end of the scale to "good," "very good," "excellent," and "outstanding." Twenty-one faculty responded to this question, and the overwhelming majority of respondents (76%) considered the outcome of their grant project "excellent" or "outstanding," with an additional 14% of respondents rating overall success as "very good." These data show a high level of agreement among faculty on the value of this professional development opportunity. (Twenty-eight faculty chose not to rate the overall success of their projects yet, noting that the projects were still "in process.")

Unanticipated outcomes. Feedback in the reports and faculty conversations with the project coordinator suggest that preparing and implementing a teaching project may have enhanced not only participants' instruction but also their perception of the entire PMYR process. One faculty member responded, "Had I not engaged in preparing my PMYR proposal and carrying out the PMYR project [with CFT], my teaching would have been considerably less effective."

Faculty also reported that "although the grant has been set up for a finite period, it will be used to acquire tools whose applications will grow over time." Another faculty member indicated his plan to use these tools "not only to improve my teaching but to enhance my professional development by locating what I do within the larger context of our digital electronic age." A senior member who had been at the institution for 35 years noted, "With small investments such as proposed here, the University and its students [through Web access] can reap substantial benefits as we enter a period of revolutionary transformation of art history teaching."

Aspects of concern to faculty. Among areas that merited attention, one-half of awardees expressed concerns about the amount of time necessary to implement a project. Many faculty did not anticipate the level of commitment required to learn new software, revise and prepare new lectures, and develop new laboratory activities. Of respondents who implemented technology-based projects, one-third mentioned technical difficulties and the setup time for computerized visual aids as another area of concern. In cases where web and email communication were introduced between students and faculty members, faculty noted a considerably increased workload in managing these out-of-class communications with students.

Implications

A review of the findings reveals some broad trends in senior faculty renewal in teaching. Given appropriate opportunities, tenured faculty will integrate modern technologies into their teaching practice, investigate pedagogies of engagement as a way to improve student learning, redesign introductory lecture courses, assess gains in student learning and their own teaching practices, and demonstrate interest in departmental priorities (i.e., interdisciplinary programs, new course development, student research internships, etc.).

The following are several implications for the design and delivery of faculty development programs as part of a post-tenure review process.

Emphasize Individual and Institutional Support

This study found that personal contact is crucial to encourage faculty undergoing post-tenure review to apply for and engage in teaching development and renewal projects. Faculty who received encouragement from department chairs and deans regarding teaching development were more positive toward applying for grants for teaching as were faculty who had engaged in other CFT grant initiatives or were personally contacted by CFT staff.

Assure Confidentiality

Confidentiality was critical to ensure faculty members' willingness to take risks. The CFT's sovereignty from departmental and school or college oversight contributed to faculty willingness to test new waters and engage in developmental activities they previously had refused to engage in within the context of the classroom or their post-tenure personnel evaluation.

Highlight Opportunity

Another factor that appears to have contributed to increased numbers of faculty participating over the years was the growing realization that many of the university's most distinguished teachers and scholars had applied for and been awarded grant funds. In this way, the program was seen as an opportunity rather than as a remedial program in which exemplary teachers as well as teachers needing improvement applied.

Encourage the Individual and the Collective

Our study results confirmed previous findings (Finkelstein & LeCelle-Peterson, 1993) that senior faculty express a keen interest in teaching and a willingness to engage in teaching development activities if they meet their instructional situation, interests, and needs. Programs should allow faculty to set out their own project goals and also stimulate faculty to address student learning problems, as well as broader institutional needs (Simpson, 1990).

Build in Flexibility as Well as Structure

Faculty reactions to the grant initiative confirm that a post-tenure development program must be well structured (e.g., processes, timelines, assessment) but flexible if it is to meet the varied needs of senior faculty as they move through their academic careers. Development programs should promote faculty potential "through processes and mechanisms that release and empower, not excessively control and supervise" (Alstete, 2000, p. 22).

Support Reflection

Study participants who approached their post-tenure review as an opportunity to pause and reflect on their teaching practice indicated a high degree of satisfaction with the process. Individually and in consultation, faculty can reexamine teaching practices as well as the underlying assumptions about teaching and learning that influence their practice (Patrick & Fletcher, 1998). As one faculty member noted,

> I will confess that, while I have remained an active and productive artist-educator over the years, I approached [my] PMYR with little enthusiasm. As it turned out, the process—coming as it did well into my university service—provided me with a timely opportunity to examine the trajectory of my career and to formulate plans to pursue new and important avenues for enhancing the quality of my teaching.

Earlier studies indicate that within the context of a post-tenure evaluation, professional development is difficult (Alstete, 2000; Licata & Morreale, 2002; O'Meara, 2003, 2004). O'Meara (2003) suggests that faculty undergoing PMYR need to "see" information and examples of positive changes in behavior or outcomes in order to view post-tenure review as less of a "sledgehammer" and more of an opportunity (p. 40). The overall findings of this study suggest that post-tenure review, when linked to a carefully designed post-tenure faculty development initiative, can have a positive influence on faculty and institutional effectiveness.

Acknowledgements

The authors gratefully acknowledge the statistical and editing assistance of Chiaki Kotori and Jung Yun, graduate interns in the CFT.

References

Alstete, J. W. (2000). *Post-tenure faculty development: Building a system of faculty improvement and appreciation* (ASHE-ERIC Higher Education Report, 27[4]). San Francisco, CA: Jossey-Bass.

Baldwin, R. G. (2002, Fall). Engaging mid-career faculty in a time of transition. *The Department Chair, 13*(2), 7–10.

Baldwin, R. G., & Chronister, J. L. (2001). *Teaching without tenure: Policies and practices for a new era.* Baltimore, MD: Johns Hopkins University Press.

Blaisdell, M. L., & Cox, M. D. (2004). Midcareer and senior faculty learning communities: Learning throughout faculty careers. In M. D. Cox & L. Richlin (Eds.), *New directions for teaching and learning: No. 97. Building faculty learning communities* (pp. 137–148). San Francisco, CA: Jossey-Bass.

Bland, C. J., & Bergquist, W. H. (1997). *The vitality of senior faculty members: Snow on the roof—fire in the furnace* (ASHE-ERIC Higher Education Report, 25[7]). Washington, DC: George Washington University, Graduate School of Education and Human Development.

Crawley, A. L. (1995, Winter). Senior faculty renewal at research universities: Implications for academic policy development. *Innovative Higher Education, 20*(2), 71–94.

Finkelstein, M. J. (1993). The senior faculty: A portrait and literature review. In M. J. Finkelstein & M. W. LaCelle-Peterson (Eds.), *New directions for teaching and learning: No. 55. Developing senior faculty as teachers* (pp. 7–19). San Francisco, CA: Jossey-Bass.

Finkelstein, M. J., & LaCelle-Peterson, M. W. (Eds.). (1993). *New directions for teaching and learning: No. 55. Developing senior faculty as teachers.* San Francisco, CA: Jossey-Bass.

Goodman, M. J. (1994, Fall). The review of tenured faculty at a research university: Outcomes and appraisals. *Review of Higher Education, 18*(1), 83–94.

Harrington, K. (2002). The view from the elephant's tail: Creation and implementation of post-tenure review at the University of Massachusetts. In C. M. Licata & J. C. Morreale (Eds.), *Post-tenure faculty review and renewal: Experienced voices* (pp. 66–79). Washington, DC: American Association for Higher Education.

Jackson, W. K., & Simpson, R. D. (1993). Refining the role of senior faculty at a research university. In M. J. Finkelstein & M. W. LaCelle-Peterson (Eds.), *New directions for teaching and learning: No. 55. Developing senior faculty as teachers* (pp. 69–80). San Francisco, CA: Jossey-Bass.

Karpiak, I. E. (1997). University professors at mid-life: Being a part of . . . but feeling apart. In D. DeZure & M. Kaplan (Eds.), *To improve the academy: Vol. 16. Resources for faculty, instructional, and organizational development* (pp. 21–40). Stillwater, OK: New Forums Press.

Karpiak, I. E. (2000, July). The "second call": Faculty renewal and recommitment at midlife. *Quality in Higher Education, 6*(2), 125–134.

Licata, C. M., & Morreale, J. C. (1997). *Post-tenure review: Policies, practices, precautions* (New Pathways Working Paper Series No. 12). Washington, DC: American Association for Higher Education.

Licata, C. M., & Morreale, J. C. (1999, Fall). Post-tenure review: National trends, questions and concerns. *Innovative Higher Education, 24*(1), 5–15.

Licata, C. M., & Morreale, J. C. (2002). *Post-tenure faculty review and renewal: Experienced voices.* Washington, DC: American Association for Higher Education.

O'Meara, K. (2003, Fall). Believing is seeing: The influence of beliefs and expectations on post-tenure review in one state system. *Review of Higher Education, 27*(1), 17–43.

O'Meara, K. (2004, March/April). Beliefs about post-tenure review: The influence of autonomy, collegiality, career stage, and institutional context. *Journal of Higher Education, 75*(2), 178–202.

Patrick, S. K., & Fletcher, J. J. (1998). Faculty developers as change agents: Transforming colleges and universities into learning organizations. In M. Kaplan & D. Lieberman (Eds.), *To improve the academy: Vol. 17. Resources for faculty, instructional, and organizational development* (pp. 155–170). Stillwater, OK: New Forums Press.

Rice, R. E., Sorcinelli, M. D., & Austin, A. E. (2000). *Heeding new voices: Academic careers for a new generation.* Washington, DC: American Association for Higher Education.

Romano, J. L., Hoesing, R., O'Donovan, K., & Weinsheimer, J. (2004, April). Faculty at mid-career: A program to enhance teaching and learning. *Innovative Higher Education,* 29(1), 21–48.

Shih, M-Y., & Sorcinelli, M. D. (2000). TEACHnology: Linking teaching and technology in faculty development. In M. Kaplan & D. Lieberman (Eds.), *To improve the academy: Vol. 18. Resources for faculty, instructional, and organizational development* (pp. 151–163). Bolton, MA: Anker.

Simpson, E. L. (1990). *Faculty renewal in higher education.* Malabar, FL: Krieger.

Sorcinelli, M. D. (2000). *Principles of good practice: Supporting early-career faculty. Guidance for deans, department chairs, and other academic leaders.* Washington, DC: American Association for Higher Education.

Sorcinelli, M. D., Austin, A. E., Eddy, P. L., & Beach, A. L. (2006). *Creating the future of faculty development: Learning from the past, understanding the present.* Bolton, MA: Anker.

Stassen, M., & Sorcinelli, M. D. (2001, February). Making assessment matter. *Advocate, 18*(4), 5–8.

Walker, C. J. (2002). Faculty well-being review: An alternative to post-tenure review? In C. M. Licata & J. C. Morreale (Eds.), *Post-tenure review faculty review and renewal: Experienced voices* (pp. 229–241). Washington, DC: American Association for Higher Education.

Wesson, M., & Johnson, S. (1991, May/June). Post-tenure review and faculty revitalization. *Academe, 77*(3), 53–57.

18

Faculty Development in Student Learning Communities: Exploring the Vitality of Mid-Career Faculty Participants

Shari Ellertson
University of Wisconsin–Stevens Point

John H. Schuh
Iowa State University

Student learning communities result in numerous benefits for students and institutions, but less is known about the influence of learning community participation on faculty renewal and development. This qualitative study examines mid-career faculty members' involvement in student learning communities to explore the degree to which the construct of vitality appropriately describes and illuminates their experiences. Findings suggest that learning communities foster vitality by serving as a boundary-spanning activity where faculty can merge various work interests, allowing them to engage in purposeful production and providing them with experiences that help generate feelings of energy, excitement, and engagement with their work.

Mid-career faculty appear to be at a point in their professional development where they are reassessing their careers, goals, and dreams (Frost & Taylor, 1996), and where it is reported that their research productivity as measured by published articles dips. These faculty members have been identified as having excellent potential for participation in student learning communities given their "stage in their careers" (Gabelnick, MacGregor,

Matthews, & Smith, 1990, p. 78) or levels of interest (Smith, 1988; Strommer, 1999). Blackburn (1985) found that research productivity over the faculty career follows a saddle-shaped curve, illustrating a dip in the mid-career. A rise, a peak, a fall, and then another rise characterize the general pattern of productivity across the career span. This pattern of productivity suggests that mid-career faculty development needs may be centered on providing opportunities for them to energize themselves and their careers by participating in new experiences. Student learning communities provide one such experience that may add robustness and energy to faculty careers.

At the core of the student learning community experience is the interaction of faculty and students working together to create learning environments. Smith, MacGregor, Matthews, and Gabelnick (2004) define learning communities as "a variety of curricular approaches that intentionally link or cluster two or more courses, often around an interdisciplinary theme or problem, and enroll a common cohort of students" (p. 67). Regardless of a learning community's structure, Shapiro and Levine (1999) assert that nothing can replace the active involvement and engagement of faculty in student learning communities.

Research on the influence of student learning communities is increasingly robust (see, for example, Epperson, 2000; Gabelnick et al., 1990; Goldberg & Finkelstein, 2002; Goodsell Love, 1999; Huba, Ellertson, Cook, & Epperson, 2003; Matthews, Smith, MacGregor, & Gabelnick, 1997). Much of what is written about learning communities focuses on institutional outcomes (i.e., retention and graduation rates, financial gains, etc.) and student outcomes (i.e., retention, skill development, academic performance, etc.); however, little is known about the influence of learning community involvement on participating faculty. Although some have speculated that learning community involvement has far-reaching potential for influencing faculty renewal and development (Gabelnick et al., 1990; Matthews et al., 1997; Smith, 1988), evidence of this impact is largely anecdotal or underreported (MacGregor & Smith, 2005). Further, Smith suggests that learning communities are particularly appealing to and have specific faculty development implications for mid-career faculty. We engaged in this study to explore the perceptions of mid-career faculty on the value of their participation in student learning communities.

While student learning communities have been employed to promote student success at major research universities (Pike, 1999; Pike, Schroeder, & Berry, 1997), participating faculty may fall outside what would be considered a traditional career path in this context, and may even be "performing a counter-cultural, even revolutionary, act" (Golde & Pribbenow, 2000, p. 38).

According to the Boyer Commission (1998), many research universities commonly expect faculty to interact only rarely with undergraduate students; thus, those who do fall outside the traditional norms of the institution.

The need for this research stems from calls to further examine mid-career faculty and to use qualitative research to better understand faculty needs and values (Kalivoda, Sorrell, & Simpson, 1994). Additionally, the learning communities "communities of practice" group from the American Association for Higher Education's 2002 assessment conference called for "case studies and personal narratives, especially ones about the changing faculty role and the effects of [student] learning communities on faculty" (J. O'Connor, personal communication, June 27, 2006).

The purpose of this exploratory study is to examine the degree to which the construct of vitality can appropriately describe and illuminate faculty experiences in student learning communities. The guiding question of the study is this: Do learning communities foster the vitality of participating mid-career faculty members?

Theoretical Frameworks

This study was situated within two main theoretical frameworks: faculty vitality as the driving content theory and constructivism as the guiding methodological theory. Vitality is a construct that is complex and not easily defined; however, it provides a more holistic exploration of faculty careers in that vitality includes but is not wholly expressed through productivity. Gooler (1991), for example, characterizes vital faculty as those

> Who are reading books and other materials, who are still very interested in their teaching, who are productive in scholarly activities. These professors carry about them a certain excitement and enthusiasm for their work and for their colleagues and students. (p. 13)

Vitality, in its essence, appears to capture a spirit of engagement that faculty members have with their work. Baldwin (1990) observes,

> Vital professors typically are individuals who challenge students academically and contribute to their overall development. . . . are curious and intellectually engaged. . . . enjoy the respect of their colleagues and are effective in the multiple roles of members of their academic profession. . . . grow personally and professionally throughout the academic career . . ." (p. 180)

The ambiguous nature of vitality allows for its complexities to emerge. Vitality, because of its abstract and multiple meanings, can best be explored through the inductive process afforded by a constructivist qualitative approach and phenomenological methodology. The basic tenet of constructivism is the inexistence of a universal truth waiting to be discovered; rather, constructivists argue that knowledge is created through active engagement of individuals with each other and their environments (Crotty, 1998). Phenomenology is concerned with the meanings that individuals ascribe to their experiences (Crotty, 1998). Furthermore, phenomenology lends itself to multiple realities, where different (and even divergent) constructions are considered meaningful (Schwandt, 1998). Because the aim of the inquiry is to understand the lived experiences and realities of mid-career faculty members, the methodology of this study is firmly grounded.

Student Learning Communities at Iowa State University

Iowa State University (ISU) is a large, research-extensive institution. Student learning communities (hereafter referenced as learning communities) began at ISU in 1995 as a grassroots movement driven by faculty and staff members who wanted to improve student learning. The learning communities were not centrally administered (Huba et al., 2003). However, they grew in number and eventually became institutionalized as the result of a three-year internal presidential grant from 1998–2001. During that time, the number of learning communities grew from 23 to 48, and student participation nearly doubled, going from 1,114 to 2,103 participants (Huba et al., 2003). In 2005, more than 50% of first-year full-time students participated in a learning community. Although most ISU learning communities are geared toward first-year students, some sophomore, transfer, and other upper-level communities have developed (Huba et al., 2003). In addition, most learning communities at ISU are discipline specific (i.e., agronomy, computer engineering, biology, etc.) and have qualities of three commonly used models: the linked courses model, clustered courses model, and freshman interest groups model (Matthews et al., 1997).

Method

We used criterion-based selection to identify participants for this study. All participants must have held at least the rank of associate professor with tenure; have had more than five years remaining to retirement; have been involved with a learning community during the current academic year; and have had a minimum of one semester of involvement as a coordinator or course instructor for a first-year learning community. The first two criteria are consistent with definitions of a mid-career faculty member. The third criterion was to ensure that participants currently were engaged in learning community work. The final criterion was essential for identifying faculty members who have experienced at least one full unit of the academic calendar—a semester—with a first-year learning community. These faculty fall outside what may be considered traditional norms of a research institution and thus provide the opportunity to explore the construct of vitality with "faculty cohorts outside the traditional career path" (Kalivoda et al., 1994, p. 269). Our selection procedure resulted in 10 participants from different learning communities and various academic disciplines.

Consistent with qualitative inquiry, a criterion for determining the adequacy of sample size is the attainment of information redundancy, which occurs when "no new information is forthcoming from newly sampled units" (Lincoln & Guba, 1985, p. 202). Informational redundancy as we achieved in this study also contributes to the overall trustworthiness of the research, which is discussed next.

We utilized three qualitative methods of data collection in this study: phenomenologically based interviews, document analysis, and observations. We conducted in-depth interviews in 75- to 90-minute timeframes using a semi-structured interview protocol. We scheduled one participant initially for an interview as a pilot study to test the protocol; after this interview, the protocol was refocused. All interviews were audiotaped and transcribed within one month. We sent transcripts to participants by email to provide them an opportunity to review transcripts for accuracy and make clarifications or corrections. This is one way of conducting member checking (Lincoln & Guba, 1985), which also contributes to the trustworthiness of the study. Two participants responded with minor corrections and/or clarifications to their transcripts. We sent two additional questions to all participants as a follow-up via email.

We analyzed the curricula vitae of participants in relation to their careers and professional experiences. Because examining learning community participation as part of the academic career was central to this study, curricula vitae provided the kind of documentation that would illuminate participants' careers from their perspectives. We also relied on documentation from the ISU learning communities office to compile descriptive information, faculty involvement data, participation rates, and so forth.

As part of an "emergent design" (Lincoln & Guba, 1985), we added participant observations as a third phase of data collection after the first two phases were completed. Observations provided an opportunity to see the faculty "in action" with the students in their learning community. Due to the timing of the observations, only two faculty members had relevant learning community events. Thus, observations were conducted with these two faculty members for approximately one hour (or the duration of the activity) in a learning community class and at a learning community picnic, respectively. We debriefed with the faculty member immediately following the activity to discuss it, ask follow-up questions, and review field notes for accuracy and completeness.

We analyzed data continuously throughout the study using the constant comparative approach that "combines inductive category coding with a simultaneous comparison of all social incidents observed and coded" (LeCompte & Preissle, 1993, p. 256). Inductive category coding, therefore, emerges from the data as opposed to the data being analyzed by predetermined categories imposed by the researcher. Various strategies assisted the data analysis process, such as analytic memos and an interview log, which provided one mechanism for immediate reflection on each interview. During an initial reading of interview transcripts, we highlighted passages of interest and items that were particularly emphasized by respondents. From this, we identified emerging patterns (e.g., working codes) and working hypotheses and filtered those back into the study. We continually refined the themes and then used categorical clustering to establish final themes.

In addition to informational redundancy and member checking (as previously discussed), we employed several other strategies to establish the trustworthiness of the study. Triangulation of sources and methods and peer debriefing with a colleague who is familiar with both learning communities and qualitative inquiry contributed to the credibility of the findings and interpretations. Although generalizability is not a goal of qualitative research, "thick descriptions" can assist readers in determining the potential transferability of the information to other settings. Thus, we have attempted to provide thick descriptions through detailed description of our method and use of participants' quotes in our findings. In addition, we strengthened the dependability (i.e., reliability) of our study by selecting appropriate methodology, utilizing feedback from colleagues and peers in the development of the study, and pilot testing the interview protocol. Finally, our audit trail consisting of detailed notes, interview tapes, and other data forms (as well as our use of a peer debriefer) aid in the confirmability of our study; that is, the degree to which the data support the conclusions.

Findings

Vitality was selected as a lens through which to examine faculty participation in learning communities because it had the potential to address faculty careers holistically rather than simply looking at productivity as measured by the number of research publications produced. Three main themes emerged from the data: energy, excitement, and engagement; merging of work interests; and purposeful production.

Energy, Excitement, and Engagement

Faculty in this study identified feelings of energy, excitement, and overall engagement with their work when interacting with students. Although the energy, excitement, and engagement seem characteristic of their work with students in general, participating in learning communities provided opportunities for interacting with students, which appears to serve as an additional stimulus for vitality. According to Joseph (all names are pseudonyms), "Any time I'm interacting with students, I find it to be . . . exciting and revitalizing. . . . And the advantage to learning communities is it provides more opportunities."

Likewise, Meredith demonstrated excitement and energy when gathering with learning community students for a picnic. While sitting on the ground in a circle with students and eating hamburgers, Meredith conversed informally with various students about everything from their summer living arrangements to the latest campus news. She was clearly comfortable with students in this informal setting, and they appeared comfortable with her as well. For the more "formal" portion of the picnic, Meredith asked students to take turns discussing their summer work plans as well as what they planned to do for fun. During the debriefing after the event, Meredith commented that the picnic was a good opportunity for her to reconnect with the learning community, say goodbye for the summer, and have some closure with the group. She viewed the "formal" portion of the picnic as a way to integrate an academic topic (i.e., summer work plans) into the conversation as well as to show the students that she cared about them by asking about their plans for fun. Meredith characterized the learning community as fostering one of her goals, which is to "make an impact in people's lives, to help students develop into professionals and good citizens." Thus, the learning community provided an environment where Meredith could interact with students in a way that was energizing and exciting for her.

Jack exhibited energy, excitement, and engagement with his learning community during their course. Jack was presenting information to the class and a student challenged him, asking, "What is the point of knowing this?" Jack responded with, "That's a good question," and then provided a rationale for why it was important they learn about the topic at hand. After Jack finished talking, another student interjected a very concise and well-thought-out point of view on why they were learning about the topic. To this, Jack responded, "That's a better response than the one I gave." Rather than being defensive or feeling "upstaged" by the student, Jack delighted in it, saying in our debriefing session, "He [the student] connected two things and that's great!" He said the apparent sparkle in his eye in the learning community class derived from the pleasure he feels when students make gains. The learning community class provided the types of interactions where he can see student gains quickly and immediately.

Finally, Kent said that he feels most active, alive, and engaged with his work when he is teaching first-year students, some of whom are in the learning community. He shared,

> Here is where I would disagree with many of my counterparts in other programs that think that it's a waste of time to work with freshmen; that's when I'm engaged. That's when I'm really alive. . . . I love first term, new 18 year olds. I love exciting them about where they're going, the challenges in their career, the controversies in their career, and the basic sciences in their career so that when I get done I hope they know a lot more about [not only the subject] but also a lot more about what they're going to be and what they're going to do.

Kent contrasted this experience with a time in his career when he felt disengaged. In other words, he was able to discuss vitality by recalling a story that illustrates an opposite experience. He said,

> And then you get into that mid-career thing where you're getting onto more committees and activities and you begin to feel a little bit disengaged. I know there was a time when I was on about five university committees, five or six college committees and seven or eight, nine at one time in my department and I felt like I wasn't being productive. I felt like I was spinning my wheels. I wasn't spending enough time on my classes. I was doing things that were important for students and committees, but boy, it was all committee work and I . . . became somewhat, I thought, disengaged. . . . [I have felt I am] kind of refocusing again the last few years. And so I really feel, especially [in] my freshman class, I just feel like I'm 100% there again.

Kent's experiences are similar to Gooler's (1991) assertion that one can identify experiences and characteristics of vitality by identifying opposite experiences and characteristics. For Kent, as with other faculty in this study, the learning community served as a venue for helping students; through helping students, he felt energy, excitement, and engagement with his work. In short, the learning community appears to provide Kent and other faculty with opportunities to experience vitality.

Energy, excitement, and engagement with one's work appear to be consistent with mid-career faculty development needs and vitality as presented in the literature. Cytrynbaum, Lee, and Wadner (1982) propose that mid-career faculty may experience "professional or personal withdrawal" (p. 16); therefore, feeling energy, excitement, or engagement with one's work seems to be opposite of some of the negative manifestations of mid-career faculty development. Clark, Corcoran, and Lewis (1986) found that highly active (i.e., vital) faculty had high self-ratings of energy. Although faculty in this study were not rating their energy levels, they described experiencing energy as characteristic of times in their careers when they felt most vital.

Merging of Work Interests

Faculty in this study described a merging of work interests that occurred for them as participants in the learning community. This is a second manifestation of vitality. Analysis of their curricula vitae revealed that most faculty identified learning community work as a separate item on their vita, and learning community work crossed all categories of the vita. For example, learning community work appeared under the categories of *teaching, grants, service, awards,* and *scholarship/publications* on vitae. Learning community work was not treated indiscriminately or as inferior; rather, it was presented purposefully and often given particular emphasis (i.e., a category of work unto itself).

The boundary-spanning nature of learning communities was further evident in faculty stories. Faculty indicated that experiences during which their work interests come together provided them with feelings of being active and alive in their work (i.e., vital). Nancy described this merging of interests as "being in the zone." According to her,

> I think when I was streamlined, when my research and my teaching and my outreach was [*sic*] in one subject area, where all I had to worry about was [my area of expertise]. I think that was when I was most alive. I think being focused.

Nancy's learning community involvement drew together various aspects of her work, including teaching, service, and scholarship. Thus, her learning community provided her with the kind of opportunity that she described as fostering her vitality.

Similarly, Byron and Joseph explained that their merging work interests provided them with experiences in which they felt particularly vital. Byron experienced enjoyment at being able to share his expertise through teaching. He said, "The things that have most engaged me is where I can provide people with my technical knowledge and [do it through] teaching." It is not just the delivery of the content that made Byron feel active and alive, but also the creativity of determining a way to share his knowledge that sparked his experience of "aliveness" (i.e., vitality). He shared, "giving them my perspective of [the topic] so they get the technical knowledge but I get to package that technical knowledge the way that I think will have the most meaning and impacting value to them." The creative challenge inherent in merging his work interests (in this case, his technical expertise and his teaching of it) was stimulating. Certainly, learning communities can provide a creative outlet that allows for the merging of expertise and teaching, particularly because of the course-based and teaching-intensive nature of them.

Joseph specifically discussed his learning community as an environment in which his various teaching interests and his passion for his discipline merged. He said,

> I would say in some ways the [learning community's service-learning project] really sort of weaves together all of the things I'm interested in. . . . [It] sort of brings all those pieces together into . . . one activity, one thing. I basically feel like I'm doing what I want to do, what I'm interested in, and what I think I'm good at. It's a pleasure to do things that you feel like "yeah, I can do that pretty well." It's frustrating to try and do things that you think "really I'm not that great at it."

Thus, Joseph derived pleasure and satisfaction from doing activities that wove together his interests and areas of work.

Learning communities can provide a boundary-spanning experience in which various aspects of faculty work can be woven together. Moreover, faculty in this study described the merging of work interests as characteristic of times when they feel most vital. While the blurring of boundaries may be common among mid-career faculty in general, learning communities seem to provide an environment where merging work interests can readily occur.

Purposeful Production

Faculty in this study described their learning community involvement as fulfilling larger overarching purposes than the outcomes realized by them or their students. They viewed their participation also as beneficial to the institution, their disciplines and departments, and even professional societies; thus, they were engaging in "purposeful production." Clark and Corcoran (1985) described vitality as "those essential, yet intangible, positive qualities of individuals and institutions that enable purposeful production" (p. 3). Essentially, purposeful production is the positive interplay between individuals and institutions, and faculty in this study viewed their learning community involvement as mutually beneficial work.

The learning community can provide experiences in which faculty feel that they are working with others toward a common purpose. According to Sharon, her "peak experiences," or experiences where she has felt the most active and alive, included the following:

> Just really getting a chance to talk with people on some of those overarching ideas, on where do we want to go, how do we want to get there? Having just occasionally the sense that we are working together to do something important. I think that some of the team meetings I've been involved in—in terms of developing a learning community or developing [a related program]—have been really great experiences along those lines. . . . I think it's just having all those points of view that you get to see and get to have a sense that with all these different points of view, you are working together for some common purpose. That you are working effectively for a common purpose.

Having a shared purpose, therefore, helped Sharon feel vital. For others, they hoped students would have positive feelings about and experiences within their departments. Harry concluded,

> I guess I feel good about it [the learning community] if the students come away from it with a positive feeling about the department. . . . I don't want them to leave because they're misinformed, let's put it that way."

In essence, the faculty viewed the learning community experience as beneficial for the students and the department.

Finally, some faculty characterized learning communities as having benefits that stretch beyond the institution, for example, to professional disciplinary associations. Mark said his learning community has positively impacted both his association and his department. He shared,

> I knew at least from working with constituents like industry that we weren't meeting their needs as far as the number of [majors] going out the door. So I thought if I can do something [the learning community] to increase our numbers, help our department because we needed to have certain numbers, and also help our professional society to meet their numbers, I feel like I'm really accomplishing something.

Overall, faculty members regard the learning community as helping them to meet purposes that are larger than themselves or their students; it also helps the institution, their departments, and their professional associations.

Vitality can occur when there is positive interplay between the faculty experience and broader interests, such as those of the institution (Bland & Schmitz, 1990; Clark & Corcoran, 1985). At Iowa State University, several institutional gains from learning communities, such as increased retention and graduation rates and financial gains, are reported (Epperson, 2000; Huba et al., 2003). Because faculty in this study indicated experiencing positive outcomes and gaining satisfaction from engaging in "purposefully productive" work, one could infer that the faculty and the institution positively intersect in learning communities.

Discussion

The extent to which learning communities provide an environment that fosters faculty vitality was the primary question explored in this study. Experiences described by faculty as making them feel vital match the types of experiences that learning communities can provide, suggesting that learning communities, in fact, can promote faculty vitality. One way in which learning communities foster vitality is by serving as a boundary-spanning activity that helps faculty bring together various elements of their work. Lamber et al. (1993) found that "the boundaries between the professional roles of teaching, research, and service become less clear" (p. 24) as faculty progress into their mid-career. Thus, learning communities may serve a developmental need of mid-career faculty, suggesting that they are an appropriate development strategy for mid-career faculty as Smith (1988) and Strommer (1999) speculated. Moreover, the boundary-spanning aspect of learning communities fosters the merging of work interests that faculty described as fostering their vitality.

Another important aspect of vitality is that it is contextual to the particular institutional setting. Several researchers suggest that vitality can occur when faculty and institutional interests intersect in a positive way (Bland & Schmitz; 1990; Clark & Corcoran, 1985; Gooler, 1991). Faculty in this study described their learning community involvement as fulfilling larger, overarching purposes than the outcomes realized by them or their students. They also regarded their learning community work as beneficial to the institution, their disciplines and departments, and even their professional organizations.

Finally, faculty in this study experienced what Clark and Lewis (1985) call the "dimension of vitality variously termed enthusiasm, energy, or esprit" (p. 249). When faculty discussed work experiences that make them feel active, alive, and engaged (i.e., vital), they identified a sense of energy, excitement, and engagement deriving from their work with students. Their learning community involvement, because it is student intensive, stimulated their energy, excitement, and engagement. Thus, because learning communities provide a venue that is rich in opportunities for student interaction, they provide an environment that fosters vitality.

Recommendations and Conclusions

Should mid-career faculty be tapped to participate in programs such as learning communities? The findings of this research suggest they should because of the potential for faculty development and the positive influence on faculty vitality. Faculty developers should identify nontraditional faculty development opportunities, such as learning communities, and make efforts to connect mid-career faculty with these programs. Faculty development benefits also are noted in related initiatives, such as first-year seminars (Barefoot, 1993) and living-learning programs (Stassen, 2000). Often, these types of programs may be coordinated by or offered in concert with student affairs, thus providing an opportunity for the faculty developer to serve as a critical link between faculty and student affairs colleagues. This outreach may be especially important in cases where teaching and learning centers are not involved directly in the student learning communities or related programs since faculty development efforts in these programs may be limited or obscured.

Student learning communities (and related programs) also provide fertile grounds for additional research on faculty development. For example, it would be instructive to know if learning communities help meet faculty development needs for faculty at different stages of their careers. Knowing this could potentially help shape various roles in learning communities for early-, mid-, and late-career faculty. For instance, is it possible that late-career faculty members may be interested in mentoring roles (which may meet their developmental needs) and early-career faculty members may be interested in scholarship opportunities in learning communities, just as the creative aspects of learning communities seem to appeal to mid-career faculty? Knowing more about the faculty development potential of learning communities for faculty at various career stages makes sense not only for development purposes but also for the purposes of identifying and recruiting faculty participants.

Faculty developers also can extend the understanding of vitality by researching its meanings and manifestations in their institutional contexts. This understanding may provide insights into the types of activities that faculty find the most energizing and revitalizing. Subsequently, faculty developers can design additional development efforts aimed at enhancing faculty vitality.

After faculty are connected with opportunities such as learning communities, we cannot assume they will automatically reap the development benefits. Faculty developers can make intentional and systematic efforts to maximize the benefits for participating faculty by providing them with adequate resources, information, and reflective experiences. In essence, we need to be in the field with our faculty to attend to their development needs as they arise. Perhaps Joseph said it best when he described how learning communities create opportunities and experiences that otherwise would not be naturally occurring:

> You've got to sort of create an environment where they [unique experiences] can happen. And learning communities, when they're done well, when they're done properly, . . . create those kind of environments . . . it's like bird watching or something. I mean, you have to be out there. You're not going to see a Cooper's hawk every day, but you know, sometimes you do, and you know, it's cool when it happens.

As faculty development professionals, we too must be "out there" for our faculty, identifying and creating opportunities for them to remain engaged in their work and enhance their feelings of vitality.

References

Baldwin, R. G. (1990, March/April). Faculty vitality beyond the research university: Extending a contextual concept. *Journal of Higher Education, 61*(2), 160–180.

Barefoot, B. O. (Ed.). (1993). *Exploring the evidence: Reporting outcomes of freshman seminars* (Monograph No. 11). Columbia, SC: University of South Carolina, National Resource Center for the First-Year Experience and Students in Transition.

Blackburn, R. T. (1985). Faculty career development: Theory and practice. In S. M. Clark & D. R. Lewis (Eds.), *Faculty vitality and institutional productivity: Critical perspectives for higher education* (pp. 55–85). New York, NY: Teachers College Press.

Bland, C. J., & Schmitz, C. C. (1990). An overview of research on faculty and institutional vitality. In J. H. Schuster, D. W. Wheeler, & Associates, *Enhancing faculty careers: Strategies for development and renewal* (pp. 41–61). San Francisco, CA: Jossey-Bass.

Boyer Commission on Educating Undergraduates in the Research University. (1998). *Reinventing undergraduate education: A blueprint for America's research universities.* Retrieved June 24, 2006, from the Stony Brook University web site: http://naples.cc.sunysb.edu/Pres/boyer.nsf

Clark, S. M., & Corcoran, M. (1985). Individual and organizational contributions to faculty vitality: An institutional case study. In S. M. Clark & D. R. Lewis (Eds.), *Faculty vitality and institutional productivity: Critical perspectives for higher education* (pp. 112–138). New York, NY: Teachers College Press.

Clark, S. M., Corcoran, M., & Lewis, D. R. (1986, March/April). The case for an institutional perspective on faculty development. *Journal of Higher Education, 57*(2), 176–195.

Clark, S. M., & Lewis, D. R. (1985). Implications for institutional response. In S. M. Clark & D. R. Lewis (Eds.), *Faculty vitality and institutional productivity: Critical perspectives for higher education* (pp. 247–256). New York, NY: Teachers College Press.

Crotty, M. (1998). *The foundations of social research: Meaning and perspective in the research process.* Thousand Oaks, CA: Sage.

Cytrynbaum, S., Lee, S., & Wadner, D. (1982). Faculty development through the life course: Application of recent adult development theory and research. *Journal of Instructional Development, 5*(3), 11–22.

Epperson, D. L. (2000). *Report on one-year and two-year university retention rates associated with first-year participation in a learning community at Iowa State University.* Ames, IA: Iowa State University, Learning Communities.

Frost, P. J., & Taylor, M. S. (Eds.). (1996). *Rhythms of academic life: Personal accounts of careers in academia*. Thousand Oaks, CA: Sage.

Gabelnick, F., MacGregor, J., Matthews, R. S., & Smith, B. L. (1990). *New directions for teaching and learning: No. 41. Learning communities: Creating connections among students, faculty, and disciplines*. San Francisco, CA: Jossey-Bass.

Goldberg, B., & Finkelstein, M. (2002, Summer). Effects of a first-semester learning community on nontraditional technical students. *Innovative Higher Education, 26*(4), 235–249.

Golde, C. M., & Pribbenow, D. A. (2000, January/February). Understanding faculty involvement in residential learning communities. *Journal of College Student Development, 41*(1), 27–40.

Goodsell Love, A. (1999). What are learning communities? In J. H. Levine (Ed.), *Learning communities: New structures, new partnerships for learning* (pp. 1–8). Columbia, SC: University of South Carolina, National Resource Center for the First-Year Experience and Students in Transition.

Gooler, D. D. (1991). *Professorial vitality: A critical issue in higher education*. DeKalb, IL: LEPS Press.

Huba, M. E., Ellertson, S., Cook, M. D., & Epperson, D. (2003). Assessment's role in transforming a grass-roots initiative into an institutionalized program: Evaluating and shaping learning communities at Iowa State University. In J. MacGregor (Ed.), *Doing learning community assessment: Five campus stories* (pp. 21–47). Olympia, WA: The Evergreen State College, Washington Center for Improving the Quality of Undergraduate Education.

Kalivoda, P., Sorrell, G. R., & Simpson, R. D. (1994, Summer). Nurturing faculty vitality by matching institutional interventions with career-stage needs. *Innovative Higher Education, 18*(4), 255–272.

Lamber, J., Ardizzone, T., Dworkin, T., Guskin, S. L., Olsen, D., Parnell, P., et al. (1993). A "community of scholars": Conversations among mid-career faculty at a public research university. In D. L. Wright & J. P. Lunde (Eds.), *To improve the academy: Vol. 12. Resources for faculty, instructional, and organizational development* (pp. 13–26). Stillwater, OK: New Forums Press.

LeCompte, M. D., & Preissle, J. (1993). *Ethnography and qualitative design in educational research* (2nd ed.). San Diego, CA: Academic Press.

Lincoln, Y. S., & Guba, E. G. (1985). *Naturalistic inquiry*. Newbury Park, CA: Sage.

MacGregor, J., & Smith, B. L. (2005, May/June). Where are learning communities now? National leaders take stock. *About Campus, 10*(2), 2–8.

Matthews, R. S., Smith, B. L., MacGregor, J., & Gabelnick, F. (1997). Creating learning communities. In J. G. Gaff, J. L. Ratcliff, & Associates, *Handbook of the undergraduate curriculum: A comprehensive guide to purposes, structures, practices, and change* (pp. 457–475). San Francisco, CA: Jossey-Bass.

Pike, G. R. (1999, May/June). The effects of residential learning communities and traditional residential living arrangements on educational gains during the first year of college. *Journal of College Student Development, 40*(3), 269–284.

Pike, G. R., Schroeder, C. C., & Berry, T. R. (1997, November/December). Enhancing the educational impact of residence halls: The relationship between residential learning communities and first-year college experiences and persistence. *Journal of College Student Development, 38*(6), 609–621.

Schwandt, T. A. (1998). Constructivist, interpretivist approaches to human inquiry. In N. K. Denzin & Y. S. Lincoln (Eds.), *The landscape of qualitative research: Theories and issues* (pp. 221–259). Thousand Oaks, CA: Sage.

Shapiro, N. S., & Levine, J. H. (1999). *Creating learning communities: A practical guide to winning support, organizing for change, and implementing programs*. San Francisco, CA: Jossey-Bass.

Smith, B. L. (1988). The Washington Center: A grass roots approach to faculty development and curricular reform. In J. G. Kurfiss (Ed.), *To improve the academy: Vol. 7. Resources for student, faculty, and institutional development* (pp. 165–177). Stillwater, OK: New Forums Press.

Smith, B. L., MacGregor, J., Matthews, R. S., & Gabelnick, F. (2004). *Learning communities: Reforming undergraduate education*. San Francisco, CA: Jossey-Bass.

Stassen, M. L. A. (2000). "It's hard work!": Faculty development in a program for first-year students. In M. Kaplan & D. Lieberman (Eds.), *To improve the academy: Vol. 18. Resources for faculty, instructional, and organizational development* (pp. 254–277). Bolton, MA: Anker.

Strommer, D. W. (1999). Teaching and learning in a learning community. In J. H. Levine (Ed.), *Learning communities: New structures, new partnerships for learning* (pp. 39–49). Columbia, SC: University of South Carolina, National Resource Center for the First-Year Experience and Students in Transition.

19

Making Meaning of a Life in Teaching: A Memoir-Writing Project for Seasoned Faculty

Kathleen F. O'Donovan, Steve R. Simmons
University of Minnesota

The University of Minnesota's faculty development project, "Making Meaning of a Life in Teaching," promotes collegiality and enhances self-reflection for those who are experienced classroom instructors. Started in October 2003, this project provides a forum that invites participants to examine specific memories from their teaching lives and to transform those recollections into a written memoir. This chapter explores the use of memoir as an effective tool for faculty development, describes the project's structure and components, and presents both co-facilitator and participant perspectives on the process and the memoir product.

Humans are storytellers and stories are intricately woven into the fabric of most civilizations and societies. Similarly, stories form the foundation of any teacher's professional life. From their first days in teaching, university faculty begin accumulating an amazing array of experiences, some of which may be informally translated into stories shared with colleagues, students, or family members. But college and university instructors seldom have opportunities to tell their teaching stories in more structured and reflective ways. "Making Meaning of a Life in Teaching" is our attempt to provide space and time for storytelling and reflection.

Since 2003, we have created communities of "seasoned" teachers for the purpose of encouraging participants to write a memoir about their lives in teaching. Since several participants in this project were not of suitable age and professional rank to be described adequately by terms such as *distinguished instructors* (Rice & Finkelstein, 1993), *senior faculty* (Jackson & Simpson, 1993), or *elders* (Finkelstein & Jemmott, 1993), we selected the term *seasoned* as an apt descriptor of the participants. Some were, in fact, senior in rank and were seeking to write memoirs as a way of telling their stories and creating a legacy. But participants, regardless of which "season" of their academic careers they happened to be living, were motivated to reflect more deeply on their lives as teachers and to glean understanding from their recollections through the process of writing their memoirs.

Why write a memoir? Personal writing, and especially memoir writing, has experienced a renaissance over the past 25 years (Barrington, 2002). We chose writer and colleague Patricia Hampl's (1999) definition of memoir, as outlined in her book *I Could Tell You Stories,* to guide us as we designed the project: "[Memoir] represents the intersection of narrative and reflection, of storytelling and essay writing" (p. 33).

From Hampl's (1999) definition and other insights provided in her book, we developed the following attributes to guide our participants in writing their memoirs of teaching.

- The style of writing for a memoir is different from other kinds of academic and scholarly writing.
- An effective memoir considers a relatively brief segment of one's life in teaching, not one's entire career.
- A memoir becomes richer through inclusion of details that appeal to all the senses.
- The "voice" of the memoirist should be authentic and express feelings, insights, aspirations, triumphs, and disappointments.
- A memoir is about both telling one's story and making meaning from it.

Professional development scholar Schön (1983) notes that reflecting on past experiences is important whenever professionals consider new situations and problems. Brookfield (1995) writes, "the influences that most shape teachers' lives and that move teachers' actions are rarely found in research studies, policy reform proposals, or institutional mission statements" (p. 39). He asserts that the most important influences for teachers are likely to be the "memories and experiences . . . the images, models, and conceptions of teaching derived from [their] own experiences" (p. 40). Karpiak (2000) proposes that autobiographical writing, of which memoir is one type, can be an effective approach for faculty in initiating "a process of self-exploration and meaning making that, in turn, can promote the development of an enlarged view of themselves" (p. 31).

We maintain that to continue to grow as teachers, academics should live "examined" teaching lives. In this regard, teachers can position themselves for personal and professional growth whenever they honestly consider what they know and believe about teaching and why. As part of examining their own stories, teachers may explore the rationale behind their professional practices. Memoir writing is a form of autobiographical writing that has great potential for prompting such self-reflection. One former participant shared her perspective on memoir writing in the project's second-year evaluation.

> Memoir was a powerful tool. True memoir takes one back into the shells or roles of the past and allows for honest memory to make a soul-level impact. Through such introspective writing, we learn what we once learned, but had forgotten. We see what we once saw, but with new eyes.

In her book, Hampl (1999) makes a distinction between describing one's life events in a memoir and making meaning from those events. She refers to the initial telling of one's story as the "first draft," which she describes as "not necessarily the truth, not even *a* truth sometimes, but the first attempt to create a shape [of the story]" (p. 28). She then describes the necessity for the memoirist to proceed to a "second draft" by which she does not mean a mere editing of the first draft text. Rather, Hampl advocates that memoirists must reexamine their "first-draft" memoirs with the intent of "waiting for the real subject to reveal itself" (p. 32).

In his recent book *A Hidden Wholeness: The Journey Toward an Undivided Life*, Palmer (2004) also addresses the importance of becoming attentive to hidden meanings within one's life. He refers to such revealed meanings as "third things" (p. 92). He describes this idea as analogous to the Rorschach inkblot test whereby the observer makes meaning from what at first appear to be meaningless blots on a page. Although Palmer does not specifically address memoir writing in his book, it is likely that he would concur that Hampl's "second draft" describes not only his "third things," but also what T. S. Eliot says of poetry, "[Poetry] may make us . . . a little more aware of the deeper, unnamed feelings which form the substratum of our being, to which we rarely penetrate; for our lives are mostly a constant evasion of ourselves " (qtd. in Palmer, 2004, p. 94).

In our project, we hoped that the process of participants writing their memoirs would help them to be more attentive to perceptions, ideas, assumptions, and feelings, some of which they might have been previously unaware. While facilitating "Making Meaning of a Life in Teaching," we realized that exploration of one's teaching story at a deeper level—one's "second draft" or "third things," if you will—resulted in the emergence of hidden principles about one's life in teaching. We also found that such intentional examination was even more significant when approached within a community of peers.

Method

Process

The "Making Meaning of a Life in Teaching" project was initially offered during the 2003–2004 academic year as part of the University of Minnesota's Center for Teaching and Learning Services' efforts to design faculty development opportunities that span the entire professional career. As facilitators, our intent was to utilize memoir writing to prompt reflection about and learning from the participants' teaching lives. Since we also undertook the writing of our own memoirs of teaching during the project, we had dual roles of participant-coach.

In the early phase of planning, we defined the following desired outcomes about the "Making Meaning of a Life in Teaching" project.

- Focus as much on the participants' aspirations as on their accomplishments.
- Involve participants relating to each other on a group basis and in pairs as writing partners.
- Engage the participants' minds and hearts.
- Feature mutual listening and responding to teaching stories of the participants in an affirming and encouraging way.
- Deepen relationships (with others and with oneself).
- Concentrate on making meaning from experience.
- Put participants' teaching stories into forms that could be accessed by broader audiences.

In addition to identifying these desired outcomes, we also developed several other broad objectives that were consistent with our university's goals for faculty development and teaching improvement.

- Encourage seasoned faculty to gain new perspectives about their teaching.

- Model a collegial community within the academy and help build trust among participants.
- Offer participants the opportunity for in-depth examination and reflection upon their teaching.
- Enhance the vitality of seasoned faculty.

Whereas conventional faculty development programs often focus on instructing or coaching participants regarding current teaching and state-of-the-art techniques and technologies—in other words, working from the outside in, the memoir project was meant to work from the inside out. Taking seriously Palmer's (1998) caveat "to correct our overemphasis on teaching technique and our obsession with objective knowledge" (p. 61), we strove to implement an approach to self-reflection that he describes as "thinking the world together" (1998, p. 62). That is, we wanted participants to engage both their heads and hearts in their writing. Thus, when designing the project's workshops and other experiences, we sought to encourage participants to journey inward in order to more deeply explore their lives as teachers. At the same time, we understood that creating one's memoir also required specific skills and techniques. We offered coaching on these as the participants defined, organized, and wrote their memoirs.

Participants

Originally, we conceived that this project would primarily serve faculty who were in the final stages of their academic careers. However, as the project developed, we realized that the profile of participants who expressed interest was much broader. Those who undertook the writing of a teaching memoir in the project's first year averaged 52 years of age with 19 years of experience in higher education. We expected to work with a small cohort of participants (between 7 and 10) each year. However, 17 participants registered for the project in its initial year. The number of participants in the second year was lower (6), but a substantial number of faculty at our institution continue to express interest in participating in this kind of professional development initiative in the future.

Our recruitment of participants for the project in both years was simple and straightforward. Most participants learned of the "Making Meaning of a Life in Teaching" project through word of mouth from us or from other participants. The Center for Teaching and Learning Services also formally announced the initiative through a mailing to all associate and full professors in the university. In both years, we made an effort to contact participants within a day of their registration and thanked them for electing to participate.

Format and Structure

Bearing in mind that one of the project's objectives was to model collegiality within the academy, we set out to create a space and a structure through which participants would experience the paradox of "being alone together" (Palmer, 1998, p. 98). In this regard, we integrated discussion topics, learning materials, and experiential exercises that encouraged group members to be both self-reflective (Brookfield, 1995) and attentive listeners to others within the writing community. We endeavored to use our time together to address the needs of individuals and to nurture connections within the group as a whole. In our roles as participant-coach, we learned firsthand the need for mutual support during the memoir-writing process. During the academic year, participants found their interactions with and feedback from writing partners to be a valuable element in the process of developing their memoirs (Simmons, 2004).

At an initial retreat held early in each academic year, we shared our desired outcomes for the project with the participants, and we invited them to add to theirs (see Table 19.1). At this retreat, we also asked participants to look broadly at their lives in teaching before deciding on a specific aspect on which to focus in their memoir-writing efforts. We then encouraged them to identify key experiences in their teaching lives that had influenced them or their classroom practice. Finally, we allocated time for participants to write a one-page "beginning" for their memoirs.

TABLE 19.1

Design Description of Initial Retreat

Title	Format	Date and Duration	Purposes	Outcomes
Reflecting on our lives as teachers	Retreat	Early October; five hours	• Foster trust • Identify key periods or memories in the participants' teaching lives • Present the memoir writing process • Begin writing	• Develop the beginnings of a prospective memoir • Instill the concepts of "first draft" and "second draft"

In each year the participants embraced the opportunity to examine their lives as teachers to varying degrees. We found that some of our desired outcomes were not viewed as being consistent with the predominant academic culture and values at our institution. For example, during the first retreat of the initial year, one participant challenged memoir writing as "not scholarship." We concurred that the memoir-writing process differed from some protocols of scholarship as they are defined by some academic disciplines, but we maintained that development of a memoir of teaching was equivalent to or surpassed such scholarship in other ways, and certainly for its potential impact on the memoirist.

On the other hand, many participants in the initial cohort expressed disappointment and frustration with their roles in the conventional academic "culture." In this regard, Palmer (1998) observed that

> . . . if we want to grow as teachers—we must do something alien to academic culture: we must talk to each other about our inner lives—risky stuff in a profession that fears the personal and seeks safety in the technical, the distant, the abstract" (p. 12).

Most participants in both years quickly warmed to the opportunity that the project provided for them to engage in "risky stuff"—to write about and discuss their inner lives as teachers within a group of trusted colleagues.

During each academic year of the project, the participants met together twice after the initial retreat. As shown in Table 19.2, we identified specific purposes and outcomes for each of these sessions.

While attending the "Listening to Each Other's Stories" session, participants were divided into small groups and asked to share excerpts from the "first draft" of their memoirs (most of these were now several pages in length). The members of each small group were asked to provide collegial responses and to help the writers consider deeper meanings of their memoirs. During this session, each writing partner also highlighted specific words, phrases, sentences, and paragraphs to which they "resonated." These responders also wrote notes in the margins of the memoir excerpts that helped explain the basis for their resonance. As a result of such feedback, participants were able to gain meaningful peer input and make better progress on their memoirs.

Also during this workshop, we facilitated a conversation around the question "Who is the intended audience for your memoir?" Hampl (1999) discusses aspects of audience within the context of memoir writing and its significance. We highlighted aspects of her perspective and encouraged the participants to consider how their own unique audience would affect the ways that they framed and wrote their memoirs. Following one of these sessions, a

TABLE 19.2
Design Description of Subsequent Sessions

Title	Format	Date and Duration	Purposes	Outcomes
Listening to each other's stories	Workshop	Early January; five hours	• Respond to selective memoir writings of participants • Discuss concept of "audience" and its implications in writing a memoir • Explore concept of "voice" in memoir • Foster collegiality	• Participants receive response to writing • Concept of writing "partners" reinforced • Advance the memoir draft and writing process
Sharing completed memoirs and identifying realized assumptions, aspirations, and goals	Retreat	Mid-May; four hours	• Read excerpts from complete (or near complete) memoirs • Share realized assumptions, aspirations, and goals • Exchange gifts • Attain closure for the community and the "shared journey" • Foster collegiality	• Complete (or near complete) memoirs presented to the community • Response to the memoirs provided by the community • Affirmation of the value of the project

participant shared the following: "Memoir can become a gift to a family or even to an institution, and it awakens parallel memories in readers."

Between the second and third sessions involving the entire group of participants, we encouraged the participants to interact with their writing partner via email or in person. As facilitators, we also met in a one-on-one session with each participant and discovered that the writing partners often provided additional relevant feedback and suggestions that took the memoirists deeper into their stories. In our one-on-one meetings with each participant, we often assumed the role of a coach and offered specific responses to the participants' writing, encouraging them to look for deeper meanings, and asking questions regarding writing style, voice, and audience.

The participants found these one-on-one coaching sessions to be both enjoyable and beneficial. For example, during one such meeting, a participant from the School of Nursing shared her intention to return to the specific place about which she was writing her memoir (a hospital in rural Appalachia) in order to gain deeper insight into her story. In another such session, a participant expressed a new insight about his life in teaching—the realization that he had been both consistent and courageous in his efforts to innovate in his teaching practice. Yet another participant realized during the coaching session that in writing his memoir he had been sidestepping his role as a university administrator and its impact on his teaching life. During that conversation, new meanings emerged for him that later influenced both the content and style of his memoir.

During the third and final session involving the entire group, participants were invited to read excerpts from their memoirs, which were completed (or nearly completed) by that time. After each participant read, others in the group wrote responses that were given to the memoirist, such as "I love the back and forth between the past and present—the changing relationship between student and teacher," "Wonderful twist—students bringing gifts from core identities and teacher embracing and supporting them," and "The idea that humility creates the conditions for soul-connection between teacher and student—speaking from the heart."

Some participants did not complete their teaching memoirs within the single academic year period for each cohort. At the final retreat, we reminded these participants that creating a memoir was an aspiration, but not an absolute expectation. Rather, we trusted that their participation in the writing process had provided new and significant perspectives about their professional teaching careers whether or not a memoir had been completed. We also expected that some would complete their memoirs at a future time and that this project will have served as a "seed." A selection of memoirs that were completed by participants during the project's first two years is available at www1.umn.edu/ohr/teachlearn/meaning/index.html.

Participant Responses

Few opportunities exist within higher education where seasoned faculty can come together to reflect on their lives as teachers. Participants in "Making Meaning of a Life in Teaching" seemed to relish their time together and appeared eager to take steps to deepen their understandings of themselves as teachers. At one of the final sessions, one participant observed that memoir writing requires courage and places a memoirist face-to-face with unconscious and conscious fears. During each session as a whole group, project participants listened attentively to each other's stories and authentically engaged with one another.

The Center for Teaching and Learning Services sponsors an event each academic year to recognize faculty, staff, and graduate students who have enhanced the university's culture of teaching and learning. Some participants from the "Making Meaning of a Life in Teaching" project have shared reflections about the project during this event. Examples of their remarks follow.

> I agreed to participate in "Making Meaning" as a gift to myself, to force me (or give myself permission) to focus on my own reactions to and feelings about what I do in the classroom. My attention is usually appropriately directed towards students and what they are experiencing, but spending time looking inward and connecting more directly with other teachers and their inward experiences turns out to be a great way to recharge my own batteries and to understand better my own position in the classroom—which of course, helps me interact more effectively and more genuinely with my students.
>
> —Participant from the Law School

> I valued the opportunity to examine, in depth, my life as a teacher. It has been a gift to rediscover why I chose this path and what influences shaped me to be the teacher I am today. I especially appreciated the facilitators . . . as they encouraged me to explore the events and emotions that give meaning to my academic life.
>
> —Participant from the School of Nursing

> One of the values of the group has been in the actual writing of the memoir. Reflecting on my own struggles, uncertainties, angers, and joys as I worked to "grow up" (in academia) reminds me what it feels like to be a young adult who is seeking to find a voice and a place in the world.
>
> —Participant from General College

Conclusion

In his book about one's calling as a teacher, Palmer (2000) advocates that an academic "must listen for the truths and values at the heart of my own identity . . . the standards by which I cannot help but live if I am living my own life" (p. 51). We have found that the "Making Meaning of a Life in Teaching" project participants' memoirs are quite personal and move well beyond descriptive accounts of events and situations. The memoirists have sincerely sought deeper understanding of their values, attitudes, and perspectives—and in the process they have been revitalized. For example, upon completing her memoir one participant noted, "Memoir can open us to someone we once were and wish we could be again."

A memoir is, of necessity, selective. Chittister (2002) suggests that while all things in life are important, they might not be of equal importance. Most teachers would agree with this idea, but we would add that it is by winnowing one's life in teaching—of deciding what is important and why—and then writing a memoir about it that one gains deeper insight about one's identity as a teacher and how one might more fully develop in the future.

We have defined a memoir as writing that is to be shared with others. This is one aspect that perhaps distinguishes memoir writing from writing a journal. We have also found that collegial discourse, based on trust, is helpful—perhaps essential—to the process of writing a memoir about teaching. We are convinced that future offerings of this kind should include aspects of both community-supported and individual writing. When reviewing our project's desired outcomes and goals, it has become evident to us that the process of reflecting on, writing about, and sharing with colleagues one's life in teaching engages the mind and heart to help make meaning as a teacher.

Finally, as we have stated, fostering trust within the community has been a central element of this project. Writing a memoir is difficult and involves myriad considerations such as what to include, whom to include, whom not to include, why it matters, and what it means. Gaining counsel about such considerations from trusted colleagues is most helpful, yet implicit in this observation is an assumption that colleagues truly care about the memoirist and seek his or her best interests above all. During the final session in one of the project years, a participant responded to this environment of trust by stating, "I feel I know people better in this group than some colleagues I've worked with in my department for more than 20 years."

As co-facilitators, we have reminded our participants—and ourselves—that building and maintaining trust is an ongoing process. For participants, one challenge was the importance of being authentic and candid in their introspections, as well as projecting a willingness to foster trust within the group of participants. And because trust begins "at home," we are pleased to note that the trust that has formed and been sustained between us as co-facilitators of this project has been most gratifying of all.

References

Barrington, J. (2002). *Writing the memoir: A practical guide to the craft, the personal challenges, and ethical dilemmas of writing your true stories* (2nd ed.). Portland, OR: Eighth Mountain Press.

Brookfield, S. D. (1995). *Becoming a critically reflective teacher.* San Francisco, CA: Jossey-Bass.

Chittister, J. D. (2002). *Seeing with our souls: Monastic wisdom for every day.* New York, NY: Sheed and Ward.

Finkelstein, M. J., & Jemmott, N. D. (1993). The senior faculty: Higher education's plentiful yet largely untapped resource. In M. J. Finkelstein & M. W. LaCelle-Peterson (Eds.), *New directions for teaching and learning: No. 55. Developing senior faculty as teachers* (pp. 95–99). San Francisco, CA: Jossey-Bass.

Hampl, P. (1999). *I could tell you stories: Sojourns in the land of memory.* New York, NY: W.W. Norton.

Jackson, W. K., & Simpson, R. (1993). Redefining the role of senior faculty at a research university. In M. J. Finkelstein & M. W. LaCelle-Peterson (Eds.), *New directions for teaching and learning. No. 55. Developing senior faculty as teachers* (pp. 69–80). San Francisco, CA: Jossey-Bass.

Karpiak, I. E. (2000, Spring). Writing our life: Adult learning and teaching through autobiography. *Canadian Journal of University Continuing Education, 26*(1), 31–50.

Palmer, P. J. (1998). *The courage to teach: Exploring the inner landscape of a teacher's life.* San Francisco, CA: Jossey-Bass.

Palmer, P. J. (2000). *Let your life speak: Listening for the voice of vocation.* San Francisco, CA: Jossey-Bass.

Palmer, P. J. (2004). *A hidden wholeness: The journey toward an undivided life.* San Francisco, CA: Jossey-Bass.

Rice, R. E., & Finkelstein M. J. (1993). The senior faculty: A portrait and literature review. In M. J. Finkelstein & M. W. LaCelle-Peterson (Eds.), *New directions for teaching and learning: No. 55. Developing senior faculty as teachers* (pp. 7–19). San Francisco, CA: Jossey-Bass.

Schön, D. A. (1983). *The reflective practitioner: How professionals think in action.* New York, NY: Basic Books.

Simmons, S. R. (2004). "An imperishable attitude": A memoir of learning and teaching. *Journal of Natural Resources and Life Sciences Education, 33,* 147–154.

20

Transforming a Teaching Culture Through Peer Mentoring: Connecticut College's Johnson Teaching Seminar for Incoming Faculty

Michael Reder, Eugene V. Gallagher
Connecticut College

This chapter describes a yearlong seminar focused on teaching that is offered to all incoming tenure-track faculty at Connecticut College, a small residential liberal arts college. This seminar is distinctive because it is facilitated by second- and third-year faculty. We argue that this peer-mentoring model has three distinct benefits. First, it avoids many of the pitfalls identified with traditional one-on-one mentoring. Second, it addresses the distinctive challenges that faculty face at small colleges. Third, it provides a strong base for faculty to pursue the scholarship of teaching and learning (SoTL). We believe that our peer-mentoring model may well be adaptable to different types of institutions. As evidence of our faculty's newfound engagement in SoTL, where previously little or no critical attention was paid to teaching, program participants have made presentations and run workshops on our own campus and at regional and national conferences, have begun to serve on teaching committees within their disciplinary organizations, and have gone on to publish their pedagogical work in a variety of national publications, both disciplinary and teaching focused.

At the Connecticut College Center for Teaching and Learning (CTL), we started out with the simple idea of giving more than mere lip service to the notion of the importance of teaching. Part of the original mandate of the CTL was to support new faculty—a straightforward if potentially paternalistic idea. Although the amount and kind of teaching experiences that incoming faculty bring to Connecticut College vary widely, all faculty face the challenge of teaching in a new environment. New faculty have undergone graduate training at large research universities where the type of teaching demonstrated is not necessarily a good fit in the classrooms of small liberal arts institutions. They may be assigned to teach new and unfamiliar courses. There are also new contexts for their work in the classroom, in their departments, and in the college as a whole.

Since 1998, Connecticut College's Christian A. Johnson Teaching Seminar for Incoming Faculty has been supporting faculty in their roles as teachers, scholars, and community members and has addressed those challenges that face new faculty members through a regularly scheduled sequence of meetings.[1] Our peer-mentoring model uses second- and third-year faculty as well as the CTL's director and faculty fellow to lead monthly seminars on topics such as local campus culture, course design, active learning, learning styles, diversity and power in the classroom, and balancing the many demands of campus life. Cohorts of new faculty—no longer isolated in their buildings and departments—are forming bonds and transforming the teaching culture at our college. Teaching has become something not only valued but also shared and discussed.

After describing the basics of our yearlong seminar, we will discuss the ways in which our peer-mentoring model addresses many of the challenges new faculty face at smaller institutions. We will then describe how our peer-based, multi-cohort approach has had unintended consequences in terms of both collaboration among faculty and their participation in the scholarship of teaching and learning (SoTL). We then offer our recommendations for promoting faculty work on teaching and SoTL, especially at a small college, and evidence of the success of our program.

The first session of the Johnson Seminar is usually held on the Friday of the week before classes begin, at the end of the college's official orientation for new faculty. We meet in the morning for breakfast, and our session begins with a nuts-and-bolts question-and-answer period that addresses any concerns that seminar members might have about teaching at Connecticut College. These questions typically range from the specific (What are the required office hours? What should my students call me? What should I call my students?) to the overarching and philosophical (What are student expectations about grades and workloads? What is it like to be a faculty member of color in a mostly white classroom?). Because the session is facilitated by second- and third-year faculty who have themselves recently made the transition to teaching at the college, they can share their own local experiences, challenges, and successes. Having second- and third-year faculty present—usually in numbers close to those of first-year faculty—also provides a larger range of experiences to share, both in terms of disciplinary focus, faculty identity, and teaching styles.

After the discussion, we break into small groups and read drafts of each other's syllabi. We ask faculty to review these syllabi as both teachers of other classes and as potential students. Is everything clear? Is the timing and amount of work reasonable (for both the faculty member and his or her students)? Each faculty member takes a turn presenting his or her own syllabus to the group, expressing concerns and answering questions. After about an hour we then reconvene as a large group and share best practices for syllabi: lateness and attendance policies we liked, the idea of being as explicit as possible in terms of learning goals and requirements, and other issues faculty might want to consider when constructing their syllabi. From our accumulated experience, we are convinced that a careful review of a syllabus can be the single most effective tool for bringing to light someone's fundamental assumptions about both the process of teaching and the nature of the subject.[2]

To end the morning, we talk about ideas for the first day of class: the importance of students getting to know each other, how to situate yourself and establish credibility (especially as a woman or nonmajority faculty member), a variety of activities to introduce students to the subject and to each other. We believe that faculty should do more on the first day of class than merely read through the syllabus. Establishing expectations and a general tone for a class is essential, and ideally each student should do a little bit of what he or she will be expected to do throughout the semester: from talking with each other and participating in discussion to engaging in small group work, in-class writing, and careful listening. We end the morning with a brief, written survey of possible topics for our upcoming monthly lunchtime meetings and workshops, and then as a group go for lunch to a local restaurant where our conversations continue.

There are several features of this first seminar that set the tone for the rest of the year. First, the entire day is collaborative, with both experienced facilitators and first-year faculty working together. The open format of the seminar clearly sends the message that "We are here to help and learn from each other," rather than "This is what you need to do."[3] Second, spending an entire day talking about teaching sends a powerful message that Connecticut College not only values teaching but also thinks of it as something that is shared and practiced critically. We have found that this introduction to teaching at the college has created a strong foundation for faculty to go on to engage in SoTL. Finally, as we discuss later, this model of peer mentoring creates a strong nexus of support for faculty that crosses both cohorts and disciplinary boundaries.

Peer Mentoring and the Specific Challenges of Institutional Type

The shortcoming of traditional one-on-one mentoring, where one member of the pair is a protégé and the other is a more senior mentor, have been well documented by Boice (1991, 1992) and others (Otto, 1994). Traditional mentoring, in the words of Boice (1992), provides "little more than socioemotional support" (p. 120). Such mentoring, Boice (1992) believes, does "little or nothing to extend the social networks of new faculty to students" (p. 121), does not directly address the improvement of teaching, and is narrow and passive, in that it can often put new faculty only on the receiving end of advice. Even taking into account the research that suggests strategies for increasing the effectiveness of such mentoring relationships, such as group meetings, pairing faculty from different departments, and written obligations (Boice, 1992), mentoring pairs are limited in their ability to create a nexus of supportive relationships within and across cohorts and departments. Such interdepartmental connections are particularly important on a small college campus, where departments range in size from 2 to 10 members, and a newly hired faculty member may be the only untenured member in his or her department.

Although the recent research into self-directed learning communities reveals that such groups successfully connect individual faculty to larger groups of faculty outside their departments, these communities, such as Cox (2001) describes, are not focused on new faculty. The most recent adaptations of faculty learning communities, such as Otterbein College's program for first-year faculty, may apply the idea of learning communities to new faculty but do so only to a single cohort and therefore do little to connect faculty *across* cohorts (Fayne & Ortquist-Ahrens, 2006). By involving recently hired cohorts of faculty we promote continuing relationships among them and their most recently hired colleagues. We believe that the power in our arrangement is that second- and third-year faculty are intimately involved in guiding first-year faculty—not as wizened mentors with all the answers, but as empathetic peers who have slightly more experience at the institution. We have found, however, that the second- and third-year faculty often get as much from their continued participation in the Johnson Seminar, particularly in the area of classroom practice and course design, as their first-year colleagues. Indeed, during the first few years of our seminars we would ask only two or three first-year faculty to return the following year to help facilitate the group, until we began to hear from second-year faculty not returning to the seminar that they were still encountering challenges and having successes they would like to share and that they missed participating. In subsequent years we made an open call for returning participants, and in most years 80%–90% of the first-year faculty return for a second year.[4]

Boice (1992) has recognized the potential effectiveness of what we term *peer mentoring,* stating that mentoring programs will fare better if they break the traditional pairing of a senior mentor with a protégé in the same discipline, noting that "junior mentors work just as well" (p. 119). Wheeler and Wheeler (1994) suggest what they term *colleague mentoring* for mid-career faculty, but we believe that early-career faculty across cohorts are also well situated to mentor each other, and that peer mentoring can be especially effective at small colleges, where most faculty must make the transition from their training at a large university to the distinctive culture of a small college.

Small liberal arts colleges in particular typically want to be known for the quality of their classroom teaching,[5] and they often attract faculty who share the tacit belief that teaching is the sine qua non of their faculty role. Yet simply valuing good teaching does not necessarily lead to good teaching. "Faculty need to be critical practitioners of their craft and critical practitioners share, discuss, and analyze their classroom practices" (Holmgren, Mooney, & Reder, 2005). By immediately devoting time and energy to the discussion of teaching—before classes even begin—Connecticut College sends the message to all its new faculty that teaching is not only something valued, but something that is actively discussed and institutionally supported.

The Johnson seminar also shows that the college devotes resources and energy toward supporting recently hired faculty members. For a new faculty member, many factors make the first year at a small college challenging, including learning about the local characteristics of the teaching and learning environment, fitting into a department, and balancing the demands of teaching, research, student contact, service, and institutional governance. In our experience, many new faculty find a small school's institutional community—identified by Rice, Sorcinelli, and Austin (2000) as a positive trait of small colleges—both limiting and frustrating. For example, the residential nature of such schools can make new faculty feel the demands of their jobs 24 hours a day, 7 days a week. Because many small schools are church affiliated, dealing with an institution's religious traditions can also pose special challenges. Diversity—among faculty, students, and even disciplines—is also a distinct issue on small college campuses. Small departments—where new faculty are often hired to diversify course offerings or the faculty itself—can quickly become oppressive if "mentoring" by more senior colleagues takes the form of micromanaging course content or teaching styles.

Faculty also need to discover the distinctive expectations of their particular students and calibrate their own expectations at least partially in response

(Smith & Kalivoda, 1998). They must learn to work with new colleagues who manifest varying degrees of engagement in their own work and different degrees of empathy for the situation of beginning faculty members. There are myriad aspects of a new setting that even the most experienced faculty member needs to discern and adjust to. As Hall (2002) notes, "Our careers are largely local" (p. 70), and one key to a faculty member's success is understanding institutional expectations (Menges & Associates, 1999). Hall also argues that a faculty member's happiness largely depends on his or her own "behaviors, attitudes, and interactions within the communities of our departments, colleges, and universities" (p. 73), and that overall success "derives from our understanding of local history and the genesis of local behaviors" (p. 77). At a small institution these issues can be pressurized: The local is more local, so to speak, and the small size of the faculty means there is less diversity and potentially fewer places in which to find one's niche. The Johnson Seminar, by creating a safe space in which faculty can explore these many issues during their early careers, helps faculty find a nexus of support and reliable sources of information about the challenges they face.

Additionally, beginning faculty face both explicit and implicit expectations for successful and productive disciplinary scholarship, and after their first year they are quickly tapped for various kinds of service. In many ways the most valuable commodity for a beginning faculty member—even more than for their senior colleagues—is time. But time often seems to be in very short supply (Menges, 1996). Even for those who have some familiarity with the current scholarly discussion of teaching and learning, it can be hard to imagine how they will be able to carve time out of their schedule to focus on their teaching. One overall effect of the seminar's conversations, however, has been to encourage an early and more sustained engagement with teaching as a critical practice, and this has had the indirect effect of creating a strong foundation for the scholarship of teaching and learning.

Promoting the Scholarship of Teaching and Learning: Creating an Atmosphere of Teaching as Critical Practice

In spite of the increasing attention that has been devoted to the scholarship of teaching and learning over the past 10 or 15 years, relatively few faculty members are interested pursuing it, especially in their early careers. Their explicit resistance is often based on the amount of time they fear they would have to invest, a professed unfamiliarity with this new field of research, the need to attend to other more pressing disciplinary commitments, and a general disdain for the field of education. Teaching-related scholarship may carry with it lower status and rewards than disciplinary scholarship, which may also account for resistance (Wright, 1995). Sometimes more forthright objections take the form of confident proclamations that one's own teaching is very successful and therefore needs no further attention. On many campuses it is difficult to create and maintain a culture that values sustained and systematic examination of teaching practices. This is particularly true at small liberal arts colleges, where "good teaching" is usually thought of as a given. The Johnson Seminar explores issues related to SoTL, sometimes directly and sometimes more indirectly, in the context of teaching at Connecticut College. It also aims to show the various ways in which engagement in SoTL might matter for individuals.

We will use definitions of SoTL given by two of its best-known advocates as reference points. Boyer (1990) argues, "The work of the professor becomes consequential only as it is understood by others. . . . Pedagogical procedures must be carefully planned, continually examined, and relate directly to the subject taught" (pp. 23–24). Building on this notion, Shulman offers a definition, first asking, "What would be a thumbnail explanation of what we mean by the scholarship of teaching?" He replies,

> The scholarship of teaching is a way of capturing teaching in a manner that makes it possible for others both to review it critically and to build on it themselves. That's all that scholarship is. What is teaching? Teaching is more than talking to students and listening to them respond. Teaching is a process of design, interaction, evaluation, and redesign. Put those two together and you have the scholarship of teaching. (Carnegie Foundation for the Advancement of Teaching, 1999)

Using these two definitions makes SoTL sound like a rather straightforward undertaking: Basically it is about shared critical practice, taking teaching and student learning as objects worthy of study and discussion among professionals. Put most simply, the scholarship of teaching and learning is about examining, refining, and promoting effective teaching and learning.

The Johnson Seminar, then, begins to connect faculty with SoTL from its first meeting, which explicitly makes teaching an object of critical reflection and discussion. Our first seminar meeting addresses issues that are imminently—even urgently—practical ("In a few days you will be in front of students teaching a class here for the first time—what can we do to help you be prepared?"). At the same time we present teaching as a topic that is complex enough to approach theoretically.

This attitude about teaching continues throughout the year and is reinforced through common readings, including *McKeachie's Teaching Tips* (McKeachie & Svinicki, 2006) and *Advice for New Faculty Members* (Boice, 2000), both of which are given to each participant.[6] One thing we do every year is to distribute a list of topics that the seminar has considered in prior years and ask the members to rank them in terms of their own interests. The survey not only gives the organizing committee a sense of the seminar members' concerns, it also orients the seminar members to the scholarly discussion of major topics in teaching and learning. During our monthly meetings, we address various issues related to teaching, such as assignment and course design, classroom incivilities, issues of power both inside and outside the classroom (including race and gender), active learning (discussion, group work), grading and evaluation, and student cultures and values (with students as guests). These issues correspond closely to the teaching topics that Seldin (2006) identifies as particularly relevant to a beginning faculty member's career. We also discuss topics related to college politics, power, promotion, and tenure, and offer seminar members additional opportunities for casual get-togethers, such as informal lunches and end-of-semester parties.

By incorporating second- and third-year faculty into the seminar each year as part of the organizing committee, the Johnson Seminar builds cohorts of faculty who have developed the habit of systematic reflection on their teaching practice; it sends the message that thinking about teaching should be an integral part of our work. Similar to the use of faculty learning communities to promote SoTL (Cox, 2003), our seminar creates a cross-cohort learning community that views teaching as critical practice. In addition, by incorporating a more experienced faculty fellow as a participant and by periodically drawing on the expertise and experience of other faculty members, the seminar connects beginning faculty members to senior faculty outside their departments and to the senior administration of the college, particularly the dean of the faculty. The seminar also puts participants into contact with the broader conversations about teaching and learning by providing funds to facilitate attendance and presentations at off-campus workshops and conferences that address teaching. Rather than offering participants a stipend paid in cash, the seminar gives money that is specifically earmarked to improve teaching.[7] This money closes the circle: We not only support teaching as a critical practice in theory, we also support faculty presenting on the topic of teaching or attending a conference focused on teaching (e.g., Association of American Colleges and Universities, POD, regional or disciplinary teaching conferences). Although a few administrators have questioned the wisdom of "paying" faculty to undertake something that is an essential part of their jobs and professional development (participating in this seminar and thinking about their teaching critically), we look at the "teaching credits" as the counterpart to the money Connecticut College offers its faculty to help them pursue their research—again, driving home the idea that small liberal arts colleges must support teaching as well as research.

Finally, the Johnson Seminar also encourages participants to apply for small grants from the CTL that will support projects related to the improvement and assessment of teaching.

In promoting SoTL, the Johnson Seminar has encountered a number of problems, not least of which is the question "Just what constitutes SoTL anyway?" There are some explicit and implied differences of opinion on this issue both across and within disciplines, including variations in the forms SoTL takes and orientations of its practitioners. Some disciplines seem more amenable to SoTL, and this disciplinary attitude can be reflected at the departmental level as well. And even if a department or wider discipline is open to the notion of SoTL, the way in which such scholarship is practiced within disciplines varies widely (Huber, 2004; Huber & Morreale, 2002). The variations among disciplines, not to mention the range of attitudes displayed by departments representing those disciplines on a local level, make any discussion of SoTL with a general audience even more challenging because the procedures, standards, and even the way in which such work is valued often change from discipline to discipline.

The scholarship of teaching and learning also takes a variety of forms, representing a range of approaches to making teaching and learning an object of critical study, sometimes even within the same discipline. Consequently, even those who would engage in SoTL have to negotiate within and between local tensions (my own classroom and practice, my own college) and global tensions (the field of SoTL, teaching in U.S. higher education). How one conceives of the task of SoTL and the models one encounters may make entry into SoTL appear either easier or more difficult.

New faculty may justifiably wonder how much SoTL actually matters to them as teachers, to their reappointment, tenure and promotion, to their senior colleagues in their department and on personnel committees. Such questions are particularly pressing to those in the pre-tenure phase of their careers. They have to consider whether the payoff from engaging in SoTL will be worth the investment, particularly when reflecting on their teaching seems inevitably to take time away from actually preparing for class, scholarly research, and the myriad service small college life requires (Gibson, 1992). Yet if we return to Shulman's definition of SoTL—simply "capturing teaching in a manner that makes it possible for others both to review it critically and to build on it themselves" (Carnegie Foundation, 1999)—then any responsible faculty member should continually be involved in critical reflection and the sharing of his or her teaching, at least at the local level. When Shulman (1999) examines the different ways in which students fail to learn, he directly links the solution to SoTL. Shulman (1999) calls for "a systematic approach" to help faculty cope with student failure to learn, and urges that "we must commit ourselves professionally to the scholarship of teaching" (p. 15).[8] In other words, the scholarship of teaching leads to better student learning, making such critical practice a necessary activity at any institution that values student learning. Hall (2002) decries what he sees as the artificial boundaries between scholarship and teaching, and also between individual work and collaboration. Our seminar challenges such divisions, encourages faculty to think critically about their teaching, and gives participants a way to maintain an engagement with SoTL.

From our work with the Johnson Seminar, we have distilled several suggestions about how to promote a small college campus culture that values the scholarship of teaching and learning.

Use Brokers

At Connecticut College, the director of the CTL and, to a lesser extent, the faculty fellow, are directly and continually engaged with SoTL. They maintain a baseline flow of information, review the literature, attend conferences, attend and conduct workshops, and generally maintain a high level of participation in the growing field of the study of teaching and learning. We believe it is essential to have a central clearinghouse for information about SoTL and a dedicated person or persons who sifts through it and funnels what is relevant to the appropriate audiences; this switching function is probably the most important element in creating a local culture that values SoTL. For the Johnson Seminar, these leaders serve as trustworthy brokers; they distill what's out there, put people in touch with thoroughly evaluated resources, keep an eye on the literature, and generally try to bring to the attention of the seminar members precisely what will be helpful to them and only what will be helpful to them. In addition, they keep an eye on which faculty are involved in SoTL and bring to the seminar both past seminar graduates and more senior faculty who have been doing interesting work in the SoTL.

Move Incrementally

The Johnson Seminar has adopted a wide view of SoTL. Its first goal is simply to get the participants talking with each other about their teaching. Beyond that, it aims to develop a system of reciprocal, nonevaluative, classroom observations in order to provide members with critical but sympathetic feedback on their teaching in addition to formal student and departmental evaluations. In addition, the seminar encourages participants to make low-stakes presentations on campus, either within the seminar itself or at other venues such as regular brown-bag "Talking Teaching" lunches. Further, the seminar encourages participants to attend nearby off-campus conferences and workshops as a group in order to become involved in broader conversations about teaching and learning.

Take the Long View

The Johnson Seminar encourages participants to plan for the medium to long term. It is designed to have faculty in their first three years maintain a steady—even if low—level of engagement with SoTL; they may, for example, start to file away ideas that they can take up again during their summers, on their fourth-year sabbaticals, or even on their post-tenure sabbaticals. The basic goal of the seminar is for participants to keep on their radar the idea that teaching can serve as an object of scholarly reflection. We hope that training in the fundamental elements of SoTL will bear fruit later in their careers. Indeed, we would argue that such early training prepares faculty for the inevitable career cycles we all experience. Our main focuses may fluctuate as our career progresses, sometimes emphasizing research, sometimes concentrating on teaching, and sometimes focusing on service. Thus, taking the long view of SoTL is essential, and preparing faculty to undertake such work is clearly the precursor for doing such work.[9]

Take Boyer's Categories of Scholarship Seriously

Faculty members arrive on campus ready, willing, and eager to pursue the scholarship of discovery. Some become interested in the scholarship of application, and others the scholarship of synthesis. Very few have seriously contemplated undertaking the scholarship of teaching in any form. The seminar encourages participants to find their own niches while being aware of other possibilities, to contemplate the rhythms and shifts of scholarly interests over a long career, and to reject the notion that they will have to or need to undertake all four types of scholarship with equal commitment and intensity at the same time. [10] The seminar acknowledges that simply staying aware of SoTL may be sufficient for certain periods during a long career or even for the entire career, so long as it promotes reflective practice.

One of the reasons that the Johnson Seminar has been successful is that it doesn't overreach. Successive organizing committees have developed a solid sense of what the seminar can and cannot do for its participants. It has been demonstrably successful in promoting and sustaining at least a minimal continuing engagement with SoTL among its graduates. By doing that, it has incrementally adjusted our own campus culture to promote SoTL. It has supported individual projects in SoTL by providing small grants, a pool of collaborators, and a sympathetic audience. It showcases local, on-campus SoTL both in the actual seminar meetings and in other programs of the Connecticut College CTL. By not requiring of faculty a certain level or kind of engagement with SoTL—beyond making their teaching public practice by sharing their teaching materials, challenges, and successes within the confines of the seminar—the seminar has helped participants to discover and pursue their own interests in reflective practice. The results of that culture of encouragement can be seen in the seminar graduates who have gone on to offer on-campus workshops and other presentations on a variety of pedagogical topics ranging from teaching critical thinking skills across the curriculum to running effective discussions, from the challenges and philosophy of grading to the effective use of technology, from incorporating information fluency assignment to diversity in the classroom.

Evidence of a Culture of Teaching and Learning

The Johnson Seminar has begun to transform the overall culture of teaching on campus. Before the founding of our Center for Teaching and Learning and the establishment of the seminar, there was no systematic attention paid to teaching and no formal mechanism for tracking faculty participation in the scholarship of teaching and learning. Although we can offer no baseline statistics for SoTL, there are some indicators of success for the seminar.

- Since 2000, more than 90% of the first-year faculty return for a second year to help facilitate the seminar for the new group of incoming faculty. Approximately 25% of those return for a third year.
- The number of participants who have attended conferences and workshops related to teaching and learning—or have presented on a teaching-related topic at a disciplinary conference—has been steadily rising.
- The number of participants who have themselves offered on-campus workshops continues to grow, as does the willingness of former participants to take on such work when they are asked to do so. At least one of

these campus workshops—on teaching students critical thinking skills—led to the faculty member writing an article on the topic in a widely distributed, national periodical that addresses teaching.

- Participants have included a number of teaching-related publications in the review files for third-year and tenure reviews, and the CTL and the Johnson Seminar in particular are prominent in faculty personal statements for these reviews.[11]

Additionally, interdisciplinary work related to teaching has flourished through connections and bonds formed through the seminar. For example, former seminar participants created an interdisciplinary course on modernism, team-taught by untenured faculty from across a variety of departments. The following year the two faculty who coordinated that course organized and ran a faculty seminar on interdisciplinarity, and arising out of that seminar, there have been faculty seminars on the state of cultural theory and living a moral life.

The 2004–2005 academic year was the first in which a full group of Johnson Seminar graduates came up for tenure. As these colleagues advance in their careers, they will infuse the school's decision-making processes with their own values. We expect, for example, as those recently tenured colleagues begin to evaluate their untenured colleagues for promotion and tenure, they will bring with them an understanding of teaching as a process worthy of critical consideration. The work done on SoTL by new candidates for promotion and tenure will get the consideration it deserves. This will encourage more faculty to take teaching as a form of scholarship more seriously. The cultural shift toward valuing teaching and learning makes a complete loop and becomes self-perpetuating. We would also argue that the Johnson Seminar models a collaborative spirit that can be easily transferred to other group undertakings, such as committee work.[12] Finally, faculty who have shared syllabi and assignments, who have been in each other's classrooms, and who know of each other's teaching successes and failures, make for sympathetic and empathetic colleagues.

It is essential for small liberal arts colleges to dedicate the resources—financial and personnel—to promoting the critical discussion of teaching. As the study of teaching and learning as a discipline expands, such schools can no longer get away with giving mere lip service to valuing teaching. Small liberal arts colleges must vigorously pursue and actively promote excellence in teaching.

In order for SoTL ever to be valued on a campus, a campus culture must explicitly value teaching by devoting time, energy, and money to its development. Merely "valuing teaching," a mantra at many small liberal arts college, is simply not enough. While the more time-intensive and even technical SoTL may not be appropriate (or even of interest) to all faculty, it is imperative that colleges provide the means and impetus for faculty to engage in SoTL at a local level. By introducing teaching as something intentional and deliberate—worthy of discussion and critical examination—our seminar has created a culture that not only explicitly values teaching, but also has begun to implicitly and explicitly engage in the scholarship of teaching and learning.

Our peer-mentoring model was created out of the exigencies particular to the setting of a small liberal arts college: in terms of scale and in terms of the need for faculty to form supportive networks beyond their often small departments or buildings. However, this model, which emphasizes multiple faculty connections that cross disciplines and cohorts, has helped bring about a major cultural shift on our campus. At Connecticut College, teaching truly has become community property.

Acknowledgments

We would like to thank the Christian A. Johnson Endeavor Foundation for their generous support of the Center for Teaching and Learning and the Johnson Teaching Seminar for Incoming Faculty. A version of this chapter was presented at the conference "Innovations in the Scholarship of Teaching and Learning at Liberal Arts Colleges" sponsored by Carleton College and St. Olaf College, April 1–3, 2005. We would also like to thank David Schodt, director of St. Olaf's Center for Innovation in the Liberal Arts and conference co-chair, for his encouragement and help in shaping our original proposal.

Endnotes

1) Since 1999, the Christian A. Johnson Endeavor Foundation has funded the teaching seminar and the majority of our Center for Teaching and Learning through two generous grants.

2) Of course, syllabi vary in content and construction, and this might shape the amount they reveal about a person's teaching. A well-constructed syllabus can reveal more than a minimalist syllabus that is little more than a course schedule—although a minimalist syllabus is revelatory in its own way. For example, a syllabus can reveal what the faculty member values and emphasizes (by how the course

weighs the variety of assignments when assigning a final grade), a faculty member's attitude toward grading and learning as a process, how he or she views the construction of knowledge, and hoped-for outcomes in terms of student learning (when a list of learning goals is included). The documents that the teaching seminar uses for its syllabus review workshop can be downloaded at http://CTL.ConnColl.edu/resources/syllabusworkshop/

3) Although the faculty fellow takes part in this workshop, his role has been as a source for information and informed opinion, as someone who possesses a strong institutional memory. Much of the success of this seminar has to do with the willingness of the faculty fellow to be the proverbial "guide on the side" rather than the "sage on the stage." His syllabus is also reviewed, and he makes it clear from the beginning that he regularly "steals" ideas and assignments from those participating in the seminar.

4) Inviting second- and third-year faculty back to facilitate the teaching seminar helps address another challenge that such first-year seminars face on small college campuses: uneven hiring from year to year. Since 1997, Connecticut College has hired anywhere from 1 to 11 new tenure-track faculty members; in some years there are too few new faculty hired to compose an active seminar (an issue not faced at larger institutions). By allowing faculty from other recent cohorts to participate, we ensure there are always enough faculty, in terms of both number and diversity, to make the seminar work.

5) It is important to note that most small liberal arts colleges are "known" for the quality of their teaching because that is the way in which they present and market themselves, often without persuasive substantiation.

6) In addition to these two books, we also provide specific articles related to the current topic under discussion. Although these are constantly changing, for a seminar meeting with the topic of "Making Our Classrooms Active," we might ask faculty to read a few chapters in *McKeachie's Teaching Tips* (McKeachie & Svinincki, 2006), and then provide short articles on running discussion (e.g., Frederick, 1981) and making lectures more effective (e.g., Desrochers 1999). Visit http://CTL.ConnColl.edu/bibliographies/ for a current bibliography of seminar readings listed by topic.

7) Visit http://CTL.ConnColl.edu/TeachingBank.html for a full explanation of how these "teaching credits" may be used and the varying amounts allotted to seminar participants.

8) It is important to note that for Shulman (1999)

> All acts of intelligence are not scholarship. An act of intelligence or of artistic creation becomes scholarship when it possesses at least three attributes: it becomes public; it becomes an object of critical review and evaluation by members of one's community; and members of one's community begin to use, build upon, and develop those acts of mind and creation. (p. 15)

9) The idea of engaging teaching at certain points in one's career seems to be working on our campus. Two faculty members recently granted tenure have decided that their next major projects will be teaching related: One had applied for outside funding to totally rethink her department's introductory course to the major; another has begun to study how discussion functions to advance knowledge in his classroom.

10) In *Scholarship Reconsidered,* Boyer (1990) identifies, in addition to the scholarship of teaching, three additional types of scholarship: discovery, integration, and application. According to Boyer, the scholarship of discovery "comes closest to what is meant when academics speak of 'research' " (p. 17). The scholarship of integration involves "making connections across the disciplines, placing the specialties in larger context, illuminating data in a revealing way, often educating nonspecialists, too" (p. 18). The scholarship of application asks and attempts to answer questions like "How can knowledge be responsibly applied to consequential problems?" "How can it be helpful to individuals and institutions?" and even "Can social problems *themselves* define an agenda for scholarly investigation?" (p. 21). Boyer argues that "What we urgently need today is a more inclusive view of what it means to be a scholar—a recognition that knowledge is acquired through research, through synthesis, through practice, and through teaching" (p. 24). It is important to understand that while Boyer divides scholarship into four separate categories for the purpose of discussion and analysis, he believes that as "intellectual functions" they are "tied inseparably to each other" (p. 25).

11) The Johnson Seminar started attracting the attention—not to mention strong support—of the dean of the faculty when, during her end-of-year interviews with first-year faculty, the seminar was consistently mentioned by those faculty as one of the best things about their first year at Connecticut College. As the positive reports continued, the dean's office started using the Johnson Seminar to help attract new faculty hires. The CTL brochure is the only brochure on the coffee table where the dean conducts her interviews. It is also worth noting that participating in the Johnson Seminar is voluntary: Since 1999, it has boasted 100% participation by incoming faculty, including faculty who arrive with years of teaching experience, faculty coming in at the associate level with tenure, and even full professors holding named chairs.

12) Interestingly, the Johnson Seminar has been identified, sometimes resentfully, among senior tenured colleagues, as a center for political power on campus, as a means by which newer faculty have connected with each other to empower untenured faculty in ways they had not previously been empowered.

References

Boice, R. (1991, January). New faculty as colleagues. *International Journal of Qualitative Studies in Education, 4*(1), 29–44.

Boice, R. (1992). *The new faculty member: Supporting and fostering professional development.* San Francisco, CA: Jossey-Bass.

Boice, R. (2000). *Advice for new faculty members: Nihil nimus.* Needham Heights, MA: Allyn & Bacon.

Boyer, E. L. (1990). *Scholarship reconsidered: Priorities of the professoriate.* Princeton, NJ: Carnegie Foundation for the Advancement of Teaching.

Carnegie Foundation for the Advancement of Teaching (Producer). (1999). *Fostering a scholarship of teaching* [Film]. Oregon: West Peak Media.

Cox, M. D. (2001). Faculty learning communities: Change agents for transforming institutions into learning organizations. In D. Lieberman & C. Wehlburg (Eds.), *To improve the academy: Vol. 19. Resources for faculty, instructional, and organizational development* (pp. 69–93). Bolton, MA: Anker.

Cox, M. D. (2003). Proven faculty development tools that foster the scholarship of teaching in faculty learning communities. In C. M. Wehlburg & S. Chadwick-Blossey (Eds.), *To improve the academy: Vol. 21. Resources for faculty, instructional, and organizational development* (pp. 109–142). Bolton, MA: Anker.

Desrochers, C. (1999, December). Multi-purpose lecture breaks. *The Teaching Professor, 13*(10), 1–2.

Fayne, H., & Ortquist-Ahrens, L. (2006). Learning communities for first-year faculty: Transition, acculturation, and transformation. In S. Chadwick-Blossey & D. R. Robertson (Eds.), *To improve the academy: Vol. 24. Resources for faculty, instructional, and organizational development* (pp. 277–290). Bolton, MA: Anker.

Frederick, P. (1981, Summer). The dreaded discussion: Ten ways to start. *Improving College and University Teaching, 29*(3), 109–114.

Gibson, G. W. (1992). *Good start: A guidebook for new faculty in liberal arts colleges.* Bolton, MA: Anker.

Hall, D. E. (2002). *The academic self: An owner's manual.* Columbus, OH: The Ohio State University Press.

Holmgren, R., Mooney, K., & Reder, M. (2005, January). *Transforming teaching cultures: The need for teaching and learning programs at liberal arts colleges.* Paper presented at the annual meeting of the Association of American Colleges and Universities, San Francisco, CA.

Huber, M. T. (2004). *Balancing acts: The scholarship of teaching and learning in academic careers.* Sterling, VA: Stylus.

Huber, M. T., & Morreale, S. P. (Eds.). (2002). *Disciplinary styles in the scholarship of teaching and learning: Exploring common ground.* Washington, DC: American Association for Higher Education.

McKeachie, W. J., & Svinicki, M. (2006). *McKeachie's teaching tips: Strategies, research, and theory for college and university teachers* (12th ed.). Boston, MA: Houghton Mifflin.

Menges, R. J. (1996). Experiences of newly hired faculty. In L. Richlin & D. DeZure (Eds.), *To improve the academy: Vol. 15. Resources for faculty, instructional, and organizational development* (pp. 169–182). Stillwater, OK: New Forums Press.

Menges, R. J., & Associates. (1999). *Faculty in new jobs: A guide to settling in, becoming established, and building institutional support.* San Francisco, CA: Jossey-Bass.

Otto, M. L. (1994). Mentoring: An adult developmental perspective. In M. A. Wunsch (Ed.), *New directions for teaching and learning: Vol. 57. Mentoring revisited: Making an impact on individuals and institutions* (pp. 15–24). San Francisco, CA: Jossey-Bass.

Rice, R. E., Sorcinelli, M. D., & Austin, A. E. (2000). *Heeding new voices: Academic careers for a new generation.* Washington, DC: American Association for Higher Education.

Seldin, P. (2006). Tailoring faculty development programs to faculty career stages. In S. Chadwick-Blossey & D. R. Robertson (Eds.), *To improve the academy: Vol. 24. Resources for faculty, instructional, and organizational development* (pp. 137–146). Bolton, MA: Anker.

Shulman, L. S. (1999, July/August). Taking learning seriously. *Change, 31*(4), 10–17.

Smith, K. S., & Kalivoda, P. L. (1998). Academic morphing: Teaching assistant to faculty member. In M. Kaplan & D. Lieberman (Eds.), *To improve the academy: Vol. 17. Resources for faculty, instructional, and organizational development* (pp. 85–101). Stillwater, OK: New Forums Press.

Wheeler, D. W., & Wheeler, B. J. (1994). Mentoring faculty for midcareer issues. In M. A. Wunsch (Ed.), *New directions for teaching and learning: Vol. 57. Mentoring revisited: Making an impact on individuals and institutions* (pp. 91–98). San Francisco, CA: Jossey-Bass.

Wright, W. A. (Ed.). (1995). *Teaching improvement practices: Successful strategies for higher educationn.* Bolton, MA: Anker.

21

Preparing Future Faculty for Careers in Academic Librarianship: A Paradigm Shift for Collaboration in Higher Education

Sean Patrick Knowlton, Laura L. B. Border
University of Colorado at Boulder

Nationwide, the number of available faculty positions represents only a fraction of the master's and doctoral degrees granted each year. Fortunately, faculty positions are available in academic librarianship, which is experiencing a decline in qualified applicants. A pioneering collaboration between a graduate student professional development program and an academic library has created a fellowship program that allows master's and doctoral students to consider careers in academic librarianship through mentored fellowships. Initial results show that participants intend to pursue librarianship as an academic career in which to use and expand their advanced subject and/or language expertise.

The Graduate Teacher Program of the University of Colorado–Boulder is working in collaboration with CU-Boulder Libraries on a sustainable mentorship program that promotes academic librarianship as an academic career goal for master's and doctoral students. To date, the Provost's Fellowship has paired nine exceptional graduate students in different academic disciplines with tenure-track librarians as their faculty mentors over the course of a semester. The mentorship introduces these students to an alternate faculty career that values teaching, research, and service. This chapter highlights the design, goals, and successes of the program with the aim of encouraging other institutions to provide their future faculty with mentorship experiences that draw attention to this academic career.

Literature Review

A confluence of information from many sources led to the development of the Provost's Fellowship. Each year, thousands of students in the United States begin their graduate education with the goal of obtaining a doctorate in a variety of academic disciplines. Golde and Dore's (2001) seminal research report, however, reveals a mismatch between graduate training and the actual careers available to them. Most (87.1%) survey respondents expressed interest in obtaining a faculty position despite the reality that the number of doctorates granted each year far exceeds the available tenure-track positions. In fact, no more than 50% of the doctoral students surveyed will find employment as full-time tenure-track faculty. This state of affairs forces many to seek employment in fields outside their area of expertise or accept lower paying nontenure-track positions as adjunct instructors.

The paucity of viable faculty positions may be a factor in current high levels of graduate attrition. Although there are no national estimates available, recent localized studies estimate graduate attrition in the sciences and humanities at 50%–65% in some programs, much higher than the 20%–40% reported in 1960 (National Research Council, 1996). Those who leave the academy with only a master's degree, a nonterminal degree in most fields, face even more limited employment options than those with a doctorate. While Golde and Dore (2001) state that the "obvious solution to this problem is both to reduce the number of doctoral recipients and to encourage them to consider careers outside of academia" (p. 11), they neglect to consider academic librarianship as a career option within academia for both master's and doctoral degree holders.

The participation of CU-Boulder's Graduate Teacher Program (GTP) in the Responsive PhD Initiative of the Woodrow Wilson National Fellowship Foundation to explore new paradigms, new practices, and new people further informed the creation of the mentorship by encouraging us to think creatively about building a new paradigm that links current graduate students with future job opportunities in academic libraries. It has also made us aware of the need to establish a pipeline for librarians that represents the current demographics in the United States. Most importantly, we have created a new partnership among the Graduate School, graduate departments, and the academic library. Lastly, the GTP's participation in the national Preparing Future

Faculty (PFF) project and the development of the Colorado Preparing Future Faculty Network Forum, together with experience in developing, monitoring, and evaluating PFF Fellow mentorships with faculty on other campuses (Gaff, Pruitt-Logan, Sims, & Denecke, 2003), helped us move quickly to define the parameters of the library mentorship, the communications and reports necessary for success, and the requirements for both fellows and mentors.

This chapter suggests that many graduate students' desire for faculty positions in higher education can be met through careers in academic librarianship. In the words of one graduate student in religion,

> During my graduate studies . . . I have come to realize that I do not want to pursue a teaching career, but still would like to remain within the academic world. A career in library studies would allow me to focus on research and deal with many different resources, all the while helping to make these accessible to others. I feel that this is what I should pursue, for it provides a synthesis of my subject area, as well as my love for books and other research materials.

Librarianship as Academic Career Goal

Academic librarianship is an attractive academic career option, yet it is often overlooked. The same interests that influence graduate students to pursue a faculty career are all present in academic librarianship: "love of teaching, enjoyment of research, and interest in doing service" (Golde & Dore, 2001, p. 9). Indeed, academic librarians often receive the same health and retirement benefits, faculty status, travel funds, and paid research leave as other faculty (Bradley, 2001). Academic libraries strongly value applicants with excellent research skills honed through advanced studies in a variety of academic disciplines. Nevertheless, recent articles (Hardesty, 2002; Hewitt, Moran, & Marsh, 2003) reveal that candidate pools regularly offer few qualified applicants at a time when demand for academic librarians is very high. Additionally, Kellsey (2003) writes that academic libraries continue to seek applicants who possess foreign language knowledge, whether in speaking or reading. Finally, nearly one-half of all recent job announcements for academic librarians are for entry-level positions (Stevens & Streatfield, 2003). The most advertised positions are in the areas of reference, cataloging, area studies, instruction, special collections, and electronic resources.

Profile of New Academic Librarians

The foundation of a successful academic librarian is a solid scholarly background and traits like a curious mind coupled with a desire to learn, adapt, and share knowledge (Tan, 2004). A survey of new librarians found that 70% of academic librarians who have been working less than five years are between 26 and 35 years old (Millet, 2005). The majority (42.9%) of new librarians work in a large research university that offers doctoral programs, 27.8% work in institutions that offer some graduate-level programs, 10.6% work in four-year colleges, and 8.5% work in community college libraries (Millet & Posas, 2005).

Unlike the profile of most academic departments, women dominate the profession of academic librarianship, even among its newest generation. Most librarians surveyed identified themselves as "technologically adept," "creative," and "intellectual" (Millet, 2005, p. 54). Additionally, most chose the profession due to their desire to research, interact with students, and work in an academic setting. Only 24.1% of new librarians possess a second master's degree in addition to a master's degree in library and information science, while only 1.9% of new librarians possess a doctorate (Millet & Posas, 2005). Despite exceptions, the possession of a master's degree in library and information science (MLIS) is a requirement to be considered for a position as an academic librarian. According to the Association of College and Research Libraries ([ACRL], 2001), a division of the American Library Association, a MLIS from an accredited program is the "appropriate terminal professional degree for academic librarians." A recent survey of Association of Research Libraries (ARL) member libraries revealed that two-thirds require a MLIS or equivalent library degree for all librarian positions (Blixrud, 2000). More than one-half of ARL member libraries grant faculty status to librarians (Blixrud, 2000). In fact, libraries that give faculty status to librarians overwhelmingly require them to possess a MLIS. ACRL (2002) and the American Association of University Professors (1990) agree that academic librarians should have faculty status. However, the definitions and realities of faculty status for librarians differ among institutions, and a small percentage of institutions that grant librarians faculty status do not offer tenure.

The Fellowship

In November 2002, CU-Boulder Libraries created a task force of academic librarians to assist in the national effort to recruit to the profession by promoting academic librarianship at the local level. Initial projects included an exhibit on academic librarianship, as well as hosting internships for current

MLIS students from other institutions. CU-Boulder does not offer a degree in library and information science. Ensuing communication between the GTP and task force members led to GTP seminars highlighting librarianship as an academic career, followed by the creation of the Provost's Fellowship.

The goal of the program is to encourage graduate students in master's or doctoral programs to explore the possibility of pursuing a career in academic librarianship by strengthening their understanding of the responsibilities of tenure-track library faculty and of faculty careers in academic libraries through a mentorship experience with an academic librarian.

Fellows are awarded "$2,500 to support their work with a faculty mentor in the libraries and to provide them with the opportunity to expand their understanding and appreciation of library faculty careers in postsecondary institutions" (GTP, 2005). The GTP provides funding for the fellowship through a special account provided by the provost. Funding is sufficient to allow graduate students to spend the time necessary to complete the fellowship, and the number of hours per dollar equates to the funding for a teaching or research assistantship, although no tuition remission was provided. In turn, fellows receive the designation "Provost's Fellow in the Libraries."

Mentor and Fellow Requirements

Expectations and requirements for the mentorship are shared with both the library faculty mentor and the fellow through the application process. Mentors are required to sign a form that states they are aware of and approve the applicant's participation. Above all, librarian mentors' primary purpose is to share their knowledge and enthusiasm for the profession. Mentors engage their fellows in librarianship by providing them with the necessary theoretical background and practical application so they may gain professional-level experience during their fellowship. Where possible, mentors integrate the fellows' subject knowledge and/or language expertise into the experience so that they develop an awareness of how their skills can be applied in academic librarianship.

For the fellows, the mentorship includes working with a librarian on assigned experiences and tasks, a library site visit, participation in Preparing Future Faculty activities through the GTP, attendance at library meetings and functions, and the preparation of a Socratic portfolio. A Socratic portfolio illustrates and explains the instructional, service, and research aspects of academic librarianship and is developed in collaboration with the faculty mentor. The faculty mentor agrees to work with the fellow to develop a mentorship plan and the Socratic portfolio and agrees to meet with the Provost's Fellow regularly throughout the mentorship. Librarians who mentor the fellows submit a written evaluation of the fellows' performance upon completion of the program.

Fellows also sign a form that clarifies expectations and participate in PFF activities including a CU-Boulder Libraries site visit, the annual Colorado PFF Forum, any mandatory meetings organized by the GTP or the libraries, and the completion of a 150-hour mentorship with an academic librarian. They provide the GTP's PFF coordinator with a current copy of their curriculum vita and transcript, which the coordinator shares with library faculty in order to set up a mentorship. Fellows must submit a plan to the PFF coordinator and set goals based on their initial meeting with their faculty mentor. At the end of the mentorship, fellows submit a detailed self-evaluative summary of their experience to the PFF coordinator and present on their library mentorship experience at the Colorado PFF Forum, a statewide conference on teaching during the spring semester. Finally, fellows submit their Socratic portfolio to the PFF coordinator, complete an online exit survey, and are asked to respond to future postgraduate assessments of the program as we attempt to track their career arcs.

Fellows are encouraged to complete the GTP's Professional Development Certificate for Preparing Future Faculty because the requirements parallel the requirements for the mentorship, except for an additional attendance requirement of 20 teaching and professional development workshops through the GTP and career services. Completion of the mentorship, the Socratic portfolio, and the faculty evaluation all count toward the Professional Development Certificate.

The Fellows

In the first two rounds of the fellowship, Provost's Fellows represented the following academic departments: art history, classics, comparative literature and humanities, English, Germanic and Slavic languages and literatures, history, and religion. Together, fellows have spoken and/or written language knowledge of French, German, Greek, Latin, Russian, Sanskrit, Spanish, and Swedish. Seventy-five percent of applicants were female, and 13% of all applicants were ethnic/racial minorities. Successful applicants were all master's students, 90% female, and did not represent an ethnic or racial minority.

During their tenure, the fellows become members of the faculty and attend faculty meetings, departmental meetings, and presentations. They also meet with the CU-Boulder Libraries' Tenure Committee in order to understand research requirements and expectations for librarians at the university. Individually, the fellows' experiences vary as widely as their academic interests and the professional activities of their mentor. To date, fellows have assisted patrons with general and discipline-specific reference questions, planned and taught library research seminars in a variety of fields, selected materials for the collection and for off-site storage, created collection development policies, used their language knowledge to catalog materials, used their subject/language expertise to create online subject guides and bibliographies to assist researchers, and evaluated materials for preservation, among many other projects.

Program Evaluations

Multiple measures effectively provide thorough evaluations of the Provost's Fellowships in the Libraries. Specifically, they reflect the standard annual evaluation mechanisms of faculty based on their performance in teaching/librarianship, research, and service. Both fellows and mentors write evaluative summaries expressing their perspectives on the experience. Fellows also detail their viewpoints on teaching/librarianship, research, and service and describe their future career goals in their Socratic portfolios. Finally, fellows respond to a program evaluation form that allows them to comment on details and generalities of their work with mentors and the program.

Fellows' Evaluative Summaries

While some applicants noted in their applications that they wanted to explore librarianship because they did not want to teach in their disciplines, they learned to appreciate a different kind of instruction from their experience. One fellow commented, "This and other micro-teaching experiences throughout my fellowship redefined my notion of pedagogical practices and helped me understand that teaching exists in many forms." Fellows reported working on teaching-as-instruction areas during their mentorship such as one-on-one instruction while working at the reference desk and participation in library instruction seminars tailored to specific academic courses. Another fellow realized that specialized instructional skills are necessary to librarians.

> Because a librarian's contact with students is mainly limited to library instruction classes and at the reference desk it is important that they work to evaluate the students' knowledge and information savvy by asking them questions and engaging them in a discussion.

Each fellow also expressed continued interest in research in their discipline despite some frustration with the way research was approached in their academic departments. They seemed to respond well to the individuality of research instruction available to them in the libraries. One noted, "showing interest in the student's work and talent is the first step in gaining their trust and a starting place for imparting research and information skills." They also gained a new understanding of how students and faculty in academic departments can benefit from research support in the libraries: "This project showed me how important it is for librarians to understand faculty and student needs and then use their own knowledge to make the information accessible." Another found the freedom to explore a personal interest that is often not supported by academic departments because of a lack of resources.

> Working as an academic librarian offers me the opportunity to help solve the research questions I have posed by increasing the amount of material on feminist art and art history that students can access and helping students to take advantage of the numerous resources available to them through individualized or classroom-based research instruction.

One fellow realized that the type of research she was most interested in was possible in the framework of the library.

> I knew from the beginning that I was not interested in teaching history and my search for other ways to channel my passion for the field led me to librarianship. I am excited about pursuing a degree in librarianship because it gives me the opportunity to work in an atmosphere of rules and constant demands for accuracy and perfection . . . while at the same time utilizing my skills as a researcher and historian.

Overwhelmingly, fellows reported that they were able to integrate their subject/language knowledge into their work in the libraries.

Academic service was not emphasized in most of the fellows' home departments, but this aspect of librarianship resonated with several of them. The service aspect of faculty work is often neglected in academic departments, yet "If graduate students actually integrate service into the articulation of their research and teaching interests, it can become a powerful vehicle for professional development" (Border, 2002, p. 741). One fellow's experience of the site visit to the library led her to note, "Many of the reasons [librarians] listed for loving their jobs are the criteria that I am looking for in my own career search as well." Others mentioned opportunities to work in a "service profession," where they can teach and interact with the public. According to one, "This combination of service and academics is exactly what I am looking for," while another reported, "Librarianship is more than supplying people with information, but a way of helping people discover the world within themselves and explore the vast world in which we live. It is an interesting, challenging, and extremely rewarding career."

Finally, one fellow articulated the summation of what a career in academic librarianship means to her.

> Academic librarianship offers the things I love most about the university environment; working closely with professors and peers, teaching and helping students, conducting research and constant exposure to new ideas, topics and information about the world. However, unlike faculty positions in many fields within the humanities, librarianship seems to offer a great deal of flexibility in terms of location and variety in duties [and] fields of study.

Mentors' Evaluative Summaries

As Golde and Dore (2001) found in their study, many graduate students lack effective mentoring. Additionally, graduate education continues to be an exploratory period during which students continue to define their specific career tracks: "it is important for graduate students to seek out multiple mentors as they begin to form their viewpoints on teaching and learning" (Border, 2005–06, p. 1). Multiple mentors were assured through the Provost's Fellowship in the Libraries. The application procedure required the applicant to meet with the director and the PFF coordinator to discuss the project, the requirements, and our goals for the mentorship experience. During the two required site visits at campuses in the Colorado PFF Forum, fellows met with librarians from the local college to talk about the expectations for teaching, research, and service on that particular campus. The next step in the mentoring of the fellows integrated a site visit in CU-Boulder Libraries in which potential faculty mentors met with and discussed their jobs with prospective fellows. Finally, an in-depth relationship with a faculty mentor was assured through one-on-one engagement throughout the semester. The fellows appreciated this mentoring experience. "Being purposely joined with a faculty mentor and working specifically towards a knowledge of librarians' full responsibilities established more open parameters than my schedule of graduate courses and focus on literary research alone."

As mentors reflected on the experience, they were self-aware of their lack of experience mentoring graduate students. "As [X's] fellowship began, [we] found that we were both feeling our way through uncertain territory, since she had obviously never been a fellow, and I had also never been a mentor." Despite these initial concerns, one effect of the mentorship experience for the librarians was a sense of accomplishment. "[Y] participated in virtually all aspects of art librarianship along side me. Of her many achievements I am most proud of the collection development policy that she created . . ." Mentors were able to comment specifically on what their fellows had accomplished, leading us to conclude that the relationships established between the faculty mentors and their fellows were strong and productive.

> Over the course of her fellowship, [Z] was able to attend various meetings of the faculty, subject librarians, and reference department to gain insights into how an organization like this functions. . . . She was also able to attend the public presentations of several library candidates, since we happened to be conducting interviews while she was here.

Upon evaluation of the first round of Provost's Fellows, library faculty mentors agreed that the experience left their fellows far better prepared than most new MLIS students and that they would make excellent academic librarians. In a profession that is widely misunderstood even within academia, one mentor proudly proclaimed that her fellow "understood what we do and why we do it." Another stated that her fellow was "a true asset to me and to the . . . collection." More importantly, all mentors believed that the mentorship deeply benefited the fellows and, according to one, the "professional level experience" received "will be critical to getting interviews and attaining positions" in academic librarianship.

Fellows' Socratic Portfolios

The Provost's Fellows create a Socratic portfolio, based on their discussions and collaborations with their library mentor, that describes their work, their aspirations for research, teaching, and service within the context of the library, and their assessment of their performance and their mentorship experience. The Socratic portfolio emphasizes the process, product, and preparation of graduate students for the next step in their academic careers and is more a reflective document than a collection of artifacts (Border, 2005–06). As beginning faculty either in their disciplines or in the library, having prepared the Socratic portfolio will help them become what Boice (2000) has described as "quick starters"— those incoming faculty who actually succeed and attain tenure. This experience is an essential step in graduate students' understanding of the evaluation procedures that faculty undergo each year on their campuses.

Fellows commented on the negative aspects of the fellowship experience and two responded negatively to the Socratic portfolio requirement itself. One expressed the opinion that "it was difficult to find relevance" in the portfolio and the other responded that fellows need more guidance in adapting the portfolio format "in light of our library fellowship experience." Even though the fellows were provided with an article detailing how and why to develop a Socratic portfolio, two understood neither its purpose nor its form and were unable to adapt the "teaching portfolio" aspect to the academic library experience. These comments point to a need for better clarification and explanation of the purpose of the requirement and better guidance from both the library mentors and the PFF mentors who assisted the fellows. It also indicates the need for specific guidance on how to prepare a portfolio for applications to library school or for job searches in librarianship. Interestingly, none of the fellows included their initial paperwork for the fellowship in their portfolios, indicating their misapprehension of what is important in assembling evidence and proof of their academic work.

Program Evaluation

Fellows evaluate the Provost's Fellowship initiative. The information gained from the program evaluation reinforces the positive information that can be gleaned from the fellows' Socratic portfolios, their reports, and the mentors' reports while pinpointing areas that need clarification and reconsideration in the program. All fellows from the first year evaluated the program. Only one was unable to attend the requisite site visits, but the others responded positively to the site visits on other campuses. They recognized that they gained a new perspective about different campus cultures and indicated that the site visits helped them to clarify the type of postsecondary institution they would choose to work in as librarians. All fellows rated their mentors very positively on helpfulness and knowledge gained. All reported high levels of satisfaction with their completed projects, and all presented their projects at the Colorado PFF Forum to an audience of faculty and graduate students from around the state.

In comparing their library experiences with their experiences in their home departments, the majority of the fellows responded that they gained new knowledge and skills but also realized they can use their disciplines in new ways. One commented, "my mentor was open and willing to discuss my development and personal interests. . . . Sadly, I never felt the same depth of commitment and support and honesty toward my professional growth from my department faculty." This comment echoes the findings of a recent study on faculty work that suggests that faculty need "orientation programs and information about college or university policies, services, and programs . . . regardless of appointment type" (Gappa, Austin, & Trice, 2005, p. 38). All reflected that their experience as a fellow in the libraries had an affirmative influence on their decisions to pursue careers as academic librarians.

Fellows' Career Plans

Of the nine fellows who participated in the first two rounds of the Provost's Fellowship in the Libraries, only two are not actively pursuing academic librarianship as a career at this time. Of those who are, one fellow is already enrolled in a MLIS program; three more have been accepted to a library program; and one has recently applied, while two more are planning on applying as they near completion of their current program. Of the two fellows who are not actively pursuing a career in academic librarianship, one is beginning a nonacademic career in which she is applying her advanced foreign language skills, and the other is working in a public library. Finally, all participants believe that the fellowship has increased their chance of success for acceptance into a MLIS program.

Conclusion

The success to date of the Provost's Fellowship in the Libraries has convinced both the GTP and CU-Boulder Libraries of the value of the program, its relevance to graduate students' careers, and its benefits to the library profession. Fellows directly benefit from their newfound perspective on their career interests and goals. They become more aware of how important it is to explore various academic career choices to find a track that best fits their needs. They realize that professional development of this nature is important to their careers and necessary to obtain job interviews and career positions. Most importantly, several of them have reconnected with the joy of learning that had brought them to the academy for graduate work in the first place.

> My personal interest in the field has grown, and I have spoken with a number of CU-Boulder Libraries faculty about their perspectives and experiences as librarians. All the librarians I have spoken with have been so overwhelmingly positive and delighted with their jobs that I feel very motivated to pursue librarianship as a career.

The experience pointed out to some what had been missing in their academic disciplines, notably a sense of community and a lack of mentoring. "Whereas I felt isolated as an academic in my department, there was a larger, more recognized sense of community and commitment to service locally and nationally in the library." The GTP and CU-Boulder Libraries intend to integrate a plan to encourage the matriculation of future librarians from diverse groups, clarify the importance of professional development through the Socratic portfolio process, and encourage all fellows to pursue the GTP's Professional Development Certificate to assure that they have a strong background in teaching as well as librarianship.

As a final point, it is our hope that the achievements of this fellowship program serve as inspiration for the development of similar programs at other institutions. The minimal elements of such a program include financial support for the graduate student participants and interested academic librarians to serve as mentors. Nevertheless, collaboration between an academic library and a graduate student teaching and professional development program sets this experience apart. Specifically, the expertise and experience of a graduate student teaching and professional development program provides a framework for graduate students' professional development and greatly enhances the mentorship experience. The ultimate outcome of such collaboration provides future colleagues in the academy who can work together for the betterment of both academic departments and academic libraries.

References

American Association of University Professors. (1990). *1940 statement of principles on academic freedom and tenure*. Retrieved June 24, 2006, from www.aaup.org/statements/Redbook/1940stat.htm

Association of College and Research Libraries. (2001). *Statement on the terminal professional degree for academic librarians*. Retrieved June 24, 2006, from www.ala.org/ala/acrl/acrlstandards/statementterminal.htm

Association of College and Research Libraries. (2002). *Guidelines for academic status for college and university librarians*. Retrieved June 24, 2006, from www.ala.org/ala/acrl/acrlstandards/guidelinesacademic.htm

Blixrud, J. C. (2000). *ARL SPEC KIT 257, the M.L.S. hiring requirement*. Washington, DC: Association of Research Libraries.

Boice, R. (2000). *Advice for new faculty members: Nihil nimus*. Needham Heights, MA: Allyn & Bacon.

Border, L. L. B. (2002). The Socratic portfolio: A guide for future faculty. *PS: Political Science & Politics, 35*(4), 739–743.

Border, L. L. B. (2005–06). Teaching portfolios for graduate students: Process, content, product, and benefits. *Essays on Teaching Excellence, 17*(4).

Bradley, G. (2001, April 20). *Careers in academic libraries.* Retrieved June 24, 2006, from http://chronicle.com/jobs/2001/04/2001042003c.htm

Gaff, J. G., Pruitt-Logan, A. S., Sims, L. B., & Denecke, D. D. (2003). *Preparing future faculty in the humanities and social sciences: A guide for change.* Washington, DC: Council of Graduate Schools and the Association of American Colleges and Universities.

Gappa, J. M., Austin, A. E., & Trice, A. G. (2005, November/December). Rethinking academic work and workplaces. *Change, 37*(6), 32–39.

Golde, C. M., & Dore, T. M. (2001). *At cross purposes: What the experiences of doctoral students reveal about doctoral education.* Philadelphia, PA: The Pew Charitable Trusts.

Graduate Teacher Program, University of Colorado–Boulder. (2005). *Provost's fellow in the libraries.* Retrieved June 24, 2006, from the University of Colorado–Boulder, Graduate Teacher Program web site: www.colorado.edu/gtp/professional/provost/library

Hardesty, L. L. (2002, January). Future of academic/research librarians: A period of transition—to what? *Portal: Libraries and the Academy, 2*(1), 79–97.

Hewitt, J. A., Moran, B. B., & Marsh, M. E. (2003, April). Finding our replacements: One institution's approach to recruiting academic librarians. *Portal: Libraries and the Academy, 3*(2), 179–189.

Kellsey, C. (2003, June). Crisis in foreign language expertise in research libraries: How do we fill this gap? *College & Research Libraries News, 64*(6), 391–392, 397.

Millet, M. S. (2005, March). Is this the ninth circle of hell? *Library Journal, 130*(5), 54.

Millet, M. S., & Posas, L. (2005). *Recruitment and retention of new academic librarians in their own words: Who they are and what they want.* Retrieved June 24, 2006, from the Trinity University web site: www.trinity.edu/mmillet/professional/NewLibProject.htm

National Research Council. (1996). *The path to the Ph.D.: Measuring graduate attrition in the sciences and humanities.* Washington, DC: National Academies Press.

Stevens, J., & Streatfeild, R. (2003). *SPEC kit 276, recruitment and retention.* Retrieved June 24, 2006, from www.arl.org/spec/SPEC276WebBook.pdf

Tan, W. (2004, June). Academic librarianship: Traveling across time lines. *Journal of Educational Media and Library Sciences, 41*(4), 431–436.

Bibliography

Abes, E. S., Jackson, G., & Jones, S. R. (2002, Fall). Factors that motivate and deter faculty use of service-learning. *Michigan Journal of Community Service Learning, 9*(1), 5–17.

Adams, M., Bell, L. A., & Griffin, P. (Eds.). (1997). *Teaching for diversity and social justice: A sourcebook.* New York, NY: Routledge.

Alstete, J. W. (2000). *Post-tenure faculty development: Building a system of faculty improvement and appreciation* (ASHE-ERIC Higher Education Report, 27[4]). San Francisco, CA: Jossey-Bass.

Altman, I. (1996, April). Higher education and psychology in the millennium. *American Psychologist, 51*(4), 371–378.

Ambady, N., & Rosenthal, R. (1993, March). Half a minute: Predicting teacher evaluations from thin slices of nonverbal behavior and physical attractiveness. *Journal of Personality and Social Psychology, 64*(3), 431–441.

American Association of University Professors. (1987). *Statement on professional ethics.* Retrieved June 17, 2006, from www.aaup.org/statements/Redbook/Rbethics.htm

American Association of University Professors. (1990). *1940 statement of principles on academic freedom and tenure.* Retrieved June 24, 2006, from www.aaup.org/statements/Redbook/1940stat.htm

American Psychiatric Association. (n.d.). *Disasters: Mental health recommendations for students and colleges.* Retrieved June 17, 2006, from http://healthyminds.org/katrinatipsforcollege.cfm

Anderson, L. W., & Krathwohl, D. R. (Eds.). (2001). *A taxonomy for learning, teaching, and assessing: A revision of Bloom's taxonomy of educational objectives.* New York, NY: Longman.

Armstrong, F., & Moore, M. (2004). Action research: Developing inclusive practice and transforming cultures. In F. Armstrong & M. Moore (Eds.), *Action research for inclusive education: Changing places, changing practices, changing minds* (pp. 1–16). London, England: RoutledgeFalmer.

Arnsten, A. F. T. (1998, June). The biology of being frazzled. *Science, 280*(5370), 1711–1712.

Arreola, R. A. (2000). *Developing a comprehensive faculty evaluation system: A handbook for college faculty and administrators on designing and operating a comprehensive faculty evaluation system* (2nd ed.). Bolton, MA: Anker.

Ash, S. L., Clayton, P. H., & Atkinson, M. P. (2005, Spring). Integrating reflection and assessment to capture and improve student learning. *Michigan Journal of Community Service Learning, 11*(2), 49–60.

Asmussen, K. J., & Creswell, J. W. (1995, September/October). Campus response to a student gunman. *Journal of Higher Education, 66*(5), 575–596.

Association of College and Research Libraries. (2001). *Statement on the terminal professional degree for academic librarians.* Retrieved June 24, 2006, from www.ala.org/ala/acrl/acrl standards/statementterminal.htm

Association of College and Research Libraries. (2002). *Guidelines for academic status for college and university librarians.* Retrieved June 24, 2006, from www.ala.org/ala/acrl/acrl standards/guidelinesacademic.htm

Astin, A. W., & Astin, H. S. (1993). *Undergraduate science education: The impact of different college environments on the educational pipeline in the sciences.* Los Angeles, CA: University of California–Los Angeles, Higher Education Research Institute.

Astin, A. W., & Sax, L. J. (1998, May/June). How undergraduates are affected by service participation. *Journal of College Student Development, 39*(3), 251–263.

Baldwin, J. (1963). *The fire next time.* New York, NY: Modern Library.

Baldwin, R. G. (1990, March/April). Faculty vitality beyond the research university: Extending a contextual concept. *Journal of Higher Education, 61*(2), 160–180.

Baldwin, R. G. (2002, Fall). Engaging mid-career faculty in a time of transition. *The Department Chair, 13*(2), 7–10.

Baldwin, R. G., & Chronister, J. L. (2001). *Teaching without tenure: Policies and practices for a new era.* Baltimore, MD: Johns Hopkins University Press.

Bamburg, J. D. (1994). *Raising expectations to improve student learning.* Naperville, IL: North Central Regional Educational Laboratory.

Banta, T. W., Lund, J. P., Black, K. E., & Oblander, F. W. (1996). *Assessment in practice: Putting principles to work on college campuses.* San Francisco, CA: Jossey-Bass.

Baptiste, I. (2000, May). Beyond reason and personal integrity: Toward a pedagogy of coercive restraint. *Canadian Journal for the Study of Adult Education, 14*(1), 27–50.

Barefoot, B. O. (Ed.). (1993). *Exploring the evidence: Reporting outcomes of freshman seminars* (Monograph No. 11). Columbia, SC: University of South Carolina, National Resource Center for the First-Year Experience and Students in Transition.

Barr, R. B., & Tagg, J. (1995, November/December). From teaching to learning—A new paradigm for undergraduate education. *Change, 27*(6), 12–25.

Barrington, J. (2002). *Writing the memoir: A practical guide to the craft, the personal challenges, and ethical dilemmas of writing your true stories* (2nd ed.). Portland, OR: Eighth Mountain Press.

Bartlett, T. (2002, May 10). Students become curricular guinea pigs. *The Chronicle of Higher Education,* p. A12.

Battistoni, R. (2002). *Civic engagement across the curriculum: A resource book for service-learning faculty in all disciplines.* Providence, RI: Campus Compact.

Bellows, L., & Weissinger, E. (2005). Assessing the academic and professional development needs of graduate students. In S. Chadwick-Blossey & D. R. Robertson (Eds.), *To improve the academy: Vol. 23. Resources for faculty, instructional, and organizational development* (pp. 267–283). Bolton, MA: Anker.

Bender, T. (1997). *Intellect and public life: Essays on the social history of academic intellectuals in the United States.* Baltimore, MD: Johns Hopkins University Press.

Benson, L., & Harkavy, I. (1996, June). Communal participatory action research as a strategy for improving universities and the social sciences: Penn's work with the West Philadelphia Improvement Corps as a case study. *Educational Policy, 10*(2), 202–222.

Bernstein, D., & Bass, R. (2005, July/August). The scholarship of teaching and learning. *Academe, 91*(4), 37–43.

Bishop, R. (1994). Initiating empowering research. *New Zealand Journal of Educational Studies, 29*(1), 175–188.

Black, B. (1998). Using the SGID method for a variety of purposes. In M. Kaplan & D. Lieberman (Eds.), *To improve the academy: Vol. 17. Resources for faculty, instructional, and organizational development* (pp. 245–262). Stillwater, OK: New Forums Press.

Blackburn, R. T. (1985). Faculty career development: Theory and practice. In S. M. Clark & D. R. Lewis (Eds.), *Faculty vitality and institutional productivity: Critical perspectives for higher education* (pp. 55–85). New York, NY: Teachers College Press.

Blaisdell, M. L., & Cox, M. D. (2004). Midcareer and senior faculty learning communities: Learning throughout faculty careers. In M. D. Cox & L. Richlin (Eds.), *New directions for teaching and learning: No. 97. Building faculty learning communities* (pp. 137–148). San Francisco, CA: Jossey-Bass.

Blake, W. (1963). *The marriage of heaven and hell.* Coral Gable, FL: University of Miami Press. (Original work published 1790)

Bland, C. J., & Bergquist, W. H. (1997). *The vitality of senior faculty members: Snow on the roof—fire in the furnace* (ASHE-ERIC Higher Education Report, 25[7]). Washington, DC: George Washington University, Graduate School of Education and Human Development.

Bland, C. J., & Schmitz, C. C. (1990). An overview of research on faculty and institutional vitality. In J. H. Schuster, D. W. Wheeler, & Associates, *Enhancing faculty careers: Strategies for development and renewal* (pp. 41–61). San Francisco, CA: Jossey-Bass.

Blixrud, J. C. (2000). *ARL SPEC KIT 257, the M.L.S. hiring requirement.* Washington, DC: Association of Research Libraries.

Bloom, B. S. (Ed.). (1956). *Taxonomy of educational objectives, handbook 1: Cognitive domain.* New York, NY: Longman.

Boice, R. (1990). Countering common misbeliefs about student evaluations of teaching. *Teaching Excellence, 2*(2).

Boice, R. (1991, January). New faculty as colleagues. *International Journal of Qualitative Studies in Education, 4*(1), 29–44.

Boice, R. (1992). *The new faculty member: Supporting and fostering professional development.* San Francisco, CA: Jossey-Bass.

Boice, R. (2000). *Advice for new faculty members: Nihil nimus.* Needham Heights, MA: Allyn & Bacon.

Bonwell, C. C., & Eison, J. A. (1991). *Active learning: Creating excitement in the classroom.* Washington, DC: George Washington University.

Border, L. L. B. (2002). The Socratic portfolio: A guide for future faculty. *PS: Political Science & Politics, 35*(4), 739–743.

Border, L. L. B. (2005–06). Teaching portfolios for graduate students: Process, content, product, and benefits. *Essays on Teaching Excellence, 17*(4).

Border, L. L. B., & Chism, N. V. N. (Eds.). (1992). *New directions for teaching and learning: No. 49. Teaching for diversity.* San Francisco, CA: Jossey-Bass.

Boyer Commission on Educating Undergraduates in the Research University. (1998). *Reinventing undergraduate education: A blueprint for America's research universities.* Retrieved June 24, 2006, from the Stony Brook University web site: http://naples.cc.sunysb.edu/Pres/boyer.nsf

Boyer, E. L. (1990). *Scholarship reconsidered: Priorities of the professoriate.* Princeton, NJ: Carnegie Foundation for the Advancement of Teaching.

Boyer, E. L. (1994, March 9). Creating the new American college. *The Chronicle of Higher Education,* p. A48.

Boyer, E. L. (1996, Spring). The scholarship of engagement. *Journal of Public Service and Outreach, 1*(1), 11–20.

Bradley, G. (2001, April 20). *Careers in academic libraries.* Retrieved June 24, 2006, from http://chronicle.com/jobs/2001/04/2001042003c.htm

Bransford, J. D., Brown, A. L., & Cocking, R. R. (Eds.). (2000). *How people learn: Brain, mind, experience, and school* (Expanded ed.). Washington, DC: National Academy Press.

Braxton, J. M., & Bayer, A. E. (1999). *Faculty misconduct in collegiate teaching.* Baltimore, MD: Johns Hopkins University Press.

Braxton, J. W., Luckey, W., & Helland, P. (2002). *Institutionalizing a broader view of scholarship through Boyer's four domains* (ASHE-ERIC Higher Education Report, 29[2]). San Francisco, CA: Jossey-Bass.

Bringle, R. G., Games, R., Foos, C. L., Osgood, R., & Osborne, R. (2000, February). Faculty Fellows Program: Enhancing integrated professional development through community service. *American Behavioral Scientist, 43*(5), 882–894.

Bringle, R. G., Games, R., & Malloy, E. A. (Eds.). (1999a). *Colleges and universities as citizens.* Needham Heights, MA: Allyn & Bacon.

Bringle, R. G., Games, R., & Malloy, E. A. (1999b). Colleges and universities as citizens: Reflections. In R. G. Bringle, R. Games, & E. A. Malloy (Eds.), *Colleges and universities as citizens* (pp. 193–204). Needham Heights, MA: Allyn & Bacon.

Bringle, R. G., & Hatcher, J. A. (1995, Fall). A service-learning curriculum for faculty. *Michigan Journal of Community Service Learning, 2*(1), 112–122.

Bringle, R. G., Hatcher, J. A., Jones, S., & Plater, W. M. (2006). Sustaining civic engagement: Faculty development, roles, and rewards. *Metropolitan Universities Journal, 17*(1), 62–74.

Brinko, K. T. (1997). The interactions of teaching improvement. In K. T. Brinko & R. J. Menges (Eds.), *Practically speaking: A sourcebook for instructional consultants in higher education* (pp. 3–8). Stillwater, OK: New Forums Press.

Britzman, D. P. (1991). *Practice makes practice: A critical study of learning to teach.* Albany, NY: State University of New York Press.

Brookfield, S. D. (1995). *Becoming a critically reflective teacher.* San Francisco, CA: Jossey-Bass.

Brookfield, S. D. (2005). *The power of critical theory: Liberating adult learning and teaching.* San Francisco, CA: Jossey-Bass.

Brookfield, S. D., & Preskill, S. (2005). *Discussion as a way of teaching: Tools and techniques for democratic classrooms* (2nd ed.). San Francisco, CA: Jossey-Bass.

Brown, J. S., Collins, A., & Duguid, P. (1989, January/February). Situated cognition and the culture of learning. *Educational Researcher, 18*(1), 32–42.

Brown, R. D., & Krager, L. (1985). Ethical issues in graduate education: Faculty and student responsibilities. *Journal of Higher Education, 56*(4), 403–418.

Brukardt, M. J., Holland, B., Percy, S. L., & Zimpher, N. (2004). *Calling the question: Is higher education ready to commit to community engagement? A Wingspread statement.* Milwaukee, WI: University of Wisconsin–Milwaukee, Milwaukee Idea Office.

Buckley, A. (2000, Spring). Tipi technology. *Teaching Tolerance, 17,* 14–17.

Callahan, D. (1982, May/June). Should there be an academic code of ethics? *Journal of Higher Education, 53*(3), 335–344.

Calleson, D. C., Jordan, C., & Seifer, S. D. (2005, April). Community-engaged scholarship: Is faculty work in communities a true academic enterprise? *Academic Medicine, 80*(4), 317–321.

Calleson, D. C., Kauper-Brown, J., & Seifer, S. D. (2005). *Community-engaged scholarship toolkit.* Seattle, WA: Community-Campus Partnerships for Health.

Campbell, P. B., Jolly, E., Hoey, L., & Perlman, L. K. (2002). *Upping the numbers: Using research-based decision making to increase diversity in the quantitative disciplines.* Newton, MA: Education Development Center, Inc.

Campus Compact. (2005). *Season of service.* Providence, RI: Campus Compact.

Carnegie Foundation for the Advancement of Teaching (Producer). (1999). *Fostering a scholarship of teaching* [Film]. Oregon: West Peak Media.

Carver, C. S., Scheier, M. F., & Weintraub, J. K. (1989). Assessing coping strategies: A theoretically based approach. *Journal of Personality and Social Psychology, 56*(2), 267–283.

Cashin, W. E. (1988). *Student ratings of teaching: A summary of the research* (Idea Paper No. 20). Manhattan, KS: Kansas State University, Center for Faculty Evaluation and Development.

Cashin, W. E., & McKnight, P. C. (1986). *Improving discussions* (Idea Paper No. 15). Manhattan, KS: Kansas State University, Center for Faculty Evaluation and Development.

Center for Public Service and Leadership, Indiana University. (1999). *Service @ Indiana University: Defining, documenting, and evaluating.* Indianapolis, IN: Author.

Center for Research on Learning and Teaching, University of Michigan. (2004). *Publications and links.* Retrieved June 17, 2006, from the University of Michigan, Center for Research on Learning and Teaching web site: www.crlt.umich.edu/publinks/publinks.html

Centra, J. A. (1976). *Faculty development practices in U.S. colleges and universities.* Princeton, NJ: Educational Testing Service.

Checkoway, B. (2001, March). Renewing the civic mission of the American research university. *Journal of Higher Education, 72*(2), 125–147.

Cherwitz, R. A. (2005, November/December). A new social compact demands real change: Connecting the university to the community. *Change, 37*(6), 48–49.

Chesler, M. A. (1990). Action research in the voluntary sector: A case study of scholar-activist roles in health care settings. In S. A. Wheelan, E. A. Pepitone, & V. Abt (Eds.), *Advances in field theory* (pp. 265–280). Newbury Park, CA: Sage.

Chickering, A. W., & Gamson, Z. F. (1987, June). Seven principles for good practice in undergraduate education. *AAHE Bulletin, 39*(7), 3–7.

Chism, N. V. N., & Szabo, B. (1996). Who uses faculty development services? In L. Richlin & D. DeZure (Eds.), *To improve the academy: Vol. 15. Resources for faculty, instructional, and organizational development* (pp. 115–128). Stillwater, OK: New Forums Press.

Chittister, J. D. (2002). *Seeing with our souls: Monastic wisdom for every day.* New York, NY: Sheed and Ward.

Chomsky, N. (2002). *Understanding power: The indispensable Chomsky* (P. R. Mitchell & J. Schoeffel, Eds.). New York, NY: The New Press.

Christian, B. (1990). The race for theory: Science, technology and socialist feminism in the 1990s. In K. V. Hansen & I. J. Philipson (Eds.), *Women, class, and the feminist imagination: A socialist-feminist reader* (pp. 568–579). Philadelphia, PA: Temple University Press.

Clark, B. R. (1987). *The academic life: Small worlds, different worlds.* Princeton, NJ: Carnegie Foundation for the Advancement of Teaching.

Clark, C. M., & Peterson, P. L. (1986). Teachers' thought processes. In M. C. Wittrock (Ed.), *Handbook of research on teaching* (3rd ed., pp. 255–296.). New York, NY: Macmillan.

Clark, D. J., & Redmond, M. (1982). *Small group instructional diagnosis: Final report.* Seattle, WA: University of Washington, Department of Biology Education. (ERIC Document Reproduction Service No. ED217954)

Clark, S. M., & Corcoran, M. (1985). Individual and organizational contributions to faculty vitality: An institutional case study. In S. M. Clark & D. R. Lewis (Eds.), *Faculty vitality and institutional productivity: Critical perspectives for higher education* (pp. 112–138). New York, NY: Teachers College Press.

Clark, S. M., Corcoran, M., & Lewis, D. R. (1986, March/April). The case for an institutional perspective on faculty development. *Journal of Higher Education, 57*(2), 176–195.

Clark, S. M., & Lewis, D. R. (1985). Implications for institutional response. In S. M. Clark & D. R. Lewis (Eds.), *Faculty vitality and institutional productivity: Critical perspectives for higher education* (pp. 247–256). New York, NY: Teachers College Press.

Clayton, P. H., & Ash, S. L. (2004, Fall). Shifts in perspective: Capitalizing on the counter-normative nature of service-learning. *Michigan Journal of Community Service Learning, 11*(1), 59–70.

Clayton, P. H., & Ash, S. L. (2005, September). Reflection as a key component in faculty development. *On the Horizon, 13*(3), 161–169.

Colby, A., Ehrlich, T., Beaumont, E., & Stephens, J. (2003). *Educating citizens: Preparing America's undergraduates for lives of moral and civic responsibility.* San Francisco, CA: Jossey-Bass.

Coles, R. (1989). *The call of stories: Teaching and the moral imagination.* Boston, MA: Houghton Mifflin.

Collins, A., Brown, J. S., & Newman, S. E. (1989). Cognitive apprenticeship: Teaching and crafts of reading, writing, and mathematics. In L. B. Resnick (Ed.), *Knowing, learning, and instruction: Essays in honor of Robert Glaser* (pp. 453–494). Hillsdale, NJ: Lawrence Erlbaum.

Committee on Institutional Cooperation. (2005). *Resource guide and recommendations for defining and benchmarking engagement.* Champaign, IL: Author.

Cook, C., Gerson, J., Godfrey, J., Kerner, N., Larsen-Freeman, D., Mullane, E., et al. (2002). *Report of the Task Force on Testing and Training Prospective GSIs.* Ann Arbor, MI: University of Michigan.

Costa, A. L., & O'Leary, P. W. (1992). Co-cognition: The cooperative development of the intellect. In J. Davidson & T. Worsham (Eds.), *Enhancing thinking through cooperative learning* (pp. 41–65). New York, NY: Teachers College Press.

Cothran, D. J., Kulinna, P. H., Banville, D., Choi, E., Amade-Escot, C., MacPhail, A., et al. (2005, June). A cross-cultural investigation of the use of teaching styles. *Research Quarterly for Exercise and Sport, 76*(2), 193–201.

Cox, M. D. (2001). Faculty learning communities: Change agents for transforming institutions into learning organizations. In D. Lieberman & C. Wehlburg (Eds.), *To improve the academy: Vol. 19. Resources for faculty, instructional, and organizational development* (pp. 69–93). Bolton, MA: Anker.

Cox, M. D. (2003). Proven faculty development tools that foster the scholarship of teaching in faculty learning communities. In C. M. Wehlburg & S. Chadwick-Blossey (Eds.), *To improve the academy: Vol. 21. Resources for faculty, instructional, and organizational development* (pp. 109–142). Bolton, MA: Anker.

Crawley, A. L. (1995, Winter). Senior faculty renewal at research universities: Implications for academic policy development. *Innovative Higher Education, 20*(2), 71–94.

Creamer, E. G., & Lattuca, L. R. (Eds.). (2005). *New directions for teaching and learning: No. 102. Advancing faculty learning through interdisciplinary collaboration.* San Francisco, CA: Jossey-Bass.

Creswell, J. W. (1998). *Qualitative inquiry and research design: Choosing among five traditions.* Thousand Oaks, CA: Sage.

Cross, K. P., & Steadman, M. H. (1996). *Classroom research: Implementing the scholarship of teaching.* San Francisco, CA: Jossey-Bass.

Crotty, M. (1998). *The foundations of social research: Meaning and perspective in the research process.* Thousand Oaks, CA: Sage.

Cutright, M. (Ed.). (2001). *Chaos theory and higher education: Leadership, planning, and policy.* New York, NY: Peter Lang.

Cutright, M. (2006). A different way to approach the future: Using chaos theory to improve planning. In S. Chadwick-Blossey & D. R. Robertson (Eds.), *To improve the academy: Vol. 24. Resources for faculty, instructional, and organizational development* (pp. 44–61). Bolton, MA: Anker.

Cytrynbaum, S., Lee, S., & Wadner, D. (1982). Faculty development through the life course: Application of recent adult development theory and research. *Journal of Instructional Development, 5*(3), 11–22.

Damasio, A. R. (1994). *Descartes' error: Emotion, reason, and the human brain.* New York, NY: G. P. Putnam.

Davis, A. Y. (1974). *Angela Davis: An autobiography.* New York, NY: International Publishers.

Davis, A.Y. (1983). *Women, race, and class.* New York, NY: Vintage Books.

Davis, B. G. (1993). *Tools for teaching.* San Francisco, CA: Jossey-Bass.

Davis, J. R. (1993). *Better teaching, more learning: Strategies for success in postsecondary settings.* Phoenix, AZ: American Council on Education/Oryx Press.

Delpit, L. D. (1996). *Other people's children: Cultural conflict in the classroom.* New York, NY: New Press.

De Russy, C. (2003, September 19). Professional ethics begin on the college campus. *The Chronicle of Higher Education,* p. B20.

Desrochers, C. (1999, December). Multi-purpose lecture breaks. *The Teaching Professor, 13*(10), 1–2.

Dews, P. (Ed.). (1992). *Autonomy and solidarity: Interviews with Jurgen Habermas* (Rev. ed.). New York, NY: Routledge.

DeZure, D. (1999). *Interdisciplinary teaching and learning.* Retrieved June 19, 2006, from the College of Charleston, Center for Effective Teaching and Learning web site: www.cofc.edu/~cetl/Essays/InterdisciplinaryTeaching&Learning.htm

Diamond, M. R. (2002). Preparing TAs to respond to ethical dilemmas. In W. Davis, J. Smith, & R. Smith (Eds.), *Ready to teach: Graduate teaching assistants prepare for today and for tomorrow* (pp. 47–50). Stillwater, OK: New Forums Press.

Diamond, M. R. (2003). How would you handle this situation? Teaching assistant responses to an ethics workshop. *Journal of Graduate Teaching Assistant Development, 9*(2), 89–96.

Diamond, N. A. (2002). Small group instructional diagnosis: Tapping student perceptions of teaching. In K. H. Gillespie, L. R. Hilsen, & E. C. Wadsworth (Eds.), *A guide to faculty development: Practical advice, examples, and resources* (pp. 82–91). Bolton, MA: Anker.

Diamond, R. M., & Adams, B. (Eds.). (1993). *New directions for higher education: No. 81. Recognizing faculty work: Reward systems for the year 2000.* San Francisco, CA: Jossey-Bass.

DiPietro, M. (2003). The day after: Faculty behavior in post-September 11, 2001, classes. In C. M. Wehlburg & S. Chadwick-Blossey (Eds.), *To improve the academy: Vol. 21. Resources for faculty, instructional, and organizational development* (pp. 21–39). Bolton, MA: Anker.

Driscoll, A., & Lynton, E. A. (1999). *Making outreach visible: A guide to documenting professional service and outreach.* Washington, DC: American Association for Higher Education.

Duffy, D. K., & Jones, J. W. (1995). *Teaching within the rhythms of the semester.* San Francisco, CA: Jossey-Bass.

Eble, K. E., & McKeachie, W. J. (1985). *Improving undergraduate education through faculty development: An analysis of effective programs and practices.* San Francisco, CA: Jossey-Bass.

Eby, K. K. (2001, Summer/Fall). Teaching and learning from an interdisciplinary perspective. *Peer Review, 3–4*(4–1), 28–31.

Edgerton, R. (1994). The engaged campus: Organizing to serve society's needs. *AAHE Bulletin, 47*(1), 2–4.

Elbow, P. (1997). High stakes and low stakes in assigning and responding to writing. In M. D. Sorcinelli & P. Elbow (Eds.), *New directions for teaching and learning: No. 69. Writing to learn: Strategies for assigning and responding to writing across the disciplines* (pp. 5–13). San Francisco, CA: Jossey-Bass.

Elden, M. (1981). Sharing the research work: Participative research and its role demands. In P. Reason & J. Rowan (Eds.), *Human inquiry: A sourcebook of new paradigm research* (pp. 261–266). Chichester, England: John Wiley & Sons.

Ellsworth, E. (1989, August). Why doesn't this feel empowering? Working through the repressive myths of critical pedagogy. *Harvard Educational Review, 59*(3), 297–324.

Epperson, D. L. (2000). *Report on one-year and two-year university retention rates associated with first-year participation in a learning community at Iowa State University.* Ames, IA: Iowa State University, Learning Communities.

Erickson, G. (1986). A survey of faculty development practices. In M. Svinicki, J. Kurfiss, & J. Stone (Eds.), *To improve the academy: Vol. 5. Resources for faculty, instructional, and organizational development* (pp. 182–196). Stillwater, OK: New Forums Press.

Eyler, J., & Giles, D. E., Jr. (1999). *Where's the learning in service-learning?* San Francisco, CA: Jossey-Bass.

Eyler, J., Giles, D. E., Jr., & Schmiede, A. (1996). *A practitioner's guide to reflection in service-learning: Student voices and reflections.* Nashville, TN: Vanderbilt University.

Eyler, J., Giles, D. E., Jr., Stenson, C. M., & Gray, C. J. (2001). *At a glance: What we know about the effects of service-learning on college students, faculty, institutions, and communities, 1993–2000* (3rd ed.). Nashville, TN: Vanderbilt University.

Faculty Center for Excellence in Teaching, Western Kentucky University. (2000). *Teaching and learning in a time of crisis.* Retrieved June 17, 2006, from the Western Kentucky University, Faculty Center for Excellence in Teaching web site: www.wku.edu/teaching/booklets/crisis.html

Fantuzzo, J. W., Dimeff, L. A., & Fox, S. L. (1989). Reciprocal peer tutoring: A multimodal assessment of effectiveness with college students. *Teaching of Psychology, 16*(3), 133–135.

Fantuzzo, J. W., Riggio, R. E., Connelly, S., & Dimeff, L. A. (1989). Effects of reciprocal peer tutoring on academic achievement and psychological adjustment: A component analysis. *Journal of Educational Psychology, 81*(2), 173–177.

Farrell, E. F. (2001, December 21). Hedging against disaster. *The Chronicle of Higher Education*, p. A40.

Fayne, H., & Ortquist-Ahrens, L. (2006). Learning communities for first-year faculty: Transition, acculturation, and transformation. In S. Chadwick-Blossey & D. R. Robertson (Eds.), *To improve the academy: Vol. 24. Resources for faculty, instructional, and organizational development* (pp. 277–290). Bolton, MA: Anker.

Feder, J. (1988). *Fractals.* New York, NY: Plenum Press.

Feichtner, S. B., & Davis, E. A. (1984–85). Why some groups fail: A survey of students' experiences with learning groups. *Organizational Behavior Teaching Review, 9*(4), 58–71.

Felder, R. M., & Brent, R. (1994). *Cooperative learning in technical courses: Procedures, pitfalls, and payoffs.* Retrieved June 16, 2006, from the North Carolina State University web site: www.ncsu.edu/felder-public/Papers/Coopreport.html#IssuesAndAnswers

Felder, R. M., Sheppard, S. D., & Smith, K. A. (2005, January). Guest editor's foreword: A new journal for a field in transition. *Journal of Engineering Education, 94*(1), 7–10.

Feldman, K. A. (1986). The perceived instructional effectiveness of college teachers as related to their personality and attitudinal characteristics: A review and synthesis. *Research in Higher Education, 24*(2), 139–213.

Fink, L. D. (2003). *Creating significant learning experiences: An integrated approach to designing college courses.* San Francisco, CA: Jossey-Bass.

Finkel, D. L. (2000). *Teaching with your mouth shut.* Portsmouth, NH: Boynton/Cook.

Finkelstein, M. J. (1993). The senior faculty: A portrait and literature review. In M. J. Finkelstein & M. W. LaCelle-Peterson (Eds.), *New directions for teaching and learning: No. 55. Developing senior faculty as teachers* (pp. 7–19). San Francisco, CA: Jossey-Bass.

Finkelstein, M. J., & Jemmott, N. D. (1993). The senior faculty: Higher education's plentiful yet largely untapped resource. In M. J. Finkelstein & M. W. LaCelle-Peterson (Eds.), *New directions for teaching and learning: No. 55. Developing senior faculty as teachers* (pp. 95–99). San Francisco, CA: Jossey-Bass.

Finkelstein, M. J., & LaCelle-Peterson, M. W. (Eds.). (1993). *New directions for teaching and learning: No. 55. Developing senior faculty as teachers.* San Francisco, CA: Jossey-Bass.

Fisch, L. (1996). *New directions for teaching and learning: No. 66. Ethical dimensions of college and university teaching: Understanding and honoring the special relationship between teachers and students.* San Francisco, CA: Jossey-Bass.

Fish, S. (2005, February 4). Who's in charge here? Retrieved May 30, 2006, from *The Chronicle of Higher Education* web site: http://chronicle.com/jobs/2005/02/2005020401c.htm

Florida, R. (2002). *The rise of the creative class: . . . And how it's transforming work, leisure, community, and everyday life.* New York, NY: Basic Books.

Florida, R. (2005). *The flight of the creative class: The new global competition for talent.* New York, NY: HarperCollins.

Forsman, A. (Director). (1984). *Amadeus* [Motion picture]. United States: Warner Brothers.

Frederick, P. (1981, Summer). The dreaded discussion: Ten ways to start. *Improving College and University Teaching, 29*(3), 109–114.

Frederick, P. (1995, Summer). Walking on eggs: Mastering the dreaded diversity discussion. *College Teaching, 43*(3), 83–92.

Frederick, P. J. (1991). The medicine wheel: Emotions and connections in the classroom. In K. J. Zahorski (Ed.), *To improve the academy: Vol. 10. Resources for student, faculty, and institutional development* (pp. 197–214). Stillwater, OK: New Forums Press.

Fromm, E. (1955). *The sane society.* New York, NY: Holt, Rinehart, & Winston.

Fromm, E. (1961). *Marx's concept of man.* New York, NY: Frederick Ungar.

Frost, P. J., & Taylor, M. S. (Eds.). (1996). *Rhythms of academic life: Personal accounts of careers in academia.* Thousand Oaks, CA: Sage.

Frost, R. (1949). *Complete poems of Robert Frost.* New York, NY: Henry Holt & Company.

Furco, A. (1996). Service-learning: A balanced approach to experiential education. In B. Taylor (Ed.), *Expanding boundaries: Serving and learning* (pp. 2–6). Washington, DC: Corporation for National Service.

Gabelnick, F., MacGregor, J., Matthews, R. S., & Smith, B. L. (1990). *New directions for teaching and learning: No. 41. Learning communities: Creating connections among students, faculty, and disciplines.* San Francisco, CA: Jossey-Bass.

Gabriele, G. A. (2005, July). Guest editorial: Advancing engineering education in a flattened world. *Journal of Engineering Education, 94*(3), 285–286.

Gaff, J. G., Pruitt-Logan, A. S., Sims, L. B., & Denecke, D. D. (2003). *Preparing future faculty in the humanities and social sciences: A guide for change.* Washington, DC: Council of Graduate Schools and the Association of American Colleges and Universities.

Gappa, J. M., Austin, A. E., & Trice, A. G. (2005, November/December). Rethinking academic work and workplaces. *Change, 37*(6), 32–39.

Gelmon, S. G., & Agre-Kippenhaan, S. (2002, January). Promotion, tenure, and the engaged scholar: Keeping the scholarship of engagement in the review process. *AAHE Bulletin, 54*(5), 7–11.

Geltner, B. B. (1993, October). *Collaborative action research: A critical component in the preparation of effective leaders and learners.* Paper presented at the annual meeting of the University Council for Educational Administration, Houston, TX.

Gess-Newsome, J., Southerland, S. A., Johnston, A., & Woodbury, S. (2003, Fall). Educational reform, personal practical theories, and dissatisfaction: The anatomy of change in college science teaching. *American Educational Research Journal, 40*(3), 731–767.

Gibson, G. W. (1992). *Good start: A guidebook for new faculty in liberal arts colleges.* Bolton, MA: Anker.

Gillespie, K. (2001, October). *Marketplace reality and our dreams of the profession.* Paper presented at the 26th annual conference of the Professional and Organizational Development Network in Higher Education, St. Louis, MO.

Gilligan, C. (1982). *In a different voice: Psychological theory and women's development.* Cambridge, MA: Harvard University Press.

Glassick, C. E. (1999). Ernest L. Boyer: Colleges and universities as citizens. In R. G. Bringle, R. Games, & E. A. Malloy (Eds.), *Universities and colleges as citizens* (pp. 17–30). Needham Heights, MA: Allyn & Bacon.

Glassick, C. E., Huber, M. T., & Maeroff, G. I. (1997). *Scholarship assessed: Evaluation of the professoriate.* San Francisco, CA: Jossey-Bass.

Gleick, J. (1987). *Chaos: Making a new science.* New York, NY: Penguin Books.

Goldberg, B., & Finkelstein, M. (2002, Summer). Effects of a first-semester learning community on nontraditional technical students. *Innovative Higher Education, 26*(4), 235–249.

Golde, C. M., & Dore, T. M. (2001). *At cross purposes: What the experiences of doctoral students reveal about doctoral education.* Philadelphia, PA: The Pew Charitable Trusts.

Golde, C. M., & Pribbenow, D. A. (2000, January/February). Understanding faculty involvement in residential learning communities. *Journal of College Student Development, 41*(1), 27–40.

Goodman, M. J. (1994, Fall). The review of tenured faculty at a research university: Outcomes and appraisals. *Review of Higher Education, 18*(1), 83–94.

Goodsell Love, A. (1999). What are learning communities? In J. H. Levine (Ed.), *Learning communities: New structures, new partnerships for learning* (pp. 1–8). Columbia, SC: University of South Carolina, National Resource Center for the First-Year Experience and Students in Transition.

Gooler, D. D. (1991). *Professorial vitality: A critical issue in higher education.* DeKalb, IL: LEPS Press.

Gouldner, A. W. (1957, December). Cosmopolitans and locals: Toward an analysis of latent social roles. *Administrative Science Quarterly, 2*(3), 281–306.

Graduate Teacher Program, University of Colorado–Boulder. (2005). *Provost's fellow in the libraries.* Retrieved June 24, 2006, from the University of Colorado–Boulder, Graduate Teacher Program web site: www.colorado.edu/gtp/professional/provost/library

Grant, G., & Riesman, D. (1978). *The perpetual dream: Reform and experiment in the American college.* Chicago, IL: University of Chicago Press.

Grasha, A. F. (1996). *Teaching with style: A practical guide to enhancing learning by understanding teaching and learning styles.* Pittsburgh, PA: Alliance.

Greenwood, D. J., & Levin, M. (1998). *Introduction to action research: Social research for social change.* Thousand Oaks, CA: Sage.

Group for Human Development in Higher Education. (1974). *Faculty development in a time of retrenchment.* New York, NY: Change Magazine Press.

Guskey, T. R. (2002, August). Professional development and teacher change. *Teachers and Teaching: Theory and Practice, 8*(3), 381–391.

Guterman, L. (2001, February 16). Student murdered in dormitory at Gallaudet University. *The Chronicle of Higher Education,* p. A49.

Haag, M., Christopher, K., Cummings, J., Dickey, J., & Gilder, B. (1999). *Effective methods of training biology laboratory teaching assistants.* Retrieved June 17, 2006, from the University of Toronto, Department of Zoology web site: www.zoo.utoronto.ca/able/volumes/vol-21/22-haag.pdf

Habermas, J. (1990). *Moral consciousness and communicative action* (C. Lenhardt & S. W. Nicholsen, Trans.). Cambridge, MA: MIT Press.

Haghighi, K. (2005, October). Guest editorial: Quiet no longer: Birth of a new discipline. *Journal of Engineering Education, 94*(4), 351–353.

Hall, D. E. (2002). *The academic self: An owner's manual.* Columbus, OH: The Ohio State University Press.

Halstead, D. K. (1974). *Statewide planning in higher education.* Washington, DC: U.S. Government Printing Office.

Hamermesh, D. S., & Parker, A. M. (2005, August). Beauty in the classroom: Instructors' pulchritude and putative pedagogical productivity. *Economics of Education Review, 24*(4), 369–376.

Hampl, P. (1999). *I could tell you stories: Sojourns in the land of memory.* New York, NY: W.W. Norton.

Hardesty, L. L. (2002, January). Future of academic/research librarians: A period of transition—to what? *Portal: Libraries and the Academy, 2*(1), 79–97.

Harkavy, I., & Puckett, J. L. (1994, September). Lessons from Hull House for the contemporary urban university. *Social Science Review, 68*(3), 299–321.

Harrington, K. (2002). The view from the elephant's tail: Creation and implementation of post-tenure review at the University of Massachusetts. In C. M. Licata & J. C. Morreale (Eds.), *Post-tenure faculty review and renewal: Experienced voices* (pp. 66–79). Washington, DC: American Association for Higher Education.

Harris, C., & Harvey, A. N. C. (2000). Team teaching in adult higher education classrooms: Toward collaborative knowledge construction. In M-J. Eisen & E. J. Tisdell (Eds.), *New directions for adult and continuing education: No. 87. Team teaching and learning in adult education* (pp. 25–32). San Francisco, CA: Jossey-Bass.

Hatcher, J. A. (1997, June). *Classroom assessment techniques: Ways to improve teaching and learning in a service learning class.* Paper presented at the American Association for Higher Education Assessment Forum, Miami, FL.

Hatcher, J. A., & Bringle, R. G. (1997, Fall). Reflections: Bridging the gap between service and learning. *Journal of College Teaching, 45*(4), 153–158.

Hatcher, J. A., Bringle, R. G., & Muthiah, R. (2004, Fall). Designing effective reflection: What matters to service learning? *Michigan Journal of Community Service Learning, 11*(1), 38–46.

Hellyer, S., & Boschmann, E. (1993). Faculty development programs: A perspective. In D. L. Wright & J. P. Lunde (Eds.), *To improve the academy: Vol. 12. Resources for faculty, instructional, and organizational development* (pp. 217–224). Stillwater, OK: New Forums Press.

Heritage University. (2004). *Heritage University catalog, 2004–2006.* (2004). Toppenish, WA: Author.

Hewitt, J. A., Moran, B. B., & Marsh, M. E. (2003, April). Finding our replacements: One institution's approach to recruiting academic librarians. *Portal: Libraries and the Academy, 3*(2), 179–189.

Hollander, J. A. (2002, July). Learning to discuss: Strategies for improving the quality of class discussion. *Teaching Sociology, 30*(3), 317–327.

Holmgren, R., Mooney, K., & Reder, M. (2005, January). *Transforming teaching cultures: The need for teaching and learning programs at liberal arts colleges.* Paper presented at the annual meeting of the Association of American Colleges and Universities, San Francisco, CA.

Holstrom, E. I., Gaddy, C. D., Van Horne, V. V., & Zimmerman, C. M. (1997). *Best and brightest: Education and career paths of top science and engineering students.* Washington, DC: Commission on Professionals in Science and Technology.

Honos-Webb, L., Sunwolf, Hart, S., & Scalise, J. T. (2006). How to help after national catastrophes: Findings following 9/11. *The Humanistic Psychologist, 34*(1), 75–97.

hooks, b. (1989). *Talking back: Thinking feminist, thinking black.* Boston, MA: South End Press.

hooks, b. (1994). *Teaching to transgress: Education as the practice of freedom.* New York, NY: Routledge.

hooks, b. (2000). *Where we stand: Class matters.* New York, NY: Routledge.

hooks, b. (2003). *Teaching community: A pedagogy of hope.* New York, NY: Routledge.

hooks, b., & West, C. (1991). *Breaking bread: Insurgent black intellectual life.* Boston, MA: South End Press.

Horkheimer, M. (1972). *Critical theory: Selected essays.* New York, NY: Herder and Herder.

Horton, M. (1990). *The long haul: An autobiography.* New York, NY: Doubleday.

Huba, M. E., Ellertson, S., Cook, M. D., & Epperson, D. (2003). Assessment's role in transforming a grass-roots initiative into an institutionalized program: Evaluating and shaping learning communities at Iowa State University. In J. MacGregor (Ed.), *Doing learning community assessment: Five campus stories* (pp. 21–47). Olympia, WA: The Evergreen State College, Washington Center for Improving the Quality of Undergraduate Education.

Huber, M. T. (2004). *Balancing acts: The scholarship of teaching and learning in academic careers.* Sterling, VA: Stylus.

Huber, M. T., & Hutchings, P. (2005). *The advancement of learning: Building the teaching commons.* San Francisco, CA: Jossey-Bass.

Huber, M. T., & Morreale, S. P. (Eds.). (2002). *Disciplinary styles in the scholarship of teaching and learning: Exploring common ground.* Washington, DC: American Association for Higher Education.

Hurst, J. C. (1999, July/August). The Matthew Shepard tragedy: Management of a crisis. *About Campus, 4*(3), 5–11.

Hutchings, P. (2000). Introduction: Approaching the scholarship of teaching and learning. In P. Hutchings (Ed.), *Opening lines: Approaches to the scholarship of teaching and learning* (pp. 1–10). Menlo Park, CA: Carnegie Foundation for the Advancement of Teaching.

Hutchings, P. (Ed.). (2002). *Ethics of inquiry: Issues in the scholarship of teaching and learning.* Menlo Park, CA: Carnegie Foundation for the Advancement of Teaching.

Hutchings, P., & Shulman, L. S. (1999, September/October). The scholarship of teaching: New elaborations, new developments. *Change, 31*(5), 10–15.

Hutchings, P., & Shulman, L. S. (2004). The scholarship of teaching: New elaborations, new developments. In L. S. Shulman, *Teaching as community property: Essays on higher education* (pp. 145–154). San Francisco, CA: Jossey-Bass. (Original work published 1999)

Iannaccone, P. M., & Khokha, M. (Eds.). (1996). *Fractal geometry in biological systems: An analytical approach.* Boca Raton, FL: CRC Press.

Inch, S., & McVarish, J. (2003, February). Across the divide: Reflecting on university collaboration. *Reflective Practice, 4*(1), 3–10.

Israel, B. A., Schurman, S. J., & Hugentobler, M. K. (1992, March). Conducting action research: Relationships between organization members and researchers. *Journal of Applied Behavioral Science, 28*(1), 74–101.

Jackson, W. K., & Simpson, R. D. (1993). Refining the role of senior faculty at a research university. In M. J. Finkelstein & M. W. LaCelle-Peterson (Eds.), *New directions for teaching and learning: No. 55. Developing senior faculty as teachers* (pp. 69–80). San Francisco, CA: Jossey-Bass.

Jacobs, L. C., & Chase, C. I. (1992). *Developing and using tests effectively: A guide for faculty.* San Francisco, CA: Jossey-Bass.

Jencks, C., & Riesman, D. (1968). *The academic revolution.* New York, NY: Doubleday.

Johnson, D. W., Johnson, R. T., & Smith, K. A. (1991). *Cooperative learning: Increasing college faculty instructional productivity.* San Francisco, CA: Jossey-Bass.

Johnston, K. (2004). *MSU thoughts on teaching #10: What undergraduates say are the most irritating faculty behaviors.* Retrieved June 26, 2006, from the Michigan State University, Teaching Assistant Program web site: http://tap.msu.edu/PDF/thoughts/tt10.pdf

Kagan, S. (1992). *Cooperative learning.* San Juan Capistrano, CA: Kagan Cooperative Learning.

Kalivoda, P., Sorrell, G. R., & Simpson, R. D. (1994, Summer). Nurturing faculty vitality by matching institutional interventions with career-stage needs. *Innovative Higher Education, 18*(4), 255–272.

Karpiak, I. E. (1997). University professors at mid-life: Being a part of . . . but feeling apart. In D. DeZure & M. Kaplan (Eds.), *To improve the academy: Vol. 16. Resources for faculty, instructional, and organizational development* (pp. 21–40). Stillwater, OK: New Forums Press.

Karpiak, I. E. (2000, July). The "second call": Faculty renewal and recommitment at midlife. *Quality in Higher Education, 6*(2), 125–134.

Karpiak, I. E. (2000, Spring). Writing our life: Adult learning and teaching through autobiography. *Canadian Journal of University Continuing Education, 26*(1), 31–50.

Kellogg Commission on the Future of State and Land-Grant Universities. (1999). *Returning to our roots: The engaged institution.* Washington, DC: National Association of State Universities and Land-Grant Colleges.

Kellsey, C. (2003, June). Crisis in foreign language expertise in research libraries: How do we fill this gap? *College & Research Libraries News, 64*(6), 391–392, 397.

King, A. (1989, October). Effects of self-questioning training on college students' comprehension of lectures. *Contemporary Educational Psychology, 14*(4), 366–381.

King, A. (1990, Winter). Enhancing peer interaction and learning in the classroom through reciprocal questioning. *American Educational Research Journal, 27*(4), 664–687.

King, A. (1992). Promoting active learning and collaborative learning in business administration classes. In T. J. Frecka (Ed.), *Critical thinking, interactive learning, and technology: Reaching for excellence in business education* (pp. 158–173). Chicago, IL: Arthur Andersen Foundation.

King, A. (1994). Autonomy and question asking: The role of personal control in guided student-generated questioning. *Learning and Individual Differences*, 6(2), 162–185.

King, A. (1995, Winter). Guided peer questioning: A cooperative learning approach to critical thinking. *Cooperative learning and college teaching, 5*(2), 15–19.

Klein, J. (2006). A collegiate dilemma: The lack of formal training in ethics for professors. *Journal of College and Character,* 2. Retrieved June 17, 2006, from www.collegevalues.org/articles.cfm?a=1&id=1416

Knapper, C., Wilcox, S., & Weisberg, M. (1996). *Teaching students more: Discussion with more students.* Ontario, Canada: Queen's University, Instructional Development Centre.

Kohl, H. (2000). *The discipline of hope: Learning from a lifetime of teaching.* New York, NY: New Press.

Kolb, D. A. (1984). *Experiential learning: Experience as the source of learning and development.* Upper Saddle River, NJ: Prentice-Hall.

Krogh, L. (2001, March). *Action research as action learning as action research as action learning . . . at multiple levels in adult education.* Paper presented at the 4th annual conference of the Australian Vocational Education and Training Research Association, Adelaide, Australia.

Kuhn, T. S. (1970). *The structure of scientific revolutions* (2nd ed.). Chicago, IL: University of Chicago Press.

Kuther, T. L. (2003). A profile of the ethical professor: Student views. *College Teaching, 51*(4), 153–160.

Lamber, J., Ardizzone, T., Dworkin, T., Guskin, S. L., Olsen, D., Parnell, P., et al. (1993). A "community of scholars": Conversations among mid-career faculty at a public research university. In D. L. Wright & J. P. Lunde (Eds.), *To improve the academy: Vol. 12. Resources for faculty, instructional, and organizational development* (pp. 13–26). Stillwater, OK: New Forums Press.

Lang, J. M. (2005). *Life on the tenure track: Lessons from the first year.* Baltimore, MD: Johns Hopkins University Press.

Langseth, M., & Plater, W. M. (Eds.). (2004). *Public work and the academy: An academic administrator's guide to civic engagement and service-learning.* Bolton, MA: Anker.

Larson, W. A. (Ed.). (1994). *When crisis strikes on campus.* Washington, DC: Council for Advancement and Support of Education.

Lazarus, R. S., & Lazarus, B. N. (1994). *Passion and reason: Making sense of our emotions.* New York, NY: Oxford University Press.

Leamnson, R. (1999). *Thinking about teaching and learning: Developing habits of learning with first year college and university students.* Sterling, VA: Stylus.

LeCompte, M. D., & Preissle, J. (1993). *Ethnography and qualitative design in educational research* (2nd ed.). San Diego, CA: Academic Press.

LeDoux, J. (1996). *The emotional brain: The mysterious underpinnings of emotional life.* New York, NY: Touchstone.

Levine, A., & Cureton J. S. (1998). *When hope and fear collide: A portrait of today's college student.* San Francisco, CA: Jossey-Bass.

Levinson, D. J., with Darrow, C. N., Klein, E. B., Levinson, M. H., & McKee, B. (1978). *The seasons of a man's life.* New York, NY: Ballantine Books.

Lewin, K. (1997). *Resolving social conflicts.* Washington, DC: American Psychological Association. (Original work published 1948)

Licata, C. M., & Morreale, J. C. (1997). *Post-tenure review: Policies, practices, precautions* (New Pathways Working Paper Series No. 12). Washington, DC: American Association for Higher Education.

Licata, C. M., & Morreale, J. C. (1999, Fall). Post-tenure review: National trends, questions and concerns. *Innovative Higher Education, 24*(1), 5–15.

Licata, C. M., & Morreale, J. C. (2002). *Post-tenure faculty review and renewal: Experienced voices.* Washington, DC: American Association for Higher Education.

Liebovitch, L. S. (1998). *Fractals and chaos simplified for the life sciences.* New York, NY: Oxford University Press.

Lincoln, Y. S., & Guba, E. G. (1985). *Naturalistic inquiry.* Newbury Park, CA: Sage.

Liverant, G. I., Hofmann, S. G., & Litz, B. T. (2004, June). Coping and anxiety in college students after the September 11th terrorist attacks. *Anxiety, Stress, & Coping, 17*(2), 127–139.

Loacker, G. (Ed.). (2000). *Self assessment at Alverno College.* Milwaukee, WI: Alverno College.

Lowman, J. (1996). Assignments that promote and integrate learning. In R. J. Menges, M. Weimer, & Associates, *Teaching on solid ground: Using scholarship to improve practice* (pp. 203–232). San Francisco, CA: Jossey-Bass.

Lyman, F. (1981). The responsive classroom discussion: The inclusion of all students. In A. S. Anderson (Ed.), *Mainstreaming digest* (pp. 109–113). College Park, MD: College of Education, University of Maryland.

Lynton, E. A. (1995). *Making the case for professional service.* Washington, DC: American Association for Higher Education.

MacGregor, J., & Smith, B. L. (2005, May/June). Where are learning communities now? National leaders take stock. *About Campus, 10*(2), 2–8.

Maki, P. L. (2004). *Assessing for learning: Building a sustainable commitment across the institution.* Sterling, VA: Stylus.

Mandelbrot, B. B. (1982). *The fractal geometry of nature.* New York, NY: W. H. Freeman.

Mangan, K. S. (2005, November 25). "Katrina" students are in every state. *The Chronicle of Higher Education,* p. A45.

Manouchehri, A. (1996, October). *Theory and practice: Implications for mathematics teacher education programs.* Paper presented at the annual forum of the Association of Independent Liberal Arts Colleges for Teacher Education, Atlanta, GA.

Marchese, T. J. (1997). The new conversations about learning: Insights from neuroscience and anthropology, cognitive studies, and work-place studies. In *Assessing impact: Evidence and action* (pp. 79–95). Washington, DC: American Association for Higher Education.

Marcuse, H. (1964). *One-dimensional man: Studies in the ideology of advanced industrial society.* Boston, MA: Beacon Press.

Marcuse, H. (1972). *Counterrevolution and revolt.* Boston, MA: Beacon Press.

Matthews, R. S., Smith, B. L., MacGregor, J., & Gabelnick, F. (1997). Creating learning communities. In J. G. Gaff, J. L. Ratcliff, & Associates, *Handbook of the undergraduate curriculum: A comprehensive guide to purposes, structures, practices, and change* (pp. 457–475). San Francisco, CA: Jossey-Bass.

McKeachie, W. J. (1994). *McKeachie's teaching tips: Strategies, research, and theory for college and university teachers* (9th ed.). Lexington, MA: D.C. Heath.

McKeachie, W. J., & Svinicki, M. (2006). *McKeachie's teaching tips: Strategies, research, and theory for college and university teachers* (12th ed.). Boston, MA: Houghton Mifflin.

McKinney, K. (2004). The scholarship of teaching and learning: Past lessons, current challenges, and future visions. In C. M. Wehlburg & S. Chadwick-Blossey (Eds.), *To improve the academy: Vol. 22. Resources for faculty, instructional, and organizational development* (pp. 3–19). Bolton, MA: Anker.

McLaren, P. (1998). *Life in schools: An introduction to critical pedagogy in the foundations of education* (3rd ed.). New York, NY: Longman.

Menges, R. J. (1996). Experiences of newly hired faculty. In L. Richlin & D. DeZure (Eds.), *To improve the academy: Vol. 15. Resources for faculty, instructional, and organizational development* (pp. 169–182). Stillwater, OK: New Forums Press.

Menges, R. J., & Associates. (1999). *Faculty in new jobs: A guide to settling in, becoming established, and building institutional support.* San Francisco, CA: Jossey-Bass.

Michaelsen, L. K., Knight, A. B. & Fink, L. D. (Eds.). (2004). *Team-based learning: A transformative use of small groups in college teaching.* Sterling, VA: Stylus.

Michigan State University. (1996). *Points of distinction: A guidebook for planning and evaluating quality outreach* (Rev. ed.). East Lansing, MI: Michigan State University.

Michigan State University Libraries. (2005). *Hurricane Katrina: Research and resources.* Retrieved June 17, 2006, from the Michigan State University Libraries web site: www.lib.msu.edu/libinstr/katrina.htm

Millem, J. F., Chang, M. J., & Antonio, A. L. (2005). *Making diversity work on campus: A research-based perspective.* Washington, DC: Association of American Colleges and Universities.

Miller, J. A. (1991, May). Experiencing management: A comprehensive, "hands-on" model for the introductory undergraduate management course. *Journal of Management Education, 15*(2), 151–169.

Millet, M. S. (2005, March). Is this the ninth circle of hell? *Library Journal, 130*(5), 54.

Millet, M. S., & Posas, L. (2005). *Recruitment and retention of new academic librarians in their own words: Who they are and what they want.* Retrieved June 24, 2006, from the Trinity University web site: www.trinity.edu/mmillet/professional/NewLibProject.htm

Millis, B. J. (1994). Conducting cooperative cases. In E. C. Wadsworth (Ed.), *To improve the academy: Vol. 13. Resources for faculty, instructional, and organizational development* (pp. 309–328). Stillwater, OK: New Forums Press.

Millis, B. J. (2002). *Enhancing learning—and more!—through cooperative learning* (IDEA Paper No. 38). Retrieved June 16, 2006, from the Kansas State University, IDEA Center web site: www.idea.ksu.edu/papers/Idea_Paper_38.pdf

Millis, B. J. (2004). A versatile interactive focus group protocol for qualitative assessments. In C. M. Wehlburg & S. Chadwick-Blossey (Eds.), *To improve the academy: Vol. 22. Resources for faculty, instructional, and organizational development* (pp. 125–141). Bolton, MA: Anker.

Millis, B. J., & Cottell, P. G., Jr. (1998). *Cooperative learning for higher education faculty.* Phoenix, AZ: American Council on Education/Oryx Press.

Mills, C. W. (1959). *The sociological imagination.* New York, NY: Oxford University Press.

Montgomery, S. M., & Groat, L. N. (1998). *Student learning styles and their implications for teaching* (CRLT Occasional Paper No. 10). Ann Arbor, MI: Center for Research on Learning and Teaching, University of Michigan.

National Research Council. (1996). *The path to the Ph.D.: Measuring graduate attrition in the sciences and humanities.* Washington, DC: National Academies Press.

National Science Board. (2004). *Science and engineering indicators, 2004* (NSB 04–01). Arlington, VA: National Science Foundation, Division of Science Resource Statistics.

National Science Foundation, Division of Science Resources Statistics. (2003). *Women, minorities, and persons with disabilities in science and engineering: 2002* (NSF 03–312). Arlington, VA: Author.

National Survey of Student Engagement. (2004). *Student engagement: Pathways to collegiate success.* Bloomington, IN: Center for Postsecondary Research, Indiana University Bloomington.

Newcomer, J. W., Selke, G., Melson, A. K., Hershey, T., Craft, S., Richards, K., et al. (1999, June). Decreased memory performance in healthy humans induced by stress-level cortisol treatment. *Archives of General Psychiatry, 56*(6), 527–533.

Nuhfer, E. B. (2003a). Content coverage, courses, and controversy part 1: Developing in fractal patterns V. *National Teaching and Learning Forum, 13*(1), 8–10.

Nuhfer, E. B. (2003b). Developing in fractal patterns I: Moving beyond diagnoses, evaluations, and fixes. *National Teaching and Learning Forum, 12*(2), 7–9.

Nuhfer, E. B. (2003c). Developing in fractal patterns II: A tour of the generator. *National Teaching and Learning Forum, 12*(4), 9–11.

Nuhfer, E. B. (2004a). Fractal thoughts on the forbidden affective in teaching evaluation and high level thinking: Educating in fractal patterns X. *National Teaching and Learning Forum, 14*(1), 9–11.

Nuhfer, E. B. (2004b). Why rubrics? Educating in fractal patterns IX. *National Teaching and Learning Forum, 13*(6), 9–11.

Nuhfer, E. B. (2005a). DeBono's red hat on Krathwohl's head: Irrational means to rational ends—more fractal thoughts on the forbidden affective: Educating in fractal patterns XIII. *National Teaching and Learning Forum, 14*(5), 7–11.

Nuhfer, E. B. (2005b). *A fractal thinker looks at student evaluations.* Retrieved May 30, 2006, from the Idaho State University, Center for Teaching and Learning web site: www.isu.edu/ctl/facultydev/extras/MeaningEvalsfract_files/MeaningEvalsfract.htm

Nuhfer, E. B. (2005c). Fractal views on good testing practices: Educating in fractal patterns XII. *National Teaching and Learning Forum, 14*(4), 9–11.

Nuhfer, E. B. (2005d). Perceiving education's temporal temperaments (part A–patterns): Educating in fractal patterns XIV. *National Teaching and Learning Forum, 14*(6), 7–10.

Nuhfer, E. B. (2005e). Perceiving education's temporal temperaments (part B–age, order, duration, frequency, rate, and magnitude): Educating in fractal patterns XIV. *National Teaching and Learning Forum, 15*(1), 8–11.

Nuhfer, E. B. (2005f). Tests as anchors that wobble: Understanding imperfect correlations in educational measurements: Educating in fractal patterns XI. *National Teaching and Learning Forum, 14*(2), 8–11.

Nuhfer, E. B., & Adkison, S. (2003). Unit level development: Teaching philosophies at the unit level: Educating in fractal patterns IV. *National Teaching and Learning Forum, 12*(6), 4–7.

Nuhfer, E. B., Chambers, F., & Heckler. (2002, June). *Teaching in fractal patterns: Recursive connections of assessment, individual faculty development, and unit level development.* Paper presented at the Pacific Planning, Assessment, and Institutional Research Conference, Honolulu, HI.

Nuhfer, E. B., & Knipp, D. (2003). The knowledge survey: a tool for all reasons. In C. M. Wehlburg & S. Chadwick-Blossey (Eds.), *To improve the academy: Vol. 21. Resources for faculty, instructional, and organizational development* (pp. 59–78). Bolton, MA: Anker. Addenda available electronically. Retrieved May 30, 2006, from the Idaho State University, Center for Teaching and Learning web site: www.isu.edu/ctl/facultydev/ADDENDUM.htm

Nuhfer, E. B., Krest, M., & Handelsman, M. (2003). A guide for composing teaching philosophies: Developing in fractal patterns III. *National Teaching and Learning Forum, 12*(5), 10–11.

Nuhfer, E. B., Leonard, L., & Akersten, S. (2004). Content coverage, courses, and controversy part 2: Developing in fractal patterns VI. *National Teaching and Learning Forum, 13*(2), 8–11.

Nuhfer, E. B., & Pavelich, M. (2001). Levels of thinking and educational outcomes. *National Teaching and Learning Forum, 11*(1), 5–8.

Nuhfer, E. B., & Pavelich, M. (2002). Using what we know to promote high level thinking outcomes. *National Teaching and Learning Forum, 11*(3), 6–8.

Nuhfer, E. B., & Pletsch, C. (2002, June). *Educating in fractal patterns: Linking development, instruction, and assessment from the individual to unit levels.* Pre-conference workshop presented at the American Association for Higher Education assessment conference, Boston, MA.

Nuhfer, E. B., & Pletsch, C. (2003, June). *Harnessing the power of fractal thinking in education, assessment, and faculty development.* Pre-conference workshop presented at the American Association for Higher Education assessment conference, Seattle, WA.

Nyquist, J. D., & Wulff, D. H. (1988). Consultation using a research perspective. In E. C. Wadsworth, L. Hilsen, & M. A. Shea (Eds.), *A handbook for new practitioners* (pp. 81–88). Stillwater, OK: New Forums Press.

O'Meara, K. (2003, Fall). Believing is seeing: The influence of beliefs and expectations on post-tenure review in one state system. *Review of Higher Education, 27*(1), 17–43.

O'Meara, K. (2004, March/April). Beliefs about post-tenure review: The influence of autonomy, collegiality, career stage, and institutional context. *Journal of Higher Education, 75*(2), 178–202.

O'Meara, K. (2005). Effects of encouraging multiple forms of scholarship nationwide and across institutional types. In K. O'Meara & R. E. Rice, *Faculty priorities reconsidered: Rewarding multiple forms of scholarship* (pp. 255–289). San Francisco, CA: Jossey-Bass.

O'Meara, K., & Rice, R. E. (2005). *Faculty priorities reconsidered: Rewarding multiple forms of scholarship.* San Francisco, CA: Jossey-Bass.

O'Reilley, M. R. (1998). *Radical presence: Teaching as contemplative practice.* Portsmouth, NH: Boynton/Cook.

Otto, M. L. (1994). Mentoring: An adult developmental perspective. In M. A. Wunsch (Ed.), *New directions for teaching and learning: Vol. 57. Mentoring revisited: Making an impact on individuals and institutions* (pp. 15–24). San Francisco, CA: Jossey-Bass.

Ouellett, M. L. (Ed.). (2005). *Teaching inclusively: Resources for course, department, and institutional change in higher education.* Stillwater, OK: New Forums Press.

Pace, D., & Middendorf, J. (Eds.). (2004). *New directions for teaching and learning: No. 98. Decoding the disciplines: Helping students learn disciplinary ways of thinking.* San Francisco, CA: Jossey-Bass.

Paine, C., & Sprague, J. (2000). Crisis prevention and response: Is your school prepared? *Oregon School Study Council Bulletin, 43*(2), 1.

Palmer, P. J. (1998). *The courage to teach: Exploring the inner landscape of a teacher's life.* San Francisco, CA: Jossey-Bass.

Palmer, P. J. (2000). *Let your life speak: Listening for the voice of vocation.* San Francisco, CA: Jossey-Bass.

Palmer, P. J. (2004). *A hidden wholeness: The journey toward an undivided life.* San Francisco, CA: Jossey-Bass.

Pappas, C. C., Kiefer, B. Z., & Levstik, L. S. (1990). *An integrated language perspective in the elementary school: Theory into action.* New York, NY: Longman.

Parini, J. (2005, April 8). The considerable satisfaction of 2 pages a day. *The Chronicle of Higher Education,* p. B5.

Park, P. (1999, June). People, knowledge, and change in participatory research. *Management Learning, 30*(2), 141–157.

Parker, W. C. (2001, March). Classroom discussion: Models for leading seminars and deliberations. *Social Education, 65*(2), 111–115.

Pascarella, E. T., & Terenzini, P. T. (1991). *How college affects students: Findings and insights from twenty years of research.* San Francisco, CA: Jossey-Bass.

Patrick, S. K., & Fletcher, J. J. (1998). Faculty developers as change agents: Transforming colleges and universities into learning organizations. In M. Kaplan & D. Lieberman (Eds.), *To improve the academy: Vol. 17. Resources for faculty, instructional, and organizational development* (pp. 155–170). Stillwater, OK: New Forums Press.

Paulsen, M. P. (2001). The relationship between research and the scholarship of teaching. In C. Kreber (Ed.), *New directions for teaching and learning: No. 86. Scholarship revisited: Perspectives on the scholarship of teaching* (pp. 19–29). San Francisco, CA: Jossey-Bass.

Pike, G. R. (1999, May/June). The effects of residential learning communities and traditional residential living arrangements on educational gains during the first year of college. *Journal of College Student Development, 40*(3), 269–284.

Pike, G. R., Schroeder, C. C., & Berry, T. R. (1997, November/December). Enhancing the educational impact of residence halls: The relationship between residential learning communities and first-year college experiences and persistence. *Journal of College Student Development, 38*(6), 609–621.

Plater, W. M. (2004, June). *What recognitions and rewards should a campus create to promote civic engagement of students?* Paper presented at the Wingspread Conference, Racine, WI.

Plater, W. M., Chism, N. V. N., & Bringle, R. G. (2005, February). *Revising promotion and tenure guidelines.* Panel presented at the meeting of the American Association of State Colleges and Universities, San Diego, CA.

Polanyi, M., & Cockburn, L. (2003, Summer). Opportunities and pitfalls of community-based research: A case study. *Michigan Journal of Community Service Learning, 9*(3), 16–25.

Professional and Organizational Development Network in Higher Education. (2002). *Ethical guidelines for educational developers.* Retrieved June 2, 2006, from http://podnetwork.org/development/ethicalguidelines.htm

Professional and Organizational Development Network in Higher Education. (2005). *The POD Network strategic plan 2005.* Retrieved June 2, 2006, from www.podnetwork.org/pdf/PODplan.pdf

Rasmussen, R. V. (1984). Practical discussion techniques for instructors. *AACE Journal, 12*(2), 38–47.

Ray, T. T. (1996). Differentiating the related concepts of ethics, morality, law, and justice. In L. Fisch (Ed.), *New directions for teaching and learning: No. 66. Ethical dimensions of college and university teaching: Understanding and honoring the special relationship between teachers and students* (pp. 47–54). San Francisco, CA: Jossey-Bass.

Reason, P. (1999, June). Integrating action and reflection through co-operative inquiry. *Management Learning, 30*(2), 207–226.

Reynolds, G., with Stevenson, K. (2003). *Leading discussions: What every student (and lecturer) needs to know!* Retrieved June 18, 2006, from the Staffordshire University, Department of Sociology and Crime, Deviance, and Society web site: www.staffs.ac.uk/schools/humanities_and_soc_sciences/sociology/leaddiss.htm

Rice, D., & Stacey, K. (1997). Small group dynamics as a catalyst for change: A faculty development model for academic service-learning. *Michigan Journal of Community Service Learning, 4*, 64–71.

Rice, R. E. (1986, January). The academic profession in transition: Toward a new social fiction. *Teaching Sociology, 14*(1), 12–23.

Rice, R. E. (1996). *Making a place for the new American scholar* (New Pathways Working Paper Series No. 1). Washington, DC: American Association for Higher Education.

Rice, R. E. (2005). "Scholarship Reconsidered": History and context. In K. O'Meara & R. E. Rice, *Faculty priorities reconsidered: Rewarding multiple forms of scholarship* (pp. 17–31). San Francisco, CA: Jossey-Bass.

Rice, R. E., & Finkelstein M. J. (1993). The senior faculty: A portrait and literature review. In M. J. Finkelstein & M. W. LaCelle-Peterson (Eds.), *New directions for teaching and learning: No. 55. Developing senior faculty as teachers* (pp. 7–19). San Francisco, CA: Jossey-Bass.

Rice, R. E., Sorcinelli, M. D., & Austin, A. E. (2000). *Heeding new voices: Academic careers for a new generation.* Washington, DC: American Association for Higher Education.

Richlin, L. (Ed.). (1993). *New directions for teaching and learning: No. 54. Preparing faculty for the new conceptions of scholarship.* San Francisco, CA: Jossey-Bass.

Robinson, B., & Schaible, R. M. (1995, Spring). Collaborative teaching: Reaping the benefits. *College Teaching, 43*(2), 57–60.

Rodgers, M. L., & Starrett, D. A. (2005, October). Is it time to get in the game? *National Teaching & Learning Forum, 14*(6), 10–11.

Romano, J. L., Hoesing, R., O'Donovan, K., & Weinsheimer, J. (2004, April). Faculty at midcareer: A program to enhance teaching and learning. *Innovative Higher Education,* 29(1), 21–48.

Rooney, M. (2002, November 8). Student kills three University of Arizona professors. *The Chronicle of Higher Education,* p. A12.

Rose, M. (1999). *Possible lives: The promise of public education in America.* New York, NY: Penguin.

Rovinescu, O. (2005). *Critical reading guide.* Quebec, Canada: Concordia University, Centre for Teaching and Learning Services.

Sanders, D. P., & McCutcheon, G. (1986, Fall). The development of practical theories of teaching. *Journal of Curriculum and Supervision, 2*(1), 40–67.

Sandmann, L. R., Foster-Fishman, P. G., Lloyd, J., Rauhe, W., & Rosaen, C. (2000, January/February). Managing critical tensions: How to strengthen the scholarship component of outreach. *Change, 32*(1), 44–52.

Savin-Baden, M., & Major, C. H. (2004). *Foundations of problem-based learning.* London, England: Open University Press.

Sax, L. J., & Astin, A. W. (1997, Summer/Fall). The benefits of service: Evidence from undergraduates. *Educational Record, 78*(3–4), 25–32.

Schank, R. C. (1990). *Tell me a story: Narrative and intelligence.* Evanston, IL: Northwestern University Press.

Schön, D. A. (1983). *The reflective practitioner: How professionals think in action.* New York, NY: Basic Books.

Schön, D. A. (1987). *Educating the reflective practitioner.* San Francisco, CA: Jossey-Bass.

Schroeder, C. M. (2005). Evidence of the transformational dimensions of the scholarship of teaching and learning: Faculty development through the eyes of SoTL scholars. In S. Chadwick-Blossey & D. R. Robertson (Eds.), *To improve the academy: Vol. 23. Resources for faculty, instructional, and organizational development* (pp. 47–71). Bolton, MA: Anker.

Schroeder, C. M. (2005, October). *Going "meta" with SoTL: Research-based frameworks as the missing link.* Paper presented at the 30th annual conference of the Professional and Organizational Development Network in Higher Education, Milwaukee, WI.

Schwandt, T. A. (1998). Constructivist, interpretivist approaches to human inquiry. In N. K. Denzin & Y. S. Lincoln (Eds.), *The landscape of qualitative research: Theories and issues* (pp. 221–259). Thousand Oaks, CA: Sage.

Seldin, P. (1997). Using student feedback to improve teaching. In D. DeZure & M. Kaplan (Eds.), *To improve the academy: Vol. 16. Resources for faculty, instructional, and organizational development* (pp. 335–345). Stillwater, OK: New Forums Press.

Seldin, P. (2006). Tailoring faculty development programs to faculty career stages. In S. Chadwick-Blossey & D. R. Robertson (Eds.), *To improve the academy: Vol. 24. Resources for faculty, instructional, and organizational development* (pp. 137–146). Bolton, MA: Anker.

Selingo, J. (2005, October 14). *U.S. spends billions to encourage math and science students, but it's unclear if programs work, report says.* Retrieved June 16, 2006, from http://chronicle.com/daily/2005/10/2005101402n.htm

Seymour, E. (2001). Tracking the processes of change in US undergraduate education in science, mathematics, engineering and technology. *Science Education, 86*, 79–105.

Seymour, E., & Hewitt, N. M. (1997). *Talking about leaving: Why undergraduates leave the sciences*. Boulder, CO: Westview Press.

Seymour, E., with Melton, G., Wiese, D. J., & Pedersen-Gallegos, L. (2005). *Partners in innovation: Teaching assistants in college science courses*. Lanham, MD: Rowman & Littlefield.

Sheehy, G. (1976). *Passages: Predictable crises of adult life*. New York, NY: Bantam Books.

Shapiro, N. S., & Levine, J. H. (1999). Creating learning communities: A practical guide to winning support, organizing for change, and implementing programs. San Francisco, CA: Jossey-Bass.

Shih, M-Y., & Sorcinelli, M. D. (2000). TEACHnology: Linking teaching and technology in faculty development. In M. Kaplan & D. Lieberman (Eds.), *To improve the academy: Vol. 18. Resources for faculty, instructional, and organizational development* (pp. 151–163). Bolton, MA: Anker.

Shor, I. (1996). *When students have power: Negotiating authority in a critical pedagogy*. Chicago, IL: University of Chicago Press.

Shulman, L. S. (1987, Spring). Knowledge and teaching: Foundations of new reform. *Harvard Educational Review, 57*(1), 1–21.

Shulman, L. S. (1999, July/August). Taking learning seriously. *Change, 31*(4), 10–17.

Shulman, L. S. (2000, April). From Minsk to Pinsk: Why a scholarship of teaching and learning? *Journal of the Scholarship of Teaching and Learning, 1*(1), 48–52.

Siegel, D. (1994). *Campuses respond to violent tragedy*. Phoenix, AZ: American Council on Education/Oryx Press.

Silver, R. C., Holman, A., McIntosh, D. N., Poulin, M., & Gil-Rivas, V. (2002, September). Nationwide longitudinal study of psychological responses to September 11. *Journal of the American Medical Association, 288*(10), 1235–1244.

Simmons, S. R. (2004). "An imperishable attitude": A memoir of learning and teaching. *Journal of Natural Resources and Life Sciences Education, 33,* 147–154.

Simpson, E. L. (1990). *Faculty renewal in higher education*. Malabar, FL: Krieger.

Small, S. A. (1995, November). Action-oriented research: Models and methods. *Journal of Marriage and the Family, 57*(4), 941–955.

Smith, B. L. (1988). The Washington Center: A grass roots approach to faculty development and curricular reform. In J. G. Kurfiss (Ed.), *To improve the academy: Vol. 7. Resources for student, faculty, and institutional development* (pp. 165–177). Stillwater, OK: New Forums Press.

Smith, B. L., MacGregor, J., Matthews, R. S., & Gabelnick, F. (2004). *Learning communities: Reforming undergraduate education*. San Francisco, CA: Jossey-Bass.

Smith, D. M., & Kolb, D. A. (1986). *The user's guide for the learning-style inventory: A manual for teachers and trainers*. Boston, MA: McBer.

Smith, K. S., & Kalivoda, P. L. (1998). Academic morphing: Teaching assistant to faculty member. In M. Kaplan & D. Lieberman (Eds.), *To improve the academy: Vol. 17. Resources for faculty, instructional, and organizational development* (pp. 85–101). Stillwater, OK: New Forums Press.

Snooks, M. K., Neely, S. E., & Williamson, K. M. (2004). From SGID and GIFT to BBQ: Streamlining midterm student evaluation to improve teaching and learning. In C. M. Wehlburg & S. Chadwick-Blossey (Eds.), *To improve the academy: Vol. 22. Resources for faculty, instructional, and organizational development* (pp. 110–124). Bolton, MA: Anker.

Snyder, G. (1990). *The practice of the wild.* San Francisco, CA: North Point Press.

Sorcinelli, M. D. (2000). *Principles of good practice: Supporting early-career faculty. Guidance for deans, department chairs, and other academic leaders.* Washington, DC: American Association for Higher Education.

Sorcinelli, M. D., Austin, A. E., Eddy, P. L., & Beach, A. L. (2006). *Creating the future of faculty development: Learning from the past, understanding the present.* Bolton, MA: Anker.

Stanton, T. K., Giles, D. E., Jr., & Cruz, N. I. (1999). *Service-learning: A movement's pioneers reflect on its origins, practice, and future.* San Francisco, CA: Jossey-Bass.

Stassen, M. L. A. (2000). "It's hard work!": Faculty development in a program for first-year students. In M. Kaplan & D. Lieberman (Eds.), *To improve the academy: Vol. 18. Resources for faculty, instructional, and organizational development* (pp. 254–277). Bolton, MA: Anker.

Stassen, M., & Sorcinelli, M. D. (2001, February). Making assessment matter. *Advocate, 18*(4), 5–8.

Steen, S., Bader, C., & Kubrin, C. (1999, April). Rethinking the graduate seminar. *Teaching Sociology,* 27(2), 167–173.

Stein, R. F., & Hurd, S. (2000). *Using student teams in the classroom: A faculty guide.* Bolton, MA: Anker.

Stevens, J., & Streatfeild, R. (2003). *SPEC kit 276, recruitment and retention.* Retrieved June 24, 2006, from www.arl.org/spec/SPEC276WebBook.pdf

Stevens, W. (1977). *Opus posthumous* (S. F. Morse, Ed.). New York, NY: Alfred A. Knopf.

St. John, E. P., McKinney, J., & Tuttle, T. (in press). Using action inquiry to address critical challenges. In E. P. St. John & M. Wilkerson (Eds.), *New directions for institutional research: Improving academic success: Reframing persistence research.* San Francisco, CA: Jossey-Bass.

Strand, K., Marullo, S., Cutforth, N., Stoecker, R., & Donohue, P. (2003). *Community-based research and higher education: Principles and practices.* San Francisco, CA: Jossey-Bass.

Strand, K., Marullo, S., Cutforth, N., Stoecker, R., & Donohue, P. (2003, Summer). Principles of best practice for community-based research. *Michigan Journal of Community Service Learning,* 9(3), 5–15.

Strauss, A., & Corbin, J. (1998). *Basics of qualitative research: Techniques and procedures for developing grounded theory* (2nd ed.). Thousand Oaks, CA: Sage.

Strenta, A. C., Elliot, R., Adair, R., Matier, M., & Scott, J. (1994, October). Choosing and leaving science in highly selective institutions. *Research in Higher Education, 35*(5), 513–547.

Streuling, G. F. (2004). Overcoming initial mistakes when using small groups. In L. K. Michaelsen, A. B. Knight, & L. D. Fink (Eds.), *Team-based learning: A transformative use of small groups in college teaching* (pp. 133–143). Sterling, VA: Stylus.

Stringer, E. T. (1999). *Action research* (2nd ed.). Thousand Oaks, CA: Sage.

Strommer, D. W. (1999). Teaching and learning in a learning community. In J. H. Levine (Ed.), *Learning communities: New structures, new partnerships for learning* (pp. 39–49). Columbia, SC: University of South Carolina, National Resource Center for the First-Year Experience and Students in Transition.

Sugar, S. (1998). *Games that teach: Experiential activities for reinforcing learning.* San Francisco, CA: Pfeiffer.

Sugar, S. E., & Willet, C. A. (1994). The game of academic ethics: The partnering of a board game. In E. C. Wadsworth (Ed.), *To improve the academy: Vol. 13. Resources for faculty, instructional, and organizational development* (pp. 121–131). Stillwater, OK: New Forums Press.

Sullivan, W. M. (2005). *Work and integrity: The crisis and promise of professionalism in America* (2nd ed.). San Francisco, CA: Jossey-Bass.

Svinicki, M. (1999). Ethics in college teaching. In W. J. McKeachie, *Teaching tips: Strategies, research, and theory for college and university teachers* (10th ed., pp. 289–300). Boston, MA: Houghton Mifflin.

Tan, W. (2004, June). Academic librarianship: Traveling across time lines. *Journal of Educational Media and Library Sciences, 41*(4), 431–436.

Tatum, B. D. (1997). *"Why are all the black kids sitting together in the cafeteria?" and other conversations about race.* New York, NY: Basic Books.

Tauber, R. T. (1998). *Good or bad, what teachers expect from students they generally get!* Washington, DC: ERIC Clearinghouse on Teaching and Teacher Education. (ERIC Document Reproduction Service No. ED426985)

Taylor, K. L., & Toews, S. V. M. (1999, July). Effective presentations: How can we learn from the experts? *Medical Teacher, 21*(4), 409–414.

Taylor, P. (1992). Improving graduate student seminar presentations through training. *Teaching of Psychology, 19*(4), 236–238.

Theall, M., Abrami, P. C., & Mets, L. M. (Eds.). (2001). *New directions for institutional research: No. 109. The student ratings debate: Are they valid? How can we best use them?* San Francisco, CA: Jossey-Bass.

Thomas, N. (1999). *The institution as a citizen: How colleges and universities enhance their civic roles* (Working Paper No. 22). Boston, MA: University of Massachusetts Boston, New England Resource Center for Higher Education.

Tobias, S. (1990). *They're not dumb, they're different: Stalking the second tier.* Tucson, AZ: Research Corporation.

Trout, P. A. (1997, September/October). What the numbers mean: Providing a context for numerical student evaluations of courses. *Change, 29*(5), 24–30.

Tuckman, B. W. (1965). Developmental sequence in small groups. *Psychological Bulletin, 63*(6), 384–399.

Tuckman, B. W., & Jensen, M. A. C. (1977). Stages of small-group development revisited. *Group and Organizational Studies, 2*(4), 419–427.

Vogler, K. E., & Long, E. (2003, September). Team teaching two sections of the same undergraduate course: A case study. *College Teaching, 51*(4), 122–126.

Walker, C. J. (2002). Faculty well-being review: An alternative to post-tenure review? In C. M. Licata & J. C. Morreale (Eds.), *Post-tenure review faculty review and renewal: Experienced voices* (pp. 229–241). Washington, DC: American Association for Higher Education.

Walshok, M. L. (1999). Strategies for building the infrastructure that supports the engaged campus. In R. G. Bringle, R. Games, & E. A. Malloy (Eds.), *Colleges and universities as citizens* (pp. 74–95). Needham Heights, MA: Allyn & Bacon.

Walshok, M. L. (2004, March). *It's not just about public service: The intellectual benefits of civic engagement.* Colloquium presented at Indiana University–Purdue University Indianapolis, Indianapolis, IN.

Ward, G. (1988). *I've got a project on . . .* Portsmouth, NH: Heinemann.

Ware, M. E., & Gardner, L. E. (1978, October). Team teaching introductory psychology as pedagogy and for faculty development. *Teaching of Psychology, 5*(3), 127–130.

Warren, L. (1998–99). Class in the classroom. *Essays on Teaching Excellence, 10*(2).

Wayment, H. A. (2004, April). It could have been me: Vicarious victims and disaster-focused distress. *Personality and Social Psychology Bulletin, 30*(4), 515–528.

Weimer, M. (1990). Successful participation strategies. In M. Weimer & R. A. Neff (Eds.), *Teaching college: Collected readings for the new instructor* (pp. 95–96). Madison, WI: Magna.

Weimer, M. (2002). *Learner-centered teaching: Five key changes to practice.* San Francisco, CA: Jossey-Bass.

Wellman, J. V. (1999). *Contributing to the civic good: Assessing and accounting for the civic contributions of higher education.* Washington, DC: Institute for Higher Education Policy.

Wesson, M., & Johnson, S. (1991, May/June). Post-tenure review and faculty revitalization. *Academe, 77*(3), 53–57.

West, C. (1999). Cornel West on heterosexism and transformation: An interview. In J. A. Segarra & R. Dobles (Eds.), *Learning as a political act: Struggles for learning and learning from struggles* (pp. 290–305). Cambridge, MA: Harvard University Press.

Westheimer, J., & Kahne, J. (2003, Winter). What kind of citizen? Political choices and educational goals. *Campus Compact Reader, 3*(3), 1–13.

Wheatley M. J. (1992). *Leadership and the new science: Learning about organization from an orderly universe.* San Francisco, CA: Berrett-Koehler.

Wheeler, D. W., & Wheeler, B. J. (1994). Mentoring faculty for midcareer issues. In M. A. Wunsch (Ed.), *New directions for teaching and learning: Vol. 57. Mentoring revisited: Making an impact on individuals and institutions* (pp. 91–98). San Francisco, CA: Jossey-Bass.

Whiting, L. R., Tucker, M., & Whaley, S. R. (2004, June). *Level of preparedness for managing crisis communication on land grant campuses.* Paper presented at the annual conference of the Association for Communication Excellence in Agriculture, Natural Resources, and Life and Human Sciences, Lake Tahoe, NV.

Wiggins, G. (1990). The truth may make you feel free, but the test may keep you imprisoned: Toward assessment worthy of the liberal arts. *AAHE Assessment Forum,* 17–31.

Wilson, E. K. (1982, May/June). Power, pretense, and piggybacking: Some ethical issues in teaching. *Journal of Higher Education, 53*(3), 268–281.

Wirth, K. R., Perkins, D., & Nuhfer, E. B. (2005). Knowledge surveys: A tool for assessing learning, courses, and programs [Abstract]. *Geological Society of America Annual Meetings Program with Abstracts, 37*(7), 119.

Witherell, C., & Noddings, N. (Ed.). (1991). *Stories lives tell: Narrative and dialogue in education.* New York, NY: Teachers College Press.

Worsfold, V. L. (2002). A workshop on the ethics of teaching. In W. Davis, J. Smith, & R. Smith (Eds.), *Ready to teach: Graduate teaching assistants prepare for today and for tomorrow* (pp. 41–46). Stillwater, OK: New Forums Press.

Wright, B. (2001). Accreditation where credit is due. In L. Suskie (Ed.), *Assessment to promote deep learning: Insight from AAHE's 2000 and 1999 assessment conferences* (pp. 49–58). Sterling, VA: Stylus.

Wright, J. C., Millar, S. B., Koscuik, S. A., Penberthy, D. L., Williams, P. H., & Wampold, B. E. (1998, August). A novel strategy for assessing the effects of curriculum reform on student competence. *Journal of Chemical Education, 75*(8), 986–992.

Wright, W. A. (Ed.). (1995). *Teaching improvement practices: Successful strategies for higher education.* Bolton, MA: Anker.

Wright, W. A., & O'Neill, W. M. (1995). Teaching improvement practices: International perspectives. In W. A. Wright & Associates, *Teaching improvement practices: Successful strategies for higher education* (pp. 1–57). Bolton, MA: Anker.

Xie, Y., & Shauman, K. A. (2003). *Women in science: Career processes and outcomes.* Cambridge, MA: Harvard University Press.

Yeats, W. B. (1940). The second coming. In P. Allt & R. K. Alspach (Eds.), *The variorum edition of the poems of W. B. Yeats* (pp. 823–825). New York, NY: Macmillan. (Original work published 1921)

Yoder, M. K. (1997, Fall). The consequences of a generic approach to teaching nursing in a multicultural world. *Journal of Cultural Diversity, 4*(3), 77–82.

Zlotkowski, E. (2000, Fall). Service-learning in the disciplines. *Michigan Journal of Community Service Learning* [Special issue], 61–67.

Zuber-Skerritt, O. (1992). *Action research in higher education: Examples and reflections.* London, England: Kogan Page.

Zuelke, D. C., & Nichols, T. M. (1995, November). *Collaborative school climate action research for school improvement: Part II.* Paper presented at the annual meeting of the Mid-South Education Research Association, Biloxi, MS.

Zull, J. E. (2002). *The art of changing the brain: Enriching the practice of teaching by exploring the biology of learning.* Sterling, VA: Stylus.